A history of the Northern Ireland Labour Party

Manchester University Press

Critical Labour Movement Studies

Series editors
John Callaghan
Steven Fielding
Steve Ludlam

Already published in the series

Jenny Andersson, *Between growth and security: Swedish social democracy from a strong society to a third way*

John Callaghan, Steven Fielding and Steve Ludlam (eds), *Interpreting the Labour Party: approaches to Labour politics and history*

Andrew Gamble, Steve Ludlam, Andrew Taylor and Stephen Wood (eds), *Labour, the state, social movements and the challenge of neo-liberal globalism*

Dianne Hayter, *Fightback! Labour's traditional right in the 1970s and 1980s*

Jonas Hinnfors, *Reinterpreting social democracy: a history of stability in the British Labour Party and Swedish Social Democratic Party*

Ben Jackson, *Equality and the British Left: a study in progressive political thought, 1900–64*
Leighton James, *The politics of identity and civil society in Britain and Germany: miners in the Ruhr and South Wales 1890–1926*

Declan McHugh, *Labour in the city: the development of the Labour Party in Manchester, 1918–31*

Stephen Meredith, *Labour's old and new? The parliamentary Right of the British Labour Party 1970–79 and the roots of New Labour*

Jeremy Nuttall, *Psychological socialism: the Labour Party and qualities of mind and character, 1931 to the present*

Lucy Robinson, *Gay men and the left in post-war Britain: How the personal got political*

A history of the Northern Ireland Labour Party

Democratic socialism and sectarianism

Aaron Edwards

Manchester University Press
Manchester and New York

distributed in the United States exclusively
by Palgrave Macmillan

Copyright © Aaron Edwards 2009

The right of Aaron Edwards to be identified as the author of this work has been asserted by him in accordance with the Copyright, Designs and Patents Act 1988.

Published by Manchester University Press
Oxford Road, Manchester M13 9NR, UK
and Room 400, 175 Fifth Avenue, New York, NY 10010, USA
www.manchesteruniversitypress.co.uk

Distributed in the United States exclusively by
Palgrave Macmillan, 175 Fifth Avenue, New York,
NY 10010, USA

Distributed in Canada exclusively by
UBC Press, University of British Columbia, 2029 West Mall,
Vancouver, BC, Canada V6T 1Z2

British Library Cataloguing-in-Publication Data
A catalogue record for this book is available from the British Library

Library of Congress Cataloging-in-Publication Data applied for

ISBN   978 0 7190 7874 3   *hardback*

First published 2009

18 17 16 15 14 13 12 11 10 09   10 9 8 7 6 5 4 3 2 1

Typeset
by Action Publishing Technology Ltd, Gloucester
Printed in Great Britain
by the MPG Books Group

For my parents

Contents

Series editors' foreword	*page* viii	
Acknowledgements	ix	
List of abbreviations	xi	
List of figures and tables	xiii	
Introduction	1	
1 Democratic socialism and sectarianism, 1924–45	7	
2 Re-appraising the origins of the 'consensus-forming strategy', 1945–58	30	
3 The Labour Opposition of Northern Ireland, 1958–65	70	
4 The failure of the 'consensus-forming strategy', 1965–69	117	
5 The NILP in retreat, 1969–72	158	
6 The fall of the NILP, 1972–75	194	
7 Squeezing the moderates, 1975–87	214	
Conclusion	227	
Index	233	

Series editors' foreword

The start of the twenty-first century is superficially an inauspicious time to study labour movements. Political parties once associated with the working class have seemingly embraced capitalism. The trade unions with which these parties were once linked have suffered near-fatal reverses. The industrial proletariat looks both divided and in rapid decline. The development of multi-level governance, prompted by 'globalisation' has furthermore apparently destroyed the institutional context for advancing the labour 'interest'. Many consequently now look on terms such as the 'working class', 'socialism' and 'the labour movement' as politically and historically redundant.

The purpose of this series is to give a platform to those students of labour movements who challenge, or develop, established ways of thinking and so demonstrate the continued vitality of the subject and the work of those interested in it. For despite appearances, many social democratic parties remain important competitors for national office and proffer distinctive programmes. Unions still impede the free flow of 'market forces'. If workers are a more diverse body and have exchanged blue collars for white, insecurity remains an everyday problem. The new institutional and global context is, moreover, as much of an opportunity as a threat. Yet, it cannot be doubted that, compared with the immediate post-1945 period, at the beginning of the new millennium what many still refer to as the 'labour movement' is much less influential. Whether this should be considered a time of retreat or reconfiguration is unclear – and a question the series aims to clarify.

The series will not only give a voice to studies of particular national bodies but will also promote comparative works that contrast experiences across time and geography. This entails taking due account of the political, economic and cultural settings in which labour movements have operated. In particular this involves taking the past seriously as a way of understanding the present as well as utilising sympathetic approaches drawn from sociology, economics and elsewhere.

John Callaghan
Steven Fielding
Steve Ludlam

Acknowledgements

I owe Professor Graham Walker an intellectual debt of gratitude for supervising the research upon which this book is based and I wish to thank him for his continued encouragement and counsel. Dr Margaret O'Callaghan also offered invaluable advice with the project at critical junctures and I thank her for helping to clarify my thinking on various issues. A special word of thanks is due here to those scholars who have discussed my research with me over the years: they include Professor Paul Arthur, Dr Paul Dixon, Dr Sydney Elliott, Dr Alan Greer, Professor James W. McAuley, Dr Niall O'Dochartaigh, Professor Henry Patterson and Dr Bob Purdie. Professor Lord Bew of Donegore and Professor Jonathan Tonge, in particular, offered suggestions on how I could improve the work for publication. Colleagues and friends also offered advice and comradeship at various points and I would like to thank Stephen Bloomer, Dr Christopher Farrington, Douglas Jamison, Dr Joanne McEvoy, Dr Aidan McGarry, Cillian McGrattan, Gareth Mulvenna, Dr John Nagle, Dr Catherine O'Donnell, Dr Eamonn O'Kane, Dr Colin Reid and Dr Kirk Simpson. None of the above share in the shortcomings of the book and I am solely responsible for any errors.

The academic breathing space provided at annual Political Studies Association of Ireland and Political Studies Association UK conferences gave me the opportunity to present my research findings and I wish to pass on my appreciation to the convenors and to the 'usual suspects' for their comments and continued support. I am grateful to the editors of the *Journal of Contemporary History* and *Irish Political Studies* for permission to use some of the material presented at these conferences and which was subsequently published in both journals. I also wish to acknowledge the Northern Ireland Department for Employment and Learning for awarding me a three-year scholarship in 2003–6 to carry out the research. Between 2002 and 2006 I received a small grant from the Academic Council Office at Queen's University Belfast which enabled me to visit various archival institutions across the United Kingdom and Republic of Ireland. I am particularly grateful to the Trustees for allocating it to me.

The real debt, of course, is to those former NILP members who permitted me valuable interview time: Professor Paul Arthur, Robert Bingham, Dr Boyd

Black, Rt. Hon. David Bleakley, Beatrice Boyd, Willie Breslin, the late Sir Charles Brett, John Campbell, Alan Carr, George Chambers, Bobby Cosgrove, Barney Deveney, Anne Foster, Brian Garrett, Erskine Holmes, Meg Holmes, Sam McAughtry, Eamonn McCann, Jim McDonald, Sydney McDowell, Douglas McIldoon, Brendan Mackin, David Morrison and Billy and Dolores O'Caomhanaigh. Other interviewees – Sir Kenneth Bloomfield, Roy Garland, Mark Langhammer, Bill McClinton, the late Billy Mitchell and Edwina Stewart – provided additional insights at various points from non-NILP perspectives.

Inevitably, a book like this accumulates huge logistical debts. Thanks to the staff of Queen's University Main Library and its Special Collections (especially the inter-library loan librarian Florence Gray); the Central Library, Belfast, and its affiliated Newspaper Library; the Labour History Archive and Study Centre, John Rylands Library, University of Manchester (especially Stephen Bird and Darren Treadwell); the Public Records Office of Northern Ireland; the Linenhall Library, Belfast (especially Yvonne Murphy and Dr Kris Brown); the National Archives of Ireland, Dublin; and the National Archives at Kew, London. Other people who helped at various points include the late Lord Blease of Cromac, Harry Donaghy Jnr, the late Billy Mitchell, Dawn Purvis and Gusty Spence. Comments from the series editors and the anonymous reader at MUP proved invaluable during the preparation of the manuscript and my thanks to Tony Mason and the production team at MUP for their assistance.

On a personal note, this book could not have been written if it had not been for the constant love and encouragement of my parents, Jim and Barbara, and I wish to dedicate this book to them for their selfless and loyal support. My brother and sister, Ryan and Stephanie, are also due a mention here for keeping my feet firmly on the ground, as too are my grandfathers Andy Edwards Snr and the late Jackie Graham who taught me the true value of hard work and determination. The remainder of the Edwards and Graham families provided much love and support through good times and bad.

Abbreviations

AEU	Amalgamated Engineering Union
APL	Anti-Partition League of Ireland
APNI	Alliance Party of Northern Ireland
ATGWU	Amalgamated Transport and General Workers Union (British based)
BICO	British & Irish Communist Organisation
BLP	British Labour Party
CCDC	Central Citizens' Defence Committee
CDU	Campaign for Democracy in Ulster
CLP	Constituency Labour Party
CLR	Campaign for Labour Representation
CPNI	Communist Party of Northern Ireland
CSJ	Campaign for Social Justice
CWLP	Commonwealth Labour Party
DCAC	Derry Citizens' Action Committee
DFA	Department of Foreign Affairs (Ireland)
DHAC	Derry Housing Action Committee
DLP	Divisional Labour Party (NILP)
DUP	Democratic Unionist Party
EC	Executive Committee (NILP)
ETU	Electrical Trades Union
FBU	Fire Brigades' Union
FLP	Falls Labour Party
GOC	General Officer Commanding
ICTU	Irish Congress of Trade Unions
IRA	Irish Republican Army
IrLP	Irish Labour Party
ITGWU	Irish Transport and General Workers Union (Irish based)
LAW	Loyalist Association of Workers
LHASC	Labour History Archive and Study Centre (Manchester)
LLP	Londonderry Labour Party (also known as the Derry Labour Party)

LPA	Labour Party Archives (Manchester, housed in the LHASC)
NAI	National Archives of Ireland
NAUK	National Archives of the United Kingdom
NDP	National Democratic Party
NEC	National Executive Committee (BLP)
NIC	Northern Ireland Committee (ICTU)
NICRA	Northern Ireland Civil Rights Association
NICRC	Northern Ireland Community Relations Commission
NILP	Northern Ireland Labour Party
NISLL	Northern Ireland Society of Labour Lawyers
NUS	National Union of Seamen
NUSWC	National Union of Shop Assistants, Warehousemen and Clerks
OIRA	Official IRA
PD	People's Democracy
PIRA	Provisional Irish Republican Army
PLP	Parliamentary Labour Party
PRONI	Public Records Office of Northern Ireland
PUP	Progressive Unionist Party
QUBLG	Queen's University of Belfast Labour Group
RLP	Republican Labour Party
RUC	Royal Ulster Constabulary
SDLP	Social Democratic and Labour Party
SLL	Society of Labour Lawyers
TGWU	Transport and General Workers Union
UDA	Ulster Defence Association
UDR	Ulster Defence Regiment
UPP	Unionist Parliamentary Party
UUP	Ulster Unionist Party
UUC	Ulster Unionist Council
UULA	Ulster Unionist Labour Association
UUUC	United Ulster Unionist Council
UVF	Ulster Volunteer Force
UWC	Ulster Workers' Council
VUPP	Vanguard Unionist Progressive Party
WLP	Woodvale Labour Party

Figures and tables

Figures

6.1	UUP–NILP local government electoral competition in Belfast, 1946–73	202

Tables

3.1	Northern Ireland general elections, 1921–69: NILP performance	72
3.2	Strikes in Northern Ireland, 1955–61	74
3.3	Occupational background of candidates in the May 1964 Belfast local government election	91
3.4	British general elections, 1945–79 (excluding by-elections): NILP performance	93
3.5	Woodvale Labour Party in the 1960s	95
3.6	Religious breakdown of the population in Woodvale (1961)	95
5.1	Falls Labour Party in the 1960s	164
5.2	Religious breakdown of the population in Falls (1961)	165

Introduction

It has often been said that the scholarly literature on Northern Irish history, politics and culture is exhaustive. Arguably, within the parameters of this huge and ever-expanding bibliography, most research tends to focus on the nature of political violence in the region and, consequently, on the ethnic antagonism existing between Protestants, who wish to maintain the Union with Great Britain, and Catholics, who hold assiduously to the aspiration of a United Ireland free from British interference. In contrast, the labour political tradition – which periodically straddled this deep ethnic, religious, cultural and national divide – has not been allotted the same degree of academic exposure. Indeed the most significant exemplar of this tradition, the Northern Ireland Labour Party (NILP), no longer exists as an electoral force in the province's politics. In many ways its destruction was a by-product of the far-reaching social and political upheaval caused by the onset of the 'troubles' in 1969. Nevertheless, as this book will explain, there were a range of other variables that contributed to its downfall, and not all of these are reducible to ethno-national tensions between Protestants and Catholics.

Despite the fact that the NILP has long since departed from the political stage, debate surrounds the reasons for both its success and its ultimate failure. Moreover there still remains an air of confusion pervading the minds of its former members about what actually happened to the party; with some claiming that the party was 'effectively wiped out by sectarian violence and inter-communal division after 1969',[1] others that it simply 'faded away',[2] or that it 'died almost without a gasp'[3] in the mid-1970s. In reality the party soldiered on into the 1980s, although it had jettisoned most of its inter-ethnic membership over the previous decade. Beyond a few anecdotal stories and some sketchy analysis, few people know anything conclusive about the NILP's political career, or, for that matter, the salient features of its ideology and discourse, the social groups which constituted its membership and support-base, or even the reasons behind its electoral successes.

In seeking to address these questions this book has two principal objectives. First, it rehabilitates and re-examines the historical record of the NILP, an understudied and poorly understood phenomenon in Irish political studies. Second, it challenges the orthodox narrative of that party's political fortunes throughout the twentieth century, by arguing that the NILP has suffered from an unfair critique in the scholarly literature. What this book does not attempt to do is to 'wish away' the deep-rooted antagonism that has been shown to exist between Protestants and Catholics in Northern Ireland. Rather it seeks to explain how a party like the NILP actually went about mobilising support across the ethnic divide and why it ultimately failed in its bid to transform the political culture operating within this deeply divided society. In seeking to meet these objectives the book advances the argument that the NILP was not destined to fail, nor was its long-drawn-out demise in the 1970s and 1980s a direct result of inter-ethnic antagonism alone.[4] Certainly the structural variables of residential segregation, polarisation and political violence, combined with the logic of the 'ethnic dual party system',[5] hastened the NILP's decline. But it was a coalescence of a number of other key factors – including a dispersal of its membership either into retirement from political life, the ranks of 'new parties'[6] or eventual absorption into 'Labour 1987' – that led to the NILP's official disbandment on 14 March 1987.[7]

Many of the more simplistic analyses of the NILP have detached the party from its proper historical and empirical context; in doing so they have been disingenuous to its genealogy and significance in Northern Irish politics. Indeed, the organised Labour movement in Ulster as a whole has a long tradition stretching back to the late 1800s. The NILP, as the political wing of that movement, was born out of the unique circumstances which converged at the time of state formation in the 1920s. During the inter-war period the local Unionist administration was constantly wary of challenges to its authority. In response the regime tirelessly stressed the need for ethnic loyalty and actively sought to erect bollards against the political opposition from the Independent Unionist and Labour forces. The abolition of Proportional Representation (PR) in the late 1920s was just one move by which the Unionist Party aimed to explicitly counter these oppositional and cross-cutting voices.[8] One by-product of imposing the plurality – or 'first-past-the-post' – electoral system in the province was the intensification of inter-communal antagonism between rival ethnic groups and the domination of local politics by the Unionist Party. Later commentators accused the Unionist Party of practising a form of 'hegemonic control' between 1921 and 1972.[9] However, such a charge must be qualified in light of the other actors existing on the political stage that presaged the need among Unionists for sustaining this regimented system.

Arguably Unionist 'hegemony' grew out of the unique nature of the party's control over the political system, wherein the reinforcing variables of religion, ethnicity and national identity could be fused together to ensure that there was little danger of cross-community voting. The tactic of gerrymandering electoral boundaries was also employed by the regime to safeguard against the possibility of a removal of Unionist power.[10] Thus, for the Unionist Party the real danger was not contained in the threat of Protestants voting for Nationalist or republican parties:

Introduction 3

Given the strength of the sectarian divide and the size of the Protestant majority, the anti-Partitionist parties did not provide any threat at all to the Unionist majority, but the possibility of the Protestant vote being further split on class issues was a much more serious challenge.[11]

However, there had always been the residual possibility that some Protestants could be persuaded to vote for a party like the NILP, which placed class interests above and beyond consideration for the constitutional question concerning the continued maintenance of Northern Ireland as a partitioned part of Ireland. The reason why Protestants found it easier to vote for Labour candidates was as much motivated by a determination to secure a 'fair share' of social, economic and political rights existing elsewhere in the United Kingdom, as any deep-seated socialist convictions. Similarly Catholics, sympathetic to the NILP in the inter-war period, tended to be motivated by similar questions of social justice, as well as an avid disdain for the existing system and, to a lesser extent, by an anti-partitionist outlook that could not be satisfied by a moribund Nationalist Party. Northern Ireland Labour provided a political alternative to Unionist 'hegemony' and Nationalist recalcitrance between 1921 and 1972.

In seeking to address the NILP's cross-cutting potential, Unionist elites tended to lump Labour – or 'socialists' as they preferred to call them – together with other oppositional forces who they considered posed an imminent danger to Northern Ireland's position within the UK, even though there were vast differences in the constitutional orientation of these groupings. As O'Leary and McGarry suggest:

Lundyism 'from below' was manifest in socialist and labourist movements which threatened to transcend sectarianism in the 1930s, and in the late 1950s and early 1960s. The threat posed by such movements was relatively easily handled by the UUP. Explicit accusations of disloyalty, reminders of the dangers inherent in splitting the unionist vote, and overt renewal of ethnic appeals usually elicited the required responses.[12]

The growing entanglement of the NILP's ideological strands – added to Unionist efforts to beat the ethnic 'loyalty drum' – eventually led to dramatic fluctuations in the party's political fortunes.

Surprisingly, few scholarly analyses of the NILP's political fortunes have emerged, in large part because of the primacy of attempts to explain the deep-seated ethnic antagonism existing between Protestants and Catholics during the recent 'troubles'. While this is certainly a legitimate academic exercise, it has subsequently obscured our understanding of politics in this deeply divided society. A key argument of the book is that, while these differences clearly exist, it is still necessary to explore episodes when ethnic differences did not lead to conflict, but co-operation. Stefan Wolff has made the point more succinctly:

Thus it would be mistaken to assume that ethnopolitics is only a matter of confrontation between different politically mobilized groups and states. On the contrary, there is a range of examples where ethnopolitics is pursued in the spirit of compromise and cooperation.[13]

Protestants and Catholics have oscillated between co-operation and conflict for generations. Given the anomaly of political co-operation across the ethno-national cleavage, then, it is puzzling that so little research has actually been completed on the NILP – an elementary glance would reveal that there have been only a handful of academic works produced over the past forty years.[14]

Throughout the seven decades of its existence the NILP represented a genuine – if often idealistic – attempt to cut across the ethno-national cleavage and unite Protestants and Catholics in a political Labour Party[15] that sought to transcend sectarianism. Recent advances in the scholarly profession of political history, as well as the release of previously untapped archival and oral sources, make it possible to plot the NILP's trajectory for the first time in a way that is impartial and sensitive to the particular context in which it operated. This book builds on the existing literature on the Northern Ireland Labour movement in general – and the NILP in particular – to offer an empirically grounded critique of an important phenomenon. The NILP's rise and fall in the twentieth century coincided with some of the most turbulent events in modern Irish history. In periods of unleashed antagonism it barely gained momentum, yet during times of relative peace it thrived and successfully built up an impressive party machinery and membership base. Above all the NILP represented a genuine attempt by Protestants and Catholics to pursue common class interests above and beyond ethnic and religious ones. This distinguishes the NILP from other parties in the region and is an anomaly worth investigating further.

In comparative perspective the NILP is far from unique. Many European societies have been divided along ethnic, religious, cultural and national lines and some of the same polities have also produced, or failed to produce, left-of-centre parties which have attempted to transcend these rigid cleavages. Cyprus provides another example of an island blighted by division between two ethnic groups with conflicting national identities and where conflict management has been complicated by the effects of partition. Intercommunal violence here has 'weakened the influence of institutions such as the trade unions that had succeeded in bridging the divide between the communities'.[16] Yet despite the entrenched nature of the island's political culture *Anorthotiko Komma tou Ergazomenou Laou* (Progressive Party of Working People) has become one of the most successful left parties in Europe, 'that (potentially) unites Greek Cypriots and Turkish Cypriots'.[17] Conversely, in Belgium, another society where the political culture has grown up around ethnic, regional and linguistic fault-lines, the division between Flemings and Walloons remains particularly marked. This division is translated into the 'conventional' political spectrum to an extent, with Wallonian nationalism traditionally situated on the left and Flemish nationalism on the right.[18] Historically, Wallonia has been the most heavily industrialised region and this has meant the Labour movement there has supported socialist politics more readily. Moreover, like Northern Ireland, Belgium is also 'a country in which workers are less likely than their counterparts in other European countries to vote on class grounds'.[19]

Political parties, like individuals, are products of the societies in which they

Introduction

grow and are nurtured. As Alan Ware has observed, 'the origins of the political parties, and the particular history of the regime in which they operate, affect the policy programmes they adopt'.[20] Labour parties face similar hurdles to other political organisations in divided societies; however the chances of failure are generally much greater in those places where socio-economic issues are subsumed within larger ethno-national frameworks. In Horowitz's view: 'So long as ethnic tensions remained in the background of politics, it was possible for left-wing parties to advocate bridging ethnic divisions by building alliances across ethnic lines.'[21] The NILP is no exception to this rule. As this book explains the party was born out of an uneasy coalition of Protestants and Catholics who set aside their ethnic differences to unite behind a democratic socialist banner. Above all these labourists were deeply committed to eradicating sectarianism and reinstating what they regarded as inalienable social, economic and political rights for all of Northern Ireland's citizens.

Ultimately, and with the benefit of hindsight, the competing national identity aspirations of most Protestants and Catholics proved irreconcilable; however that does not preclude us from investigating the reasons which brought them together in the first place. By and large the NILP's uniqueness in a society divided along ethnic, national, cultural and class lines is only surprising when viewed within the traditional paradigm of Western understanding of political parties as static products of the late nineteenth to the mid-twentieth centuries.[22] Fortunately the study of political parties has developed exponentially over the past few decades to better reflect the fluidity and diversity of these political actors as they exist in a wealth of complex environments. This book not only offers students and scholars an informed history of the NILP, but also provides an illuminating glimpse into the much broader phenomenon of left-of-centre parties that operate in ethnically-divided societies.

Notes

1 Interview with Brian Garrett, 30 September 2003.
2 Interview with David Bleakley, 21 March 2006.
3 Interview with Robert Bingham, 24 February 2005.
4 Those analysts who emphasise sectarianism as a major factor in the NILP's political downfall include Mitchell, Paul, 'The Party System and Party Competition', in Mitchell, Paul and Rick Wilford (eds), *Politics in Northern Ireland* (Boulder: Westview Press, 1999), pp. 91–116; McGarry, John and Brendan O'Leary, *Explaining Northern Ireland: Broken Images* (Oxford: Blackwell, 1995); and Rumpf, Erhard and Anthony C. Hepburn, *Nationalism and Socialism in Twentieth Century Ireland* (Liverpool: Liverpool University Press, 1977).
5 The term was coined by Paul Mitchell. See his 'Party Competition in an Ethnic Dual Party System', *Ethnic and Racial Studies*, Vol. 18, No. 4 (October 1995), pp. 773–96.
6 These 'new parties' include: the Democratic Unionist Party, founded in October 1971; the Social Democratic and Labour Party, founded in August 1970; and the Alliance Party of Northern Ireland, founded in April 1970.
7 Northern Ireland Political Collection, Linenhall Library, Belfast (NIPC), NILP Box

1, 'Internal NILP Memorandum', 14 March 1987.

8 Pringle, D.G., 'Electoral Systems and Political Manipulation: A Case Study of Northern Ireland in the 1920s', *Economic and Social Review*, Vol. 11, No. 3 (April 1980), p. 204.

9 See O'Leary, Brendan and John McGarry, *The Politics of Antagonism: Understanding Northern Ireland: Second Edition* (London: Athlone, 1996), pp. 108–11.

10 Elliott, Sydney, 'The Northern Ireland Electoral System: A Vehicle for Disputation', in Roche, Patrick J. and Brian Barton (eds), *The Northern Ireland Question: Nationalism, Unionism and Partition* (Aldershot: Ashgate, 1999), pp. 122–38.

11 Pringle, 'Electoral Systems and Political Manipulation', p. 203.

12 O'Leary and McGarry, *The Politics of Antagonism*, p. 141.

13 Wolff, Stefan, *Ethnic Conflict: A Global Perspective* (Oxford: Oxford University Press, 2007), p. 3.

14 Published works on the NILP include: Rutan, Gerard F., 'The Labor Party in Ulster: Opposition by Cartel', *Review of Politics*, Vol. 29, No. 4 (October 1967), pp. 526–35; Walker, Graham, 'The Northern Ireland Labour Party in the 1920s', *Saothar* 10, (1984), pp. 19–29; Walker, Graham, *The Politics of Frustration: Harry Midgley and the Failure of Labour in Northern Ireland* (Manchester: Manchester University Press, 1985); Cradden, Terry, 'Labour in Britain and the Northern Ireland Labour Party, 1900–1970', in Catterall, Peter and Sean McDougal (eds), *The Northern Ireland Question in British Politics* (Basingstoke: Macmillan, 1996); Walker, Graham, 'The Northern Ireland Labour Party, 1924–45', in Lane, Fintan and Donal Ó Drisceoil (eds), *Politics and the Irish Working Class, 1830–1945* (Basingstoke: Palgrave, 2005), pp. 229–45. See also Edwards, Aaron, 'Democratic Socialism and Sectarianism: The Northern Ireland Labour Party and Progressive Unionist Party Compared', *Politics*, Vol. 27, No. 1 (February 2007), pp. 24–31; and Edwards, Aaron, 'Social Democracy and Partition: The British Labour Party and Northern Ireland, 1951–64', *Journal of Contemporary History*, Vol. 42, No. 4 (October 2007), pp. 595–612.

15 NILP, *Constitution* (Revised 1964).

16 Guelke, Adrian, 'Northern Ireland and Island Status', in McGarry, John (ed.), *Northern Ireland and the Divided World: Post-Agreement Northern Ireland in Comparative Perspective* (Oxford: Oxford University Press, 2001), p. 234.

17 Dunphy, Richard and Tim Bale, 'Still Flying the Red Flag? Explaining AKEL – Cyprus's Communist Anomaly', *Party Politics*, Vol. 13, No. 3 (2007), p. 300.

18 See Erk, Jan, 'Sub-state Nationalism and the Left-Right Divided: Critical Junctures in the Formation of Nationalist Labour Movements in Belgium', *Nations and Nationalism*, Vol. 11, No. 4 (2005), p. 551–70.

19 Urwin, Derek W., 'Social Cleavages and Political Parties in Belgium: Problems of Institutionalization', *Political Studies*, Vol. 18, No. 3 (1970), p. 321.

20 Ware, Alan, *Political Parties and Party Systems* (Oxford: Oxford University Press, 1996), p. 48.

21 Horowitz, Donald L., *Ethnic Groups in Conflict* (London: University of California Press, 2000), p. 337.

22 See Gunther, Richard and Larry Diamond, 'Species of Political Parties: A New Typology', *Party Politics*, Vol. 9, No 2 (2003), pp. 167–99.

1

Democratic socialism and sectarianism, 1924–45

No party, proceeded Mr. Midgley, could serve the interests of the people better than a party of their own creation and kind. The Labour party did not appeal to them on the ground of religion, and their message to every creed in society was to cease to dwell on the things that were of no importance and remember the things that were of importance, at least on six days of the week. If Belfast, and indeed Northern Ireland, were not careful there was a danger that they would be left hopelessly behind in the march of working class emancipation.[1]

Introduction: the crisis of state formation

The birth of the Northern Ireland state in 1920–21 coincided with the rapid return of thousands of soldiers from front-line service in the British military campaign during the First World War. Their homecoming laid bare an early challenge to the newly-constituted Unionist regime in Belfast in relation to its ability to absorb these demobilised troops back into the local workforce. Although Ireland had been traumatised by the war, with whole towns and villages decimated by the slaughter of their sons along the Western Front, nothing could prepare the country for the impact of partition. Partition had hitherto been piloted by the British as a conflict management device in the Middle Eastern colonial outposts of Iraq, Transjordan and Palestine, which were soon given the status of 'mandates'.[2] In 1918, despite Home Rule legislation being suspended, the rise of Sinn Féin continued unabated and the violence of the Irish Republican Army (IRA) in the South eventually intensified, leading to the Anglo-Irish war of independence between 1919 and 1921. The conflict had placed tremendous pressure on the British state to free itself from the problem of Ireland and it soon found itself in political negotiations with plenipotentiaries from Dáil Éireann to negotiate a truce and, to a lesser extent, to streamline the handing over of power.[3]

The violent transition from one institutional arrangement to another was keenly felt elsewhere in Europe, as revolution and civil unrest continued to grip defeated powers like Germany and Hungary. In the wake of the Great War radical communist and fascist groups contributed to 'a new brutalization of public life, a routinization of violence and authoritarianism, and a heightening of nationalist conflict and ambition'.[4] In Germany the new-fangled Weimar Republic was moving from one crisis to another, while in Russia the clatter of Soviet guns during the October revolution in 1917 sounded the death knell of an *ancien regime* built on generations of an autocratic Tsarist dynasty. Radical political forces also began to take root in the fabric of democratic societies convulsed by chronic economic instability, poverty and high unemployment. In short, liberal regimes were in crisis.[5]

Amidst these cataclysmic events Northern Ireland was experiencing its own difficulties, as the Unionist regime took over the reins of power from the British in the wake of the Government of Ireland Act (1920). Like most of the rest of Europe the province had suffered irreparably for its role in the war, as well as from the high stakes of political diplomacy which presided over the partitioning of the island. Despite its commitment to alleviate unemployment, the Unionist administration struggled to meet the basic needs of the working classes and failed in its self-proclaimed quest to 'treasure those heroes who fought in the Great War'.[6] The historian Brian Follis has detailed how the Unionist administration set about the huge and unrewarding task of laying state foundations. In his words:

> Isolated and alienated from the policymakers in London, and threatened by the ambitions of Irish nationalism, the new Government of Northern Ireland took office uncertain of its future and unsure of its friends.[7]

On the other hand Bew *et al.* are a little more circumspect. As they make clear the hand-over of power was perhaps a little more forthright and deliberate: 'The strategy of class alliance pursued by the Unionist middle class, together with the diplomatic strategies of the British government, were responsible for the establishment of a Northern Ireland state with a sectarian-populist flavour.'[8] For these scholars Unionism had reluctantly grasped the nettle of Home Rule for the six north-east counties, an option it had hitherto resisted, though one that it would soon come to master. Furthermore, the new state's unique demographic imbalance, favouring the majority Protestant community, fed directly into the Unionist Party's quick-paced decision to strengthen its hand both politically and militarily.

Yet it was by no means absolutely guaranteed that Unionist authority would go unchallenged. Intra-ethnic fissures did exist and these were met by and large with the determination on the part of the local regime to play up the dangers of 'socialism', which they frequently equated with its Bolshevik variant in Russia, and rather oddly, with the conservative Catholic regime in the Irish Free State.[9] Indeed, political and electoral competition threatened the ruling party's hegemony to such an extent that the messiness of state formation allowed it to exploit the ethnic enmities – existing between Protestants and Catholics – for its own ends. One means by which the Unionist regime could maintain its power-base was to grant patronage to those with a proven loyalty to the new state. As a consequence the locally-raised security apparatus – consisting of the Royal

Ulster Constabulary (RUC) and the Ulster Special Constabulary – became almost exclusively Protestant, despite it being envisaged that one-third of the RUC should be made up of Roman Catholics.[10] Paul Bew reminds us that Unionism's 'highly controversial line of thinking' was based on the incremental loss of control over the Protestant working class, which began to slip, 'as the challenge from the IRA became more intense and British irresolution was all too visible'.[11]

Believing itself to be fighting a rear-guard action, the Unionist regime set about preparing further bulwarks to disloyal Catholic Nationalist and left-wing opinion. The reality behind such imperatives was complex and, in large part, remained for the Unionist leadership 'the product of exaggerated fears of the other side's unity of resources and objectives, and a pessimistic appraisal of its own collective strength and political stamina'.[12] The strategy of circumventing working-class disgruntlement, while emitting the appearance of unity (rather than its actuality) was sustained by making popular appeals along sectarian lines. Thus, in the first election to the Northern Ireland House of Commons, where 'loyalty' became the foremost watchword, the Unionist Party polled comfortably, amassing some 343,347 votes (66.9% of the total vote) and winning 40 seats; the remaining 12 seats going evenly to the Nationalists and Sinn Féin, who immediately boycotted the new parliament.[13] Disastrously, the five Independent Labour candidates received only 4,001 votes and lost their deposits.[14]

James Craig, Northern Ireland's first Prime Minister, claimed in his opening remarks to the newly established Belfast Parliament that 'we have nothing in our view except the welfare of the people'.[15] Nonetheless, the Unionist regime's position was precarious and prone to fissures, and was not monolithically 'Orange' as some commemorators have claimed.[16] More reflective commentators have reminded us that 'in reality, while there was agreement on the fundamental issues of the constitution and Ulster's right to self-determination, unionism was a coalition of personalities, and classes'.[17] Thus a plurality of oppositional voices did exist outside of the official Unionist camp, often manifesting themselves in distinctly class terms. Indeed one is struck when reading contemporary newspaper reports from the time just how 'shot through by conflicts'[18] the regime actually was in the 1920s. Furthermore, Unionism remained deeply divided over issues of social service expenditure and the adoption of welfare legislation emanating from Westminster. Christopher Norton has emphasised how keeping in step with Great Britain was a calculated political decision, taken by the Unionist leadership to 'guarantee to its Protestant working class supporters that devolution would not mean the lowering of standards'.[19] Needless to say, this deliberate strategy did leave the door open to future challenge should the government default on its commitment to implement welfarist legislation.[20]

Unionism recognised the danger of the labour interests harboured by a significant portion of working-class Protestants and set about meeting these by establishing its own trade union organisation. The Ulster Unionist Labour

Association (UULA) was formed in 1918 and actively sought out ways to placate the Protestant working class in industrialised parts of Belfast. Above all the UULA was an elite-driven venture designed to maintain the constitution and preserve Unionist unity by providing a controlled outlet for loyalist-labour interests.[21] In a speech to a large social gathering of 2,000 UULA members in 1923 the organisation's honorary patron Sir James Craig articulated the need for unity at a time of deep-seated unease brought about by the impending report from the Boundary Commission. He said:

> We are only on the stage for a certain time, sympathetically to endeavour to inter-pret the will and the wish of the people, and with any commonsense we may possess to endeavour to guide them along what we consider will be the path that will lead to the improvement of all – not one class, not one interest in one particular section of the people, but that the whole people may benefit and benefit by trade, by bring-ing in work to our yards and factories, and to endeavour to make everybody swing along as they used to do in the good old times before the war (Applause).[22]

As the Unionist Party became more and more enmeshed with the Northern Ireland state it sought to portray any challenge to Unionist authority as an attack on the Union with Great Britain itself. This tactical ploy was to gain significance as the years progressed.

The roots of the Northern Ireland Labour movement

Prior to the formation of the six-county state the Labour movement in Ulster had a long lineage stretching back over 200 years to when the first craft union was set up in Belfast.[23] At first, trade unionists and socialists congregated in tiny groups in and around the Lagan Valley, but their network soon mushroomed. As it did it encountered two communities frequently at odds with one another, principally in terms of their incompatible constitutional aspirations. Nevertheless, these ethnically different groupings were not beyond indulging themselves in collaborative enterprises to raise awareness of socio-economic grievances. What is important to remember, however, is that despite building up this measured consensus, such periods of relative calm did not maintain momentum for long. As John Harbinson points out:

> With a large proportion of the electorate belonging to the working-class, and the high level of unemployment, it might be imagined that the Labour Party would have received considerable support, both in terms of members and votes. Yet this was not so.[24]

Labour's difficulty in neutralising the ethno-national antagonism prevalent among the working classes would remain a constant barrier to its future devel-opment.

Harbinson has traced the NILP's immediate roots back to the late nineteenth century, when Home Rule was being floated as a radical new dispensation in Irish political life. Home Rule became a massive stumbling block for Labour, particularly from the so-called 'third crisis' (1912–14) onwards. Even though many working-class Protestants were sympathetic to the idea of Ireland remaining within the United Kingdom, working-class Catholics were deeply committed to Irish self-government. Although not the formal policy of the British Labour Party (BLP), most members were plainly in favour of Home Rule within the British Empire.[25] This posed something of a conundrum for the local Labour movement that would forever remain insoluble. The Northern Labour movement's close association with British Labour can be dated to 1893, when the British Trades Union Congress held its annual conference in Ulster and 'left behind it a branch of the Independent Labour Party which was so successful that it made Belfast the chief centre of socialist thought in Ireland'.[26]

Home Rule had a lasting legacy for the Irish Labour movement, with the well-known Irish socialist leaders William Walker and James Connolly becoming implacable enemies on the issue. As a consequence, it wrought tremendous havoc on Labour organisation in Belfast – Ireland's most industrialised city and the place where, conterminously, workplace solidarity was most pronounced. In Harbinson's view it became 'impossible for a political party to operate normally, and particularly a labour party with is emphasis on social and economic problems. Politics, in this sense, and nationalism did not mix'.[27] The stage was set for a conflict between the predominant ideological traditions; Labour was left spectating on the sidelines.[28]

According to Norton the Belfast Labour Party carried with it into the new state its internal divisions over Home Rule.[29] Several of the local party's senior activists had a penchant for indulging in anti-partitionist rhetoric,[30] while remaining just as sceptical of their British Labour connection. At a meeting of the 'Connollyite' Falls and Smithfield Labour parties in the wake of the British Labour Party's victory in the 1924 British General Election the Irish Transport and General Workers Union (ITGWU) official and Belfast Labour spokesman, William McMullen, observed how '[t]he great fault of labour, so far as the North was concerned, in the past was that they had always directed their gaze to Great Britain. That was a grievous mistake. (Hear, hear)'. On the other hand, those prominent members who constituted what might be termed the NILP's 'mainstream' – Sam Kyle, Hugh Gemmell and Harry Midgley – 'concentrated on supplying a non-sectarian opposition to the governing unionists with British Labour as their model and ideological base'.[31] Nevertheless, as Norton points out, 'regardless of this fundamental division, these groups were prepared to put their differences to one side in pursuit of the common goal of social reform'.[32]

While Belfast Labour remained 'a rather hybrid organisation'[33] in its political and constitutional orientation, it had grown primarily out of the reaction to social and economic discontent caused by unemployment and the competition for jobs. At the beginning of 1922, 25% of the North's insured population were unemployed. Significantly, unemployment stood at 48,355 at the end of February 1923,[34] a steady increase from the Unionist government's own estimation of 32–33,000 in 1920.[35] Despite pressing difficulties the Unionist regime survived the years of mass unemployment, according to Norton, by pursuing a series of strategies involving sectarian rhetoric and the endorsement of exclusivist practices.[36]

Throughout these years the Protestant working class formed the backbone of the Labour movement in Belfast, though it was prone to the populist rhetoric of Unionist politicians who continued to conjure up the spectre of what became known as the 'border bogey' at convenient moments.[37] For Henry Patterson this was a combination of endogenous ideological tensions within the Protestant community and the exogenous irredentist threat posed by the Southern government, which loomed like a dark cloud over the province's political culture in these years. In his view:

> As in the pre-war period, the development of the labour movement must be related closely to the wider field of intra-Protestant conflicts, so in the immediate post-war period, widespread economic and social discontent must be related both to the specific ideological traditions of Protestant workers and the intensifying political and military conflict in the rest of Ireland.[38]

How the Unionist Party managed these conflicts within the Protestant bloc had far-reaching effects for the development of the Labour movement in the inter-war period.

The socialist challenge and the Unionist response

Almost immediately the Unionists recognised Labour as a threat to the political stability of Northern Ireland. Proportional Representation (PR) was promptly abolished in 1922 for all future local government elections, with the consequence that Labour's representation in Belfast was slashed from eleven to two councillors.[39] Notwithstanding these structural inhibitors Labour took two seats in the Dock and Court Ward by-elections the following year. Budge and O'Leary have argued that these 'victories might be attributed to the gradual increase in Labour strength in Belfast as a whole (as evidenced by the election of three Labour MPs in the Stormont election of 1925), and the corresponding decline in Nationalist effort and propaganda'.[40] Nonetheless, the successful return of Labour MPs 'confirmed Craig in his determination to be rid of the PR system at the earliest opportunity. This he did in 1928 as a deliberate strike at both Labour and the Independents.'[41] PR had been a source of Unionist angst for some time, for none more so than Sir Edward Carson, Craig's predecessor as Unionist leader, who complained bitterly about its potentially destabilising effects and frequently pondered the rationale behind its introduction in the first place.[42] Indeed the Ulster Unionist Council established a committee in 1921 to 'review the Unionist position in the six-counties', reporting back that PR made unity in the Protestant ranks imperative - 'otherwise under PR undesirable candidates may succeed in being elected'.[43]

Electorally, Labour declined to contest elections in the new state until 1923, although Independent Labour candidates did run in the May 1921 poll. With limited resources at its disposal the Belfast Labour Party decided to challenge 'the powers that be in an electoral contest' shortly after the announcement of an Imperial general election in November 1923.[44] Midgley was nominated as the candidate for West Belfast and chose to use the platform to address the legacy of the First World War and the resultant socio-economic fall-out gripping working-class communities in the North. While unemployment formed the main plank of his campaign he did pay even-handed attention to other concerns raised in Labour's official manifesto. These included:

The Right to Work, or Full Maintenance.
The Establishment of a National Minimum Wage.
A Universal Eight Hour Day.
Pensions for Widowed Mothers.
Full Recognition of the Claims of Ex-Service Men and their Dependents, on the Basis of "Fit for Service, Fit for Pension."
And, The Reduction of the Age Limit for Old Age Pensions to 60, irrespective of the applicant's Income.[45]

For Midgley, the 'fight for Labour' was 'the fight for Human Justice, Truth, and Right'. It made for an impressive rallying call. Indeed, his campaign reflected his own military service along the Western Front, where he 'realised from bitter experience how dearly the workers have to pay in blood and money, for the harvest of Secret Diplomacy carried on by Conservative and Liberal Governments'.[46]

Collectively Labour was calling for a number of changes to the existing political dispensation and Midgley used his individual personality and charisma to press home the message. Voicing his support for Midgley on the Falls Road in West Belfast, the Labour Party's President Sam Kyle said that

the time had come for the workers to unite irrespective of creed or class to sweep away the differences that existed and remove the stigma that had so long rested upon them. (Cheers.) The issues that divided them in the past had now been solved in some way, so that they had now the opportunity of uniting and returning a Labour man for West Belfast – a Labour man without prefixes, neither a Nationalist Labour man nor Unionist Labour man, but a Labour man pure and unadulterated. (Cheers.)[47]

Even though Midgley subsequently lost the election, he did come within 2,000 votes of unseating his Unionist opponent. And as Walker points out Midgley 'took on the sectarian forces which were inevitably directed against him, and emerged with a personal triumph having won votes in equal numbers from Protestants and Catholics'.[48] For the emerging Labour Party (NI) the contest

rallied the sympathisers of Labour in a fashion never previously excelled in the City, and revealed to what extent the people will subscribe both morally and financially in a fight for genuine Labour principles.[49]

Notwithstanding Midgley's defeat the party chose to contest the municipal elections in January 1924. Out of its four candidates it successfully returned one,

Clarke Scott, to Court Ward in West Belfast. This ward would become the hub of party activity in West Belfast for the next half century.

The Labour Party of Northern Ireland was officially constituted at the beginning of 1924, though those activists who subsequently served on its interim 19-strong management committee – including Sam Kyle, William Boyd, Dawson Gordon and William McMullen – had been busy establishing two divisional parties on the basis of individual membership in East and West Belfast during the previous 12 months.[50] Midgley also confidently reported how a new branch had been formed in Newtownards and that seven societies had since affiliated to the party. Financially, the books were healthily balanced and the party remained confident that it was on the cusp of a 'harvest' that 'shall yet be garnered'. In Walker's opinion:

> The new party was independent of both the British and Irish Labour parties ... it clearly modelled its aims and its approach on the former, and had an indirect link with the latter by virtue of a number of trade unions and other organisations being affiliated to the ITUC [Irish Trades Union Congress] of which the Irish Labour Party was part.[51]

According to the party's official records its name and objectives were officially adopted on 8 March 1924 at a conference attended by over 40 delegates who represented the country districts, the party locally and representatives from the Shipbuilding and Engineering Federation.[52]

The Labour Party (NI) entered a crowded political arena, made up of official Unionists, Independent Unionists, Nationalists and republicans. Throughout the 1920s and 1930s there were a number of hard-fought campaigns between the party of government and these oppositional forces. The unseating of the head of the Orange Order, Sir Joseph Davison, by the Independent Unionist Colonel P.J. Woods, in West Belfast in 1923, for instance, illustrates the delicate nature of Unionist Party hegemony. Woods appealed to the same core constituency as the established party by directly challenging 'the old clique', who, he claimed, 'had done every conceivable thing to destroy the initiative and lull to sleep the thinking capabilities of the working class and ex-servicemen'.[53] Craig was quick to recognise the threat posed by Independent Unionists, and he tarnished them 'as dangerous and disloyal' in a bid 'to simplify Protestant politics to maintain hegemonic control'.[54] One way of stymieing opposition was to alter the electoral system to extinguish intra-Protestant competition.

By 1927 Craig was seriously considering abolishing PR for elections to the Northern Ireland Parliament. In the annual Orange Order demonstration at Finaghy, outside Belfast, he invited support for official Unionist candidates 'against all comers – Republicans, Nationalists, Socialists, or so-called "Independents"'. Playing to rapturous applause and cheers Craig made the bald assertion that 'Mr Devlin and his party are the natural Opposition. Why, then, should any Loyalist constituency add strength to it and weaken the influence of my colleagues and myself?'[55] Responding to Craig's speech in the House of Commons after the summer recess Kyle stated:

The Prime Minister says that the Nationalists are the natural Opposition. What exactly does he mean if he does not mean that his conception of Government is based on the different views held by the sects of the Christian religion.[56]

Craig's reasoning for 'doing away' with PR was simple:

What I want to get in this House, and what I believe we will get very much better in this House under the old-fashioned plain and simple system, are men who are for the Union on the one hand or who are against it and want to go into a Dublin Parliament on the other.[57]

Labour MP Jack Beattie accused the Unionist leader of 'sectarianism', a label the PM rejected out of hand. Perhaps most disturbing of all was Craig's patronising view of the people of Northern Ireland, who, in his mind, 'are plain, simple honest folk, and they deserve and are entitled to get a plain simple method of recording their votes' in a general election.[58] Notwithstanding his condescending rhetoric, Craig displayed a calculated understanding of intra-Protestant political challenges to his party's stranglehold over the locally devolved administration.

However, it was something that the Labour Party set out to challenge in its oppositional role within the Belfast Parliament. In many ways it had measured success. Overall, however, Labour's parliamentary record remained mixed. In an official report to its Fifth Annual Conference on 31 March 1928 the Parliamentary Labour Party (PLP) reported on its track record as Official Opposition. A range of social and economic issues were covered, including the party's purported 'constant watch' on the Rent Restriction Act, agricultural wages and the employment of ex-servicemen. Perhaps the most important piece of legislation challenged by Labour was the Trade Dispute and Trade Union Bill, which was eventually carried by the government and its supporters in 1927. Labour saw the Bill as a direct threat to its political interests and the PLP was quick to call for both its rejection and the party responsible for bringing it before the House:

How can the Government say that they have the welfare of the working classes at heart, when they introduce a Bill of this character. We hope the organised workers will at the next opportunity pay back to the representatives of re-action their due reward by giving all Unionist candidates their discharge note.[59]

The knock-on effect of the legislation was obvious, in that it introduced 'contracting in' to the political levy. In other words the workers automatically 'contracted out' unless they explicitly stated that they wished to 'contract in' and pay their trade union dues. One way that the NILP sought to traverse this hurdle in the post-war period was to raise the party's profile by forming Labour Groups in the Harland and Wolff shipyard, as well as in other industrial workplaces throughout the province. Another way was to lobby the BLP for a financial assistance, a matter that was given little serious consideration by the latter until the late 1940s.[60] According to Labour the Unionists were attempting to make it 'as difficult as possible to prepare for a general election' and in many ways 'deliberately inciting the trade unions and the labour party to become unconstitutional'; a line, Kyle intimated, that his party would never cross.[61]

Outside of the House of Commons, and despite these structural constraints, the party's local government representation continued to mushroom, albeit tentatively. In January 1928 Labour contested six seats in the Belfast Borough, where both Clarke Scott and Harry Midgley retained their seats. In Derry Frank Callaghan was returned unopposed as Chairman of the Labour Group on the local Corporation, which had successfully returned 16 councillors in 1926.[62] Meanwhile, in the Triennial Poor Law and Urban Council Elections in Newry, Labour successfully returned five members; in Belfast it returned three out of its four candidates. Newtownards and several other outlying areas also returned Labour members. Affiliated membership was healthy too, with 26 unions on the membership books, including the National Union of Vehicle Builders, the Amalgamated Engineering Union and the United Patternmakers Association, three sizable British-based unions. Importantly, the Belfast and District Trades and Labour Council and the Londonderry, Enniskillen and Newry Trades Councils soon affiliated. All of these areas had established Labour parties.[63] Additionally, the NILP affiliated to the ITUC in 1927, and set up a joint council with the Irish Labour Party in 1930.[64]

The hungry Thirties

The 1930s presented a range of unique challenges and opportunities for the Northern Ireland Labour movement and it soon became exercised by developments on the political front. By now the NILP had branches established in most of the province's major towns, with Belfast, Derry and North Antrim becoming hotbeds of activity. Several branches made submissions to the party's eighth annual conference in 1931 calling for, among other things, a greater redistribution of material support for unemployed workers and the establishment of maternity and child welfare clinics.[65] In direct correlation with the broader party's policy, the North Antrim Labour Party called upon the Unionist administration to 'immediately extend the Unemployment Insurance Act so as to include Agricultural Workers'.[66] It was an indication that the Labour Party did not view itself in Belfast-centric terms, but to this end it had only limited success.[67]

The following year the Minister of Labour John Miller Andrews boasted that he wished to see 'prosperity for our farmers and for our industrial and commercial undertakings, with full-time employment for all our people'.[68] Disappointingly the hotly anticipated prosperity soon gave way to the reality of economic hardship in the key manufacturing industries. Over 100,000 industrial and agricultural workers were to be rendered unemployed during the 1930s, something which hastened greater co-operation between the unions, the NILP and Belfast Trades Council and resulted in a concerted campaign of protest.[69] However this did not always manifest itself in electoral terms. For example, in the 1932 municipal elections in Belfast the NILP still faced two major challenges: voter apathy and ethnic loyalty. In Court Ward Labour's Armand Wallace ran against the official Unionist candidate Malcolm Mercer. Wallace was promptly defeated by a majority of 1,464, although in Dock the Unionists regained the seat from the NILP with a slimmer majority of just 568 votes. In both wards turnout was as low as 47% and 48% respectively, demonstrating the apparent lack of interest among voters.[70]

Meanwhile in Derry, Frank Callaghan, the former leader of the local Municipal Labour Party, was beaten into third place by his two Nationalist opponents in the South Ward.[71] According to Walker the Derry party had an anti-partitionist outlook,[72] though surprisingly contemporary newspaper reports pointed to the fact that eligible Protestants were expected to cast their votes in favour of Labour in the absence of a Unionist candidate.[73] Despite the local Waterside Unionist Association calling on loyalist electors to abstain in the South Ward,[74] Labour did succeed in polling some 1,618 votes, indicating strong support from among the 587 Protestant voters residing there. During the campaign Callaghan had publicly questioned the right of 'gentlemen who belonged to the employing class to adequately represent a working class Ward like the South Ward' and said that he would campaign vigorously on social issues, like greater provision of amenities for elderly and infirm people and children, and improved sewage and refuse services. In the run-up to the election the Labour candidate promised that, if elected, he 'would look after the interests of the working classes and make every effort both by voice and vote to improve their condition'.[75] The limited advances on the local government front, however, indicated that the NILP's ambitious rhetoric had yet to be channelled into an electoral high-tide of support for the party. Nevertheless, the Unionist Party in Derry and elsewhere was conscious of the fact that it had to guard against losing any further ground to Independent Unionists and Labour by continually emphasising 'how it was not down on the working man'.[76]

Conversely, these limited Labour successes led some Unionist elites to question the usefulness of democratic participation more emphatically. In a particularly insensitive speech delivered to a meeting of the Strandtown Women's Unionist Association in East Belfast, the local Unionist MP for Belfast Dock, Major Charles Blakiston-Houston, called into question the benefits of universal franchise:

> The democratic system is grand in theory but not in practice, he said, and pointed out that in business concerns the shareholders voted according to the number of shares held, whereas in the Parliamentary and municipal voting lists it was one man one vote no matter whether the voter paid 2s 6d in taxes or sixteen times that amount. He considered the man who paid the piper should call the tune.[77]

Few in the Labour movement needed reminding that they were fighting for an extension of democratic rights several years after their comrades had sacrificed their lives on the battlefields of France and Belgium for just that ideal. Utterances by some high-ranking Unionists only added grist to the mill for populist challenges from oppositional politicians seeking to win over the working-class vote. In a further twist Blakiston-Houston challenged the right of the Labour movement to act as a vanguard for the working class: 'Trade unions, the Major declared, were the curse of the country. Their "go-slow" policy had prevented men getting on with jobs, and had made shipbuilding so expensive that foreigners were securing the trade'.[78] Blakiston-Houston was rewarded for his dogmatic attitude by defeat at the hands of Harry Midgley in the contest for Belfast Dock at the 1933 Northern Ireland General Election.

Ethnic exclusivist feelings among certain sections of the Unionist elite manifested themselves in more draconian ways too. For instance, in the internal chamber election of the Londonderry Corporation's chairman in 1932 Nationalist calls for their candidate, a successful local businessman in the city, to be returned were flatly rejected by the Unionists. Instead, the Unionist incumbent Senator Dudley McCorkell was re-elected. Accepting the defeat of their candidate the Nationalists stated that 'we claim to represent 30,000 out of a population of 50,000 ... in this Corporation. If Proportional Representation were restored the position would be reversed'. McCorkell's re-election was effortlessly secured by 20 votes to 12, with three abstentions.[79]

Subsequent critical commentators have claimed that the issue of gerrymandering was the direct result of rational thinking on the part of the Unionist leadership, insofar as they 'encouraged anti-Catholicism because they wanted to stay in power and thereby to preserve the economic position of their class'.[80] While the Unionists certainly governed Derry from a selfish, ethnic and materialistic standpoint, the precarious minority regime enjoyed little legitimacy, even amongst a sizeable section of the working-class Protestants in the city. Nor was the Corporation in any way representative of the latter's class interests; rather it reflected the narrow economic interests of the entrepreneurial, mercantile and landowning elite. Unionist misrule in Derry would return to haunt the regime once again a generation later.[81]

Another bone of contention for the working classes in the 1930s was the introduction of legislation in the form of the Anomalies Act which applied a 'means test' to the allocation of pensions and other sources of financial help from the state. The Unionists claimed that 'it was in the interests of the unemployed as much as the taxpayer that a means test should be applied'.[82] In Sam Kyle's words it was 'the most degrading and iniquitous system ever imposed on the workers of Northern Ireland'.[83] Indeed, the NILP used the occasion of the annual May Day demonstrations in 1932 to call for its abolition. Jack Beattie made an impassioned plea from the Custom House steps for the workers to 'demand a decent standard of living. There were thousands of workers on the verge of starvation', he said; while Robert Getgood – a future MP for Belfast Oldpark – appealed to the workers to protect themselves by joining a union. Meanwhile, Kyle's wife reminded those gathered that they belonged to 'an international organisation' and that 'as women and as mothers they should protest against their children being brought up, trained, and sent into the ranks to shoot down their fellow workers in other countries'.[84]

By the end of the year Protestant and Catholic workers were coming together

Democratic socialism and sectarianism, 1924–45

to protest against the scourge of unemployment.[85] The October 1932 demonstrations ended in riots against the authorities, a cross-community venture 'which caused consternation within government circles'.[86] This realignment did not last long as inter-communal polarisation became an unfortunate by-product of the street demonstrations.[87] Ironically, within a few tumultuous years the Protestant and Catholic workers of Belfast were training their sights on each other. By 1934 individual murders were being carried out by loyalist para-militaries in a bid to whip up tension among the working classes. Predictably, sectarian rioting followed in 1935 and 'inevitably strengthened northern Catholics' sense of themselves as a besieged minority within a hostile society and with a government that was, at best, indifferent to their fate'.[88]

The brittle rigidity of inter-ethnic co-operation had thrown into sharp relief the NILP's obvious difficulty in bridging the divide at the political level. Added to this was the party's continual espousal of its dogmatic aim to become the main opposition in Northern Ireland, a fruitless pursuit which, as Walker points out, was doomed to failure, especially in light of the party's equivocation on the question of Northern Ireland's constitutional position. Another obstacle blocking the NILP's progress, besides flag-waving by the Unionists, was the latter's 'approach to devolution under the leadership of Craigavon' that 'had the effect of nullifying much of the appeal of a party like the NILP around social and economic policies'.[89]

In a further bid to stymie working-class political advances the Unionists used the occasion of the 1938 election to mobilise their supporters against the adoption of an Irish Constitution by Eamonn De Valera in 1937, which gave a special position to the Roman Catholic Church and laid claim to the entire island of Ireland in Articles Two and Three. Meanwhile another party sympathetic to working-class interests had emerged in Belfast. The Ulster Progressive Unionist Party was led by the liberal Unionist William J. Stewart and sought to improve the lot of those who opposed the local regime's socio-economic policies. Although defeated in all of the constituencies it contested, Stewart later claimed that the 40,000 votes polled by the PUP represented something of an achievement, especially since the Unionist Party had effectively truncated opposition to its rule by playing up the danger to Northern Ireland's constitutional position. As Stewart disappointedly observed in his post-election speech:

> It was represented to our people that the only issue was that of partition, and as this was done very thoroughly by the Press and canvassers, the question of unemployment for the time being made little impression.[90]

The threat to the border would be repeatedly played upon by the Unionists as a vehicle to remove dissent and drive a wedge between the common interests of the working classes. Furthermore, the issue also impacted negatively on the NILP's efforts to build up fraternal relations with the British and Irish Labour movements, while keeping its own supporters' divergent national identity issues in check; a particularly 'difficult balancing act', writes Niamh Puirséil, that 'seems, however, to have been wasted on its southern counterparts who broke off relations with the NILP on two occasions during the late 1930s'.[91]

Even though the odds were heavily stacked against it, the NILP successfully returned its candidate for the Stormont seat of South Armagh. Paddy Agnew was one of the NILP's most articulate spokesmen. Originally from a rural background, he was deeply motivated by a Christian compassion for the plight of his fellow worker. Though a devout Roman Catholic, he rarely allowed the Church to interfere with his political decisions and often rallied against those whom he thought were acting on behalf of the Church's interests. One commentator has described Agnew as 'a nationalist on the right wing of the party'.[92] And in many of his speeches in the Stormont debating chamber it is difficult to downplay the fact that he was an extremely proactive campaigner on issues affecting the socio-economic well-being of the people of South Armagh. He frequently highlighted the plight of those who led protest marches calling on local authorities to employ local workers as labour on local projects.[93] Agnew's adversarial style was imbibed with the notion that political power should be decentralised in favour of those in the outlying areas of the province.

Other topics of interest that Agnew raised in the House included road improvements, pension rights for workers, the 'unjust' poor law system, housing and the school leaving age. Agnew was also a champion of the non-industrial worker and could often be found lamenting how: 'At a time like this, when progress and prosperity are so much talked about, surely it is not too much to ask that the agricultural labourer should receive his due reward.'[94] He had experienced long-term unemployment first-hand at the height of the 1929 Great Depression and brought this to bear on all of his public speaking engagements as a local councillor and as MP for South Armagh a decade later between 1938 and 1945. The following excerpt from one of his speeches illustrates how his background shaped his labour discourse:

> Whilst poverty and unemployment remain, it is an indication that the Government are unable to tackle the problem after so many years in office. They evade their responsibilities, and I, as a representative of the labour movement, demand justice and security for my class.[95]

Agnew personified the Christian socialist ethos that would continue to permeate the NILP's ranks in the post-war years, although unlike those from Protestant Methodist roots, who were elected after 1958 in Belfast constituencies, he adhered to a uniquely Roman Catholic concern for social justice. Agnew was one of the most vocal opponents of the Unionist government's track-record on trade union issues in the Stormont Parliament.

According to Boyd Black the outbreak of war in 1939 provided a great shock for the Northern Ireland labour market. While unemployment had been falling since 1932 in Great Britain, it had peaked at 28% in Northern Ireland in 1938,[96] leaving almost half of all textile workers unemployed.[97] Yet total employment in construction, shipbuilding and textiles doubled between 1939 and 1942, a rate of mobilisation which was, as Black points out, 'bound to bring considerable disturbance in its wake'.[98] In fact, it could be argued that the continual disgruntlement among unemployed labour would soon be translated into voting capital for the NILP.

'Paying the piper:' war and welfarism in Northern Ireland

Northern Ireland had proven a strategic asset in the British war effort, but at a hefty price. Political life almost ground to a halt, with the Ulster Unionist Party (UUP) suspending its electoral organisation and calling upon its opponents to do likewise, at least for the duration of the emergency.[99] Some commentators blamed the ineptitude of John Miller Andrews (Prime Minister from 1940 to 1943) for the political economic downturn, though others insisted that structural implications were equally as debilitating. Above all the Andrews years indirectly exposed the inability of some Unionist leaders to sacrifice narrow sectarian concerns in favour of sustaining allied industrial output.[100] The collapse of public morale following the Belfast Blitz of April and May 1941 led one senior official 'to predict attacks on the Parliamentary buildings at Stormont by an irate and frightened populace'.[101] Brian Barton has claimed that the province's defences 'were hopelessly inadequate and the public psychologically unprepared for aerial bombardment'.[102]

Growing industrial unrest compounded these difficulties and even led some Unionists to demand the introduction of conscription as a disciplinary measure. Nonetheless Unionism was prevented from taking this option by London and easily faced down charges from its parliamentary backbenchers that it was 'spineless' in the face of socialist agitation.[103] Coincidentally, the NILP did pursue conciliatory measures designed to maximise war production, a course of action favoured by many leftists following the entry of the Soviet Union into the war. Indeed there is much evidence to suggest that the Unionist administration relied upon the NILP to appeal to the workers 'to utilise existing negotiation and arbitration machinery in the settlement of differences with their employers'.[104]

Scholarly writings on Northern Ireland's 'forgotten' premiership (of which there are few) are typically unsentimental, either hinging on Andrews's deftness for 'populist' rhetoric or on his equally woefully insular political outlook.[105] A common argument runs:

> As Chairman of the UULA and Minister of Labour, Andrews ensured that the Government did not lose touch with its urban supporters. In the midst of global war, however, Andrews' concentration on the domestic needs of the province only served to weaken his administration.[106]

Consequently, assessments have ranged from outright hostility to downright vilification: he was purportedly regarded by officials in the British Treasury as 'a dangerous demagogue';[107] by one contemporary political opponent as 'the arch apostle of private enterprise',[108] and by his only academic biographer to date as 'the archetypal Stormont politician, with a keen understanding of local needs, but lacking the ability to see beyond the practical concerns of 1920'.[109] One

Round Table commentator even suggested that the odds were stacked against Andrews from the beginning when:

> Deprived of Lord Craigavon's leadership, a Cabinet whose average age was remarkably high, and the majority of whose members had been in office for more than 20 years, became tired and its policy lost its resilience.[110]

Life got more difficult for Andrews as the war wore on, particularly as it became clearer that the Protestant working class was just as promiscuous in its political preferences as it had been before 1939.

The death of Lord Craigavon in 1940 robbed the Unionist Party of one of its most iconic figures. It also raised the possibility of an imminent by-election to fill his Stormont seat of North Down. This was held in March 1941. The Unionist Party, which had called on all parties to suspend electioneering during the war, now found itself facing the prospect of having to fight a general election, something especially troubling given the NILP and Independent Unionists' decision to contest the constituency. According to Walker, 'the NILP victory by 7,209 votes to 2,435 constituted the biggest electoral upset in Northern Ireland's political history'.[111] For many contemporaries, including the Unionist press, it was a serious threat that served to portray Andrews as a weak Prime Minister. Arguably, Andrews's fate was sealed when NILP leader Harry Midgley subsequently beat Unionist councillor Fred Lavery in Willowfield.[112]

Success was short-lived for the NILP. In 1942 Midgley resigned from the party after an aborted attempt to persuade it to adopt a definite pro-partitionist position on the constitutional question. Midgley had been party leader for 10 years and in that time he had gradually moved the party closer to accepting the border.[113] On 20 November, as Walker points out, 'at a meeting of the Willowfield labour group, he issued a "Declaration of policy" which committed the NILP to support for the constitutional position of Northern Ireland within the United Kingdom'.[114] It provoked consternation within the ranks of the party. George H. Simpson, secretary of the North Derry Labour Party, summed up the dismay felt by many of Midgley's 'staunch friends' when he said that the forcing of the issue had 'done us a world of good down here and we at least appreciate the stand that you have taken'. Simpson intimated that Midgley had highlighted a 'matter of vital importance to the future of the Labour movement in Northern Ireland'.[115] Nonetheless, with two out of three NILP MPs at Stormont now anti-partitionist, Midgley – once described as "the Solomon of socialism"[116] – was 'convinced that he had to sever the ties with the party he had been so instrumental in founding'[117] and pursue a more pro-British agenda. Within weeks Midgley announced the formation of the Commonwealth Labour Party.

Several months later Midgley would lament his expulsion from the NILP in a letter to the Manchester-based General Secretary of National Union of Distributive and Allied Workers (NUDAW). In what he saw as a calculated termination of his services Midgley thought:

> That such action should be taken against one whose only crime has been that he has

Democratic socialism and sectarianism, 1924–45   23

endeavoured to build up closer association between Northern Ireland and Gt. Britain in the stress of war's adversities is almost beyond comprehension and will certainly not redound to the credit of N.U.D.A.W. in this area.[118]

The action against Midgley had set a precedent that would later have repercussions for Jack Beattie who had also come into conflict with NILP policy in the same year, following his defeat of the Unionist Party candidate in a by-election for the Westminster seat of West Belfast and his subsequent aborted attempt to take the BLP whip at Westminster.[119]

Beattie's by-election victory in January 1943 inflicted one further mortal wound on the regime's integrity. Within months rebellious backbenchers and junior ministers were actively calling for Andrews's resignation.[120] The threat from Independent Unionists and the NILP loomed large in these years, as much as at any other time before the war, and such danger was not lost on certain elements in the Unionist establishment. Indeed, despite the successful absorption of unemployed workers into the labour market during the war years, the Unionist Party remained unpopular. Andrews's hand was forced and his capitulation made way for a man of sterner military bearing: Sir Basil Brooke was installed in office.

Internally the transition from war to peace threatened to upset the balance of power within the Unionist Party. The fall of Andrews failed to placate dissension within Unionist ranks. Maintaining loyalty, while fending off the threat from Labour and other oppositional forces, was a pressing priority for the new Prime Minister. However, unlike his predecessor, Brooke's excellent man-management skills, most pronounced in his ambidextrous handling of backbench revolts, soon became apparent and were indicative of his strong leadership abilities. The following extract from his diary, written shortly after a meeting of the Ulster Unionist Council in March 1945, captures his thinking well:

> I told them that I was afraid the general teamwork was not what it should be and that I was not prepared to lead a party who, knowing the problems, refused to face them with the hope that they would solve themselves. I said a Prime Minister was like a runner in a relay race, that at some time he would hand the torch on. The question was did they want me to hand it on now. If not, they must establish a strong and firm government.[121]

Placing these remarks in their historical context, it is not difficult to discern Brooke's rationale: the climb-down in war production meant that Ulster faced the very pressing prospect of mass redundancies in its traditional staple industries.

Many Unionists were adept too at drawing comparisons with his hapless predecessor at this time. Something had to be done. Impending realities goaded the Prime Minister into action. He lobbied the British government directly, actively seeking ways to diversify the hamstrung staples.[122] By his actions 'he showed greater enterprise and activity than his predecessors'.[123] Brooke's remarkable 'ability, confidence and imagination'[124] may adequately explain how these political difficulties were quickly remedied, but Northern Ireland's proneness to economic fluctuations could not be solved by continually cashing in on ethnic loyalty dividends: structural economic faults necessitated long-term planning. Inevitably, attempts by the NILP to inflate the twin barrage balloons of unemployment and poor housing were targeted by Brooke's administration when it reanimated a series of social welfarist initiatives that had been lying in cold storage since Andrews's premiership. Not for the last time had Labour been outmanoeuvred by its Unionist opponents.

Conclusion

The forward march of Northern Ireland Labour was checked by the fusion of ethno-national sentiment and the ability of the Unionist regime to portray itself as the only true defender of the Union. By following a policy of 'step-by-step' with respect to socio-economic legislation emanating from Westminster, the Unionists effectively stymied NILP advances and created a situation in which devolution could be used to win over Protestant working-class support.[125] Consequently, Labour had only reasonable successes at the ballot box in the inter-war period and remained plagued by ideological fluctuations over the constitutional issue. Yet, the Labour movement as a whole remained strong and it was perhaps the power of the militant trade unionist wing of the Labour movement, and its propensity for strike action, that inevitably led to the British criticism of the Unionist regime that Northern Ireland was only 'half in the war'. Despite workplace solidarity the ethnic antagonism between Protestants and Catholics – which the Unionists stoked up to their political advantage in the inter-war period – remained a recurrent problem for the NILP and somewhat stunted its growth in the greater Belfast area.

The experience of a war-time economy prompted a major sea-change in the NILP's ideology and discourse. With the introduction of welfare state initiatives the party soon became more deliberately focused on the benefit provided by partition. Strands of 'unionism', 'anti-partitionism' and 'ambivalence' continued to weave their way through the party and allowed it to gain some electoral headway in ethnically diverse constituencies. That Labour continued to win votes and seats meant that it could present the electorate with an alternative voice at the political expense of Unionism and Nationalism. However, while successes in Willowfield and West Belfast should have been welcomed by the party rank and file they 'proved instead to be the pretext for the intensification of dilemmas over the national question and the relationship of labour politics to it'.[126] Harry Midgley's enduring quarrel with Jack Beattie eventually earned the latter a second expulsion from the NILP, perhaps less in terms of his ardent anti-partitionist convictions (for these were in plentiful evidence[127]) and more because of his refusal to accept party policy. The party's ability to suspend or expel those enigmatic personalities who chose to branch out from – or gainsay – official policy would remain a consistent feature throughout its history. Further external challenges continued to unfold during the post-war period, but the ingredients for the NILP's success and ultimate failure were contained in the first two decades of its existence.

Notes

1 *Northern Whig*, 3 January 1924.
2 Ferguson, Niall, *Empire: How Britain Made the Modern World* (London: Penguin Books, 2004), p. 315.
3 Townshend, Charles, *The British Campaign in Ireland, 1919–21: The Development of Political and Military Policies* (Oxford: Oxford University Press, 1975), pp. 196–9.
4 Payne, Stanley G., *A History of Fascism, 1914–45* (London: Routledge, 2001), p. 79.
5 Paxton, Robert O., *The Anatomy of Fascism* (London: Penguin Books, 2004), p. 78.
6 James Craig, Northern Ireland's first Prime Minister, speaking after the opening of the local Parliament. Northern Ireland House of Commons Debates, Vol. 1, Col. 37, 23 June 1921.
7 Follis, Bryan A., *A State Under Siege: The Establishment of Northern Ireland, 1920–1925* (Oxford: Oxford University Press, 1995), p. 189.
8 Bew, Paul, Peter Gibbon and Henry Patterson, *Northern Ireland, 1921–2001: Political Forces and Social Classes: Revised and Updated Version* (London: Serif, 2002), p. 27.
9 *The Northern Whig*, 10 and 11 January 1924 and *Northern Whig*, 13 July 1927.
10 See Follis, *A State under Siege*, p. 86. For a more detailed history of the USC see Hezlet, Arthur, *The 'B' Specials: A History of the Ulster Special Constabulary* (Belfast: Mourne River Press, 1997).
11 Bew, Paul, *Ireland: The Politics of Enmity, 1789–2006* (Oxford: Oxford University Press, 2007), p. 402.
12 Walker, Graham, *A History of the Ulster Unionist Party: Protest, Pragmatism and Pessimism* (Manchester: Manchester University Press, 2004), p. 55.
13 Budge, Ian and Cornelius O'Leary, *Belfast: Approach to Crisis: A Study of Belfast Politics, 1613–1970* (Basingstoke: Macmillan, 1973), p. 142.
14 Follis, *A State Under Siege*, p. 44.
15 Northern Ireland House of Commons Debates, Vol. 1, Col. 36, 23 June 1921.
16 Farrell, Michael, *Northern Ireland: The Orange State* (London: Pluto Press, 1976); O'Dowd, Liam, Bill Rolston and Mike Tomlinson, *Northern Ireland: Between Civil Rights and Civil War* (London: CSE Books, 1980).
17 Follis, *A State Under Siege*, p. 42.
18 Bew *et al.*, *Northern Ireland*, p. 65.
19 Norton, Christopher, 'Creating Jobs, Manufacturing Unity: Ulster Unionism and Mass Unemployment, 1922–34', *Contemporary British History*, Vol. 15, No. 2 (Summer 2001), p. 2; see also Walker, *A History of the Ulster Unionist Party*, p. 64.
20 Follis, *A State Under Siege*, p. 147. Walker, Graham 'The Northern Ireland Labour Party, 1924–45' in Lane, Fintan and Donal Ó Drisceoil (eds), *Politics and the Irish Working Class, 1830–1945* (Basingstoke: Palgrave, 2005), p. 235.
21 Walker, *A History of the Ulster Unionist Party*, pp. 42–4, 73.
22 *Belfast Telegraph*, 8 March 1923.
23 Bleakley, David, *Trade Union Beginnings in Belfast* (Unpublished MA Thesis, Queen's University Belfast, 1955).
24 Harbinson, John, *A History of the Northern Ireland Labour Party, 1891–1949* (Unpublished MSc Thesis: Queen's University Belfast, 1966), p. 261.
25 Cradden, Terry, 'Labour in Britain and the Northern Ireland Labour Party, 1900–1970', in Catterall, Peter and Sean McDougal (eds), *The Northern Ireland Question in British Politics* (Basingstoke: Macmillan, 1996), p. 71.

26 Harbinson, *A History of the Northern Ireland Labour Party*, p. 10.
27 Ibid., p. 260.
28 The most extensive analysis of the difficulties facing the Ulster Labour movement during this period is contained in Morgan, Austen, *Labour and Partition: The Belfast Working Class, 1905–23* (London: Pluto, 1991).
29 See Norton, Christopher, 'The Left in Northern Ireland, 1921–1932', *Labour History Review*, Vol. 60, No. 1 (Spring 1995), p. 3.
30 See the comments of William McMullen about the creation of 'an artificial boundary', *Northern Whig*, 7 January 1924.
31 Walker, 'The Northern Ireland Labour Party, 1924–45', p. 233.
32 Norton, 'The Left in Northern Ireland, 1921–1932', p. 3.
33 Walker, Graham, *The Politics of Frustration: Harry Midgley and the Failure of Labour in Northern Ireland* (Manchester: Manchester University Press, 1985), p. 47.
34 *Belfast Telegraph*, 6 March 1923.
35 Norton, Christopher, 'Worker Response to the 1920 Belfast Shipyard Expulsions: Solidarity or Sectarianism?', *Etudes Irlandaises* (Spring 1996), p. 154.
36 Norton, 'Creating Jobs, Manufacturing Unity', p. 11.
37 Walker, *The Politics of Frustration*, p. 34.
38 Patterson, Henry, *Class Conflict and Sectarianism: The Protestant Working Class and the Belfast Labour Movement 1868–1920* (Belfast: Blackstaff, 1980).
39 Budge and O'Leary, *Belfast*, p. 145.
40 Ibid., p. 149.
41 Walker, 'The Northern Ireland Labour Party, 1924–45', p. 237.
42 Lewis, Geoffrey, *Carson: The Man who Divided Ireland* (London: Hambledon and London, 2005), p. 223.
43 Report cited in Reid, Colin, *Independent Unionism and the Ulster Unionist Party State, 1925–1939* (Unpublished MA Thesis: Queen's University Belfast, 2004), p. 17. I am grateful to Colin Reid for drawing my attention to this point.
44 Public Records Office of Northern Ireland (PRONI), D/3702/B/1–3. *The Labour Party (Northern Ireland) Annual Report for 1923–1924*. The first report was written by the Secretary Harry Midgley and dated 28 March 1924.
45 PRONI, D/4089/4/1/1, 'Personal Manifesto for Harry Midgley, Parliamentary Elections: West Belfast, 6 December 1923'.
46 Ibid.
47 *Northern Whig*, 28 November 1923.
48 Walker, *The Politics of Frustration*, p. 33.
49 PRONI, D/3702/B/1–3. *The Labour Party (Northern Ireland) Annual Report for 1923–1924*. The first report was written by the Secretary Harry Midgley and dated 28 March 1924.
50 Ibid.
51 Walker, *The Politics of Frustration*, p. 34.
52 PRONI, D/3702/B/1–3. *The Labour Party (Northern Ireland) Annual Report for 1923–1924*.
53 *Irish News*, 1 May 1923.
54 Reid, *Independent Unionism and the Ulster Unionist Party State*, p. 16.
55 *The Londonderry Sentinel*, 14 July 1927.
56 Northern Ireland House of Commons Debates, Vol. 8, Col. 2259, 25 October 1927.
57 Ibid., Col. 2276, 25 October 1927.
58 Ibid., Col. 2272, 25 October 1927.

59 PRONI, D/3702/B/2, *The Labour Party (Northern Ireland) Report of Executive Committee, 1927–28*, Presented to the Fifth Annual Conference, 31 March 1928.

60 Labour Party Archives (LPA), Northern Ireland Policy Box (1980–1990), *Northern Ireland Liaison Committee: The Labour Party and Northern Ireland – An Historical Account of the Relations between the Labour Party and the Northern Ireland Labour Party* (BLP: Research Department, February, 1984).

61 Northern Ireland House of Commons Debates, Vol. 8, Col. 2095, 18 October 1927.

62 Walker, 'The Northern Ireland Labour Party, 1924–45', pp. 231–2.

63 PRONI, D/3702/B/2, *The Labour Party (Northern Ireland) Report of Executive Committee, 1927–28*.

64 O'Connor, Emmet, *A Labour History of Ireland 1824–1960* (Dublin: Gill and Macmillan, 1992), p. 182.

65 PRONI, D/3702/B/1–3, *Final Agenda: The Labour Party (Northern Ireland), Eighth Annual Conference, 6–7 April 1931*.

66 Ibid.

67 Walker, 'The Northern Ireland Labour Party, 1924–45', p. 232.

68 *Northern Whig*, 1 January 1932.

69 Cradden, Terry, *Trade Unionism, Socialism and Partition: The Labour Movement in Northern Ireland, 1939–1953* (Belfast: December Publications, 1993), p. 18.

70 *Northern Whig*, 15 January 1932.

71 *The Londonderry Sentinel*, 19 January 1932. The turnout was high at 76%.

72 Walker, *The Politics of Frustration*, p. 51.

73 *The Londonderry Sentinel*, 19 January 1932.

74 *The Londonderry Sentinel*, 14 January 1932.

75 *The Londonderry Sentinel*, 12 January 1932.

76 *The Londonderry Sentinel*, 27 February 1932.

77 *Northern Whig*, 19 January 1932.

78 Ibid.

79 *Northern Whig*, 25 January 1932.

80 McCann, Eamonn, *War in an Irish Town* (London: Pluto, 1993), p. 247.

81 See the comments of a high-ranking Unionist Edmund Warnock in Bew, *Ireland*, p. 491.

82 *Northern Whig*, 1 March 1932.

83 *Northern Whig*, 25 February 1932.

84 *Northern Whig*, 2 May 1932.

85 For more detailed coverage of this inter-ethnic co-operation see Bew, Paul and Christopher Norton, 'The Unionist State and the Outdoor Relief Riots of 1932', *Economic and Social Review*, Vol. 10, No. 3 (1979), pp. 255–65.

86 Walker, *A History of the Ulster Unionist Party*, p. 75.

87 Devlin, Paddy, *Yes, We Have No Bananas: Outdoor Relief in Belfast, 1920–39* (Belfast: Blackstaff, 1981).

88 Patterson, Henry, *Ireland Since 1939: The Persistence of Conflict* (London: Penguin, 2007), p. 29.

89 Walker, *A History of the Ulster Unionist Party*, p. 76.

90 *Belfast Telegraph*, 11 February 1938.

91 Puirséil, Niamh, *The Irish Labour Party, 1922–73* (Dublin: UCD Press, 2007), p. 137.

92 Walker, Graham, 'The Commonwealth Labour Party in Northern Ireland, 1942–7', *Irish Historical Studies*, Vol. 34, No. 93 (1984), p. 71.

93 Northern Ireland House of Commons Debates, Vol. 21, Col. 488, 29 March 1938.

94 Ibid., Col. 351, 22 March 1938.

95 Ibid., Col. 88, 2 March 1938.

96 Black, Boyd, 'A Triumph of Voluntarism? Industrial Relations and Strikes in Northern Ireland in World War Two', *Labour History Review*, Vol. 70, No. 1 (April 2005), p. 8.

97 Budge and O'Leary, *Belfast*, p. 144.

98 Black, 'A Triumph of Voluntarism?', p. 8.

99 Ibid., p. 87. The natural lifecycle of the Stormont Parliament was prolonged for the duration of the Second World War. The last general election was held in 1938. Cultural activities, like Orange Order parades, were also suspended – thus considerably alleviating sectarian tensions between 1939 and 1945.

100 There were 513 strikes in Northern Ireland between 1939 and 1945. See Black, Boyd, 'Industrial Relations', in Harris, R.I.D., C. Jefferson and J.E. Spencer (eds), *The Northern Ireland Economy: A Comparative Study in the Economic Development of a Peripheral Region* (London: Longman, 1990), pp. 207–33.

101 Barton, Brian, 'The Impact of World War II on Northern Ireland and on Belfast–London Relations', in Catterall, Peter and Sean McDougal (eds), *The Northern Ireland Question in British Politics* (Basingstoke: Macmillan, 1996), p. 50.

102 Ibid., p. 50.

103 Ibid., p. 51. Barton also informs us that 'the most serious of these strikes was in October, 1942, and affected 20,000 workers in the strategic industries'.

104 PRONI, CAB4/484/3, Draft Conclusions of a Cabinet Meeting Held at Stormont Castle, 14 October 1941.

105 For more on 'populism' and 'anti-populism' see Bew *et al.*, *Northern Ireland*, especially Chapter 3.

106 Richardson, David *The Political Career of John Miller Andrews 1871–1956* (Unpublished PhD Thesis: Queen's University Belfast, 1998), pp. 298–9.

107 Bew *et al.*, *Northern Ireland*, p. 77.

108 Hugh Downey, Northern Ireland House of Commons Debates, Vol. 29, Col. 84, 24 July 1945.

109 Richardson, *The Political Career of John Miller Andrews*, p. 303.

110 *The Round Table*, No. 132 (September 1943), p. 370.

111 Walker, *A History of the Ulster Unionist Party*, p. 91.

112 Walker, *A History of the Ulster Unionist Party*, pp. 89–91; Buckland, Patrick, *A History of Northern Ireland* (Dublin: Gill and Macmillan, 1981), p. 83; Bew *et al.*, *Northern Ireland*, p. 75. The results were 6,268 to 5,137 in favour of Baillie and 7,209 to 2,435 in favour of Midgley.

113 Walker, 'The Commonwealth Labour Party in Northern Ireland, 1942–7', p. 70.

114 Ibid., p. 72.

115 PRONI, D/4089/1/1/4, George Simpson to Harry Midgley, 23 November 1942.

116 *Northern Whig*, 3 August 1927.

117 Walker, 'The Northern Ireland Labour Party, 1924–45', p. 241.

118 PRONI, D/4089/1/1/5, Harry Midgley to J. Hallsworth, 18 February 1943.

119 Edwards, Aaron, 'Social Democracy and Partition: The British Labour Party and Northern Ireland, 1951–64', *Journal of Contemporary History*, Vol. 42, No. 4 (October 2007), p. 600.

120 Patterson, *Ireland since 1939*, p. 43.

121 PRONI, D/3004/D/36, *Brookeborough Diaries*, 7 March 1945.

122 This was not a completely novel idea as Brooke had previously exercised this

approach when he held the cabinet portfolio of Minister for Commerce and Production, 1941–43.

123 Barton, 'The Impact of World War II on Northern Ireland and on Belfast-London Relations', p. 54.
124 Ibid., p. 56.
125 Walker, *A History of the Ulster Unionist Party*, p. 77.
126 Walker, 'The Northern Ireland Labour Party, 1924–45', p. 243.
127 For a further illustration of Beattie's dogmatic anti-partitionism see the United Kingdom House of Commons Debates, Vol. 393, Col. 701–02, 3 November 1943.

2
Re-appraising the origins of the 'consensus-forming strategy', 1945–58

> The Northern Ireland Labour Party will maintain unbroken the connection between Great Britain and Northern Ireland as part of the Commonwealth, and to implement this hereby instructs the Executive Committee to proceed at once to take all necessary steps to seek the closest possible means of co-operation with the British Labour Party.[1]

Introduction: the welfare state

Historians have generally viewed the ending of the Second World War as a watershed in British politics because it announced the closure of one highly destructive era and the heralding of a new, more prosperous, epoch.[2] As embattled soldiers gradually returned from frontline combat, hopes were high that their demobilisation into civilian life would be facilitated by the state which had cajoled them into action. For the most part the Unionist administration was well aware of its obligations before Germany's surrender in May 1945. Sir Basil Brooke spoke in forward-thinking terms:

> My Government is resolved that Northern Ireland, having shared the struggles and sorrows of war, shall not stop at the half-way house but will press on to participate fully with the rest of the Kingdom in the benefits of a prosperous and progressive peace ... Our people, especially our men and women from the fighting forces, are entitled to this and it is the one goal to which they now aim.[3]

Despite the tactical deployment of these 'rhetorical sorties', hopes were soon dashed. Chronic unemployment – on a similar par to that experienced in the aftermath of the First World War – quickly transpired to become a monumental feature of everyday life until its peak in the late 1950s. Moreover, an intensification of industrial militancy among the local labour force, low levels of war production, the absence of conscription and Unionism's general apathy towards civil defence all impacted negatively on the local regime.[4] Doubts were soon raised over the province's actual contribution to the war effort. True to form, many Unionist leaders began to make the calculated sectarian argument

Origins of the 'consensus-forming strategy', 1945–58

that such despondency was largely attributable to the influx of Southern migrant workers into Belfast.

An extension of the British social welfare state to Northern Ireland and the tackling of acute unemployment were huge undertakings for the Unionist administration. Yet Brooke remained optimistic, claiming that 'by the end of July, 1945, Ulster would have turned the corner'.[5] Unemployment would be dissipated if only 'goodwill and collaboration' were fomented between workers and the local state: in other words, labour pacification was essential. 'There is no avoiding that fact,' asserted Brooke, 'and we must face it, fairly and squarely, realising and remedying to the best of our ability the dislocation which it is bound to cause.'[6]

The transition from war production (when cost was of secondary importance) to labour absorption in peace-time industries would now be his administration's chief priority. Displaced workers would be reimbursed with new jobs, new housing and the promise of better healthcare and educational provision. Although this ambitious social services programme had been in the pipeline since the obliteration of housing stock by the German *Luftwaffe* in 1941 it had taken a renewed radicalisation in working-class mindsets before the regime began to return the province's employed workforce to its war-time peak. These promised undertakings emphasised how well Unionism had anticipated the desires of the working classes, who sought to build a 'New Jerusalem' like that being constructed elsewhere in the United Kingdom. Brooke's plea to the Labour movement for compliance captures this mood well:

> What I want to urge upon you with all the earnestness at my command is this: that the success of all the efforts, all the plans, which the Government are making for the transitional period, must ultimately depend upon the goodwill and collaboration and, above all, the steadiness of our people in the critical months ahead.[7]

However, the radicalisation in working-class politics was by no means revolutionary and was premised firmly on socio-economic realities. Coincidently it occurred during an upsurge in trade union membership and British Labour government promises to lift the United Kingdom out of impoverishment. The number of unionised workers rose steadily from 109,000 (spread over 72 unions) in 1941 to 142,000 (across 78 unions) in 1945,[8] with David Bleakley estimating that by the early 1950s 90% of Ulster's trade unionists belonged to British-based unions – giving the Labour movement an overall membership strength of 196,000 (spread over 92 unions).[9]

Pre-empting a housing drought Brooke appointed a Housing Trust in February 1945 to oversee the mammoth task of 'building homes for heroes'.[10] Those heading up the initiative were pooled exclusively from the Protestant Grammar School-educated layer of local bourgeois society.[11] In fact four of its board members held key executive or managerial positions within Northern Ireland's textile industry, while the fifth was the daughter of a linen manufacturing doyen. It was recognised, at its inaugural meeting, that:

For a time most of the houses the Trust will build will inevitably be occupied by the better-paid workers, leaving the houses they vacate to relieve overcrowding amongst the worst-housed sections of the public.[12]

From its inception the Trust courted controversy. Independent Unionist MP for Belfast Shankill (and long-time thorn in the side of the government) Tommy Henderson remained the most hostile critic of Brooke's drive for post-war reconstruction. His damning indictment of the lackadaisical way by which the organisation replenished housing stock spiced up parliamentary debates on the issue.[13] Together with unemployment, education, health and social services, the issue of housing generated most heat in the immediate post-war period. Although the Trust was successful in offsetting minority Catholic charges of sectarian discrimination, intra-Unionist scepticism nevertheless remained vibrant. 'From the outset,' writes Henry Patterson, 'to the chagrin of many Unionist councillors, Housing Trust allocations were based on a points system and the system was free from allegations of discriminatory intent.'[14] The only leeway now given for preferential treatment in this system was that ex-servicemen, merchant seaman, bombed-out families and those more affluent workers would be given priority. Tension between the Housing Trust and local authorities remained considerable over the next 25 years in terms of housing allocation, and indeed was to provide grist to the mill for those engaging in civil rights agitation in the 1960s.[15]

The formation of the Housing Trust came at a time when the public appetite for post-war reconstruction, prosperity and security had been whetted through-out the UK.[16] It had been triggered by welfare state legislation tabled at Westminster during the darkest days of the war and later served as a beacon of light for those who had sacrificed most for the war effort.[17] Northern Ireland was expected to receive a generous windfall for its exhibition of hardy patriot-ism during the Second World War. In line with the strategy followed by his predecessor, Lord Craigavon, Brooke opted to reproduce Westminster social service legislation. As Walker has concluded:

> However, this was a solid commitment on which the Unionist Party could base its pledges to take Northern Ireland into the new British welfareist and socially trans-formed era. Arguably, such pledges were to be crucial to the party's continuing dominance of Northern Ireland politics.[18]

There was now an onus on Unionism not to depart from its commitment to introduce 'socialist' planning measures: 'step-by-step' with Britain became the imperative.[19] In Patterson's view:

> World War II produced a significant alteration in British elite attitudes to Northern Ireland, at the same time as it allowed a strong Labour challenge to the Unionist regime. The rigidities of the local regime laid it open to a challenge that combined class and a sense of Britishness betrayed by provincial conservativism.[20]

To those oppositional forces, hostile to Unionist one-party rule, future audits of British welfare legislation would have to take into account Unionist reluctance to sacrifice the one vital ingredient (i.e. equal citizenship) holding together its cross-class alliance.

Walker has studiously observed that the 'Unionist election campaign in 1945 had to concern itself much more than previously with issues other than the constitution'.[21] Yet partition still remained a crucial vote winner and, for Sir Basil Brooke at least, 'the old hardy annual, the border, was the one linchpin that mattered'.[22] In a speech to Orangemen in Enniskillen in March 1945 Brooke aptly conveyed to those gathered how Unionist ideology could be modified for projection onto different audiences. While those in the outlying areas were encouraged to ask prospective candidates, 'Are you prepared to maintain our position within the British Empire or not?',[23] those in the industrialised centres were constantly being reminded that the local regime was faithfully implementing British welfarist policies. However, what united Unionist Associations east and west of the Bann was their shared antipathy towards socialism, coupled with a desire for strong party leadership. The appeal to small-town provincialism was more successful in those places close to the border for obvious demographic reasons, but it simply would not wash in Belfast. As far as Brooke was concerned 'it was complete folly ... to vote for Labour when they could get nothing and might lose a great deal'; the only choice open then was to vote for the Unionist Party.[24] Unionism had directed its considerable propaganda resources towards emphasising the contrast between the socio-economic backwardness of the South (not to mention the special place for Roman Catholicism in the Irish Constitution of 1937) and the more socially progressive north-east. For most of the time this enabled Unionism to 'fire-fight' policy wavering in its constituency associations, where most of its grass-roots support could be found. Éire's wartime neutrality also permitted Unionists to reinforce these perceptions more starkly.[25]

In the minds of those who voted for the Unionist Party, Independent Unionists, NILP and other left-wing candidates in the June 1945 election, Ulster's constitutional position appeared secure. There is little evidence to suggest otherwise. Surprisingly, the 1945 poll did not double as a referendum on partition, as the 1949 election was to do four years later. Moreover, the Anti-Partition League of Ireland (APL), formed in 1945, and the internationally orchestrated propaganda campaign against partition were both still relatively weak-kneed.[26] When the Stormont results were finally announced on 10 July the left's vote had rocketed. This result proved a marked improvement on earlier NILP efforts in April when it had 'concentrated on social and economic issues and failed to come out definitely on the constitutional question',[27] thereby allowing the UUP to outflank it in both the Carrickfergus and Larne by-elections.

An autopsy of the UUP's electoral performance shows that a radicalisation among the working-class electorate had indeed taken place (a phenomenon, incidentally, which had also followed in the wake of the First World War), contributing almost certainly to the Unionist Party's poor showing. Patterson suggests that:

While the electoral system ensured that the NILP won only two seats, the vote for the left helped to convince Brooke that his government had to embrace the welfare state no matter how much this enraged many of the region's middle class.[28]

A shift to the left was now a vivid reality in Belfast. Although, in overall terms, the NILP's vote (66,053 or 18.6%) was around a third of the Unionist Party's, it secured double that of the Nationalists and, along with other left-orientated parties, such as the Communist Party (CPNI) and the Commonwealth Labour Party, easily superseded the total Nationalist vote.[29] NILP concentration on unemployment paid off and it returned two of its candidates to Stormont. Yet despite this welcome success 'the Labour Party remained small and fairly ineffective in the new Parliament'.[30] Westminster elections in July did not hold much promise and all its candidates were defeated. Nevertheless, William Leeburn spoke for the entire Ulster Labour movement when he said:

> We salute British Labour for the lead they have given us here in Northern Ireland and other countries where the capitalist class are still in power. British Labour by its victory has added the most thrilling page in the epic of human progress.[31]

The close ties with the BLP would prove crucial for the NILP's continued success.

The Stormont parliamentary record of Bob Getgood (Belfast Oldpark) and Hugh Downey (Belfast Dock) demonstrated their commitment to improving the lot of the working classes. Much time was spent agitating on unemployment, housing and basic workers' rights. Unfortunately Labour's efforts were rebuffed by the Unionists who consistently harried the party for its ambiguous stance on the border. Strangely, even though the NILP did not officially declare in favour of partition until 1949, Downey felt compelled to respond to his Unionist critics on the issue during his maiden speech:

> Let me say this, the party to which I have the honour to belong has never questioned the constitution of Northern Ireland. It has not at any time declared other than it is prepared to accept things as they are, but the party opposite all through its history, being bankrupt in policy and barren in statesmanship, and having nothing to offer the masses of the common people, have made the border a sort of smoke screen.[32]

'Smoke screen' or not, it was the chief bulwark Unionism deployed to good effect in maintaining its hegemony over the local state.

The Parliamentary Labour Party (PLP) found itself handicapped by Unionism's stress on the ethnic connotations of the link with Great Britain. Nevertheless, the party remained undeterred:

> The foundation of the welfare state and the conjectures as to the province thriving under socialist overlordship encouraged visions of a socialist government at Stormont. The idea of developing the party grew, for a potential government needed to be something more than a parliamentary pressure group.[33]

Downey's protestations, like Getgood's, were delivered with ability and gusto, but he frequently found himself out of his depth. Moreover, the Unionist

Parliamentary Party, by sheer weight of numbers, was largely successful in outmanoeuvring the small PLP, especially on legislative matters of a socio-economic hue. This agility was another crucial prerequisite for the maintenance of Unionism's position over the Protestant working class.[34] Angela Clifford has persuasively written:

> The fact that the Unionist Government was implementing Labour policy had a very disorientating effect on the Labour members. Up till then, the British policies which the Stormont administrations had repeated were mostly right-wing. Now, they were repeating the policies of the Left. The Labour members had got into the simplistic habit of regarding the Unionists as Tories. This was not true and in fact, William Grant was not simply rubberstamping the NHS, he was revealing himself to be a socialist of ability and calibre. The Debate shows him fighting for the NHS against its detractors. This confused the Northern Ireland Labour Party.[35]

Meanwhile, outside of the confines of the debating chamber, Northern Ireland was experiencing severe unemployment problems, which no amount of skilful oratory could overcome. Brooke again sought conciliation with the Labour movement:

> In order to prevent mass unemployment in the aircraft industry we must press for a new type of aluminium houses. The building of aircraft at the moment is out of the question and probably it is as well to have a break.[36]

Not everyone agreed with Brooke on this point and on 19 July the Minister of Home Affairs, Edmund Warnock, warned the Prime Minister of an impending protest march by workers from the Shorts aircraft factory on Queen's Island to Stormont. Within 24 hours a deputation of trade unionists had been received by government officials. Such direct action stood in contrast with events only a few days earlier when 5,000 overjoyed and patriotic workers greeted King George VI at a 'workers' garden party' in Botanic Gardens.[37] Disgruntlement with the government's handling of unemployment explains why a few hundred aircraft workers downed tools and marched to Stormont. It seems that promised improvement in material standing failed to completely placate the Labour movement in these years.[38]

By receiving this protest delegation Unionism was able to circumvent mass industrial unrest on this occasion – further demonstrating how the local regime could manage its clientalist links with the trade union movement without having to enter into negotiation with its opponents in Labour's political wing. Maurice Goldring informs us how:

> The Unionist government managed to feel its way through the conflicts created by the war in a way that protected its privileged relations with the loyalist working class ... Despite considerable hostility towards the government the majority of the population remained staunchly Unionist and 1945 was not the major turning-point in the history of Belfast and the North as it was in Britain. What the Blitz, Auschwitz, Stalingrad, Dresden and Hiroshima did not achieve, Burntollet did a generation later.[39]

Turbulence within the Protestant cross-class alliance was anticipated and had, arguably, been pre-empted by the appointment of two ministers with strong working-class credentials.[40] In many ways it was symptomatic of the intra-ethnic tensions which remained constant within the Unionist state until its eventual unravelling in 1972. Nevertheless, Labour had flexed its muscles, politically and industrially, and sent out a clear signal that state loyalty was a prerequisite for socio-economic improvement.

The announcement by Irish Taoiseach, John A. Costello, in September 1948 that Éire intended to leave the Commonwealth was greeted with suspicion and uncertainty by Unionists. Sir Basil Brooke's response had been well rehearsed and was delivered instantaneously: 'Ulster is in the Commonwealth because it is in the United Kingdom. To all who would try to thrust us out or entice us out our reply is the same – we stay where we are.'[41] Prior to Costello's announcement the NILP had held its annual conference at Warrenpoint, County Down, on 18 September. The pro-Unionist *Belfast Telegraph* came out against the NILP for its deliberate avoidance of the partition issue.[42] The editorial claimed that Labour had defaulted on two counts: first, by remaining uncommitted on partition (or 'sitting on the fence' as it was termed), and, second, by presenting itself as a credible alternative to Brooke's government; moreover, in the view of the newspaper's editor, the NILP had confused the electorate by its ambiguous stance and its day of reckoning bordered the horizon.

In fact at a special session of the NILP's 1947 annual conference, held somewhat belatedly in February 1948, disagreement on partition had already come to a head. The West Belfast Labour Party proposed a resolution which advocated that the NILP actively seek ways to abolish the border. It put forward the following recommendation:

> That the Northern Ireland Labour Party recognises that the partition of Ireland is the greatest barrier to the political and economical development of both parts of the country, and to the free, full and friendly relationship which could exist between Ireland and Britain and therefore resolves to adopt all constitutional means to secure its removal.[43]

Countering this anti-partitionist motion the South Antrim Labour Party advocated that a pledge be drawn up to support the link:

> That for the achievement of the objectives as set out in the party constitution, the Party fully accepts the present constitutional position of Northern Ireland, and will not seek to alter it when elected to power, but will endeavour to remove the abuses of the democratic expression of the will of the people and the liberty of the subject, at present in force in Northern Ireland.[44]

Costello's speech in late 1948 may have upset Unionists, but it came as no surprise to those liberal NILP activists frantically applying adhesive to the cracks now appearing in the ceiling of the party's 'broad church'.[45] Stephen McGonagle, Chairman of the Foyle Labour Party, later sparked considerable unease when he told the NILP's 1948 conference that his local branch would once again invite back Geoffrey Bing to address its membership, despite the

Executive Committee's protestations that the 'Friends of Ireland' were 'trouble-makers'.[46] 'Partition', he said, 'was what the Northern Ireland Labour Party was afraid of and not Geoffrey Bing.'[47] In a reprisal move Getgood was refused admittance to the BLP's annual conference in December.[48]

The constitutional debate shook the NILP to its very core. Not only did individual members begin to leave the party in late 1948 and early 1949, but whole branches disaffiliated or were expelled (like West Belfast) and soon switched their allegiance en masse to republican-orientated parties and collectives such as the Irish Labour Party (IrLP) and the APL. Factional disputes had been a recurring nuisance for the NILP throughout the 1940s and had, arguably, contributed directly to the later 1949 split along pro- and anti-partitionist lines, although as Graham rightly points out, 'it would not be complete to describe the 1949 declaration [in favour of partition] as the outcome of the showdown between the two factions'; other factors were at play here also.[49] One such gestating factor had been the conflict between party policy and personality. The NILP, like other political parties in the region and elsewhere, had larger than life characters at its helm, and who frequently over-shadowed policy initiatives by their own personal egotistical pursuits. As mentioned in the previous chapter the fate of Harry Midgley is instructive here. Midgley had been an NILP figurehead for over a decade and had allowed it to acquire the 'reputation of being a Midgley centred Party'.[50] Pro-British in outlook and uncharacteristically internationalist for a local politician Midgley attempted on more than one occasion to force the NILP to adopt a like-minded position, but to no avail. He resigned in 1942. In the 1940s the party refused to take an official line on partition, thereby allowing various ideological strands to co-exist within it.[51] Midgley's eventual departure did not silence debate on the NILP's pro-partitionist character. Senator Luke Duffy, the IrLP's General Secretary, stunned his BLP counterpart, Morgan Phillips, by claiming in a private letter 'that a group of crypto-Orangemen has taken possession of the Belfast Labour Party'.[52]

The breaking away of anti-partitionist activists in 1948–49 ensured that party policy would now take precedence over the private consciences of individual members. Consequently, the authority of annual conference resolutions became a *de rigueur* characteristic of the NILP's operations and in this regard it imitated the broader British Labour movement's commitment to the sovereignty of conference.[53] Terry Cradden's description of the NILP in the 1940s as 'a socialist-reformist broad church', is certainly true to an extent, though one must remember that by the 1949 crisis simmering internecine tensions had been brought to a boil. Whereas previously two factions co-existed in relative harmony, Graham argues:

> One, a small but actively committed anti-partitionist group, whose line of thought descended from James Connolly in that socialism and nationalism were regarded as essentially complementary; the other, the trade unionist bulk, predominantly loyalist but animated to an extent by the notion of a brotherhood of working men transcending political and religious differences. The latter was generally pro-British

as opposed to pro-partition, and thus by nature amenable to co-operation with the Connollyites.[54]

1949 spelt the beginning of the end for the 'broad church' and its replacement by a decidedly pro-British ethos – an ethos, moreover, which envisaged Northern Ireland enjoying 'the benefits of the social and economic reforms promised by Labour for the new post-war Britain'.[55] Nevertheless, allying itself more closely with a greater British project did not necessarily mean becoming a confessional party and the NILP – from its new centrist political position – continued to barrack its Unionist opponents on their attitudes towards the minority.

The 'Chapel Gates Election' of 1949: prelude and aftermath

The analysis of electoral paraphernalia produced by political parties is a profitable way of gauging attitudes on important policy matters. Sloganeering became a useful vehicle for promoting Unionist cohesion, particularly at a time of great constitutional uncertainty. *Ulster Holds the Fort, Ulster at the Crossroads* and *This we will Maintain* are three examples of slogans deployed by Unionism on the campaign trail in 1949.[56] Interrogating these adages in light of the historical context in which they were produced we find a Unionism preoccupied with 'toning down' the ethnic-exclusivist nature of its political programme in a bid to broaden the acceptance of the socio-economic dividends attached to continued support for the constitutional link with Great Britain. Patterson has observed how:

> The sharp disparity between social conditions North and South created by Northern Ireland's integration into the British welfare state was undeniable and while Unionists made much of it in their propaganda war with Dublin, there was a genuine, if myopic hope that such clear material advantages would lessen Catholic alienation from the state.[57]

The border issue occupied a vital position in Unionist discourse and was a spectre conjured up at opportune moments to haunt electoral campaigns since the infant days of the state. Any sign of class-based agitation – which threatened to unravel the 'brittle rigidity'[58] of the Unionist all-class alliance – could be neutralised by emphasising Ulster's privileged position in direct contrast to Éire's dire economic backwardness. Thus, a purely economic argument served to solidify Unionist unity in times of political uncertainty. The archetypal response by Unionist leaders, when faced with a class-based challenge, was to underline the disparity between wage levels North and South: the 'border bogey' was again wheeled out to enthusiastic flag-waving.

In the run-up to the 10 February election enthusiastic professions of loyalty were predictably commonplace. Brooke's manifesto rallied the Unionist community behind partition with such intensity that all other political issues paled into insignificance:

> It is therefore imperative that our determination to remain under the Union Jack

Origins of the 'consensus-forming strategy', 1945–58

should be immediately and overwhelmingly reaffirmed. Your vote will reinforce the action I have taken on your behalf so that our enemies can point to no weakening of Ulster's purpose ... No surrender. We are the King's men.[59]

Northern Ireland Labour had little scope to out-manoeuvre Unionism's ethno-sectarian appeal. Although the NILP had come out in favour of partition by the end of January, this decision had yet to be ratified by its annual conference. On the eve of the poll, NILP organiser Arthur Johnson[60] reported that 'the biggest weapon in the hands of the Unionist Party which has been exploited to the full has been the border question. People have been whipped into a frenzy in this matter.'[61] Labour now found itself in a quandary. Although the NILP had effectively dealt with the constitutional question by accepting the 'consent principle', it was still perceived to be ambivalent. A credibility gap opened up between the party and its core Protestant working-class support-base.

The advances made in trade union organisation when war production was at its peak were scuppered as ethnicity and national identity fused. Northern Ireland's divided working class retreated to a tribalistic position.[62] Above all these events 'convinced socialists who were particularly committed to anti-partition or pro-Union views that they must declare themselves more clearly'.[63] Difficulties were magnified for the party when the IrLP passed a resolution indicating that it would now organise and contest elections on a 32-county basis.[64] The formation of IrLP branches in Belfast would prove to have an adverse effect on the NILP's electoral performance. Indeed, former NILP activists went on to take up leading roles in the new organisation.[65] Although only one IrLP member was returned to Stormont, a more successful entrance into local government politics beckoned.[66] This provided a hub around which both confessional and labourist sympathies could be channelled – to the detriment of the non-sectarian democratic socialist programme espoused by the NILP.

Within the available literature there appear to be conflicting assumptions about the BLP's relationship with the NILP. In fact Rumpf and Hepburn have concluded negatively, though not without some justification, that 'even British socialism has been unable to intervene in Northern Ireland affairs outside the sectarian framework'.[67] A more accurate view would show that in fact British Labour's policy towards Northern Ireland has been more complex and contradictory than this. Not only did the BLP finance its 'sister' party by way of a substantial maintenance grant from the 1920s, but it saved the NILP from winding up its political operations on more than one occasion.[68]

Generally, though, fraternal connections were predicated on a good working relationship with the agent on loan to the party, who, according to Bleakley, 'was the first man to bring us up to date on the methods of organisation'.[69] The report from the NILP's 26th annual conference carried a unanimous vote in favour of strengthening its ties with the British party:

As instructed by the Special Conference, the Executive Committee have proceeded to strengthen the ties with the British Labour Party. Mr A.A. Johnson, who is on loan from the British Party, has worked unsparingly during the year to develop organisation here. There have been consultations with the British Party on the Imperial Election seats, and the policy to be pursued jointly at the 1950 Election. For the first time a number of members of the NILP attended the British Labour Party Conference as visitors.[70]

Former NILP Chairman William Leeburn was one of a number of leadership figures who called for stronger foundations to be laid between both parties. His suggestion that the NILP be allocated regional council status by the BLP's National Excutive Committee (NEC) fell on deaf ears.[71] The available archival evidence suggests that BLP Secretary, Morgan Phillips, was a central figure holding the NILP together as it weathered the storm whipped up by the APL. Throughout its term in office British Labour had remained 'broadly supportive of the Unionist leadership and responded with genuine sympathy to its requirements'.[72]

The Ireland Bill (hastily drafted up to reaffirm Northern Ireland's place in the UK) was negotiated with businesslike fashion by Brooke and Attlee and later processed by the Labour government with considerable ease, despite fierce objections from the backbench pressure group the 'Friends of Ireland'.[73] Labour in government was a much more chameleon-type entity from Labour in parliament. Geoffrey Bell has offered a resounding indictment of Attlee's administration:

> The Labour Cabinet's decision to turn a blind eye to what was happening in Northern Ireland was to prove crucial ... One thing is certain: by extending the authority of the Northern Ireland parliament in 1949 while at the same time refusing to challenge its flouting of democracy, the Labour Government was truly washing its hands in the blood which had flown and would continue to flow from partition.[74]

It is often assumed that the NILP remained seriously split on the partition issue; however upon closer inspection we can apportion some blame at least to the hostile socio-political environment in which the party had to operate. Anti-Labour feeling among loyalists had reached such a height in the opening months of 1949 that it was a logistical nightmare for some Labour candidates to canvass in their prospective constituencies, let alone to project their views onto an attentive audience. Similarly, the party's decision to delete all reference to the constitutional question in its manifesto, in favour of 'bread and butter' issues, was a self-inflicted wound that proved extremely difficult to heal. NILP fears were confirmed by widespread personation and verbal and physical intimidation. Furthermore, the electorate had been bombarded by a well-drilled propaganda machine commanded with military precision from Unionist Party Headquarters in Glengall Street.

Although acts of intimidation were widely reported by Northern Ireland's daily newspapers, the *Belfast Telegraph* predictably relegated Labour's gripes to a tiny inconsequential paragraph.[75] Johnson promptly issued a statement condemning what he viewed 'as an attempt by Unionists to create a religious struggle and not a political one', concluding that:

Origins of the 'consensus-forming strategy', 1945–58

The campaign of misrepresentation of Labour, the policy of intimidation of the electorate – an electorate imbued with a fear that 'Ulster' would be swallowed by Éire and that the Protestants of Northern Ireland would be sunk in a Catholic State, and that the children of Northern Ireland would become foreign-speaking citizens in their own province – all these things have had their effect ... The Unionists would claim that this was a smashing victory, but such a claim was only an idle dream because the only political issues raised in the election were those introduced by the Labour candidates ... Sectarianism in its starkest and most dreadful form had been the Tory battle-cry.[76]

On the same day that Brooke announced the date for the Stormont election the *Belfast Telegraph* claimed that it would in fact 'be regarded as a referendum on the issue of joining the Irish Republic or remaining part of the United Kingdom'.[77]

Carrying a typically pro-Unionist line on this occasion the newspaper continued to lambast the NILP on its ambivalent attitude towards partition:

Next month has many added advantages. It means that the Labour Party, which is the chief Unionist opposition in Belfast, will have to make haste if it is not caught out on the Border issue ... At present its policy is being redrafted and in view of the divergent opinions with the movement it is doubtful whether it will prove a satisfactory formula.[78]

The following day the *Belfast Telegraph* carried an article on Brooke with a thoroughly populist message in its subtext:

This year it has been obvious that events demand a renewed declaration of Unionist principles and the next task that falls on Sir Basil Brooke's shoulders is to lead the rally that will show the people of Ulster to be still true to themselves.[79]

The newspaper's editorial was no less explicit in its political predictions, claiming that February's election 'would give people here an opportunity to express their preference for remaining in the Commonwealth or getting out of it'. Those from the Opposition benches in Stormont were branded 'childish' for complaining that the election was merely a tactic employed to resuscitate a failed administration. Likewise, the Irish Taoiseach's claims that Ulster remained 'an occupation zone' ruled by 'an intractable class' were rebuked:

The Government here has always had the support of all classes of the people ... In terms of bread and butter the choice in this election for every creed and class is a higher or lower living standard. No republic in prospect or in being can offer the ordinary family the benefits they enjoy today as part of the United Kingdom. That is a simple, stubborn fact and no amount of emotional speechifying can alter it.[80]

However, as with most documentary sources, one must interrogate the context in which this article was produced. Walker posits a caveat that 'an assessment of the Unionist Party in this period has to take full account of the "pressure cooker" created politically by the global profile of the APL'.[81]

The APL had been formed in 1945 and was 'inspired by hopes of major political changes in the post-war world and in particular by the election to power of the Labour Party'.[82] It was a peculiar entity, comprising a diverse range of interests – from devout Catholic Nationalist politicians to anti-clerical Labour representatives – all of whom were united in their opposition to partition. Purdie contends that the APL was 'primarily a purely Northern initiative',[83] yet the Irish government had financed its campaign directly, thereby ensuring that it took on a global agenda in terms of raising passions among Irish diasporas for a United Ireland. The APL's significance lies in its failure to penetrate the secular political sphere of industrialised Belfast. As Purdie pointed out 'the political environment of Belfast, with its class-based politics and strident party competition, was inimical to the League'.[84] It fizzled out by the mid-1950s.[85]

With the considerable resources of the Unionist press now deployed in full support of Brooke's partitionist policy it was hardly surprising that the NILP found it difficult to get its voice heard. Nevertheless Labour put on a brave, but totally unavailing, showing. All 12 of its candidates were defeated and two candidates lost their deposits (one by only three votes). The party managed only to muster a meagre 26,831 votes, most of which were in marginal Belfast constituencies.[86] There can be little doubt that the NILP had reached a stationary position by late 1949, but nonetheless 'they kept going in the hope that their new position on the constitution would enable them to make a breakthrough among the Protestant working class'.[87]

Internal wrangling over partition had led to ambivalence, confusion and downright inertia, and contributed to the NILP's poor public profile among an embattled Belfast working class. The special party conference held on 9 April eventually reaffirmed the NILP's commitment to partition by 2,000 votes to 700.[88] Under such an intense sectarian atmosphere it was unrealistic for the party to expect an overnight reversal in its electoral fortunes. The proposal to shift working-class mindsets from antagonism to co-operation along socio-economic lines was a transition dogged by suspicion, danger and uncertainty: the events of 1949 served only to magnify problems for the party. A report compiled by a Belfast-based representative of the National Union of Seamen (NUS),[89] who attended the 1949 conference, gives us an outsider's impression of party business at a time when internal division was most evident. According to the NUS's delegate, the problems facing the party were exacerbated by a lack of talented individuals in the leadership cadre: 'the breakaway from the party has left a serious mark on its solidarity', he claimed.[90] Other internal divisions centred on NILP–BLP relations. Visitations by high-profile Labour Party representatives had always served as a morale-boosting exercise for the NILP rank-and-file, but in the late 1940s it had a very debilitating effect. On a recent trip to the province Herbert Morrison had apparently 'spent more time in the company of Tory bosses and this naturally incurred the wrath of some Conference delegates'.[91] It was regretted in the report that these outbursts occurred in the presence of British Labour fraternal delegates, Mr Windle and Mr Webber.[92]

An unhappy strain in the marriage between both parties ensued. Ill-timed, impromptu speeches delivered by Labour ministers on Northern Ireland affairs did little to bestow confidence on the NILP after their routing by the Unionists. Sam Napier, the NILP's Secretary, was convulsed into writing a strongly-worded directive to Morgan Phillips:

a. References to Northern Ireland should be qualified in the light of the policy of the NILP, and the criticism of the Northern Ireland Government supplied by the NILP.
b. In so far as possible, it should be remembered that political democracy in Northern Ireland is very far behind that in Britain.
c. In political broadcasts the opportunity should be taken to specifically mention Northern Ireland affairs on a party basis.
d. In the Commons the "conservative" attitude of Ulster Unionist members should be stressed and not treated as above "party reproach", and their questions and observations dealt with on a "Northern Ireland" basis.
e. Care should be taken that Labour Ministers and prominent party members should not be used by Unionist "stooge" organisations and clubs in Britain.
f. On the overall policy to be pursued it would appear that while Northern Ireland affairs should be dealt with on a fair basis, it should, in so far as is possible, be made clear that the Labour Party in Northern Ireland is other than a Tory party, and that, on a party political basis, it is not satisfied with [the Unionist government's current] policy.[93]

Research by Bob Purdie has certainly indicated the huge divergent opinions on Ireland emanating from the Labour backbenches.[94] However, the occasional bungling comment by a Labour MP or cabinet minister obscured a much deeper grievance harboured by those who constituted the 'rump' of the NILP in 1949. The source of this grievance can be found in the legislation agreed between Belfast and London, which to all intents and purposes showed a gratifying relationship having developed.[95]

By the close of 1949 it was obvious that Unionists had only grasped at British welfare legislation as a means of keeping their working-class supporters in check. In a letter to Morgan Phillips, Sam Napier accurately conveyed NILP disgruntlement at this Unionist ploy:

My Executive Committee are particularly anxious about this matter in view of the fact that the Unionist Party here are continually claiming credit for legislation which has been introduced at Westminster by the Labour Party, and which on many occasions has been opposed by the Unionist Party representatives here.[96]

In fact this was typical of Unionist strategy. The leverage established over the Protestant working class was crucial for the state's continued existence and would not be sacrificed lightly, even if this necessitated embracing British socialist measures. W.B. Topping, in a speech delivered to a group of Young Unionists in 1948, typified the regime's catchall policy by stating that 'the Unionist Party did not represent one class, nor a sectional interest, but was the party of the people and legislated for all'.[97] Napier and his colleagues faced an uphill struggle in their bid to return to their happy electoral hunting grounds among the Protestant working class.

Conversely, the chameleon-type discourse projected by Unionism camouflaged deep intra-party uneasiness on socialism. It must be stressed, however, that, in 'carbon-copying' progressive British policies, the Unionist regime left the door open to challenge if there was any wavering on their self-professed obligation to introduce the full fruits of material prosperity. Unionism could not have it both ways. In any case many working-class Protestants had willingly bought into the idea that their interests were bound up in a UK context. For them the choice was summed up by Captain Willy Orr, Unionist MP for South Down:

> Are you for the King or are you for the Republic? Are you for the United Kingdom, British freedom, the British standard of life and social services or are you for a United Ireland, a lower standard of living and lower social services? And are you for remaining part of the great Commonwealth and Empire that can still lead the destinies of the world or are you for joining an isolated little Republic cut off from the rest of mankind?[98]

Unionism had ample opportunities open to it to perpetuate a vibrant myth. The reproduction of their 'progressive' ideology could now be gainfully consolidated. Working-class Protestants voting for Orr, like their co-religionists in other constituencies across Northern Ireland, had very little option. Labour had been branded by Unionist elites as 'misleading'. 'The party had sat on the fence for so many years,' claimed Topping, 'it could not be trusted.'[99]

Party policies and political realities, 1950–52

The prevailing historical interpretation of the 1950s is that of a golden age, when progressive politics and new departures overshadowed sectarian animosities. Community spirit returned to the province from whence it was banished in 1949. One historian has even gone so far as to claim that this decade was 'the most successful period in the experiment of devolution'.[100] In complete contrast Paddy Devlin has offered a much gloomier picture:

> Northern Ireland and Belfast had changed very little in the thirty years since partition. Sectarianism was still assiduously fostered by the Unionist Party to maintain division. Virtually all the political energy in the community was focused on preserving or questioning Northern Ireland's position, a futile obsession, for there was no real possibility of change.[101]

It is difficult to write about the NILP in the context of the 1950s without seeing the party's development as more opportunistic than strategic. Even though chronic unemployment, poverty and an upsurge in sectarian tensions had a polarising effect on the working classes, it did work to the advantage of Northern Ireland Labour. Electorally the decade opened unpromisingly for the NILP and there was certainly no real indication that by March 1958 the party would have returned four MPs to the Northern Ireland House of Commons. Like the 1950 outing, the February 1951 British general election had caught the party on the back foot, leading to a similar outcome to those elections held over

Origins of the 'consensus-forming strategy', 1945–58

the previous two years when Labour candidates were all defeated outright.[102] But it did show that the NILP was willing to challenge its opponents in their heartlands of support.

British Labour's return to office in 1950 was a short-lived affair and in October 1951 the Conservatives, under Sir Winston Churchill and Anthony Eden, were installed in power on a slender majority of 17. The victory of the IrLP's Jack Beattie in West Belfast threw the Irish question into sharp relief. Beattie had been elected on a firm anti-partitionist platform, snatching back his seat from the Ulster Unionist, Thomas Teevan, by a narrow majority of only 25 votes. His arrival at Westminster was greeted with unease – but not surprise – in many Unionist quarters; Beattie had after all held the seat between 1943–50, first on an NILP ticket after the 1943 by-election, and then as an Independent Labour politician following his expulsion. Beattie's attempt to take the Labour whip a second time failed due principally to his expulsion from the NILP: this was perhaps the most graphic illustration of Labour's pro-NILP policy in the wake of the latter's split over partition in 1948–49. Arguably it showed the extent of the NILP's influence on the PLP at Westminster. Beattie would not be the last Independent Labour politician from Northern Ireland to seek the PLP whip – as Gerry Fitt was later to prove in 1966.

Thanks principally to the partition issue the NILP had little prospect of returning parliamentary representation anytime soon. Its weak organisational structure and deflated membership all pointed to the party having entered a period of decline. There was no sign that the Unionist Party was about to be challenged on constitutional or economic grounds. By September 1951 matters had come to a head. John F. Hill's report to the BLP's NEC reinforced an abysmal view of a party in 'a very weak state'.[103] A pervasive air of unreality gripped Northern Ireland over the exact nature of its misfortunes, with many activists believing that it was now entering a spell in the political wilderness. But this decline should not be examined in isolation. The formation of the IrLP sapped away a significant amount of Catholic working-class support and left the NILP confined mainly to Protestant areas. To Hill this meant 'that any votes the Irish Party takes must come from us and not the Government Party, and therefore, our position in the future will be weakened'.[104] One historian, however, has judged the IrLP's move north in 1950 to have been a far more limited affair:

> Thereafter, the Irish Labour Party began to describe itself as Ireland's only '32 county party'. Of course, it was nothing of the sort – with branches in Derry and Newry as well as a couple of wards in Belfast, it was a '29 county party' at best – but the fact remained that for all its rivals' anti-partitionist claims, the Irish Labour Party was the only constitutional party organised north of the border at that time.[105]

The NILP's reputation for being a 'broad church' had always been ingrained in many people's minds, but now, with a split in its membership and support-base, sectarian variables once again became compatible with a working-class disposition.

In 1950 a small rump of 300 individual members were left behind to rebuild the party, not only financially but also in terms of prestige and organisation. To this end a more effective means of communicating the NILP's policies was sought out and the crucial appointment of Sam Napier as party secretary in December 1949,[106] following the departure of Joseph Corrigan, marked its rebirth. Significantly, John Harbinson was appointed as the party's research officer in early 1950, initially to lead a team of researchers (pooled from the Queen's University Labour Group) in a bid to reformulate party policy. This 'think-tank' soon folded, leaving Harbinson to undertake most of the research on his own. Yet, despite these difficulties, a press officer was quickly appointed to help boost the NILP's profile and Charles Brett took over editorship of the party's new journal *The Rising Tide*. Unfortunately insufficient funds and soaring production costs meant that regular publication of this organ became impossible and it was wound up in July 1951.[107]

Finance had always been a thorny issue for the party. Its main source of income was from its trade union affiliation fees. Disastrously, in the wake of the special conference in April 1949, the Amalgamated Transport and General Workers Union (ATGWU), which accounted for 5,000 of the party's affiliated members, disaffiliated at a loss of £200 per annum in subscription dues, a substantial amount vital for party coffers. As with any other political party finance overwhelmingly dictated how effective election campaigns could be, but equally important in this respect was organisation. Structurally, Divisional Labour Parties (DLPs) were established to correspond with Northern Ireland's parliamentary constituencies. In theory four DLPs made up a single Westminster constituency. These divisions were lumped together with women's branches and the League of Youth. In practice, however, such hypothetical boundaries 'did not function at all outside Belfast and were not that well organised within the city either'.[108] Despite Graham's passing remark that 'rural developments continued to be prominent by their absence, bearing out the view that the party's title was ideologically rather than geographically descriptive',[109] attempts were made during the summer of 1951 to canvas beyond the Belfast urban area in outlying parts of the province.[110]

Admittedly this was based on false optimism; the NILP seemed to be punching above its weight. Recently unearthed evidence suggests that by late 1951 several party officers had considered the state of the organisation so bad and 'the difficulties ... so serious that they may necessitate the complete winding up of the party here at an early date'.[111] On paper at least the party looked healthy enough (individual membership was estimated to have risen to 900 in 1951),[112] though its poor showings at the polls and a dire financial situation (it had accumulated a substantial deficit of £600 by September 1951 and was bordering on bankruptcy according to Napier)[113] all conveyed a view to a British Labour audience that the NILP would not make it beyond 1952 unless further financial assistance was forthcoming. Arguably, Graham fails to convey the full gravity of this crisis in his thesis. Instead we get a rather stoic version of the state of the party in these years, conveyed by Napier in a retrospective interview; from

Origins of the 'consensus-forming strategy', 1945–58

contemporary BLP–NILP correspondence though we can make a reasonably rounded judgement on the endogenous and exogenous challenges facing the party. Despite the NILP's earlier misfortunes it had emerged emboldened and at an opportune time to mount successful challenges against the Unionist Party in the 1953 and 1958 elections.

Towards a constructive and constitutional Opposition, 1953–57

Under the direction of Sam Napier the NILP sought to promote a political culture which was non-sectarian, democratic socialist and constitutionally reliable. A civic partnership between Protestants and Catholics, based on British liberal democracy, was clearly advocated by the mid-1950s.[114] Arguably the party's attempts to jockey for a lead political position can be traced back, albeit in skeletal form, to the war years:

> It is with mixed feelings that I look forward to the post-war period ... The means to carry out these imperative needs [social transformation] are far beyond the will and the desires of most of our present day statesmen. They must be replaced from our own ranks. To our members and to the country we must give a clear lead. Private enterprise has failed. It must be replaced by public ownership and co-operative effort. The potentialities of this country must be developed. The wealth produced must be used for the benefit of all, not the enrichment of a few. The standard of life must be raised. The poor must no longer remain objects of charity, rather we must abolish the causes of poverty.[115]

Napier reaffirmed this again under rather different circumstances in October 1952 when he made a valiant, but unsuccessful, challenge against the elderly Unionist incumbent Sir David Campbell for the South Belfast Westminster seat. Graham has written that Napier's intervention afforded him 'an opportunity to test his detailed plans'.[116] His 'plans' concerned the party's future. Beyond stabilising its morale in the medium term, they were relatively underdeveloped at this time. Imposing financial practicalities, not to mention a weakness in organisation, greatly impinged upon the NILP Executive's ability to think beyond the next election and forced the party onto the defensive. Labour now recognised that it had to project an image of itself as sound on partition before it lost further ground to Unionism.[117]

The real problem facing the party was that a credibility gulf had opened between it and the Protestant working class. It was a gulf which urgently required bridging before any advance could be made from what was a precarious political position. Napier's eve of election address set the precedent for Labour's future direction:

> The NILP is in favour of the maintenance of the present constitutional position of Northern Ireland. The economic life of the country depends upon it; more than that, nearly four-fifths of the people of Northern Ireland want it that way. The market for Northern Ireland's manufactured goods is in Great Britain; tariff barriers or trade restrictions between Northern Ireland and the rest of the United Kingdom would cause a fall in Northern Ireland's standard of living.[118]

Charles Brett made a similar impassioned plea in the party's *South Belfast Elector*:

> The Northern Ireland Labour Party stands for the maintenance of our present position within the United Kingdom. We support the constitution because we think it is best for the community as a whole. But we want to see good use made of it; we want good government and not just pious talk.[119]

Voters were faced with a stark choice, Brett said, between 'Labour and Conservative, rather than Nationalist and Unionist'. A vote for Napier would help to prove:

> The existence of a large section of the community here who want a return to 'fair share' policy; who want to see effective steps taken to reduce the enormous number of unemployed in Ulster.[120]

By prioritising both socio-economic issues, as well as much bulkier political-constitutional ones, Labour set out in 1952–53 on an ambitious mission to wrest power from Unionism and replace it with a programme of government which was 'radically alternative'.[121] Marshalled along class lines, the logic behind this enterprise was intended to be simple and effective, but it inadvertently posed a dilemma for the party: how could it articulate radical socio-economic policies, while also appearing to be 'safe' on the constitution? Graham's extrapolations from the available empirical data led him to identify four key 'predictive elements' - or conditions – necessary for the success of the 'consensus-forming strategy':

- Firstly, that there would be a diminution of sectarianism and a relaxing of polarised voting behaviour.
- Secondly, and complementary, that there would be a trend within the Roman Catholic community towards acceptance of the constitutional position, predominately due to an improvement in the province's economic situation vis-à-vis Éire.
- Thirdly, that the Unionist Party would be willing to engage in a British-style political dialogue.
- Fourthly, that there would be a gradual relinquishing of Protestant privileges towards a situation of civil equality.[122]

Yet before the party could settle into this long-term role as a constructive constitutional Opposition it had to demonstrate that it had a significant electoral mandate. Electoral recognition, in the medium term at least, had to be high among the party's list of priorities. By courting acceptability in the eyes of the Protestant working class (a constituency which traditionally, and overwhelmingly, voted on the basis of preserving the constitutional status quo), the party could manoeuvre itself into a position from where it could exercise power. As Graham points out, 'essentially the task facing Napier was two-fold – he had to sustain the party against its immediate perils and to project it along a path towards the goal of government'.[123]

Arguably the practicalities of making Ulster Labour more electorally appealing had been considered several years earlier in 1949:

> PROPAGANDA is vital! Perhaps in the past few years our movement has become too respectable. Not enough street corner meetings or door-step canvassing. But even if you do neither of these things you can still be active for the way of life in which you believe – by talking constantly about it and explaining frequently what it will mean to the people of Northern Ireland.
>
> HOW do your friends think? Tory? Well, what are you doing about it? What about your fellow Trade Unionists, the members of your tennis club or even your own family?
>
> IT'S easy to begin. There must have been a beginning for the greatest figures that the movement has produced. Everyone began with a soap-box – maybe at a bench, in a workshop, drawing room or street corner he began talking about the things he knew – that's how it all began![124]

From this article we can gather that Napier viewed the popularity of socio-economic grievances in everyday public discourse as an essential part of the NILP's recovery.

Graham's retrospective analysis of this shift in party policy is theoretically driven by his overbearing reliance on modernisation theory. Put succinctly this theoretical approach anticipated the triumph of material wealth over ethnic tribalism.[125] Politically, this would be reflected in the party system:

> Ideally their objective was to be attained as follows – by a movement in public opinion on the dominant political divide towards a diminishing of bi-polarity and the creation of a consensus, combined with the creation of another significant political issue effectively cross-cutting the community cleavage, and thereby uniting Protestants and Catholics against Protestants and Catholics. The chosen cross-cutting cleavage – the attempt at a consensus – was a complex of working-class economic consciousness and governmental accountability.[126]

The question about whether the NILP formulated a coherent political strategy during these years was something originally posed and corroborated in a retrospective manner by Graham. Yet one could argue that the NILP was fortunate just to have survived the 1948–49 split; a split so severe it threatened to destroy the party. Moreover, a 'consensus-forming strategy' was not conceived until the late 1950s when it seemed likely that the party would be propelled into a more entrenched position, despite Graham's findings that:

> The period, 1949–1958, saw the party attain a strategic first phase. This was perhaps its greatest achievement, for in terms of strategic requirements it had serious organisational, financial, policy and communications problems with the recent constitutional declaration the only positive indication of strategic viability ... Realisations of these predictions would make viable modernising the political system through the development of a consensus upon economic and welfare issues, and hopefully one favourable to a radical alternative.[127]

With the benefit of hindsight it is possible to maintain a healthy scepticism without necessarily being dismissive of the party's record during these post-war years. It is not difficult to see how Graham's interpretation of the NILP's role throughout the period was anchored in a pragmatic proviso, insofar as NILP energies were evidently being directed towards establishing a firm foothold in majority Protestant areas in industrial Belfast before spreading the tentacles of party organisation beyond the city's boundaries.

Furthermore, Graham claims that the party was going through a transitional period of 'strategic reorientation' in policy-making during these years. Evidence which has recently come to light contravenes this interpretation. Strategic imperatives do not convincingly explain why 23,067 constituents rejected Sam Napier in favour of the Ulster Unionist candidate in the 1952 South Belfast by-election, or why the NILP was once again given the cold shoulder by the Protestant working class in October 1953. The truth of the matter is that the campaign undertaken by the party was more *ad hoc* and opportunistic than Graham's analysis allows. Even though 'the party's ambitions were, by now, firmly focused on Stormont, where the success or failure of the consensus forming strategy would be decided',[128] the situation's political realities militated against it. The tide was by no means rising in the NILP's favour just yet. Only by giving equal weight to socio-economic policies and constitutional priorities could the NILP manoeuvre itself back onto the political radar screen. Clearly Napier's intervention in South Belfast constituted a litmus test, but the stigma had not yet dissipated from the NILP's public profile.

Most party members still clung to their belief that a non-sectarian democratic socialist Ulster was achievable, despite frequent ethnic polarisation amongst the working classes. To an extent, their focus now shifted towards exploring the possibility of laying down a challenge to Unionism on its own terms. However, a note of caution must be appended here: these imperatives were moulded in political realism, not idealism, and the advent of a 'dominant ideological triumvirate'[129] coincided with a changeover in the party's Executive Committee (EC). Older party leaders, like Getgood and Leeburn, vacated the scene and were replaced by an emergent 'younger generation of party ideologues, chief among whom were Sam Napier, Tom Boyd, David Bleakley and Charles Brett'.[130]

The pragmatic shift in policy towards an acceptance of the constitutional status quo gave party activists much-needed legroom to work towards what Sam Napier termed the 'radical alternative' to Unionist one-party rule, but at a cost. Undoubtedly, the 'radical alternative' combined realism with pragmatism and was coherent insofar as it aimed for the goal of a pluralist democratic politics in Northern Ireland. In its initial phase it necessitated prioritising the majority Protestant section of a divided working class ahead of their Catholic counter-parts:

> The immediate task was two-fold ... propagation as a radical party on economic and social issues, and projection as a safe unionist body. In the years 1949–1953, the former dominated affairs.[131]

Napier recognised that he faced an uphill struggle to meet Unionist propaganda on its own terms. The NILP finally set about canvassing on a pro-Union ticket.

A coherent electoral programme was drawn up for the 1953 Stormont election, due to be held in October, and canvassing was begun in earnest. Napier claimed in his post-election report that the party had set off on the campaign trail in July 1952.[132] Nonetheless, nominations had only been received from each constituency in early 1953, that is except for Carrickfergus, which had delayed selection until June. 'An unusual feature of the campaign,' claimed Napier, 'was the great amount of space given in the press to the party's policy statements, spokesmen and candidates.'[133] Four separate pamphlets were produced and about 27,100 copies issued. Financially Willowfield, Woodvale, Oldpark, Shankill and Victoria had small credit balances while Carrick and Pottinger remained in debt – information was patchy for Ards. Similarly, Napier's unsuccessful bid for a seat at Queen's University Belfast cost £12:10:0 in a lost deposit, although this was recovered from donations made to central party funds. The actual election itself saw nine seats contested but all bids were unsuccessful. 'The important conclusions to be drawn from the contest', wrote Napier in his report, included:

a. The eclipse of Éire Labour when all its candidates were bottom of the poll in the five divisions in which it contested. One candidate lost his deposit.
b. The failure of the independents to regain Woodvale and their losing Shankill after 28 years. This was offset by their gain in Clifton.
c. The creation of marginal seats in Belfast.
d. The increase in the Labour vote.
e. The fact that the vote against the Government in the contested seats far exceeded the Unionist vote.
f. The appearance in the province of what might be termed a floating vote.[134]

It is obvious from this report that the NILP's problematisation of the unemployment issue by itself did not win it votes, and disgruntlement with more confessional parties probably won it considerable numbers of floating voters.

Graham insinuates that the NILP's performance was influenced by three overlapping factors: 'the efforts of the rank and file'; 'the *Belfast Telegraph's* retreat to a community outlook'; and the 'inability to create a winning electoral issue and thereby frustrate the Unionist Party's determined advocacy of the constitutional cleavage'.[135] On two counts Graham is accurate. Party activists were conspicuous by their absence, except for those who sat at the apex of the NILP, and the press seemed detached from its previous cheerleading role behind the Unionist regime. But the party's winning electoral issue *was* present: unemployment had reached a crescendo, becoming even more pressing as the decade progressed. Sir Basil Brooke (created Viscount Brookeborough in 1952) emerged to offset pressure on his regime by currying favour with Conservative ministers in London. This staved off a wholesale political defection to the NILP by disgruntled Protestant workers. However, it did not plug all the leakages which had now sprung up, as Patterson has shown:

> As early as the 1953 Stormont election, the Unionist Party headquarters at Glengall Street was bemoaning the fact that 'our Party is losing the support of the lower paid

income group and the artisans to the NILP'. The lack of any working class Unionist MPs and the domination of Belfast Unionist representation by the local bourgeoisie were important in encouraging defections.[136]

Obviously NILP agitation on unemployment failed to reach the kind of tempo it would display in the 1956–58 period, though conditions were favourable for a challenge. The question must be asked: why did the party fail to win any parliamentary seats?

The relative failure of the IrLP, which by now had been eclipsed by the NILP in those constituencies with minority Catholic support, may provide a clue.[137] There can be no doubt – even though Graham[138] and Patterson[139] make no explicit mention of the fact – that IrLP intervention inhibited the NILP's performance in 1953. With the virtual elimination of the IrLP by the late 1950s Northern Ireland Labour found itself the main beneficiary of a more favourable set of circumstances. It is a central argument of this book that the NILP's success depended on an absence of confessional sentiment among the Catholic working class, as much as their Protestant counterparts, especially in Belfast constituencies. Another vital ingredient was the availability of a space into which the NILP could move: the winding up of the IrLP explains this at least in part. This argument surpasses earlier claims made by Farrell[140] and others who have said that a lull in the constitutional issue and the corresponding dramatic rise in unemployment radicalised the Protestant working class into voting for the NILP, because admittedly Catholic support proved just as decisive.[141]

What aided the NILP in its attempt to woo supporters from the minority community was the electoral rejection of ethnic nationalism in Belfast. 'Green' Nationalists had been banished from Belfast in 1945 because of an ignition in class-based sentiment.[142] When Nationalists were returned in the late 1960s they failed to make an impact on the Catholic working class. Rather it was 'red' republican socialists, like Harry Diamond and Gerry Fitt, who were rewarded with most Catholic working-class support. Even though the NILP had wholeheartedly endorsed partition it took the pressing empirical reality of industrial strikes and dole queues, coupled with further government complacency,[143] to galvanise working-class people into voting for it.

The 1953 election also emitted the impression that the party had a centralised command, something it appeared to lack from the time of internal wrangling in 1949.[144] Admittedly, in terms of policy, pragmatic thinking was beginning to set in. With a lack of parliamentary representation it was imperative that the NILP could demonstrate its political relevance. Two documents were drafted with this in mind. *Spotlight on the Unionist Record* (1953) and *It's a High Price: A Survey of the Cost-of-Living in Northern Ireland* (1953) framed discussion of socio-economic issues firmly within existing British parameters and neatly complimented the central tenets of the NILP's democratic socialist ideology, which, to all intents and purposes, was an imitation of the BLP's ethical socialism and labourism.

These two reports shored up, by now, familiar themes in NILP discourse: Unionist Party 'ineptitude' in strict contrast to NILP responsibility in the face of

Origins of the 'consensus-forming strategy', 1945–58

pressing economic disparities between Great Britain and Northern Ireland. 'The post-war years have displayed incompetence and a real lack of interest by the Unionist Party. Despite proposals from the NILP which, had they been accepted, would have helped, little has been done.'[145] Hitherto the major crisis posed by redundancies in the staple industries was duly audited in a forthright manner; the charge for Ulster's high levels of unemployment was laid firmly at Unionism's door.

> Post-war Britain, on the other hand, enjoyed prosperity. For a long time the figure was less than 1%. In June, 1953, Northern Ireland had some 37,000 out of work. This was 7.9%, and at the same time the figure for Great Britain was 1.4%.[146]

Against this background Labour did actually possess a strong case.[147] The message being articulated was intended to be easily digestible for the average working-class wage earner. *Spotlight on the Unionist Record* reserved much criticism for Major Ivan Neill (the Minister for Labour and National Insurance) because of his department's mishandling of the emigration problem. The total number of people estimated to have left the province between 1946 and 1952 stood at a 'startling' 22,568.

The NILP – and Napier in particular – was making the connection between high unemployment and so-called 'economic emigration'. Napier wrote how:

> In the face of the magnitude of the problem the Government appears to be stunned into complete inaction. Indeed it would appear from Government spokesmen that the Government, having recognised that 'the population is increasing out of all proportion to the number of jobs which can be found' choose emigration as a solution to the unemployment problem rather than making serious endeavours to create work.[148]

Unionist promises on housing targets were also subjected to scrutiny here: the total number of houses built (including 2,000 prefabs) stood at 44,167, 'less than one quarter of what is required'.[149] Of much greater impact on working-class material interests was the revelation that:

> In June, 1951, although no such legislation had been planned by the Westminster Government, the Unionist Minister of Health and Local Government introduced the Rent Restriction Law (Amendment) Act. This increased house rents by amounts averaging 5/- per week.[150]

Further audits noted the lack of 'parity' in legal aid benefits, industrial and agricultural wage earnings and prices, education, national assistance, coal importation levies and public service transport costs. Overall the document lambasted the Unionist regime for failing to provide work for its citizens, presenting a reasonably informed caveat that about 100,000 people (including dependents) bordered on the poverty line.[151] It is clear from *Spotlight on the Unionist Record* that the dire economic situation was played up by the NILP for voting capital.

Similarly, *It's a High Price: A Survey of the Cost-of-Living in Northern Ireland* (1953) detailed the intolerable burden imposed by these regional disparities in terms of cost-of-living. Those from the non-wage-earning sections in society were targeted at the outset – 'the old-age pensioner; the person in retirement; the unemployed; the sick; the less fortunate in our community – they were all compelled to live at bare subsistence level'.[152] Labour even utilised the archetypal 'housewife's budget' as an illustration of how working people were struggling to make ends meet. 'This, of course, means that the family standards of life must inevitably fall, because as we all realise *wages* are not keeping pace with the *cost-of-living*'.[153] The principal point being made by the NILP, of course, was that the local Unionist regime was badly out of step with its British partner and must therefore be apportioned some of the blame for the dramatic fall in living standards. Although international market forces aided and abetted local difficulties, the NILP remained adamant that it knew where ultimate blame lay: 'The Unionist Party at Stormont by its support for such measures as their Tory friends in Britain have introduced for the benefit of one section of the community only, stands condemned.'[154]

Both of these policy documents fed into the rationale informing the party's recently published manifesto: *What Ulster Labour Would Do* (1953). Ostensibly based on a British Labour ethos it gave explicit assurances that the practical implications of its subscription to a province-wide nationalisation scheme would 'not merely maintain the standards of living but also raise them'. Northern Ireland's natural resources would be harnessed for the future material security of its people, leading ultimately to health, happiness and prosperity. Although these socio-economic policy documents appeared radical they were in fact framed realistically within 'the present constitutional position'.[155] Above all Labour believed 'that better use should be made of the constitution we already possess'. No departure from current British financial arrangements, welfare state legislation or trade agreements was advocated. The NILP's aim was – put simply – to raise the standard of living, to pursue a policy of full employment and to make the best possible use of the province's home-grown assets. Overall the NILP's rationale for publishing these pamphlets was:

> To counteract the erroneous and illogical comparisons between Northern Ireland and the Éire Republic which are made deliberately by the Northern Ireland Unionist Party to support their case and which in fact bear no relation whatever to Northern Ireland, because of the differences in wage rates, taxation, and economic and social structure of the two countries.[156]

By now NILP mathematics was bound up in the economic logic of partition and it could propagate its 'radical' economic synthesis with a greater degree of confidence.

While *What Ulster Labour Would Do* encapsulated perfectly the NILP's recalculation of Northern Ireland's economic accounts, the accompanying pamphlet *Where Ulster Labour Stands* (1953) focused on making the party's commitment to partition more transparent. It was issued as: 'A challenge to those who seek to make political capital for themselves by misrepresenting its views; above all a challenge to the ordinary voter' and it had a dual purpose: to demystify Unionist rhetoric that Labour was suspect on the constitution, while simultaneously demonstrating its progressive-reformist attitude. Similarly, the party went to great lengths to reassert its political independence, stating that it 'owed allegiance to neither Moscow or Dublin. It fights elections and formulates policy in association with the British Labour Party.'[157] In a Cold War context it was vital for class-based parties, hopeful of electoral success in Western European liberal democracies, to put clear blue water between democratic socialism and authoritarian communism. It was especially pertinent in Ulster where Unionists were all too accustomed to tar the NILP with a red republican brush at a time when Northern Ireland's strategic position provided Great Britain with a safe back door. Its anti-Tory and anti-communist stance committed the party to a middle road. The appeal of its small 'u' unionism was now being projected for the benefit of the Protestant working class. Moreover, it could stress its soundness on the constitution while, conterminously, appearing to break with austerity on pressing socio-economic issues. Thoroughgoing planning measures outlined in *What Ulster Labour Would Do* were steeped in a long lineage of British labourist initiatives, but purposely adapted for applicability to local circumstances. The NILP's pledge to openly challenge the UUP on socio-economic issues was now based on an ostensible 'socialist unionist' ticket.

Over the next two years party activity was dominated by the campaign on unemployment and the pressing task of projecting a pro-unionist image onto the Protestant electorate.[158] The benefits reaped by the NILP on unemployment were not won easily. The visit by a high-ranking BLP delegation to Northern Ireland in November 1954 included the former Minister for Labour, Alfred Robens. This trip was planned by Napier in conjunction with Phillips and its main purpose served to add weight to NILP agitation on unemployment, while embarrassing those Unionists prone to make speeches on the province's buoyant economic fortunes. Much political credibility was generated for the NILP by the visit, especially when Robens delivered his 'ten-point plan' for economic recovery and development in the region. The plan stressed the need for a Development Corporation as a way of streamlining efforts to 'attract and establish new industries; [while] investigating freight rates; encouraging efficient marketing and co-operative enterprises'.[159] Provisions for a dry dock were mooted as a boost-port for short- to long-term employment along with governmental prioritisation for new aircraft orders, a textile council, and the appointment of a Secretary of State for Northern Ireland. Even though the main Belfast dailies welcomed Robens's proposals with open arms things might well have been different if Napier had been unveiled as the real author.[160]

Most of the economic misfortune experienced in these years can be attributed to a credit squeeze initiated by the British Chancellor of the Exchequer, which left less money around to finance new industrial initiatives. Regional difficulties were exacerbated by the slowdown in post-war royalties gravitating from central British government coffers 'and the threat to the balance of payments that developed during the investment boom of 1954–55'.[161] For Unionism it was a double-edged sword:

The pressure began to mount for the Unionist Government when hopes that the Conservative Government in London, in office from 1951, would interfere to help came to nothing; in fact, the Tory counter-inflationary measures of the time resulted in a credit squeeze and further blows to Northern Ireland's staple industrial base.[162]

These economic problems had complex political connotations too and were manifest in rumours of disquiet in Unionist ranks.[163] Furthermore, the province's 'remoteness from major markets meant that transport costs were somewhat higher ... than in more centrally located regions'[164] leading to the levying of additional surcharges on the importation of essential goods such as fuel (especially coal) and raw materials.

NILP election paraphernalia like *Ulster First* (1955), the NILP's manifesto for the 1955 Westminster election, played upon the Unionist–Conservative relationship as one of 'blind alliance'. It claimed that Northern Ireland's needs were being jettisoned for a foolish endorsement of reactionary Tory legislation. Primarily, it sought to advance the view that Unionist MPs were out of touch with ordinary people, pointing out that:

> Unionist members have included experts on the Balkans, on commercial television, on Oscar Wilde, on Malta, and on Kenya. They have not included a single expert on Ulster affairs. They do not include anyone with first hand knowledge of shipbuilding; nor of aircraft building; nor of textiles.[165]

Criticism did not merely stop at the character assassination of sitting UUP MPs. The structural deficiencies linking Westminster and Stormont were fully analysed, and the semi-radical idea of appointing a Secretary of State for Northern Ireland was again floated.[166] The very idea of a British cabinet minister acting as a legislative chaperone to the Unionist regime was not mooted simply to cause embarrassment to Brookeborough, but reflected genuine NILP angst over Ulster's devolved impotence.

Billy Boyd's unsuccessful bid in spring 1955 for the West Belfast seat at Westminster was not his only electoral defeat of that year. A Stormont by-election in Woodvale held on 15 November saw him defeated by just 436 votes by the Unionist candidate Neville Martin,[167] though his performance was a strong indication of NILP popularity among the Protestant working class. In his next outing Boyd would actually defeat his opponent on an even more slender majority of 80 votes. The 1955 results highlight how the NILP's new twin-track approach of critiquing the Unionist regime on its handling of a pressing unemployment situation and its failure to build the promised 'New Jerusalem' was beginning to reap rewards. The NILP began its emergence from its earlier exile in the political wilderness.

These attacks on the Unionist government's economic track-record were a central component of NILP discourse in the post-war period. Such thinking was especially potent when it involved exploiting the 'parity' deficit, i.e. the argument that Northern Ireland should be brought closer into line with other regions of the UK, particularly in the socio-economic sphere. The NILP argued consistently throughout the post-war period for realignment towards British standards of democracy and a greater share in UK-wide prosperity. Throughout almost its entire history NILP preoccupation with the 'parity' issue governed the flow of its discourse:

> 'This is the Answer' (1949), 'The Reform of Local Government' (1950), the 'Education Policy Statement' (1951), and 'There's a Job to Do' (1952). The radical stance these constituted served the party for the subsequent ten years. Image-wise the early Fifties were not the occasion to project the NILP alternative upon the Protestant electorate. The party was still on the defensive, protecting itself against repercussions of the 1949 electoral polarisations and accusations of former anti-partitionist leanings. To appear 'safe' and 'unionist' were the immediate concerns publicly.[168]

It is a matter of debate as to whether NILP appeals at this time were made directly to Protestant working-class hearts and minds or indirectly to their pockets. The document entitled *Rents and Houses* (1956), for example, was a counter-attack on Unionism's apparent departure from 'parity' in family allowances and housing legislation. Analysis of the document, essayed chiefly by Charles Brett,[169] uncovers an altogether more impressive critique than previously published propaganda. The underlying focus was on exposing Unionism's failure to demonstrate compassion for the most needy in society or to appreciate the local intricacies of Northern Ireland's economy.

Set against the immediate political backdrop, *Rents and Houses* appeared at a time when the debate over the Housing Miscellaneous Provisions Bill, or the 'Rent Bill', caused most intra-Unionist difficulties over the prerogative of landlords to raise the rent of their properties independently.[170] The NILP supported the right to private ownership by occupants, but advocated a more comprehensive co-operative public ownership scheme. A publicly funded body, 'existing for that purpose, making no profits, but bound to see that existing uses are preserved, and new houses built to take the place of those that had outlived their usefulness',[171] would not be formed until 1970. NILP challenges to Unionist ineptitude over the Rent Bill did constitute a direct appeal to working-class material interests. Security of tenure for those who were denied it under the existing scheme was emphatically called for: 'We can see no justification whatever, so long as the famine lasts, for abolishing this security, as the Rents Bill proposes to do immediately for houses over £40 valuation, and progressively for those over £8 valuation.'[172] A trumpeting of 'fair rents for all' was the raucous tune played by Labour for the benefit of working people and it served to win over many undecided voters.

In retrospect, 1956 is an easily recognisable date on the province's historical calendar because it brought 'the most serious physical force campaign launched against the Northern state since 1922'.[173] The tendency to overlook those decisive socio-economic issues, alluded to above, can imperil our historical understanding of the period. The fact that they caused a debilitating effect on Unionism's dominance over the Protestant working class exposed inherent weaknesses. Those government ministers hailing from the upper echelons of

Unionism were cast in a new light, particularly by the NILP and Independent Unionists, as being 'out of touch with the realities of ordinary peoples' lives'.[174]

A strong policy base was now in place by 1956. The very fact that the party had been consistently formulating its policies to meet the existing and impending realities showed that it was in touch with where working people were coming from in the 1950s. It also exemplified its capacity to adapt and harness working-class resentment of Unionism's mishandling of the economic situation, including the Rent Bill fiasco. Boyd's attempt to capture the Woodvale seat in 1955 heralded a more nuanced shift in support away from the Unionist Party and towards the NILP's critique.[175] By 1957 Brookeborough had not been successful in staving off a barrage of criticism emanating from the local Unionist associations in Belfast. Further intra-Unionist disquiet was prompted when the embattled Prime Minister lobbied Whitehall for an increase in economic subsidies from London, though the deployment of additional military resources to tackle the resurgent IRA threat did materialise. Although Brookeborough saw off the IRA threat – while arguably keeping his party united – he could not prevent the favourable wind from blowing in the NILP's direction.[176]

The 1958 Stormont election campaign

A worsening economic situation by late 1957, allied to Unionist government hesitancy over Family Allowance and Rent Bill legislation the previous year, led to increased enthusiasm for NILP policies. In the months running up to the election it was obvious to political commentators and the electorate alike that intra-Unionist conflict was clogging up Unionist Parliamentary Party (UPP) machinery. An attempt to play up the constitutional question as a way of reining in wavering working-class doubters did little to offset the NILP challenge now evident. The UUP's manifesto declared:

> We have built our house upon the rock of our constitutional position. Upon that rock depends all that we have achieved and all that we hope to achieve in the future. We are guardians of our own house … The maintenance of the constitutional issue is the vital issue.[177]

The chief electoral weapon in the hands of the NILP was the dire economic situation, and more precisely Unionist ineptitude in dealing with the acute unemployment problem.

Traditionally a sore point for the Unionist Party, the NILP's calls for a Development Corporation 'was used as an effective stick with which to beat the Government in the run up to the election'.[178] David Bleakley, speaking to party activists two weeks before the poll, fired the first shot across Unionist bows:

> The General Election has got off to a good start by arousing attention on Ulster's greatest menace – mass unemployment. In the debate now taking place, glaring defects in Northern Ireland Government policy are being revealed.[179]

This was a familiar theme in NILP discourse. Indeed, when the NILP began its

Origins of the 'consensus-forming strategy', 1945–58

electoral campaign back in 1957, criticising the Unionists was a crucial prerequisite for raising awareness among sceptical working-class Protestant voters, but of necessity it had to be clearly articulated within a partitionist framework. Successive election defeats over the last decade had taught the party this much. Billy Boyd had been more evangelical about this than most other candidates:

> The NILP takes its stand in favour of the maintenance of partition and at the same time demands a full programme of social justice and economic prosperity ... Let us forget trying to solve the affairs of the world, let us try to build a 'united Ulster' where prosperity, security and contentment shall be the birthright of every citizen.[180]

Boyd spoke from a firm Christian socialist platform, yet his brand of Labourism was non-sectarian – a trait he retained until his death.[181]

The party's policy base was solidified by a string of consistent and competent responses to local economic misfortune. A shift in leadership cadre brought to the forefront individuals firmer in their pro-British convictions; most of whom were imbibed with a tough working-class demeanour. 'Northern Ireland Labour stands unshakeably for the maintenance of the link with Britain' was the line trumpeted by the NILP's 1958 manifesto.[182] Socially, economically and politically this made sense to those party members who had become involved with Labour from the early 1950s and who were pro-Union in sentiment. But it was more than just pinning hopes on a closer economic and political integration with Great Britain. To the NILP the 'real danger is that, by neglecting "bread-and-butter" politics, the Government may allow economic disaster to overwhelm us. Year by year Stormont falls farther behind Westminster.'[183] There can be little doubt that by now leading figures such as Bleakley and Boyd had become the public face of the NILP.[184] By 1958 they were clear and unambiguous advocates for the Union and 'socialists outside the frame of Ulster's sectarian politics, though a Protestant Sabbatarianism, of strong non-conformist origins'.[185] By now the NILP's constitutional-friendly discourse had projected an image that was vastly different from the party of 1949.

By 1958 it was about establishing a non-sectarian style of political discourse – to make Northern Ireland more democratically acceptable; in short to realign the province's politics along a conventional left–right basis, as was the norm elsewhere in the UK. Issuing his party's first election communiqué, David Bleakley revealed the NILP's primary objective:

> Labour would provide Stormont with an effective Opposition. In our opinion, the experiment of running Parliament without such an Opposition has failed. What is needed is a core of pro-British Labour Members who will fearlessly, yet constructively, keep the policies of the Unionist Administration under constant supervision.[186]

In all it targeted four major issues inhibiting the lives of working people: first, it consolidated its position on the constitution; second, it lambasted Unionist efforts to minimise unemployment by plagiarising Labour calls for a Development Corporation; third, it dealt with socio-economic issues, including health and social services; and fourth the NILP played up its challenge over Rent Bill legislation. Thus:

> By the 1956 Rent Act, the Unionists raised nearly everyone's rent. At the same time Northern Ireland Labour organised mass protests. There can be no doubt that they were supported then by the vast majority of electors in these protests. They still represent the tenants' point of view. Did your Unionist MP protest? Did he vote against the Rents Bill?[187]

Again the NILP's critique of government ineptitude was counterbalanced by a constructive list of remedies. The 1958 manifesto represents a culmination in NILP grievances against the Unionist government. It appealed to working-class disgruntlement in a way previous documents had not. Having said that, the vital ingredients introduced into the party's earlier culinary serving up of critiques to the Unionist government can all be found repeated in this manifesto. This is at least an indication of consistency in its policies, if not a sign that the NILP saw itself as riding on the crest of a wave of working-class resentment at the Brookeborough regime.

The party of the late 1950s was an altogether different species from that left behind in 1949. More robust on the constitutional question, non-sectarian and democratic socialist in ideological outlook, it coveted a more pluralistic agenda for Northern Ireland. By 1958 most of its policies were couched in a constructive pragmatism. This lay in strict contrast to the stormy anti-imperialist rhetoric espoused by the old guard of ambivalents, such as Getgood. Equally important was the radically different socio-economic–political environment in which the party now found itself. Mass redundancies, twinned with industrial unrest, had been a constant feature of working life in Belfast throughout the 1950s. By 1957–58 the storm that had been brewing finally broke, leaving 10% of the province's workforce unemployed. A massive platers strike in the shipyard led to 2,000 being rendered idle.[188] Following the downing of tools the yard's management ruthlessly dismissed 1,000 other workers, mainly platers' helpers. The key demand articulated by shop stewards was for increased wages on a par with other British yards. The NILP, through its close liaison with its trade union comrades, was well disposed to offer its guidance and support to those laid-off workers. Its assistance to the Belfast working class in their 'hour of need' was rewarded at the polls in March 1958 when the NILP saw four of its number elected to Stormont. Out of these four constituencies Labour polled a clear majority in Pottinger, but won on only slender majorities in Oldpark, Woodvale and Victoria.[189] Overall the NILP vote stood at an impressive 16%, a significant increase on the 1953 figure of 12.1%.[190]

Conclusion

The NILP's tendency to label Unionists 'Tories' was based on the tacit assumption that they shared an unbreakable connection with the Conservative Party. However, as shown above, the introduction of welfare state legislation was by no means a painless process for the Unionist Party to champion any more than it was a pain-free process for the NILP. Indeed, welfarism illuminated intra-Unionist disputes to a greater extent than allegations of ethno-sectarian exclusivism. Dissension in the ranks of political parties is arguably a healthy sign of democracy, but to Unionist leaders it reinforced the tensions between its bulky middle-class membership and the ideal of a devolved administration under local authority. Clifford's persuasive anti-clericalist reading of the debates on welfare legislation provides us with a more sympathetic interpretation of Unionist efforts to bring progressive change to Northern Ireland, but she has indirectly produced an unflattering picture of the PLP's performance on the Opposition benches. It did not help matters much that Labour defiantly 'stuck to its guns' in a fruitless attempt to outbid Unionists for ownership of the welfare scheme. Arguably it left the NILP transfixed by a mood of despondency until its final acceptance of partition in 1949. By becoming 'light orange',[191] however, it manoeuvred itself into a much stabler political position from where it could later lay down a robust challenge to Unionism. With little reason to depart from the economic logic of partition Labour settled into its new oppositional role.

1953 may have been the year that witnessed the first tentative steps to square NILP policies with where the Protestant working class was coming from; by 1958 conditions were favourable for these gains to be consolidated. Protestant workers had clearly suffered economic impoverishment at the hands of an 'inept' Unionist regime but they were not prepared to throw in their lot with a socially retrogressive Republic, which, via the Unionist propaganda medium at least, was repeatedly characterised as politically backward, economically autarkic, firmly irredentist and deeply clerical. Following its withdrawal from the British Commonwealth it was all these things and more to the Protestant working class. Their ties to the economic logic of partition would bind them firmly to a pro-British sentiment. By alleviating working-class angst – vis-à-vis the inability of Unionism to remedy Ulster's socio-economic ills – the NILP provided both a diagnosis and a panacea.

Notes

1 PRONI, D/2704/A4/4/1, *NILP Documents*, NILP Executive Committee Report: Special Conference, Wellington Park, Belfast, Saturday 9 April 1949.
2 Addison, Paul, *The Road to 1945: British Politics and the Second World War* (London: Pimlico, 1994) and Hobsbawm, Eric, *The Age of Extremes: A History of the World, 1914–1991* (New York: Vintage, 1996).
3 *Belfast Telegraph*, 27 February 1945.
4 Barton, Brian, 'The Impact of World War II on Northern Ireland and on Belfast–London Relations', in Catterall, Peter and Sean McDougal (eds), *The Northern Ireland Question in British Politics* (Basingstoke: Macmillan, 1996), p. 48.
5 *Belfast Telegraph*, 31 January 1945.
6 Ibid.
7 Ibid.

8 Data taken from Bleakley, David W., 'The Trade Union Movement in Northern Ireland', *Journal of the Statistical and Social Inquiry Society of Ireland*, Vol. 19 (1954), p. 2.

9 Ibid.

10 'The Housing Act of 1945 provided for the first time for a large expansion of subsidized local authority housing, breaking with the pre-war policies that had relied on private enterprise.' Patterson, Henry, *Ireland Since 1939* (Oxford: Oxford University Press, 2002), p. 123. The Trust's immediate aim was to provide 5,000 houses, rising to a target total of 25,000 within five years.

11 The Minister of Health and Local Government, Dame Dehra Parker, later extended the Trust's tenure in 1950.

12 *Belfast Telegraph*, 14 February 1945.

13 Northern Ireland House of Commons Debates, Vol. 29, Col. 146, 25 July 1945.

14 Patterson, *Ireland Since 1939*, p. 123.

15 For an outline of the discrimination issue see Whyte, John, 'How much Discrimination was there Under the Unionist Regime, 1921–68?', in Gallagher, Tom and James O'Connell (eds), *Contemporary Irish Studies* (Manchester: Manchester University Press, 1983), pp. 1–35.

16 See Callaghan, John, 'The Welfare State: A New Society?', in Firth, Jim (ed.), *Labour's Promised Land? Culture and Society in Labour Britain 1945–51* (London: Lawrence and Wishart, 1995), pp. 115–31, for a detailed synopsis of British welfarist legislation.

17 The British Labour Party won a massive victory at the July 1945 British general election taking 393 seats (47.8% of the vote), compared to the Conservative's 213 (39.8% of the vote). Addison, *The Road to 1945*, p. 267.

18 Walker, Graham, *A History of the Ulster Unionist Party: Protest, Pragmatism and Pessimism* (Manchester: Manchester University Press, 2004), p. 100.

19 Important legislation included: the Family Allowances Act (1945); the National Insurance Act (1946); the Industrial Injuries Act (1946); the National Health Service Act (1946) and the Education Act (1947).

20 Patterson, Henry, 'Socialism in Ulster', in Patten, Eve (ed.), *Returning to Ourselves: Second Volume of Papers from the John Hewitt International Summer School* (Belfast: Lagan Press, 1995), p. 162.

21 Walker, *A History of the Ulster Unionist Party*, p. 104.

22 *Belfast Telegraph*, 9 March 1945.

23 Ibid.

24 Ibid.

25 See Kennedy, Denis, *The Widening Gulf: Northern Attitudes to the Independent Irish State, 1919–49* (Belfast: Blackstaff, 1988).

26 See Purdie, Bob, 'The Irish Anti-Partitionist League, South Armagh and the Abstentionist Tactic 1945–58', *Irish Political Studies*, Vol. 1 (1986), pp. 67–77.

27 Harbinson, J.F., *A History of the Northern Ireland Labour Party, 1891–1949* (Unpublished M.Sc. Thesis: Queen's University Belfast, 1966), p. 178.

28 Patterson, *Ireland Since 1939*, p. 50.

29 The UUP gained 178,662 votes (50.4% of the total vote), while the NILP gained 66,053 votes (18.6% of the total vote). Overall the left of centre parties gained 113,413 (31.9%) of the total vote. The Nationalists managed a meagre 32,546 votes, with most of these confined to the outlying areas.

30 Harbinson, *A History of the Northern Ireland Labour Party*, pp. 184, 258.

31 NILP, 22nd Annual Conference of the NILP, Carrickfergus, 27–28 October 1945.
32 Northern Ireland House of Commons Debates, Vol. 29, Col. 81, 24 July 1945.
33 Graham, J.A.V., *The Consensus-Forming Strategy of the Northern Ireland Labour Party 1949–1968* (Unpublished MSc Thesis: Queen's University Belfast, 1972), p. 5.
34 See Bew, Paul, Peter Gibbon and Henry Patterson, *The State in Northern Ireland: Political Forces and Social Classes* (Manchester: Manchester University Press, 1979), pp. 114–25.
35 Clifford, Angela, *The Mater Hospital (Belfast) and the National Health Service: Past, Present and Future* (Belfast: Athol Books, 1990), p. 15.
36 PRONI, D/3004/D/36, *Brookeborough Diaries*, 7 February 1945.
37 PRONI, D/3004/D/36, *Brookeborough Diaries*, 18 July 1945.
38 Andrews's populist appeals to the innate loyalty of workers can be contrasted with Brooke's realistic outlook. A further illustration of this point can easily be found – when a large strike broke out at the Harland and Wolff shipyard in February 1945 the arrest of five shop stewards 'revealed a growing feeling that organised labour looked on the prosecution as a threat to the Trades Union movement'. PRONI, CAB 4/578/1. The government, anxious for a quick return to war production, was prepared to allow clemency in exchange for a return to work. The strike proved the most successful in 30 years, winning all the concessions its leaders had initially sought.
39 Goldring, Maurice, *Belfast: From Loyalty to Rebellion* (London: Lawrence and Wishart, 1991), pp. 96–7.
40 Harry Midgley was Minister for Public Security 1943–44 and William Grant was Minister for Health and Social Services from 1944.
41 *Belfast Telegraph*, 15 September 1948.
42 *Belfast Telegraph*, 20 September 1948.
43 NIPC, *NILP Box 1*, Special Session of the 1947 Annual Conference: Final Agenda.
44 Ibid.
45 For a detailed analysis of the split see Cradden, Terry, *Trade Unionism, Socialism and Partition: The Labour Movement in Northern Ireland, 1939–1953* (Belfast: December Publications, 1993), pp. 170–213.
46 *Belfast Telegraph*, 20 September 1948.
47 Ibid.
48 LPA, GS12/NI/9i–ii.
49 Graham, *The Consensus-Forming Strategy of the Northern Ireland Labour Party*, p. 4.
50 See Walker, Graham, *The Politics of Frustration: Harry Midgley and the Failure of Labour in Northern Ireland* (Manchester: Manchester University Press, 1985), especially Chapter 7.
51 Midgley's rivalry with Jack Beattie is indicative of the competing ideological outlooks harboured by many party members at that time. Harbinson (p. 276) cautions us against seeing these divisions as centring on personalities. Rather the cause of the difficulties, he insists, was due to 'disunity previously apparent in the leadership, [which] became evident in the rank and file. It was from then centred on groups, not individuals'.
52 LPA, GS12/NI/9i–ii, Senator Luke O'Duffy to Morgan Phillips, February 1949.
53 The party's programme was decided at the Annual Party Conference. Delegates from all affiliated organisations were invited to submit matters for consideration, following which an agenda was sent out. The members of each Constituency Labour Party (CLP), and affiliated group, then chose which motion to support or oppose.

All matters were determined in the end by majority vote. Ascertained from the document: *The Labour Party and How it Functions*, PRONI, D/3702/C/9. As we will see the paramount importance of party policy precipitated the split of 1948–49 and would later be raised again when policy jarred with the local concerns of elected representatives during the 'Sunday Swings' debacle of 1964.

54 Graham, *The Consensus-Forming Strategy of the Northern Ireland Labour Party*, p. 4.

55 Cradden, Terry, 'The Left in Northern Ireland and the National Question: The "Democratic Alternative" in the 1940s', *Saothar* 16 (1991), p. 36.

56 It was reported at the time that the UUP's Propaganda Department had issued 350,000 posters, leaflets and booklets. In addition to the eight different posters (five in colour) 200,000 buttonhole badges, featuring Brooke alongside the slogan: 'Vote Unionist–We Are the King's Men', were also distributed. *Belfast Telegraph*, 3 February 1949.

57 Patterson, *Ireland Since 1939*, p. 121.

58 Bew, Paul, Peter Gibbon and Henry Patterson, 'Some Aspects of Nationalism and Socialism in Ireland: 1968–1978', in Morgan, Austen and Bob Purdie (eds), *Ireland: Divided Nation–Divided Class* (London: Ink Links, 1980), p. 155.

59 *Manchester Guardian*, 25 January 1949.

60 Arthur Johnson (BLP Agent for Newcastle Central) was appointed by the British Labour Party's National Executive Committee in April 1948, following an endorsement on 23 March 1948. He was initially paid 'an annual salary of £500 rising by three yearly increments of £20, £20 and £10 to a maximum of £550'. Taken from a document entitled: *Northern Ireland Liaison Committee: The Labour Party and Northern Ireland – An Historical Account of the Relations between the Labour Party and the Northern Ireland Labour Party* (BLP: Research Department, February, 1984), p. 9. LPA, British Labour Party, Northern Ireland Policy Box (1980–1990).

61 *Belfast Telegraph*, 12 February 1949.

62 See Cradden, *Trade Unionism, Socialism and Partition*, p. 222.

63 Cradden, 'The Left in Northern Ireland', p. 39.

64 See Norton, Christopher, 'The Irish Labour Party in Northern Ireland, 1949–58', *Saothar* 21 (1996), pp. 47–59. Graham has also written that these difficulties 'reached a peak at the Chapel Gate election, in February, 1949, when electoral polarisation along community lines squeezed Labour out, both Parliamentary seats (Dock and Oldpark) being lost. The election was so-called because funds were collected outside Roman Catholic churches in Éire and Northern Ireland to support anti-partitionist candidates.' Graham, *The Consensus-Forming Strategy of the Northern Ireland Labour Party*, p. 5.

65 See 'Letting Labour Lead: Jack MacGougan and the Pursuit of Unity, 1913–1958', *Saothar* 14 (1989), pp. 113–24.

66 In Belfast the party won all seven seats contested, leaving it as the main opposition to the Unionists on Belfast Corporation (the NILP and the Nationalist Party were both left with one solitary representative each). The IrLP also returned councillors to Armagh, Dungannon, Newry and Warrenpoint. See Norton, 'The Irish Labour Party in Northern Ireland', p. 51.

67 Rumpf, Erhard and Anthony C. Hepburn, *Nationalism and Socialism in Twentieth Century Ireland* (Liverpool: Liverpool Univeresity Press, 1977), p. 208.

68 The full extent of this maintenance grant can be found in LPA, Northern Ireland Policy Box, 1980–1990, *The Labour Party and Northern Ireland: An Historical Account of the Relations between the Labour Party and the Northern Ireland Labour Party* (1984).

69 Interview with Rt. Hon. David Bleakley, 21 March 2006.

70 LPA, GS12/NI/6/XXVII, Report of the 26th Annual NILP Conference (1949).

71 For full details of the BLP's response to the NILP's request for affiliation as a regional council see LPA, *The Labour Party and Northern Ireland: An Historical Account of the Relations between the Labour Party and the Northern Ireland Labour Party*, pp. 16–19.

72 Barton, Brian, 'Relations Between Westminster and Stormont During the Attlee Premiership', *Irish Political Studies*, Vol. 7 (1992), p. 19.

73 See Purdie, Bob, 'The Friends of Ireland: British Labour and Irish Nationalism, 1945–49', in Gallagher, Tom and James O'Connell (eds), *Contemporary Irish Studies* (Manchester: Manchester University Press, 1983), pp. 81–94.

74 Bell, Geoffrey, *Troublesome Business: The Labour Party and the Irish Question* (London: Pluto, 1982), p. 98.

75 *Belfast Telegraph*, 12 February 1949.

76 Ibid. In NILP discourse Unionists were referred to as 'Tories'. Some scholars have accepted this description, stating, 'There is clearly considerable justification for such a view: the 1927 Trades Disputes Act, which impeded the political activities of trade unions, was repealed in Great Britain in 1946, but in Northern Ireland not until 1959; plural voting in parliamentary and local elections was retained until 1969, long after it had been done away in Britain. The political representatives of the party have been drawn mainly from the social and economic elite of the province'. Rumpf and Hepburn, *Nationalism and Socialism in Twentieth Century Ireland*, p. 177.

77 *Belfast Telegraph*, 20 January 1949.

78 Ibid.

79 *Belfast Telegraph*, 21 January 1949.

80 Ibid.

81 Walker, *A History of the Ulster Unionist Party*, p. 101.

82 Purdie, Bob, *Politics in the Streets: The Origins of the Civil Rights Movement in Northern Ireland* (Belfast: Blackstaff, 1990), p. 67.

83 Ibid., p. 68.

84 Ibid., p. 69.

85 See Staunton, Enda, *The Nationalists of Northern Ireland, 1918–1973* (Dublin: Columbia, 2001), pp. 158–229.

86 A detailed election post-mortem can be found in the document entitled: *State of the Labour Movement in Northern Ireland*, compiled in June 1949 by the NILP's chairman James Morrow and party secretary Sam Napier, LPA, GS12/NI/45i–vi.

87 Farrell, Michael, *Northern Ireland: The Orange State* (London: Pluto, 1976), p. 195.

88 LPA, GS12/NI/45ii, *State of the Labour Movement in Northern Ireland*, June 1949.

89 LPA, GS12/NUJ/40i–ii, Covering Letter and Report sent to Morgan Phillips by the National Organiser of the National Union of Seamen.

90 Ibid.

91 Ibid.

92 Ibid.

93 LPA, GS12/NI/69/ii–iv, Napier to Phillips, Difficulties raised by authoritative statement from British Labour sources dealing with Northern Ireland, December, 1949.

94 Purdie, 'The Friends of Ireland: British Labour and Irish Nationalism, 1945–49'.

95 See Barton, 'Relations Between Westminster and Stormont During the Attlee Premiership'.

96 LPA, GS12/NI/23, Napier to Phillips, 2 March 1949.

97 *Belfast Telegraph*, 3 January 1948.

98 *Belfast Newsletter*, 17 February 1950.

99 Ibid.

100 Wichert, Sabine, *Northern Ireland Since 1945* (Harlow: Longman, 1991), p. 55.

101 Devlin, Paddy, *Straight Left: An Autobiography* (Belfast: Blackstaff, 1993), p. 67.

102 Candidates in North, South and East Belfast all polled respectably and managed to obtain second place in each constituency.

103 LPA, GS12/NI/ADD/22–3. Napier to Phillips, 10 September, 1951. See attached report signed by Sam Napier and John F. Hill.

104 LPA, GS12/NI/ADD/29v.

105 Puirséil, Niamh, *The Irish Labour Party, 1922–73* (Dublin: UCD Press, 2007), p. 138.

106 Sam Napier became acting Party Secretary following the resignation of Joseph Corrigan on 12 December 1949. He remained in that capacity until appointed on a full-time salary in 1952. He was the principal architect of NILP electoral campaigns in these years, together with Arthur A. Johnston (Party Organiser, 1948–51) and John F. Hill (1951–52). See correspondence in LPA, GS12/NI/1–100.

107 LPA, GS12/NI/ADD/22–3, 29iii–xi.

108 LPA, GS12/NI/ADD/22–3. The North Belfast Federation had four constituency Labour parties contained within it. However, Duncairn DLP had party machinery, but no secretary. The South and East Belfast Federations had two DLPs each, but the West Belfast Federation had only one. Two branches of the League of Youth existed, but one was under-strength. There were about six women's sections in the City. South Antrim Federation consisted of two parties (Carrickfergus and Lisburn) with 24 active members and County Londonderry consisted of two, Coleraine and Londonderry. Both these parties were 'in a very bad way' according to contemporary reports and it was doubted if they had more than 36 members between them. North Down branches consisted of Cregagh, Dundonald, Bangor and Comber.

109 Graham, *The Consensus-Forming Strategy of the Northern Ireland Labour Party*, p. 17.

110 LPA, GS12/NI/ADD/iii, Memo from Napier to Phillips, 5 April, 1951. The NILP indicated that it wanted to purchase a small van to enable them 'to carry literature, loud speaker equipment, and workers, into rural areas'.

111 LPA, GS12/NI/ADD/22i, Memo from Sam Napier to Morgan Phillips, 10 September 1951.

112 LPA, GS12/NI/ADD/22iii.

113 Ibid.

114 Edwards, Aaron, 'Democratic Socialism and Sectarianism: The Northern Ireland Labour Party and Progressive Unionist Party Compared', *Politics*, Vol. 27, No. 1 (2007), p. 26.

115 PRONI, D/3702/D/4, *NILP Documents*, Address by Robert Getgood to the 50th Irish Trade Union Congress in Drogheda, 7–8 July 1944.

116 Graham, *The Consensus-Forming Strategy of the Northern Ireland Labour Party*, p. 27.

117 Robert Bingham set up the St Annes Labour Party in 1954. Interview with Robert Bingham, 24 February 2005.

118 *Belfast Telegraph*, 10 October 1953.

119 NILP, *South Belfast Elector* (October 1952).

120 Ibid.

121 The term 'radically alternative' was attributed to Sam Napier by J.A.V. Graham.

Origins of the 'consensus-forming strategy', 1945–58   67

However, it is unclear whether the term was in common usage among NILP activists.

122 These points are taken from Graham, *The Consensus-Forming Strategy of the Northern Ireland Labour Party*, pp. 7–8.

123 Graham, *The Consensus-Forming Strategy of the Northern Ireland Labour Party*, p. 9.

124 PRONI, D/3702/C/9, *Sam Napier Papers*, Napier, Sam, 'Soapbox Socialism', *The Rising Tide*, Vol. 1, No. 1 (August 1949).

125 A critique of the logic of modernisation can be found in Dixon, Paul, *Northern Ireland: The Politics of War and Peace* (Basingstoke: Palgrave, 2001), pp. 47–66.

126 Graham, *The Consensus-Forming Strategy of the Northern Ireland Labour Party*, p. 8.

127 Ibid., p. 274.

128 Ibid., p. 27.

129 Graham (ibid., p. 10) claims here that: 'Napier dominated party thinking during the Fifties, although along with Tom Boyd, the future party leader, and Charles Brett a dominant ideological triumvirate had already formed.'

130 Ibid., p. 6.

131 Ibid., p. 274.

132 LPA, GS12/NI/181–2.

133 Ibid.

134 LPA, GS12/NI/181ii, *Foreword by Party Secretary to Report for Executive Committee on Northern Ireland General Election* (1953).

135 Graham, *The Consensus-Forming Strategy of the Northern Ireland Labour Party*, p. 29.

136 Patterson, *Ireland Since 1939*, p. 144.

137 These constituencies included Oldpark and Pottinger. Conversely an Independent Unionist ran in Woodvale in 1953, but not in 1958.

138 Graham, *The Consensus-Forming Strategy of the Northern Ireland Labour Party*, pp. 27–33.

139 Patterson, *Ireland Since 1939*, pp. 143–6.

140 Farrell, *Northern Ireland*, p. 225.

141 McGarry, John and Brendan O'Leary, *Explaining Northern Ireland: Broken Images* (Oxford: Blackwell, 1995), p. 156.

142 See Rumpf and Hepburn, *Nationalism and Socialism in Twentieth Century Ireland*, pp. 188–9.

143 Farrell, *Northern Ireland*, p. 225, makes a similar point.

144 See GS12/NI/183i–ii, Napier to Phillips, 14 December 1953.

145 LPA, GS/NI/11/xi, *Spotlight on the Unionist Record* (1953).

146 Ibid.

147 Unemployment rates for the previous three years in Northern Ireland stood at 5.8% in 1950, 6.1% in 1951 and 10.4% in 1952, while in Great Britain the figures were 1.5%, 1.2% and 2.0% respectively. Source: Isles, K.S. and Norman Cuthbert, *An Economic Survey of Northern Ireland* (Belfast: HMSO, 1957), Statistical Appendix, Table 1: Twelve Month Average Unemployment, pp. 566–7.

148 PRONI, D/3702/D/5, *Sam Napier Papers*, untitled article on emigration.

149 NILP, *Spotlight on the Unionist Record* (1953).

150 Ibid.

151 The party took this figure from the *Belfast Telegraph*, 18 March 1953.

152 NILP, *It's a High Price* (1953).

153 Ibid.

154 Ibid.

155 NILP, *What Ulster Labour Would Do* (1953).

156 Ibid.

157 NILP, *Where Ulster Labour Stands* (1953).

158 Graham, *The Consensus-Forming Strategy of the Northern Ireland Labour Party*, p. 33.

159 NILP, *North Belfast Elector* (May 1955).

160 Graham, *The Consensus-Forming Strategy of the Northern Ireland Labour Party*, p. 36.

161 Bew, Paul, Peter Gibbon and Henry Patterson, *Northern Ireland, 1921–2001: Political Forces and Social Classes: Revised and Updated Version* (London: Serif, 2002), p. 140.

162 Walker, *A History of the Ulster Unionist Party*, p. 126.

163 Bew et al, *Northern Ireland*, p. 141.

164 Harris, Richard, *Regional Economic Policy in Northern Ireland, 1945–1988* (Aldershot: Avebury, 1991), p. 35.

165 NILP, *Ulster First* (1955).

166 Ibid. The rationale behind NILP calls for a new Ministry were grounded in a UK-wide perspective. 'In the late Government the Home Secretary was also Minster for Welsh Affairs. There was a Secretary of State for Scotland, a Minister of State, and three Under-Secretaries for Scotland. Why should not Ulster benefit from a similar appointment?'

167 Elliott, Sydney, *Northern Ireland Parliamentary Election Results, 1921–1972* (Chichester: Political Reference Publications, 1973), p. 50.

168 Graham, *The Consensus-Forming Strategy of the Northern Ireland Labour Party*, p. 275.

169 Interview with Sir Charles Brett, 30 January 2004.

170 See Walker, *A History of the Ulster Unionist Party*, pp. 124–6.

171 NILP, *Rents and Houses* (1956).

172 Ibid.

173 Farrell, *Northern Ireland*, p. 202.

174 Walker, *A History of the Ulster Unionist Party*, p. 12.

175 Boyd polled 5,173 votes, while his opponent polled 5,609. In 1958 Boyd polled 7,529 votes, while his opponent polled 7,449. Elliott, *Northern Ireland Parliamentary Election Results, 1921–1972*, p. 50.

176 Walker, *A History of the Ulster Unionist Party*, p. 124.

177 *Belfast Telegraph*, 6 March 1958. See also the criticism levelled at the NILP by the Unionist Candidate for Oldpark, W.J. Morgan, who said that the NILP had failed in the past to announce a 'clear-cut and straightforward' decision on the constitutional issue. *Northern Whig*, 13 March 1958.

178 Walker, *A History of the Ulster Unionist Party*, p. 127.

179 *Belfast Telegraph*, 6 March 1958.

180 *Northern Whig*, 5 August 1957.

181 Interview with Douglas McIldoon, 30 January 2004; interview with Beatrice Boyd, 21 February 2005.

182 PRONI, D/4276, *Tom Boyd Papers*, Pottinger Special: Stormont Election Manifesto (1958).

183 Ibid.

184 Billy Boyd was a 'born and bred' Shankill Road man with firm roots in the local

Labour movement. He was a shipyard worker and a member of the British-based National Union of Vehicle Builders. In 1954 he had been elected to serve on the Irish Congress of Trade Unions Northern Ireland Committee, for the term 1954–55, almost certainly contributing to an elevation in his profile in the trade union circuit in Northern Ireland.

185 Morgan, Austen, *Labour and Partition: The Belfast Working Class, 1905–23* (London: Pluto, 1991), p. 324.
186 *Northern Whig*, 1 March 1958.
187 Ibid.
188 *Belfast Telegraph*, 1 March 1958.
189 The voting majorities were: Oldpark, 155; Pottinger 1,333; Victoria, 147 and Woodvale, 80. Elliott, *Northern Ireland Parliamentary Election Results, 1921–1972*, pp. 43, 44, 47, 50.
190 Ibid., p. 93.
191 Morgan, *Labour and Partition*, p. 324.

3

The Labour Opposition of Northern Ireland, 1958–65

The Northern Ireland Labour Party candidates will do everything possible to preserve and strengthen the link with Britain. Unlike the Unionist Party we will not use the border as an excuse for doing nothing.[1]

Ulster cannot afford to stand still in the Sixties, nor can she afford constant backward glances over her shoulder ... Labour believes that Northern Ireland can become a prosperous and united community if its people so decide; that unemployment can be beaten; that social justice can be achieved; that the gulfs between our people can be bridged. The process can neither be swift nor easy. It will never come if a beginning is never made. Only a strong, constructive, constitutional Labour opposition can make that beginning. The electors must choose between Ulster's past and Ulster's future.[2]

The Northern Ireland Labour Party fights this election in association with the British Labour Party: our candidates support and share British Labour's high ideals and practical policies. And Northern Ireland Labour believes deeply, as does the British Labour Party, in the fundamental rights of human beings without regard to the barrier of religion, race or colour. Both are wholly non-sectarian parties, striving for the betterment of our people without distinction.[3]

Introduction: the 1958 Stormont election

In the run-up to the 20 March polling date Belfast newspapers were rife with speculation over whether or not the ongoing IRA threat would serve as the cleft stick in the forthcoming elections. The *Northern Whig* seemed assured that 'None of the parties, Unionist, Independent Unionist, Northern Ireland Labour or any of the varieties of Nationalism, can or will omit the border from their programmes'.[4] For the NILP a reaffirmation of support for Ulster's constitutional status quo was an important component on the election trail.[5] It had now become mandatory for Labour candidates to present themselves as safe on the constitution in order to challenge the UUP's increasingly sophisticated and well-oiled propaganda machine on its own terms. In Belfast the Labour candidate for Victoria, David Bleakley, repeated a familiar précis to all NILP electoral communiqués by reiterating his party's commitment to the Union,[6] though flag waving by itself was insufficient to reel in those yearning for a fresh electoral alternative. Simultaneously the party sought to boost working-class resilience with promises of future job creation, economic development and healthier standards of living: social justice would now be placed at the apex of the NILP's post-election priorities.[7] There would be no attempt to shirk from their responsibilities to their constituents, especially when observers had forecast the emergence of a Unionism more willing to advocate social reform to head off the Labour challenge.[8]

Labour was greatly facilitated in its bid to direct public attention away from the border issue by Nationalist indifference towards the IRA's campaign. IRA activities were largely rural-based affairs; republican paramilitaries refrained from launching a large-scale offensive on Belfast.[9] Nevertheless, the constitutional question had been thrown into sharp relief by republican actions and would persist in clouding the minds of most voters for some time yet. Where it could, Labour attempted to deal with the issue head-on by calling unambiguously for the 'gun to be removed from Irish politics',[10] while conterminously appearing reluctant to rely disproportionately on its small 'u' unionist credentials.[11] For Paddy Devlin – the IrLP's newly elected councillor in Belfast – the NILP's position was a sham, a cheap ploy exploited by a party claiming an affinity to the founding principles of democratic socialism. 'This is surely a contradictory position,' Devlin complained, 'as a socialist could not stand for the continued existence of a State founded on a fundamental injustice, i.e. allowing a minority to contract out of a majority decision.'[12] In fact it was the NILP's unique blend of social radicalism – articulated through a pro-unionist framework – which quickened its rapid ascendancy in the minds of many working-class voters.[13] For NILP strategists this was to be the beginning of a transitional period in which Protestant working-class support could be prolifically consolidated.[14] Once this phase of the 'consensus-forming strategy' was complete tentative moves could then be made to embrace the Catholic minority.

Before polling had closed there were signs that many working-class voters were making their decision based on calls from trade union leaders to vote on 'bread and butter' issues.[15] Of the eight Belfast constituencies contested by the NILP in 1958 half returned Labour MPs, notwithstanding the fact that the NILP's relatively small share of the vote (37,748) meant that its overall percentage was only slightly higher than its 1953 total.[16] The *Belfast Telegraph* welcomed Labour's encroachment in Belfast industrial divisions as an indication that '[t]hese are changing times, and the public has decided to give Labour a say, not in the main, we believe, for socialist purposes, but to see the effect of opposing constructive criticism at Stormont'.[17] Such favourable press coverage undoubtedly aided the NILP, as Bleakley points out:

> We were also very lucky in the Labour Party that our most difficult times coincided with a great editor on the *Belfast Telegraph*, John E. Sayers. And John Sayers was a man who (he was no socialist) but he was a man who believed in fair play. That was

of considerable importance – and you got a crack of the whip in other words. Before that it was very difficult [with] the *Belfast Telegraph* because it was a pillar of Unionism. But it became … [fairer] across the board.[18]

Table 3.1 Northern Ireland general elections, 1921–69: NILP performance

Election	Candidates	MPs elected	Forfeited deposits	Total votes	%
1921	0	0	0	N/A	N/A
1925	3	3	0	18,114	4.7
1929	5	1	0	23,334	8.0
1933	3	2	0	14,436	8.6
1938	7	1	1	18,775	5.7
1945	15	2	1	66,053	18.6
1949	9	0	2	26,831	7.2
1953	9	0	0	31,063	21.1
1958	8	4	0	37,748	16.0
1962	14	4	0	76,842	26.0
1965	17	2	0	66,323	20.4
1969	16	2	2	45,113	8.1

Source: Adapted from Elliott, Sydney, *Northern Ireland Parliamentary Election Results, 1921–1972* (Chichester: Political Reference Publications, 1973), p. 116.

It was in the 'sectarian cockpit' of Belfast where a significant turn towards Labour was most evident. The impact of cross-sectarian voting power in Oldpark and Pottinger, when taken in conjunction with the loss of solidly Unionist seats in Woodvale and Victoria, had far-reaching effects for Unionism beyond the loss of two marginal seats. After all these latter two constituencies were mostly Protestant and working class, while the other two (in Oldpark and Pottinger) were more evenly divided along ethnic lines, between Catholics and Protestants.[19] Reasons for the UUP's dire performances in Belfast constituencies are multiple, but it was undoubtedly the unemployment issue, as well as intra-Unionist division over family allowances and rents legislation, which secured the NILP's ambition to become a constructive Opposition at Stormont. Graham Walker has stressed the dislocation of some Unionist politicians from the socio-economic concerns of their constituents:

> By this time, against a background of economic gloom in the province's traditional heavy industries, the Unionist Party appeared too distant from working class concerns, and, even more damagingly, insufficiently equipped to deal with the problems.[20]

However it would be wrong to attribute the NILP's successes in these constituencies solely to the UUP's blasé attitude on socio-economic issues. Their ideological allies in the Conservative government must also shoulder some of the blame because of their refusal to buoy up the Unionist position on economic matters. Local Labour politicians were not the only critics of this unprofitable alliance. Belfast Unionists, such as Edmund Warnock and Neville Martin (the defeated candidate in Woodvale) saw their party's identification with the Conservatives as 'a liability'.[21]

Morgan Phillips was the first British Labour Party representative to travel to Northern Ireland to congratulate the NILP on its electoral success.[22] Accordingly he addressed the party's victory celebrations in its Royal Avenue headquarters, conferring on those gathered the fraternal gratitude of the NEC on a modestly successful assault on the 'Tory' Unionist position. Yet Phillips's visit had an ulterior purpose: the 1959 Westminster election loomed large on the horizon and early planning was essential if a replication of NILP success was to continue.[23] These talks displayed few of the self-congratulatory attitudes one might expect to be manifest in the wake of an electoral triumph. Phillips's report to the NEC was equally subdued:

> The Executive of the party feel that their efforts in the Imperial election should be confined to possibly two but no more than three seats, all of which are in Belfast. If this is done, they believe they can win one, or possibly two. They are severely handicapped by the lack of sufficient candidates of the calibre required to win but what is even more important, their organisation could not handle more than two or three constituencies successfully in the course of the next eighteen months.[24]

Nevertheless the NILP had much to console it in this election in that it opened up a new front against the Unionist position in Belfast. Unionist recrimination could not disguise the fact that marginal seats had been won in Woodvale and Victoria. Contrary to previous scholarly accounts of the BLP's disinterest in Ireland there was no disguising the firmness of that party's support for its Ulster comrades during these critical junctures: much would hinge on NILP success in the parliamentary arena.

The Parliamentary Labour Party as Official Opposition

At the inaugural meeting of the Parliamentary Labour Party (PLP) held in Parliament Buildings, Stormont, Tom Boyd (MP for Pottinger) was elected leader and David Bleakley his deputy.[25] The party was formally recognised as Her Majesty's Official Opposition by the Unionist Speaker of the House, Captain Sir Norman Stronge, on 5 April 1958.[26] Stronge had taken the decision without government assent, but it was done primarily as a way of expediting business in the House.[27] The *Irish News* reacted by belittling the NILP's new position as Official Opposition: 'it can hardly be regarded as an historic event, unless history descends to the trivialities of political life'.[28] Grass-roots Labour activists, on the other hand, were more upbeat. At the annual meeting of the Oldpark DLP in February 1959 the return of four members to Stormont was saluted; Labour's victory had 'shown in no uncertain manner the way in which the electorate was thinking politically'.[29] The newly elected MP for Oldpark, Vivian Simpson, was congratulated on his electoral performance and tribute was paid to the PLP for adding 'zest and purpose to the Parliamentary Debates and other procedures in the House'.[30] In Woodvale the local secretary, Hugh Stockman, reported that the past year had been 'eventful' with the successful election of Billy Boyd. Owing to the steep increase in party business in the area it was deemed necessary to appoint an organiser to manage constituency work on a full-time basis.[31] Most activists now felt enamoured by the party's good showing at the Stormont election; their imagined vision of a future where parliamentary socialism held onto the levers of power was now within reach.

One example of how the NILP envisaged its parliamentary career panning out came within its first three weeks of taking its seats. The platers' strike, which had broken out in February 1958, was still ongoing by late April 1958 and there were few signs of workers reaching an amicable accommodation with their bosses.[32] Amidst a deteriorating economic situation the NILP used its influence as Official Opposition to draw attention to the problems facing the workers. As Table 3.2 shows, strike activity was particularly severe between 1955 and 1961. It is remarkable for the number of days lost in 1957, which stood at a massive 565,000. The NILP was riding on the crest of a wave in its critique of Unionist mishandling of the industrial unrest.

Table 3.2 Strikes in Northern Ireland, 1955–61

Year	Number of workers involved	Days lost in strike action
1955	3,000	7,000
1956	32,000	44,000
1957	64,300	565,000
1958	11,100	258,000
1959	20,500	92,000
1960	19,000	156,000
1961	49,000	39,000

Source: ICTU, Research Department, Trade Union Information, Vol. 1, Nos. 13–14, (August 1961), cited in Mulholland, Marc, *'Stolen Thunder!': The Northern Ireland Labour Party in Context, 1958–1965* (Unpublished MA Thesis: Queen's University Belfast, 1994), p. 14.

These strikes not only exposed the potency of class-based agitation prevalent among Belfast's proletariat during this period[33] but they also highlighted the failure of Northern Ireland's heavy industries to adapt (or diversify) in the face of global economic rationalisation and in terms of higher inflationary changes within the UK.[34] Collectively, the new Labour MPs – Tom Boyd, David Bleakley, Billy Boyd and Vivian Simpson – seized on working-class misfortune as a means of displaying their organic working-class credentials, something they did with tremendous flair. Their close proximity to the directly affected workers meant that they could make intuitive speeches on the matter despite considerable harrying from political opponents.

As the newly elected MP for Woodvale, Billy Boyd made frequent representations on behalf of those employees who had been affected by the strike for many months. His stark forecast that it 'was only a matter of time until the entire ship-yard closes down and every worker is out on the street'[35] was interpreted by the affected workers as an indication of Labour's deep-seated concern for its working-class brethren. Yet some politicians, like former NILP chairman and by then Unionist MP for Shankill, Henry Holmes, accused Boyd of over-exaggerating the level of support for striking workers. The decision to down tools was by no means unilateral, he remonstrated; indeed many of those affected were willing to reconcile themselves to their employer's terms and conditions if it meant a return to proper pay.[36] Boyd's shrewd interpretation of the underlying problems fuelling the strike came from his work as a local coun-cillor in Belfast's Court Ward – something which earned him substantial favour in West Belfast. Boyd's election agent, Robert Bingham who, incidentally, served as the party's chairman in 1959–60, vividly recalls the day of the election:

> On polling day, when Billy Boyd was elected (1958 that was), I was working in Shorts and I virtually emptied that factory. The boys came out to work on polling day (you would never get that again) ... That's a fact ... And they came out wanting to do it ... Billy Boyd was first put forward in a by-election and he didn't win it, and then he was put forward in a general election and did win it ... The great thing about winning Woodvale and Victoria was they were Unionist seats. Oldpark and Pottinger were probably in [and around the] 50:50 kind of [figure] - they could have swung. Pottinger always had a Labour tradition – Jack Beattie. Jack eventually became Irish Labour. The two seats – Victoria and Woodvale – were a big victory because of the religious composition. But on those [victories] we failed to build, in the sense that we made gains at the next two but not sufficient ... That was 1962. I had been elected ... in 1961 ... to Castlereagh here. We did very well but we didn't do well enough. And that's where the growth of the Labour Party seemed to become stunted. To be going anywhere we would have needed to have a couple of more seats. But we didn't do it. And you know the religious thing was deteriorating ... We didn't notice this.[37]

It is impossible to confirm with any clear certainty what motivated people to vote for Boyd on both occasions, though in the interviews with the author most former party activists from Woodvale emphasised the feeling that there were many people who were eager to repay Boyd for his erstwhile and energetic constituency work.[38]

Parliamentary sessions dealing with instances of industrial unrest demonstrated just how effective the NILP could be as the Official Opposition. NILP MPs proved willing and able to draw attention to workers' issues in day-to-day parliamentary business. They were well placed to take an accurate barometer reading of wider Labour movement interests. The fact that the party's link with trade unionism was not as strong as its mainland British counterpart was due mainly to structural and legislative differences which have their roots in the inter-war period.[39] However, the one conduit through which the unions could speak was when one of their number was elected to public office. The four Labour MPs were members of British-based trade unions operating in Northern Ireland and all sought to provide a platform for both wings of the Labour movement. As Graham rightly surmises it was their eagerness 'to work for the advancement of trade union ends, which gave the party its bargaining power' in Stormont.[40]

As a high-ranking regional official in the British-based Boilermakers Union Billy Boyd had served as a member of the Northern Ireland Committee (NIC) of the Irish Congress of Trade Unions (ICTU) in the mid-1950s and like his fellow Labour MPs he had been imbibed with a strong trade union ethos through his association with the movement. Even though the NIC's newest officer Billy Blease was also a card-carrying member of the NILP, the NIC and PLP still lacked the quality of formalised institutional links which made their British political allies so unique.[41] The Unionist government's refusal to recognise the NIC as the trade union movement in Northern Ireland because its headquarters was in Dublin - 'a foreign country'[42] – did much to preclude a more active engagement at the institutional interface between the Labour movement and the local administration.[43] The NILP's financial dependency on trade union levies meant that interest groups occupied integral positions within the local DLPs, as well as links to the EC and the rejuvenated PLP.[44] The Labour movement still did not enjoy unfettered access to the corridors of power: an organisational shake-up was needed to bring the PLP and trade unions closer together. It was not until 1960 that Blease and Napier formed the Joint Unemployment Committee[45] in order to bring into line the coalition between party and unions. The Blease–Napier initiative pre-empted the formation of a joint liaison committee by almost six years – coincidentally the same year that Terence O'Neill's government eventually recognised the NIC's authority.[46]

Despite the many constraints imposed on them, Labour's parliamentarians settled into their oppositional roles with considerable ease. Nonetheless, they frequently experienced a frigid reception from the Unionists because of their proactive style. David Bleakley's forced withdrawal from the Public Accounts Committee, amidst much political recrimination, pointed to the NILP's precariously inflated position in the House, even though the rules stated that one Opposition member should be appointed.[47] In November 1958 the party staked its claim as an integral part of the wider Labour movement when it tried unsuccessfully to challenge the Unionist government's Trades Disputes and Trades Unions Bill (1958). This Bill proposed the biggest overhaul of trade union legislation since 1927 – and was arguably drawn up by Unionists as a way of quelling recent industrial unrest.[48] In consultation with their trade union comrades the NILP requested the complete repeal of the 1927 Act[49] but its lobbying failed to persuade Brookeborough's administration which pressed ahead with its plans to retain the Act. Nevertheless PLP business during these years was noteworthy for the amount of research that had gone into preparing its detailed cases against unfavourable government legislation such as this.

One strategy adopted by the party as a means of reaching out across the ethno-religious division in Ulster society was to champion those social welfarist issues, such as health and social service provision, which mattered most to people. In this – as in much else – the NILP shared an ideological philosophy with British Labour. Just as both parties had consistently lobbied for the automatic right of every citizen to enjoy free access to education, so it was with the NHS. Introduced by Clement Attlee's Labour Government (1945–51) in the aftermath of the Second World War, the NHS was the BLP's greatest political achievement. When legislation was passed in Britain to include private hospitals in the full financial backing of the state system the Unionist regime departed from its step-by-step policy, instead deciding against extending the provision to privately managed hospitals, thereby excluding the Catholic-maintained Mater Hospital. Situated on Belfast's Crumlin Road, yards from the 'Crum' (Belfast's main prison at the time), the Mater served both sides of the community regardless of creed and without request for payment.[50] NILP policy had been consistent on the Mater situation: it should be included under the NHS scheme.[51] As MP for Oldpark, and also party spokesman on Health and Local Government, Vivian Simpson was responsible for the party's handling of the Mater issue. He raised the Mater's predicament several times in the House but each time the issue was downplayed by a government eager to placate the most reactionary elements of its parliamentary cadre.

Despite Simpson's tireless lobbying over the Mater and other cross-sectarian issues there were instances when Nationalist politicians charged the NILP with being an 'Orange tinged' party. In one notable instance a motion tabled by Eddie McAteer in October 1958, calling on a review of the conditions inside Crumlin Road prison, was met with obstruction from the Labour Opposition bench. On this issue Unionist obstinacy was replaced by Nationalist hostility. Most indignation was reserved for Bleakley by the Nationalists who complained about his pro-government demeanour. But Bleakley's objection to the motion had less to do with the actual content of McAteer's proposed review; instead it had more to do with the context in which it was issued, after all it had been proposed that an independent reappraisal of prison conditions take place while the IRA's so-called border campaign was in full swing against the Northern state. Bleakley explained his party's thinking on the matter:

> While we of the Labour Opposition are against this Motion it is not so much because of what it says – I will deal with tensions behind the Motion. Whether it comes from that side of the House or this side of the House in our opinion the intentions behind Motions of this kind are basically sectarian. We in the Labour Party will have no part in motions which group the people of Northern Ireland into two sections depending on where they worship on Sundays.[52]

His remarks incurred considerable criticism, including a rebuttal by McAteer and the Nationalist leader Joe Stewart. The Nationalist MP for South Down, Joe Connellan, went as far as to charge the NILP with 'making political capital out of this motion'.[53] Labour members, it was said at the time, were 'living in a glasshouse and should not throw stones'.[54] Sir Norman Stronge was forced to intervene on several occasions to prevent Nationalist criticism from spiralling out of control. One might also single out the electoral competition between Northern Nationalism and absentionist republicanism as a further reason for Nationalist anxiety over the issue.

Further clashes were to come as the NILP won little Nationalist support for its stance on internment. Michael Farrell, in a typically downbeat critique, argued that Labour's policies cloaked its rightist underbelly:

> The four MPs consistently supported internment and the actions of the RUC and Specials, and voted against motions for the release of internees and political prisoners. And in November 1961 when the last RUC man was killed, Bleakley suggested using capital punishment against IRA men. The NILP men were fairly accurately described as 'pale pink' unionists.[55]

In fact Farrell is misleading here on two points. Official NILP policy, as set out in its 1962 election manifesto, recommended that 'The Government should review the existing law and if it is not prepared to abolish the death penalty, at least bring the law into step with that in Britain.'[56] The party had consistently lobbied Unionism to extend the Homicide Act (1957) to Northern Ireland since it first entered parliament in April 1958.[57] Indeed the BLP, in a report entitled *Civil Liberties and Administration of Justice* (1962), recorded the NILP's position on this very matter.[58] Apart from capital punishment other crucial tenets of the NILP's socio-economic reform programme included the inauguration of a think-tank to enquire into the causes and effects of crime, highlighting the implications for the province in the British Chancellor's recent 'little budget', and reporting on recent discussions at Chequers relating to Britain's application to join the Common Market.[59] In July 1961 all four NILP MPs, as well as the latest addition to its parliamentary team, Senator Arnold Schofield,[60] signed a recall notice to bring Stormont out of recess in order to debate capital punishment and recommended a cessation of all executions pending the reform of the law on the matter. Unfortunately the NILP's eagerness to bring the province back into step with the remainder of the UK was stingingly rebuked by Brookeborough.[61]

There can be little doubt that many Unionists harboured an antipathy for the NILP's proactive political style, especially as it played up the local regime's complacency in the economic field.[62] The disobedient streak displayed by Protestant workers at times of economic uncertainty was incomprehensible for those Unionist Associations with bulky bourgeois memberships. At the 1959 annual meeting of the Ulster Women's Unionist Council, presided over by Lady Brookeborough, Mrs Unity Lister of the Executive Committee viewed the high unemployment rate in Northern Ireland with alarm, berating Whitehall for not doing more to remedy the situation. But the solution in her opinion would not be found by voting for Labour. Socialism, by its appeal 'to the half-hearted, semi-literate, and the ignorant', would serve only to inflict damage on Ulster's constitutional standing.[63] Speeches like this are extremely revealing as they permit a glimpse into the thinking of some elements in the upper echelons of Unionist society at a time when Labour was making significant inroads into Unionism's citadel of power.

It could be argued with some justification that the NILP's gains goaded many Unionists into yearning for a return to a populist Unionism which stressed the renewal of cross-class alliances.[64] Young Unionists like John Taylor were quite perceptive in this regard, and even contemplated a compromise arrangement to give *de facto* recognition to the trade unions.[65] The essence of such progressive thinking was captured perfectly by the Belfast Unionist Major John Kerr: 'the days of the country squire as a public representative are gone', he said in an address to the Woodvale Unionist women's group, 'the people should have Members of Parliament who [are] prepared to go into kitchen houses' and speak with their electors. It was the MP's job to remain 'in touch with the people of the city, if necessary night and day', something past MPs had not been doing.[66] Presumably Kerr's address was meant as a means of stymieing further dissent among working-class voters, yet it only really served to paper over the cracks already appearing in the Unionist monolith. By mounting a rear-guard action Unionist politicians were attempting to insulate themselves against a possible Labour upset in Belfast, especially as the NILP made no bones about its willingness to fight future electoral contests on an unemployment ticket.[67] Regardless of Kerr's window dressing the fact remained that Westminster Unionist MPs were materially much better off than the vast majority of their electors, a differential, moreover, which also existed between Unionist and Labour candidates. In his study of the social class and occupational backgrounds of Unionist MPs at Stormont John Harbinson found that overwhelmingly they were attracted from the higher administrative, managerial, professional and farming class,[68] while Labour candidates were overwhelmingly drawn from the skilled trades.[69]

Endorsement or ambivalence? Fraternal relations with British Labour[70]

NILP candidates received the full backing of the BLP in all post-war Westminster elections between 1949 and 1974. In fact its leader from 1955 to 1963, Hugh Gaitskell, visited the province just prior to the 1958 contest to wish the party well in the forthcoming poll. Herbert Morrison was equally impressed by what he saw on his visit in October 1959, sensing 'a distinct improvement in the organisation, coherence and outlook of the Northern Ireland Labour Party since I met the Executive some years ago'. He reserved much criticism for the Westminster Unionists 'stressing that it was damaging to Northern Ireland to have a solid block of right-wing Tory MPs'.[71] Nevertheless Morrison's inspirational speeches to NILP candidates and workers, while ensuring a 'good press',[72] did little to offset the comfortable return of Unionist MPs in those Belfast constituencies where Labour candidates were fielded. Even the BLP's fraternal messages of support and the personal visit by Gaitskell[73] as well as endless hours of proof-reading policy documents completed by Transport House officials were insufficient guarantees of winning across all sections of Ulster's working class. The BLP was once again thwarted in its bid to wrest power from its Tory rivals who won the 1959 election with a convincing majority lead of 99 seats.[74]

The existence of such evidence has done little to sway the prevailing interpretation of BLP policy towards Northern Ireland as anything other than anti-partitionist. The efforts of backbench pressure groups, such as the early

Friends of Ireland[75] grouping and the later Campaign for Democracy in Ulster (CDU), which attempted to bring Northern Ireland business to the forefront of parliamentary proceedings at Westminster despite the 'Northern Ireland convention',[76] has been overemphasised in the literature. Peter Rose has dramatically reinforced the orthodox interpretation of British Labour's active disinterest in Irish affairs during its spell in Opposition,[77] while Graham Walker is equally dismissive of NILP–BLP relations in this period.[78] In fact every election manifesto published by the NILP from 1949 until at least 1974 was drafted in conjunction with the BLP.[79]

The party's 1962 manifesto *Ulster Labour and the Sixties* is just one example where Transport House officials nudged their Northern Irish comrades into maintaining a closer policy-making alliance.[80] In a note written for the Labour Party's Home Policy Committee by the *apparatchik* Joan Bourne, the NILP was praised for its vast array of sophisticated policies.[81] Bourne also commended the party's effective electioneering during the last general election in 1959. Terry Cradden has been fixated with the unimportance of the fraternal relationship: 'The main reason for the lack of solidarity with the NILP, however, was that there was never anything in it, either electorally or organisationally, for the British Labour Party.'[82] To some NILP leaders a closer liaison with the BLP was more aspirational than real:

> I always felt that there was an ambiguity in the relationship between the British Labour Party and the Northern Ireland Labour Party. We were not fully members of the family as it were. I can recall going to conferences for instance and happening to sit on the platform with other members of my party, but we never had the right to speak – never to intervene in the debate – so that there wasn't that kind of close arrangement with it.[83]

Arguably such retrospective thinking is tinged with a sense of guilt at having been fooled into consenting to the long-term frigidity of an unconsummated marriage.[84]

Bi-partisanship was the most consistent policy adopted by British political parties towards Ireland from the signing of the Treaty in 1921.[85] Although in practice its main function was to contain the Irish question it did give the Opposition considerable leverage for influencing governmental decision. Above all bi-partisanship was a tool of the elites; as Dixon explains 'the official view of the Labour Party was that contained in the Ireland Act of 1949 – that Irish unity could not come about without the consent of Stormont'. Moreover:

> Growing economic integration and the emerging civil rights movement conspired to involve British politicians more closely in Northern Ireland's affairs and break down that region's 'splendid isolation' from the rest of the UK. The deteriorating state of the Northern Ireland economy and the fashion for economic planning gave both major British parties a closer interest in the region.[86]

It is easy to draw the conclusion that the events of the late 1960s and early 1970s transformed the BLP–NILP relationship, but a green-tinged lens is not the only one through which to observe the parties' fraternal relationship. That said, it is impossible to dismiss the existence of anti-partitionist sentiment among local Constituency Labour Parties (CLPs) in Great Britain. Resolutions were proposed at Labour Party conferences calling for the repeal of the Ireland Act (1949), the withdrawal of British troops and indeed the deterrence of Northern Ireland MPs from taking their seats at Westminster – something accelerated during Wilson's weak administration of 1964–66.[87] Nevertheless, as Dixon writes, 'the average number of resolutions and amendments submitted to Labour Party conference during the years 1958–69 was 58. The average total of resolutions and amendments debated at each conference was just 31.'[88]

The Labour Party's Archives are bristling with letters and resolutions sent to Morgan Phillips and other Labour Party officials by local CLPs and affiliated trade unions. For Phillips (and his successor at Transport House Len Williams) the key to soothing fears among the party's rank-and-file was to obtain accurate and up-to-date information on the province's security situation, social and economic issues and also general political activities. As a matter of course Transport House turned instinctively to Napier for accurate briefings on these issues.[89]

When one London-based branch of the Amalgamated Engineering Union (AEU) sent a letter to Phillips protesting at the detainment without trial of terrorist suspects during the IRA's border campaign, Labour's deputy general secretary Len Williams suggested that the 'use of Special Powers by the Northern Ireland Government is not a matter that comes within the jurisdiction of our own Parliament and is not therefore one in which the Labour Party has any right to intervene'. The letter then went on to explain how thorough research had been undertaken to ascertain accurate facts on the matter:

> The Northern Ireland Labour Party, with which we maintain close association, has in fact made every effort to secure improvements in the situation with regard to political detainees. In reply to our enquiries, the Secretary of the Northern Ireland Labour Party has reaffirmed that it is their policy to get rid of special powers at the earliest possible date. We were glad to be informed that the number of people interned had fallen from nearly 200 at the beginning of 1960, to 27 at the beginning of this year [1961].[90]

This kind of response by Transport House was by no means atypical.[91] The weekly correspondence between Napier and Phillips helped to shape BLP policy on Northern Ireland.

The conduct of the Unionist government administration in its fight against the IRA caused a major headache for British political parties. The problem was substantially magnified for those MPs holding seats where a bulky proportion of their constituents claimed Irish lineage. Notable MPs with Irish interests included Harold Wilson (Huyton Merseyside), Stan Orme (Salford West) and Frank Allaun (Salford East). The diasporas were concentrated mostly in Liverpool, Manchester and Glasgow. Frank Allaun, for instance, represented a constituency heavily populated by second- and third-generation Irish immigrants and, like Wilson, was commonly subjected to pressure on matters of Irish interest.[92] In fact Wilson had displayed his anxiousness about the criticisms levelled at the BLP by the London-based Anti-Partition League of Ireland (APL) in a letter to Morgan Phillips. 'In common with other members of the NEC,' he said, 'I have received the enclosed circular letter. As you know, this problem affects my constituency more than almost any other.'[93] Wilson may have harboured anti-partitionist sympathies, but as far as official BLP policy was concerned Northern Ireland representation at Westminster was legitimate:

> It is unfortunate that these representatives should at present all be numbered among our political opponents, but the remedy for this state of affairs lies in our continued fraternal support for the Northern Ireland Labour Party, who have already succeeded in securing the election of four of their number to the Northern Ireland Parliament.[94]

Although later BLP policy on Northern Ireland was perforated by a deep-seated disappointment over the failure of their Ulster comrades to secure further electoral gains at the expense of their Unionist opponents, for the time being support for the NILP (and along with it the province's constitutional position) was assured.

Since the inter-war years BLP fraternal delegates had received a warm reception at the NILP's annual conferences. The former also made reciprocal gestures – most NILP elites were permitted an exchange visit, although their status was often ambiguous – but their attendance was in an observer capacity only.[95] An illustration of this congeniality can be garnered from a report submitted by Bessie Braddock, BLP fraternal delegate, on her return from the NILP's conference in 1960.[96] Braddock said it 'was the strongly expressed desire of the Northern Ireland Labour Party to have more liaison with and more visits from the National Executive Committee'.[97] She also noted the party's acceptance of a non-sectarian approach to politics. However, it was the NILP's critique of the Northern Ireland government's refusal to grant recognition to the Leader of the Opposition at Stormont, to provide buildings to be used as community centres, the setting up of local health centres and group practices, free legal aid and the party's call for the introduction of legislation covering office regulations as recommended by the Gowers Committee Report, which sparked most interest among members.[98] However, the single item which fixed the NILP's attention was sectarianism and the desire to seek the support and involvement of more working-class Catholics in party affairs.[99]

The NILP: policies and practice

The NILP's policies were grounded in the wealth of professional and trade union expertise possessed by a talented cadre of newly elected MPs and behind-the-scenes *apparatchiks*.[100] Beyond official policy documents individual activists sought to draw attention to the socio-economic and political grievances confronting Ulster's citizens. One of the NILP's most prolific writers was David Bleakley. Bleakley, a former economics lecturer at Queen's University Belfast, resigned his academic post to fight the electoral campaign. He pledged to his prospective constituents that if elected he would pursue workers' rights with vigour and determination. In a paper delivered to the annual Industrial Medical Officers' Conference in 1961 Bleakley articulated the kind of humanist concern for working-class people common to many European non-communist social-democratic intellectuals at the time.[101] His text is distinguished by its Christian socialist overtones – echoes of pre-eminent British socialists like R.H. Tawney and George Lansbury are not difficult to detect. Bleakley made little attempt to disguise his concern for the moral and spiritual values of the working classes. The desire to actively pursue social justice dividends for the disadvantaged and marginalised in Ulster society animated much of his intellectual thinking at the time. Yet his blend of socialism is particularly noteworthy for its relevance to the local neighbourhood activism practised by all NILP politicians since the party's formation. Free from aggrandised notions of global Marxist revolution, the NILP's socialism was forged out of an ideology tainted by a moral obligation to empower its constituents. It sought the removal of all social, political and religious obstacles at grass-roots level; although that is not to say that the NILP believed no less in 'the brotherhood of man', nor did it 'draw a distinction between man and man on the basis of religion'.[102] Rather the party's aim was 'to work within the framework of the existing constitution to achieve a prosperous and unified community in Ulster'.[103]

On a more practical level Bleakley's constituency work was marked by a hands-on down-to-business attitude towards the Victoria electorate. In his first four years as MP he recorded over 4,000 drop-ins to his surgery and notched up over 100 home visits. His constituency surgery work ranged from 'helping pensioners, looking into benefit problems, attending at Appeals Tribunals, investigating housing difficulties [to] dealing with employment questions'. In a digest of his activities he claimed that '[t]his kind of activity matters because it touches upon the personal lives of our people'.[104] Bleakley possessed a common touch with ordinary working-class people. He enjoyed helping others because it was in his nature as a Christian to do so. Above all he was a community-based leader who possessed charm, charisma and intellect which left him a cut above his political opponents, but which also earned him criticisms from those who opposed his overbearing Sabbatarianism.[105]

According to Labour intellectuals, like Bleakley, Northern Ireland's poor socio-economic prospects suffocated the unique qualities of homegrown talent. He suggested that individuals only got a chance to thrive once they left these restrictive confines.[106] Indeed one of Bleakley's central beliefs (and something continually spotlighted by NILP propaganda) was that at times of high unemployment emigration levels rose, to the detriment of working-class material prospects.[107] Many of his writings in this period paint a gloomy picture of the province's socio-economic fabric, though it is important to point out how his writings frequently went beyond elementary statistical measurement by stressing the lonely predicament of the unemployed. Bleakley spoke for the NILP at large when he said that the social evil of unemployment sapped at the very lifeblood and vitality of community spirit.

In its submission to the Conservative Home Secretary, Rab Butler, the party expressed its reservations at the announcement that a Parliamentary Committee was to be set up to investigate unemployment in Northern Ireland.[108] Overall the memo was relatively downbeat about the province's economic prospects, but it did again emphasise the party's willingness to present both a critique and a panacea. Of the three industries examined – agriculture, textiles and heavy engineering – the party recommended future development and diversification to alleviate the pressure on existing staple industries. Included in its submission were proposals for a new dry dock and a Development Corporation – something conceded by Butler following a positive meeting with NILP representatives.[109] Similarly, in the shipbuilding industry, the exploration of new designs and the locating of new markets all pointed to a potential step back from the abyss. It seemed likely that the emerging success of Japanese and German shipyards would continue to have knock-on effects for locally-based industries in Belfast, Clydeside and Merseyside.[110] According to the NILP, transport costs were aggravated by credit restrictions imposed by the Conservative government.[111] It was obvious that Ulster's remoteness from British markets was taking its toll: if a solution was not forthcoming then local industries risked going under.

The working party (taken over by Sir Robert Hall after the death of Sir Herbert Brittain) finally released its report in 1962. At a meeting of leading industrialists and trade unionists in Bangor, County Down, Norman Cuthbert (co-author of the 1957 government-sponsored economic report) suggested that 'the unemployment problem would be very greatly eased if training facilities were better'.[112] Meanwhile at Stormont, Unionist backbenchers became more and more restive. In combination with the newly elected Unionist MP for Shankill, Desmond Boal, David Bleakley proposed an unemployment motion querying Unionism's failed economic policy, prompting Brookeborough's personal intervention on the matter.[113]

Consolidation: the 1962 Stormont election

The NILP entered the campaign trail in good spirits. Party finances were in reasonable shape and organisationally at least vast improvements had been made at local branch level since 1958. The party now had 14 councillors scattered across local authorities in three of the six counties, in places like Belfast, Newtownabbey, North Down, Derry and Portadown.[114] New NILP branches were formed in the old Labour-dominated ward of Belfast Dock and it was clear from incursions into Mid Down and Larne that an overhaul of party organisation beyond the Belfast urban area would be forthcoming.[115] According to Vivian Simpson individual membership had risen to around 1,500 in early 1962, two-thirds of that figure being Protestant and the other third Catholic.[116] Further developments during the previous 12 months included the bolstering of the PLP's ranks with the election of Arnold Schofield to the Stormont Senate in June 1961.

Unsurprisingly the incoming chairman, Charles Brett, addressed his party's

1962 annual conference in confident mood. Predicting a Labour government at Stormont within 20 years, he announced the NILP's timetable for government by appealing explicitly across the sectarian divide. By highlighting the Unionist Party's ethnic exclusivism he sought to play up the NILP's anti-sectarian credentials:

> The change is slow, but it will come ... The electors are going to wake up to the fact that we believe in principles of social justice. They are going to realise that sectarianism is a waste of time. We do not believe, as the Unionists believe, that Roman Catholics should not be taken into the party. Our party is open to everyone.[117]

Stormy anti-partitionist rhetoric, like that indulged in at impromptu moments by Labour parliamentarians Bob Getgood and Hugh Downey, had been replaced by a purely non-sectarian pro-Union ethos. Having successfully projected itself as a 'Protestant party'[118] the NILP turned its attention to the second phase of its so-called consensus-forming strategy: working-class Catholics would now be wooed.

There had been early warning signs that the 1962 Stormont election might be fought primarily on non-constitutional issues.[119] Further credence was given to this view when the Confederation of Shipbuilding and Engineering Unions (CSEU) staged a huge one-day strike to draw attention to the government's White Paper denying the unions the right to negotiate on behalf of their members. This stoppage was the biggest in nine years, effectively keeping at home 30,000 of the 36,000 shipyard workers in Belfast.[120] In January 1962 public attention had shifted away from the irredentist challenge posed by the IRA and four weeks later the organisation eventually called a halt to its campaign – complaining of the overwhelming strength of the state forces mobilised against it.[121] Notwithstanding the repressive measures adopted by the Republic's government in spiking IRA guns on their side of the border most credit was reserved for Brookeborough and his Minister for Home Affairs Brian Faulkner.[122] Brookeborough's speech to his party's Executive reiterated his government's defeat of the IRA to the rapturous applause of rural Unionists. Curiously he did not shirk from providing a frank assessment of the main political challenge now facing his administration:

> Hitherto our principal opposition had been from those who were opposed to Northern Ireland's constitution. Today, however, particularly in Belfast, the fight had been shifted to the economic field and the socialists who profess support for the constitutional position were bent on discrediting the economic and industrial achievements of the Government in order to triumph at the Government's expense.[123]

It was obvious that NILP agitation on working-class material concerns had made significant inroads into the Unionist position in Belfast and fears had been growing among Unionists that the party would expand its base of operations out into Greater Belfast at the next available opportunity.[124] The NILP nominated 14 candidates for the forthcoming election, unveiling its manifesto *Ulster Labour and the Sixties* to favourable media coverage.[125] The *Belfast Telegraph* said that *Ulster Labour and the Sixties* was a 'radical and even visionary' document[126] but the newspaper's initial optimism for the NILP had waned considerably since March 1958. In any case its editor Jack Sayers had been plumping, not for a potential Labour government, but for a moderate Unionist one.[127] Overall the NILP polled 76,842 votes in Northern Ireland (26% of the total vote, some 67,350 in Belfast alone) compared with the total Unionist share of 143,740 (48.6%).[128] In 1962 they were the second largest party in voting terms, and in Belfast 'the total vote of opposition groups within the city, the vast majority Northern Ireland Labour, outnumbered the Unionist figure'.[129]

The consolidation of the party's position in Belfast was not won lightly. Its involvement in the 'Save Shorts campaign' – a mobilisation by the trade unions to stave off further unemployment during a downturn in the economic fortunes of the Belfast firm – gained it much gratitude from rank-and-filers in Ulster's Labour movement. Rapid improvement in party organisation (facilitated greatly by an increase in party membership) shored up the NILP's electioneering capabilities:

> This sort of [organisation] eventually gave the NILP a canvassing muscle second only to the Ulster Unionists. In the 1962 election, when the latter mobilised six to seven hundred cars to bring voters to the polling stations, Labour could muster some five hundred vehicles, including twelve minibuses in Duncairn alone.[130]

Labour now had at its disposal an experienced cadre of politicians and candidates. Most of these individuals were convincing in front of a television camera, which meant that the party's message could be accurately (and unambiguously) broadcast into most homes. The party's chief policy writer Charles Brett had been the backroom strategist chiefly responsible for the NILP's socially progressive *Rents and Houses* (1956) document.[131] With the advent of television Brett set about building up the party's PR kudos, while attempting to counter Unionist domination of the airwaves. A policy sub-committee created in the 1950s, under Brett's direction, assumed the task of disseminating the NILP's non-sectarian message across the divide.[132] Arguably Brett's sophisticated policy formulations contributed directly to the party's successful showing at the 1958 and 1962 electoral bouts. Furthermore, Brett's political acumen was beginning to convince younger Catholics that perhaps the time was ripe to join a political party which was finally making a stand for non-sectarian democratic socialist principles.

'Paying for our inertia': Unionism on the back foot

Brookeborough's inability to plug the leaks now manifest in the UUP's electoral bulkhead damaged his premiership irreparably. Despite Unionist attempts to tone down the more critical elements of the *Hall Report* (1962)[133] the fact could not be denied that Northern Ireland's economy was in crisis. Last-ditch appeals to the Conservative government in London for more aircraft orders to ease the burden of threatened job losses at Shorts, in the weeks and months prior to the release of *Hall*, aroused little response.[134] The lobbying of Treasury officials for further subsidies to prop up Ulster's remaining crippled staple industries was similarly greeted with little in the way of reciprocal enthusiasm. Graham is notably blunt on this point: 'The report was a considerable disappointment to the government, offering no means of extradition from the atmosphere of economic gloom.'[135] Matters were not helped by party dissidents who claimed a clairvoyant talent for forecasting further electoral gains for Labour in the city, should the misfortune continue. The elderly Prime Minster proved increasingly incapable of deflecting intra-party criticism away from his policies, giving rise to the widespread feeling that perhaps a younger politician was needed to take over the reigns of office.

At first though it was not immediately clear who would succeed Brookeborough in light of his long service and good conduct as Prime Minister. David Bleakley saw the liberal Unionist figure William Morrison May as perhaps the likeliest candidate for the post, but May's premature death in March 1962 removed the strongest contender from the frame.[136] Consequently, Terence O'Neill was proposed as a composite choice after Bill Craig took 'soundings' from inside the Unionist Parliamentary Party.[137] Arguably, the decision by Lord Wakehurst to appoint O'Neill as Prime Minister on 26 March 1963 delayed Brian Faulkner's entry into office, thereby aggravating an already incendiary atmosphere in the cabinet. Faulkner would not become Premier until James Chichester-Clark's resignation in March 1971.

Initially O'Neill's appointment was greeted with surprise, though this very quickly turned to rumblings of dissent attributable mainly to the lack of consultation undertaken within the wider party.[138] Doubly unfortunate for O'Neill was that he had succeeded Brookeborough at a time when the economic situation in the province was at its bleakest since 1952. Unemployment stood at a high of 7.4% in 1963 (compared to 5.9% in 1956), far outstripping the overall UK average.[139] The new premier was therefore under an obligation to remedy the situation before any further political hostages to fortune presented themselves. As Bew *et al.* have emphasised:

> The NILP victories of 1958 and their consolidation in 1962, together with a massive rate of actual and threatened redundancies, seemed to presage large-scale working class defection if drastic action was postponed.[140]

One might have expected the NILP to have reduced O'Neill's room for manoeuvre by challenging him on his government's poor economic track record, though a confrontation failed to materialise. At first the PLP appeared reluctant to support a Nationalist censure motion exploiting Unionism's devolved impotence; instead Labour adopted what Graham has called a 'sober viewpoint' – claiming that 'Ulster's misfortune was to be shared by all – to appear to be making political capital from it would be to risk appearing anti-Ulster'.[141] With one eye on the impending Westminster election Labour was anxious to display its constructive oppositional credentials, judging it more prudent to win over voters with its persuasive hypothetical arguments. Placing country before party

'Stealing Labour's thunder': O'Neillism and modernisation

Terence O'Neill assumed the Northern Ireland premiership at a time when the NILP looked like it was poised to breach the Unionist electoral bulkhead in Belfast. Consequentially, he had a clear remit from the local Unionist Associations in the city: either halt the Labour advance or face stiff opposition to his leadership. Intra-Unionist revolt became a spectre that would continue to haunt him throughout his time in office. One backbencher who sought to defy the Unionist whip at every turn was the MP for St Anne's, Edmund Warnock. Warnock had been an arch-critic of the government for many years, believing firmly that the Unionist administration had failed to trump the forward march of Labour in Belfast. He harboured real fears of a hostile takeover by the NILP in the city and expressed these potently in a letter to party colleague Major John Kerr on the eve of the 1962 Cromac by-election:

> I am just as anxious about the position in Belfast. The opposition hold 7 of the 16 Belfast seats, and our people are not getting the vigorous leadership which I would like to see. We have had three serious industrial crises in the past two years. Ten thousand men paid off in the shipyard, the closure of several of our great textile concerns, the threat to Short and Harlands. The inactivity of the Government has left a vacuum and a group of shop stewards has filled the vacuum, and has assumed the leadership of the industrial workers. The last election showed they wanted to be led by the Unionist Party, but they have looked to us in vain. The threat of further redundancy in Harland and Wolff will be a powerful weapon in the hands of the Labour Party in the coming election in Cromac. It is most unfortunate that we should have let the initiative pass to the Labour crowd, and I only hope that we won't have to pay for our inertia.[142]

Historians of the Unionist Party view Warnock as something of a 'siren voice', more concerned with his own personal ambitions than with his party's electoral vitality.[143] Warnock's behind-the-scenes moves to undermine O'Neill's position led him to concede in his memoirs that his actions were 'indicative of how the right wing were not willing to accept change and still yearned for the good old days'.[144]

O'Neill's plan to counter-attack the NILP's position was by no means an elaborate piece of political strategising, though it was conducted with a certain amount of tact and precision. Stripped bare it necessitated the employment of a whirlwind of modernising rhetoric to woo Protestant working-class doubters back into the arms of the Unionist Party.[145] For some commentators, however, it was wishful thinking built on an overambitious technocratic programme which relied disproportionately on a thin veil of style more than substance,[146] the focus of which was fixed firmly on solving the unemployment situation that continued to give much grist to the mill of the NILP's indictment of Unionist economic policies. O'Neill's liberalism sought to steer a middle course between the right of his party and the left of the NILP. However he could only do this by tackling the most pressing threat to his position at the time, as Paul Bew explains:

> The liberal Terence O'Neill made it clear in his memoirs that he assumed, when he took over as premier in 1963 that the Northern Ireland Labour Party, not Nationalism, was the main problem. The question of politics was why is Northern Ireland the least prosperous part of the United Kingdom? The issue of Irish unity was apparently marginalized.[147]

The Conservative government's patience had been stretched by Brookeborough's frequent lobbying for subsidies without making significant steps towards modernising the Northern Ireland economy. As a former Finance Minister O'Neill had a thorough grasp of the province's devolved impotence and knew only too well the limitations of British assistance. By the late 1950s Ulster's ailing staple industries 'were in long-term decline. There was, consequently, an urgent need to diversify the region's industrial "mix" by selectively encouraging the setting up of new industries in the province.'[148] In an era when Britain was switching to long-term planning as a way to avoid future arresting developments in the UK economy, Northern Ireland too would be required by central purse-holders to move with the times.[149] O'Neill was quick to realise that the only way to secure the passage of his plans through Stormont was to convince business and trade union leaders of the long-term benefits of pulling together for the sake of Northern Ireland's economic prosperity.[150]

A new mood of goodwill appeared to prevail. At the outset of O'Neill's ambitious enterprise there were signs that his own party were convinced of their leader's potential and there were even pleas by Young Unionists at the Unionist Party's 1963 annual conference for conciliatory dialogue to be opened up with the ICTU's Northern Ireland Committee (NIC).[151] The appetites of business leaders were also being whetted at the prospect of accommodation on the issue, especially in light of the recently published government document *Blueprint for Ulster* (1963) – a document which openly advocated the implementation of Labour ideas.[152] However, O'Neill's plagiarism had far-reaching consequences:

> By adopting Labour ideas, Captain O'Neill was making it difficult for the NILP to maintain a profitable and distinctive stance on economics. Yet the cautious Labour leadership were reluctant to be drawn into adopting a more extreme position where they might be criticised for rash socialism.[153]

Judging the tide of liberalism to be flowing in his direction O'Neill set about trying to secure the co-operation of the trade unions in his bid to 'transform the face of Ulster'. However it was not until August 1964 that he could confidently claim that, 'We were finally able to achieve recognition of the Northern Ireland Committee of the Irish Congress of Trades Unions.'[154]

In preparation for the anticipated Westminster election the NILP again drafted its manifesto in co-operation with the BLP. The changeover in leadership following Gaitskell's death did not immediately alter the fraternal alliance, perhaps best illustrated by the BLP's continued preoccupation with regionalism in its election manifesto *The New Britain* (1964).[155] Northern Ireland was given its own distinct regional identity on an equal par to that of Scotland and Wales.[156] *The New Britain* further flagged up the BLP's deliberate shift to embrace the modernisation project on a UK-wide scale. Wilson inspired many beyond his party's rank-and-file when he talked of the impending 'white heat' of progress and scientific revolution during his inaugural leadership speech at the 1963 BLP conference.[157]

To an extent Wilson's drive for socio-economic modernisation animated the NILP's own version of *The New Britain*, similarly entitled *Signposts to the New Ulster*, a document with the express intent of playing down the significance of the Stormont administration as a key decision-making institution. The NILP's early drive in the mid-1950s to emphasise Unionism's mishandling of the controls of devolution once again took centre stage: the importance of Westminster as a place where 'the decisions with the most far-reaching effects on the lives of Ulster men and women are taken' was deemed much greater.[158] This was the institutional interface where the economic fortunes of Northern Ireland would be determined and the NILP's thinking was reflected to a large degree by official BLP discourse at the time. In its annual report for 1964 the Westminster PLP reported that 'the Opposition thought that Northern Ireland ought to be regarded as a region of the United Kingdom whose economy was of vital importance, and in need of modernisation just as that of other regions'.[159] Planning was showcased by the NILP as the means by which the province could escape its economic misfortune. 'High interest rates – such as we have had under Tory rule – immediately cut back public works of every kind, including housing, and slow down our already sluggish economy.'[160]

Yet it remains ambiguous just how committed the BLP was to taking a more active role in Northern Ireland. The desire of Transport House to steer clear of signalling approval of the NILP's agitation on citizens' rights issues (by instead advocating non-interference) is something brought to the fore in Graham's study of the party. That said, there is little sign that the Labour alliance was anything other than affable. In the BLP's Annual Report for 1963–64 the section on Ulster reads:

> On 14 July 1964 the Opposition initiated a debate on Northern Ireland. The Opposition spokesman said that it was a pleasure to learn that proposals which the Northern Ireland and United Kingdom Labour Parties had advocated over a long period were now being accepted and placed before the House as original ideas of the Government. As long ago as 1955 the Northern Ireland Labour Party had campaigned to get a dry dock at Belfast, and the belated acceptance of the proposal was now welcomed. The Opposition also raised the question of the Stranraer–Larne crossing and again welcomed the Government's announcement.[161]

Not all historians are convinced by the amiability of Wilson's strategy in these years and prefer to see BLP policy in the 1960s as a double-edged affair.[162] Nevertheless practical aid did reach the NILP in the months running up to the October 1964 election in the form of a £1,200 grant to help pay campaign costs. Despite the fact that funding was received, additional policy clauses were built

Labour Opposition of Northern Ireland, 1958–65

into it, which precluded the NILP from exploiting controversial reform issues (including the marked departure from parity on electoral boundary changes). The restrictions did not seem to shatter the NILP's will to expose Unionist misdemeanours.

Since 1962 new NILP branches had been formed in Dungannon, Omagh, Ballymena, Newry, Enniskillen, Lurgan and Armagh and older established parties were strengthened and reformed.[163] As a way of bolstering the party's ranks the EC issued directions to all local DLPs and Federations to embark on a fresh recruitment drive. Some local parties even took the initiative of readdressing the gender imbalance by reorganising their women's sections.[164] In the local government elections 130 candidates were nominated, many in areas hitherto uncontested by the party in a generation, such as Enniskillen, Omagh and Newry. By the close of polling the party had increased its representation from 18 to 30 local councillors, with seven elected in Belfast out of the 24 nominated.[165]

Table 3.3 Occupational background of candidates in the May 1964 Belfast local government election

Occupational class	Unionist	NILP	Other	Total
Professional, managerial	21	3	2	26
Lower-grade non-manual	9	6	7	22
Skilled manual	4	10	5	19
Semi-skilled manual	5	1	2	8
Unskilled	5	4	5	14
Total	44 (3)	24 (1)	21 (1)	89 (5)[a]

Source: Compiled from data given in the *Belfast Telegraph,* 6 May 1964. 'Other' includes Independent and Republican Labour candidates as well as Communist, World Socialist, Independent Unionist and Protestant Unionist candidates.
[a]Figures in brackets indicate the number of female candidates.

Prior to the impending Westminster election Terence O'Neill met with Harold Wilson in London to test the water in the event of a Labour return to power. O'Neill's account of the meeting makes for interesting reading in light of traditional UUP antipathy for Labour's socialism: 'When I tell him how well we were treated by the last Labour Government, he assures me we shall be equally well treated by the next,' he boasted.[166] Yet O'Neill was not the only Northern Irish politician to anticipate a Labour victory. In January 1964 a delegation of Nationalist politicians, headed by McAteer, sought an audience with Wilson and other leading Labour MPs, though they were met with a frosty reception. As the following secret memo reveals:

On their arrival they went to the Irish Club ... At the reception given in the Club Messrs. McAteer and Lennon outlined their plans for their visit in London and other representatives also spoke. There was a certain lack of agreement between the Nationalist and the Labour Party Representatives. Lord Longford suggested that perhaps it would be possible to work in harmony with the Six County Labour Party but this idea was indignantly rejected by the Nationalists who said that in fact they got no cooperation at all from the Six County Labour Party and could, if they wanted to, put out three at least of the four sitting Labour MPs. This mild clash was, perhaps, occasioned by some expressions of bitterness on the part of the Six County men at the failure of Mr. Wilson to receive them.[167]

There is certainly some truth in the argument that rural Nationalist politicians overestimated their political influence in the Belfast urban area at this time, so much so that they frequently engaged in bellicose language designed to play down the strength of the NILP vote in the city.[168]

The BLP won the October election by only a slender majority of 13 seats over their Tory rivals. Wilson's arrival in Downing Street in 1964 caused a major upset among Unionist elites fearful of a socialist backlash. The new Labour leader had been viewed with hostility because of his Irish Nationalist sympathies and there was a feeling that his publicised promises to Nationalists in the Dungannon-based Campaign for Social Justice (CSJ) would extend from aiding socio-economic and political reform (by bringing Ulster into line with the rest of the UK) to an all-out move authorising Irish unity by stealth.[169] Promisingly, the October election pointed towards an electoral high tide for the NILP. Notwithstanding several arrests for personation and the intimidation of Labour activists by Protestant ultras[170] the party still managed to gain an impressive 102,759 votes, thereby further consolidating its gains in the previous three contests. It even inspired a considerable number of Catholics to join the party in areas – like Dock, Falls and Derry – traditionally known for their 'red' republican allegiances. Most success came in East Belfast where Sam Watt gained 15,555 (36.87%) votes against the Unionist S.R. McMaster's 24,804 (58.80%), a majority later significantly narrowed to 3,633 in 1966. The NILP made gains attributable mainly to Nationalist abstention in the election and the poor showing of the four republican candidates in Belfast who all lost their deposits. The Belfast correspondent of *The Round Table* provided this sobering analysis:

> Labour cannot look back on events with satisfaction. It did not advance in Belfast so much as it had claimed to have done, and cannot look forward with any certainty to sending a member to Westminster in support of Mr. Harold Wilson, a long-cherished ambition. Its misfortune is that its vote in the new housing areas round Belfast, though substantial, is swallowed up in County constituencies with the largest Unionist majorities in the Country.[171]

Above all this election pointed to a stabilisation in the left-of-centre vote across Belfast. McGarry and O'Leary's argument that the NILP vote was 'transient and vulnerable to rapid erosion in periods of communal tension' must be qualified in light of the 1964 result, which was attained despite considerable sectarian animosity and rabid (often violent) outpourings of fanaticism among Paisleyites.[172]

'Sunday swings' and political roundabouts

The political competition between the UUP and its rivals came to a head in the closing months of 1964. The return of a Labour government under its new leader Harold Wilson in October ended 13 long years of 'Tory misrule' at Westminster but in Northern Ireland there was little indication that a new spirit of social or political progress was visible on the horizon. In what was a sectarian-charged month Protestant and Catholic rioters took to the streets of Belfast to protest. Following the unfurling of a republican tricolour in the window of Liam McMillan's constituency office in Divis Street a loyalist mob, headed by Ian Paisley (who in the early 1960s had only begun to make his presence felt in Belfast) and supported by Unionist candidate Jim Kilfedder,[173] threatened to march into the largely Catholic area and remove the flag. In response the RUC intervened and presided over its lowering. However, when a replacement was found and re-erected, further confrontation was sparked off between rival mobs which culminated in several more nights of serious rioting.[174] The police responded by deploying a water canon in the Lower Falls for the first time; it would not be the last.[175]

The NILP recognised the potential for a polarisation of voting behaviour and pleaded directly to the people of Belfast to put 'the Divis Street troubles behind them'.[176] Graham has criticised the party's 'doveish' response to the sectarian riots, which he blames on internal ideological haemorrhaging, though it could be argued that he overplayed the extent of disunity gripping Labour at this time. In hindsight, the principal variable seems to have been the temporary polarisation in voting behaviour, something Graham argues Boyd had not anticipated.[177] Moreover, it is important not to underestimate the electoral dividends generated by Kilfedder's demands for the removal of the tricolour, especially since he paraded his staunch loyalist credentials in a constituency-wide leaflet drop prior to the election.[178]

Table 3.4 British general elections, 1945–79 (excluding by-elections): NILP performance

Year	No. of seats	No. contested	Total votes
1945	13	5	66,459
1950	12	5	67,816
1951	12	4	62,324
1955	12	3	35,614
1959	12	3	42,222
1964	12	10	102,759
1966	12	4	49,941
1970	12	7	98,194
1974 (Feb)	12	4	15,483
1974 (Oct)	12	3	11,539
1979	12	3	4,411

Source: Compiled from data provided in Kimber, Richard, Elections Archive: British Governments and Elections since 1945, www.psr.keele.ac.uk/area/uk/uktable.htm.

Meanwhile another conflict was brewing in West Belfast involving Boyd, this time in his capacity as a local councillor, and it revolved around the Corporation debate on whether children's play parks across the city should be opened on Sundays. Ultimately it brought into question how NILP policy could be translated into empirical reality. Robert Bingham (who was close to Boyd, and who also served as a councillor on Castlereagh District Council at the time) explains what impact the controversy had on Boyd's standing:

> Billy Boyd came in for a big lot of criticism. I think myself that at times he was ill-advised. It was the Shankill Road [after all] ... I never fell out with him or anything. We remained friends until he died. But I didn't always agree with him. And I would certainly claim I had a hell of a big hand in his elections in the first place. Simply ... because then I worked in the factory and had been a Shop Steward and I was able to bring most of the workers out of work to vote for the Labour Party. He would have lost that kind of [vote]. You know. That's the kind of thing that divided people in the sense of being kind of acrimonious in the sense – if that's the word – because they were just issues. And they shouldn't have necessarily created ... [that] kind of ... recrimination ... I don't think ... that we were big enough in attitude and mind ... We allowed ourselves to look for [an easy way out] ... Not having the courage to stand up and say this is what we believe and to hell with [it] – we believe this and this is what we are saying.[179]

The dilemma now facing Boyd had a simple solution in that he could either choose to toe the party line, which stipulated that there ought to be open access to play parks, or he could opt to support the wishes of his constituents who purportedly did not want playgrounds open seven days a week. For those close to Boyd the decision he took was the result of much soul-searching. Beatrice Boyd (Billy's wife and a member of the women's section of the Woodvale DLP) recalls:

> Well that time of the swings was very painful really to us all because it ended up with Billy being dismissed from the Labour Party for a while because he insisted on voting for the swings being closed ... The people said that was the only time that they got peace from all the noise of the children playing ... Billy took not a referendum but a survey of what those people wanted and the majority (nearly all) said no to the opening of swings on a Sunday. So Billy was discharged from the Labour Party. And that was very painful for someone who was an MP and a councillor. He was an MP so it was a very difficult decision because many of the Labour Party wanted the swings open. So he wouldn't have had much support from the Labour Party.[180]

If nothing else the conflict exposed the clash between official policy and private conscience and threw into sharp relief the democratic nature of the party.

Labour Opposition of Northern Ireland, 1958–65

Table 3.5 Woodvale Labour Party in the 1960s

Constituency of residence	Males	Females	Total
North Belfast	15	11	26
West Belfast	40	40	80
East Belfast	6	6	12
South Belfast	5	0	5
Miscellaneous	9	4	13[a]
Total	75	61	136

Source: The data shown in this table were compiled by comparing the membership list in the Woodvale minute book with the Belfast and Northern Ireland Street Directory for the years 1958 and 1964, the dates when the first and last entries were made.

[a]11 of these individuals lived outside the Belfast municipal boundary.

Table 3.6 Religious breakdown of the population in Woodvale (1961)

Religion	Male	Female	Total
Roman Catholic	3,367	3,472	6,839
Protestant	14,815	15,655	30,470
Other	1,189	1,253	2,442
Total	19,371	20,380	39,751

Source: Census of Population, 1961: Belfast County Borough (Belfast: HMSO, 1963), p. 33. NB: Statistics from the Woodvale and Court local government wards were added together for accuracy.

The three councillors involved – Billy Boyd, David Walsh (Boyd's brother-in-law) and John Black – refused to give an undertaking that they would subscribe to party authority. Faced with a clear challenge to its constitution the party's EC had no other option open to it but to suspend its three Belfast councillors. At a special meeting – called to make a decision on the actions of the three Court Ward representatives – the following hastily assembled resolutions were carried:

a. That all party members serving on public bodies must realise that their first loyalty is to party policy on all issues – other than matters of conscience.
b. That if the conscience clause is [claimed] the party members shall abstaining [*sic*] from voting and refrain from discussion.
c. That in the interests of party unity and preserving the good public image which has been strenuously striven for and built up since 1949 such extreme measures as have been sought by way of punishment of individuals should not *de facto* be imposed but *de jure* a severe reprimand be recorded or undertaking signed that these resolutions be notified to all parties.[181]

In response Billy Boyd sent a letter to the *Belfast Telegraph* protesting at his unfair dismissal.[182] The letter did little to aid his cause and instead led party officers to complain about the adverse publicity now accumulating in the local print media.

It was with some displeasure that Billy Blease issued a statement on behalf of the Northern Committee of the ICTU expressing his disappointment that a minority of party members were unwilling to toe the party line on the 'Sunday swings' issue. He said: 'It is to be regretted that commonsense has not prevailed in this matter, and that the three persons concerned have rejected all overtures made on their behalf.'[183] Blease devoted considerable personal time and energy to helping the party resolve the issue. Regardless of his personal standing within the party and the wider Labour movement, his brokerage was insufficient to prevent a split developing in the NILP's ranks between confessionally-driven elites and those harbouring a more secular and inclusive political strategy. Blease displayed great skill and tenacity during the controversy, but despite his best efforts he could not heal the rift now palpable within the NILP. Nevertheless internal wrangling did not preclude the NIC from continuing to offer its support to its political partners:

> The trades unions will continue to support and assist the Northern Ireland Labour Party in achieving the political objectives of the movement and the NI Committee, ICTU will actively cooperate with the Parliamentary Labour Party on all matters of mutual interest.[184]

The NIC failed to heal divisions now besetting the party. Billy Blease had to rest contented with a personal apology from Billy Boyd that 'he was sorry for the trouble his actions had caused and declared he still wished to be a member of the Northern Ireland Labour Party and did not want to be expelled'.[185] However, Boyd had little to worry about as David Bleakley intervened on his behalf to block the Executive taking any further steps against the Woodvale MP. It is impossible to overestimate the far-reaching consequences of the internal ruptures occasioned by the 'Sunday swings' incident: relations in the party would continue at a low ebb well beyond November 1964. Retrospectively, Charles Brett expressed his regret that the whole issue had been permitted to get out of hand; he claimed he had not been on speaking terms with Bleakley since the latter chose to walk a confessional route in 1964.[186]

Coincidentally, Billy Boyd had found himself embroiled in a similar dispute six years earlier, when in 1958 (shortly after his election to the Belfast Corporation) he locked horns with a religious fundamentalist collective known as the 'Sunday Observance Vigilance Committee'. Interestingly Boyd had supported the right for citizens to stage musical concerts in Belfast parks on Sundays.[187] By 30 votes to 17 the motion to open the parks was defeated. The 'self-proclaimed champion of workers' rights' Tommy Henderson asserted that Boyd was forcing something on the people of Belfast's Court Ward which was not wanted. One female Unionist councillor, who supported Boyd's stance, retorted: 'The playgrounds were closed on Sundays, and now they had the spectacle of the children playing in the gutter on Sunday, while the swings were tied up.'[188] That Boyd should be supporting a more liberal motion than the one he later favoured seems curious in light of his subsequent unrepentant attitude.

In 1966, whilst completing an empirical study of Belfast politics, Budge and O'Leary found that 80% of NILP aligned councillors and 78% of NILP aligned residents in their survey were in favour of play parks being opened on a Sunday.[189] There is some basis in the argument made by local people that they didn't want open-ended access to the parks because of the danger of anti-social behaviour;[190] if this is the case then the issue was less a Sabbatarian one and more a practical community safety matter. It is impossible to know for certain what animated Boyd's thinking on the swings issue, but in light of the historical evidence and secondary testimony it is likely that it was not dictated by narrow sectarian interests. In other words, if he was acting on behalf of his constituents as a local representative then the NILP's image as a non-sectarian party should be vindicated. However, if the reverse is true, subsequent criticism of the NILP as a Sabbatarian party would appear justified.

However, the clash of personalities could not disguise the fact that the Protestant working class was becoming more susceptible to the outcries of petit bourgeois theologians warning of the dangers of ecumenicalism at street corners. Billy Boyd and David Bleakley undoubtedly saw this agitation as an erosion of their political power-bases and reacted with a predictable retreat to the whims of the Protestant camp. As one analyst put it:

> Considering themselves subjected to the strains of militant Protestantism they became as sensitive to the strategic danger of a Protestant reaction as to a Catholic frustration with the pace of reform. Hence the different emphasis in their reading of the changing political situation from that of ideologues Napier and Brett. Protecting the party's Protestant base appeared paramount.[191]

Paddy Devlin, who served on the NILP's EC from 1963–69 (becoming party chairman in 1968), claimed retrospectively that Boyd's decision to pander to the whims of reactionary Protestants was a 'risky strategy because such tactics, while winning Woodvale for Boyd, compromised the NILP vote in other constituencies where the Catholic vote was important'.[192] It was at this point that tensions between the party's practitioners and theoreticians collided.

The Nationalist eclipse

Nationalist opposition to Labour had its origins in ideological antipathy but was nurtured in the spirit of political calculation. It was only following the O'Neill–Lemass summit of January 1965 that Irish government representatives applied pressure on Nationalist MPs to take up occupancy on the Opposition benches. It could be argued that Nationalist antagonism towards Labour fed on the NILP's endorsement of minority grievances in those areas where few Catholics would have voted for 'green' Nationalist politicians. Labour's political lobbying on such emotive issues as the status of the Mater Hospital, the Rent Bill and the antiquated electoral franchise allowed it to emit an air of consistency throughout the 1960s in comparison to Unionist provincial conservativism.

David Bleakley had made some play of Unionist attempts to strike an inter-ethnic alliance with the Nationalist Party back in 1962. Now it seemed that O'Neill's plan to counter-attack Labour's position involved incorporating the old adage of 'the enemy of my enemy is my friend' into his campaign as a means of ferreting out non-sectarian voting habits (based along socio-economic lines) which had periodically cropped up in Belfast. O'Neill's shift towards addressing working-class social welfarist issues was a tactical ploy designed, on the one hand, to woo Catholic political representatives back into the frame while, on the other, allowing Unionism to reel back in some of the floating voters who had supported the NILP in the previous two elections.[193] Arguably, Nationalist politicians were forced to reveal their hand because of the rise of groups that placed socio-economic grievances before any immediate calls for the removal of the border.[194] Faced with continuing challenges to its political stranglehold of Catholic Nationalist politics from individual republican Labour MPs like Harry Diamond and Gerry Fitt, not to mention Independent Labour MP Frank Hanna, the Nationalist Party chose to 'evolve in order to maintain the Catholic middle ground'. In February 1965, 'after seven years' equivocation, it claimed the status of Official Opposition by virtue of being the largest opposition group'.[195]

Internal splits and factionalism

The 'Sunday swings' incident generated much negative publicity for the NILP and served to reinforce the public perception that the party was no longer a solidified unit like it had been when it first entered parliamentary politics in 1958. The sacking of Sam Napier from the PLP secretaryship in 1964[196] and his aborted candidature at the Senate election of May 1965 (in favour of the ATGWU official Norman Kennedy)[197] further alienated those who had endeavoured to build up the party's constructive public profile since 1949. These ruptures served to aggravate the conflicting nature of the agnostic, liberal and Christian socialist strands underpinning the party's ideology – something previously masked by its united front against Unionism's socio-economic conservativism.[198] Moreover, recent evidence has come to light which suggests that Tom Boyd considered retiring from public office as early as 1964, and had shifted his attention towards finding a suitable successor as party leader.

The NILP's failure to secure any parliamentary representation at the 1964 Westminster Election only sapped at Boyd's political energy. The following is an extract from a confidential letter he sent to Napier at the time:

> The failure to elect additional members is one for which I consider the EC is in large measure responsible and my mind has been ranging into the future as it always tends to do and the big question for me, as I put it last night, is what political legacy can I leave behind me at Stormont and who is the potential leader of the party.[199]

Tom Boyd's observations were indeed thought-provoking and his belief that David Bleakley and Billy Boyd craved power beyond Stormont proved damning:

> As I see it with our two younger members setting their eyes on Westminster I must look outside the Parliamentary Party for a successor and in my view you are the person to undertake that task ... That is why I want you to go into the Senate so that

you can not only train a team but also become more familiar with the workings of Parliament.[200]

It is clear from Boyd's support for Napier's Senate candidature that as leader he had identified himself more with one side of the split than the other. By January 1965 problems within the party escalated when Boyd's leadership and man-management decisions were challenged by Vivian Simpson. Simpson criticised Boyd's new shadowing arrangements – whereby Labour MPs shadowed main government departments – in a virile attack on the decision to announce the changes to the press, apparently without first consulting his team.[201]

The spirit of camaraderie which had prevailed across party ranks during its darkest years in the 1950s was now under increasing strain. Douglas McIldoon further highlighted how:

> It got to be the sort of secular bit of the party versus the part of the party which (alright it was Christian socialist) but it was actually in many ways much more in touch with the mind or the emotions of (I suppose) where the Protestant working class was coming from. And that then meant that the sort of secularists also, in a sense, were regarded as being more open to a more Catholic agenda as well. And they should have been able to manage that. They didn't, and I think if they had managed that better they would have created a more solid, robust political entity in Northern Ireland which might have been better able to resist the 'troubles', or indeed to stop them happening.[202]

Meanwhile the poor relations between the PLP and the EC were enough to prompt Napier to tender his resignation (a destabilising factor overlooked by Graham in his thesis) exactly a decade since his last threatened walkout. Napier's decision plunged the party into further disarray as it convulsed at the prospect of losing the one person who had held the ship together as it weathered the storm of successive electoral defeats in the 1950s. Napier had sacrificed much in his personal life to build up the NILP since he was appointed full-time secretary in 1955 and his decision was not one arrived at on a whim. As he noted in his resignation letter:

> My decision has not been arrived at hastily as I have seen and worked for this party in good times and in bad: I have been with it in its successes and setbacks. And I have at all times been conscious of its great contribution to the life of Northern Ireland.[203]

It was now obvious that the atmosphere in the party was touching on despondency. This had a hugely negative effect on the party's finances, which, according to Napier, had been almost destroyed – leaving it in a comparable position to 1955 when it had only managed to put forward a token number of candidates for the Westminster election.

Napier confessed that he had 'just lost my enthusiasm for the job … After eight months wrangling within the party, I can see no end to it.'[204] His deliberations came just 48 hours after the party's EC passed a vote of confidence for his sterling work. The *Belfast Telegraph* declared that his resignation would 'have an extremely adverse effect on party morale generally, as he was a widely respected and popular figure in the province'.[205] What made the issue so damaging to Labour was that no extenuating political circumstances were actually at stake. It centred round whether the PLP could take action independently of the EC. Bleakley was quoted as having said that every progressive person in Northern Ireland would deeply regret Napier's defeat at the Senate election, but that 'Mr Kennedy's election is a symbol of an increased closeness between political Labour and the unions. It is the sort of development which would provide the beginning to a great leap forward in Labour organisation and influence.'[206] Moreover, these internal ruptures came towards the end of a successful seven-year battle to breathe new life into Northern Ireland's political institutions. Dismissing a whispering campaign against Labour, David Bleakley instead offered a summary of his party's impressive parliamentary résumé:

> In parliamentary affairs Labour has breathed life into the conventions of the consti-tution. In communal affairs we have built up a reputation as a progressive and moderating influence. In economic matters we have pushed and prodded a reluc-tant Unionist Party towards the outline of a planned society. These are the enduring things which really matter in politics. In the days ahead Labour will continue to demonstrate that it can produce the kind of political enterprise without which our province cannot hope to survive.[207]

Labour's troubles were certainly domestic but they had far-reaching effects for both communities. 1964 would prove to be one of the last high tides for the party.

Historians of the period have concluded that O'Neill's anti-NILP crusade 'unin-tentionally sharpened community antagonisms'.[208] Additionally: 'The sectarian polarisation created by the Divis Street riots was still operating and a fall in the unemployment rate deprived the NILP of its major issue.'[209] But it had deeper implications for the NILP. Working relations between the PLP and the EC, in particular, hit an all-time low and it was unsurprising that it was failing to project a positive image ahead of a very public internecine power struggle.

Furthermore, it could be argued that O'Neill was greatly facilitated in his counter-attack of the NILP by the BLP. Despite providing its sister party with much ideological and financial assistance, British Labour contended that the NILP accepted that 'the present constitutional position, and our relations with it, are based on the principle of non-interference'.[210] That is if one regards the BLP in the 1960s as a wholly 'socialist party'. Ralph Miliband argued – some-what critically – in the early 1960s that socialist goals played second fiddle to Wilson's desire, when he was elected to power, to wrest the British economy from aristocratic hands, while turning loose social, economic and political entrepreneurs to oversee modernisation projects across the UK.[211] It could be argued that Wilson's liberalising agenda found many converts, including O'Neill, whom he regarded as having 'carried through a remarkable programme of easement' in Northern Ireland.[212] For Wilson, O'Neill's problems were largely engineered by the 'black reactionary group in his cabinet';[213] the Unionist leader's position would have to be shored up by stabilising both his authority and his economic proposals. Nevertheless, Wilson's chief concern during his first term was a damage limitation exercise aimed at curtailing the unruliness of the 12 Unionist MPs at Westminster, not the building up of the NILP as an alternative parliamentary-based government.[214]

Wearing Labour's clothes: O'Neill and the 1965 Stormont election

The political conflict which had been bubbling to the surface between labourism and loyalism, particularly in inner-city districts, was to reach a crescendo by October 1965 with profoundly damaging consequences for sitting MPs David Bleakley and Billy Boyd. Both men had beaten Unionist Party candidates by slender majorities, in Victoria and Woodvale respectively, in the March 1958 election. In 1962 they confidently doubled their majorities in both constituencies, though as the closing months of 1965 were to confirm, electoral loyalty in these areas was conditional upon an absence of anti-partitionist feeling and the prevalence of 'bread and butter' issues. By challenging the NILP on socio-economic grounds (while stealing its germane policies) O'Neill was administering a *coup de grace* to its political fortunes.

By the mid-1960s the spectre of loyalism had once again reared its head in Woodvale, this time under the guise of the *nom de plume* Ulster Protestant Action (UPA). The threat from within the Protestant community to the NILP's position was so great that Sam Napier produced a detailed report on its influence.[215] In many ways Napier overestimated the fascistic basis of the UPA and its potential for orchestrating militant activism among the grass-roots. To one of those involved in its activities, the recently demobilised soldier Gusty Spence, '[t]he UPA was a ginger group. They had no firearms or anything remotely like that.'[216] Its main purpose was to channel grass-roots disgruntlement in a populist direction for the benefit of Ian Paisley's personal political ambitions and public profile. However, by October, an even more deadly conspiracy emerged in the form of a rejuvenated Ulster Volunteer Force.

The susceptibility of working-class Protestants to Paisleyite populism made conventional politicking difficult for NILP activists. Jack Sayers later noted in *The Round Table* that:

> The dangers of Paisleyism are not only that it provokes communal strife, but that the belief in its leader's 'fundamentalism', in politics as well as religion, colours as much as half of the working class backbone of unionism.[217]

Walker has indicated that the sort of working-class culture which the NILP had to work with in these districts 'often co-existed with sectarianism and with an unshakeable suspiciousness about the intentions of the Nationalist minority, and was thus vulnerable to Paisleyite populism'.[218] The cultivation of an alternative non-sectarian Labour political culture rarely exuded any kind of longevity whilst Unionists continually warned of an 'imminent' IRA atrocity or the dangers of Irish constitutional irredentism.

The weeks running up to the 1965 Northern Ireland general election were therefore a difficult period for the NILP. This can be attributed directly to the internal friction by then persisting among the party's leadership which was made worse by an increase in sectarian feeling across Belfast. Graham attributes the party's difficulties to O'Neill's successful bid to gain the middle ground by rejuvenating the Ulster Unionist Labour Association (UULA), an organisation reformed by plundering the deluge of the past for ways to woo working-class Protestants back to the broader Unionist alliance.[219] However it is not clear whether the UULA actually functioned beyond the successful paper exercise initiated by O'Neill.[220] Nevertheless, O'Neill was greatly facilitated in his bid to win back despondent workers by the construction of new housing estates in the Greater Belfast area. Over 10,000 new homes were circulated with a personal message from the premier appealing for workers to join with him in his imaginative journey towards the 'new Ulster'.

Although flawed on many levels O'Neill's modernisation rhetoric was an ambitious piece of political theatrics. As Bew *et al.* point out:

> The ideology of modernisation could function quite simply to defend sectarian activity by defining nationalist and NILP concern as 'reactionary' or 'living in the past' ... O'Neill's economic policies bore no relation to intercommunity relations. Their *raison d'être* lay only in political conflicts within the Protestant bloc.[221]

At the heart of this latest Unionist appeal was the need to reconstruct Northern Ireland and to permit a wider share in the lucrative new industrial schemes cropping up across the province. In the run-up to the November 1965 poll O'Neill intended to spike Labour's guns by portraying its class-based analysis as vulgar and suspect:

> In a particularly silly speech, the Labour candidate for this constituency [Carrick] described the Unionist candidate, Captain Ardill, as 'upper crust'. I say to you that a man who was good enough to fight for his country and to be decorated for gallantry is good enough to seek the support of the electors of Carrick without having this sort of class-conscious rubbish thrown at him ... I hate to see the ugly, strident note of class warfare creeping into Ulster politics. This is a society in which we have always held one man to be as good as another.[222]

Furthermore, O'Neill's attempts to stall Labour's advance was given backing by powerful bourgeois allies within Northern Irish society. In a letter from Captain O.W.J. Henderson, Chairman of Century Newspapers Ltd (which incorporated the *Belfast Newsletter*), to O'Neill, unconditional support was pledged to the Unionist campaign: 'you may be certain that everything that we can do in influencing the electors will be dealt with', he maintained.[223] Unionism had always had at its disposal a plethora of resources which it could marshal at crucial political moments. In this latest bout it was obvious that much favourable media coverage would be given to the Unionist Party's manifesto despite Labour's newly refined public relations strategy.

It is clear from recently unearthed private correspondence that O'Neill was gravely concerned about Labour's inroads into Protestant working-class areas:

> In the last 15 years the trend has been towards increased Labour support in Belfast and unless this can be in some measure contained the danger looking up during the next 10 years is the one of Coalition Government. You will doubtless recall the

ghastly consequences of coalition in Dublin … There are some so-called Unionists who see (a) Coalition as a possible vehicle for office (b) Coalition as a road towards a United Ireland.[224]

In subsequent correspondence to Henderson (who, incidentally, had represented Belfast Victoria between 1955 and 1958) O'Neill was uncharacteristically frank in his assessment of the NILP challenge:

> In Belfast we shall have a big problem in containing the gravitational pull which the Labour Party are bound to exert in a highly industrialised area. This effect has been well illustrated by the increasing support which the local party have managed to achieve over the past three elections … I am in no doubt that it is in the city constituencies that the real contest will take place and we shall certainly be grateful for your support, which I can see having an important influence on the result.[225]

O'Neill's fears about the NILP threat would soon be channelled into a personal campaign by him against its MPs in Woodvale, Victoria, Oldpark and Pottinger.

Arguably, O'Neill had been planning his counter-attack on the NILP's electoral positions for some time. Within six months of becoming Premier he publicly announced that he had commissioned a series of high-profile government audits into the economic state of play in the province. In his first three years in office the Matthew, Wilson and Lockwood reports all returned open-ended verdicts on the need to expand Ulster's industrial base and to improve its infrastructure. The Matthew Report had advocated the construction of new growth centres within the range of the Belfast stop-line (the catchment area which ran from the city to the limits of Belfast Rural District Council). In response O'Neill appointed Thomas Wilson, a Professor of Economics at Glasgow University, to head up the planning think-tank which would augment the methodology for implementing Matthew's proposals. Wilson's report, released in December 1964, formed the 'basis of the Government's economic policy'[226] and essentially crystallised new thinking on how best to diversify Northern Ireland's staple industries in an era of unprecedented decline and misfortune.

The decision to sacrifice the unprofitable staple industries – which had long symbolised the prosperity of Ulster's unique economic circumstances, in contrast to Southern Ireland – was a risky enterprise, but O'Neill felt much emboldened by his emphasis on 'self-help' in contrast to the failed overtures to successive British governments by his predecessor.[227] However, this change in the economic fabric of the region did not herald a transfer in power from the 'old-established family firms to new British, American or continental firms', nor did it signal a wresting of political influence from traditional segregationists to 'a modernised, less sectarian Unionism', as Farrell has claimed.[228] Rather it strengthened the socio-economic fortunes of the working class and made them more affluent and willing to disperse from traditional segregatory living conditions and into new housing estates, like Rathcoole, situated on the northern outskirts of Belfast, or Ballymurphy in the west of the city.[229] The revitalisation of Ulster's infrastructure for O'Neill was a prelude for future socio-economic success and with it greater community harmony.

It is a source of contention what actually drove O'Neill to make such cosmetic changes. However Mulholland leaves us in little doubt:

> O'Neill knew what he was doing and his intention was never to adopt planning, but rather to steal the modernising, technocratic clothes of the NILP and, more important still, to construct new levers for winning a greater British subvention.[230]

As noted above, O'Neill's approach marked a crucial new departure in the economic strategy pursued during the Brookeborough era. He saw his task simply to 'set out to develop a new persuasiveness around the theme of regionalism'.[231] Walker's analysis is broadly similar, though he has concentrated much more on explaining the inner mechanics of this core–periphery relationship operating throughout the UK in this period. With a £230 million dividend announced by the Conservative government in November 1963 for the regeneration of regional areas of the UK O'Neill rightly anticipated a move by the centre to breathe new life into the ailing peripheral economies. As far as the NILP was concerned the new Premier second-guessed the party with great perceptiveness – the theft of Labour's clothing had begun.

The NILP's 1965 manifesto expressed dismay at Unionist isolationism. It issued an indictment against O'Neill's brainchild modernisation project on the basis that it was largely cosmetic. And it called for tighter legislative transference between Stormont and Westminster, though it attached the caveat that:

> Parity does not mean the wholesale duplication of Westminster legislation. The advantages of devolution must be seized; there are many matters upon which Stormont might well be the legislative pioneer. In fact, it is the legislative laggard – as witness the introduction only now, seventeen years late, of so basic a piece of social legislation as the legal aid scheme.[232]

Having been active in Stormont for the past seven years the NILP was suitably poised to make purposeful claims about the legislative system from raw experience. Its list of requirements neatly mirrored what it had been articulating convincingly in the debating chamber. Parity was demanded in social service benefits, the electoral franchise, criminal compensation, and in the fundamentally important field of Citizens' Rights. Significantly, Billy Boyd's tabling of the Racial Discrimination Bill (which reached a second reading before being overturned by the Unionists[233]) and Tom Boyd's lobbying for a criminal compensation scheme had succeeded in gaining cross-party consensus. The mid-1960s brought a distillation in NILP policies. Alongside calls for the acceleration of the government's house-building scheme the party sought allocation of new housing stock on 'a fair and non-discriminatory basis. A standard points system, fair to all parties, should be hammered out at Government level and rigidly imposed throughout the whole of Northern Ireland.'[234] Above all it called for O'Neill's pledges on reform to be honoured.

O'Neill's repudiation of Labour policies stood him in good stead as he attempted to navigate his party past the right – now typified by Paisleyism – and the left of the NILP. The crux of his political argument was that his government had performed nothing less than a miracle in the two years since he had taken over at the helm from Brookeborough. A campaign speech he made in Oldpark underlined this:

> There is one very good reason for the efforts of the Northern Ireland Labour Party to make this an election of false 'scares' and political stunts. They are afraid to fight us on our record of achievement, because in their hearts they know that the last few years have been years of concrete progress. Jobs, houses, hospitals, roads, agriculture – these are the *real* issues of this campaign. Our policy document is a statement of achievement and a declaration of intention. It tells the electorate very clearly what we propose to do with another five years of power. It embodies realistic yet imaginative policies. We have the will to put these policies into effect ... So you do not have to take *my* word for it; take, instead, if you wish, the word of leading financial journalists in London and Dublin, or the word of the United Kingdom Government ... Progress in Ulster is a fact; small wonder, then, that the Northern Ireland Labour Party want to fight on a basis of fancy![235]

Few contemporary political commentators doubted the return of a Unionist government. The party's inbuilt majority was premised on making every election a referendum on the border and it was almost inconceivable that they would fail to steady supporters' nerves on this cardinal issue once again.

The NILP's emphasis on socio-economic issues was further checked by a Premier who wished to broaden the accountability (and with it the acceptability) of his regime. This was a risky tactic, according to Cornelius O'Leary:

> Cut off from its Protestant moorings, as it would be if O'Neill were successful, the Unionist Party would lose the main guarantee of its permanence in office and an alternative government would soon be in sight. This was understood by O'Neill, but he did not regard it as an excessive price for normalcy. However, the grassroots politicians did.[236]

O'Neill's mistake was to consider Northern Ireland politics as conventional in the British sense. His doggedness to repel Labour's advances revealed his impressive skills as a politician, though arguably the principal motivation behind O'Neill's cosmetic alterations was his determination to lead the UUP back onto the electoral battlefield, thereby challenging the NILP for its monopolisation of the political centre ground. This was a plan which was designed, according to Walker, to 'appropriate much of the ideological armoury of the NILP which then found its room for making a distinctive political appeal on social and economic questions further constricted'.[237] Nonetheless, O'Neill largely dismissed out of hand the seriousness of the Paisleyite 'O'Neill Must Go!' campaign and left his flank open to attack from the right. Many scholars have criticised O'Neill's modernisation programme because of its blasé attitude towards the Catholic community, especially those west of the Bann. Understandably O'Neill's pompous and aloof personality placed him in the firing line of those who found his liberal Unionism shallow, though as Cochrane states, 'it rather overstates O'Neill's Machiavellian credentials'.[238]

In his bid to preserve Unionism's hegemony O'Neill sought to dilute the Labour electoral challenge by meeting it on its own terms. Surprisingly, some former NILP activists refused to condemn O'Neill for his actions.[239] Most activists, while refusing to see the UUP contender in Woodvale, Johnny McQuade, as a weak choice,[240] claimed that the Unionist candidate 'was actually very strongly backed' in his campaign to oust Boyd:

> It's odd that O'Neill (who was Prime Minister at the time) was supposed to be trying to modernise Northern Ireland and you know make parliamentary democracy work and so on. Yet in the 1965 election the main thrust of the election campaign seemed to be directed towards destroying the NILP which was the only possibility of making the Stormont Parliament work. The two seats he targeted, in part, were David Bleakley's in Victoria and Billy Boyd's in Woodvale and that was done for short-term narrow party political interests. He clearly recognised that Nationalist politics was no threat to the Unionist powerbase but the NILP was beginning to win a significant Protestant working class vote in North Belfast and East Belfast and that was the seats that were targeted.[241]

In the November election Boyd polled 5,067 votes, trailing in behind McQuade's 6,791. Compared with the previous election voter turnout was down from 71.9% to 57.3%. Some NILP activists, including George Chambers, thought that this was due to the awful weather the province had experienced that week.[242] In Victoria the NILP result was equally miserable. Bleakley was defeated by newcomer Roy Bradford who won his seat with a majority of 426 votes. Elsewhere in Belfast O'Neill's counter-attack had only measured success. Both Vivian Simpson and Tom Boyd held on to their seats, though it was undoubtedly the poor turnout which lessened Unionism's electoral challenge.[243]

Outside East and West Belfast the NILP seemed more emboldened by the prospect of winning more seats following its massive pool of 102,759 votes in the October 1964 election. Consequently the party's revitalised self-confidence outside marginal seats pushed it into direct confrontation with the Unionist Party, especially in those constituencies where Unionist incumbents had traditionally been guaranteed a clear run. One high-profile example was the challenge thrown down by Sydney Stewart, who entered into the South Antrim contest with Brian McConnell. McConnell (who had been the MP since 1951) now faced his first opponent in what had hitherto been an uncontested seat, at least since the abolition of PR in 1929.[244] Douglas McIldoon, who was Stewart's election agent, vividly recalled how:

> The election in South Antrim was against Brian McConnell – the Minister for Home Affairs – and I think we got 4,000 votes and he got 14,000 roughly on a very low turnout. It was a very big constituency but it had never been contested. I don't think it was ever contested. I think they were returned unopposed from the beginning of time. So to that extent it was breaking new ground and was great fun. Disappointing election of course because Labour – [David] Bleakley and Billy Boyd lost their seats – I think events in Northern Ireland started to unravel at that point. [245]

Elsewhere in Northern Ireland the party faced stiff opposition from Nationalists reluctant to give any ground at a time when their positions were under threat from republicans eager to capitalise on rural Catholic discontent at the pace of reform.

Conclusion

Sam Napier's annual review of the NILP's political development in 1965 sought to do two things. First, it audited the party's electoral performance. Second, it took stock of the 'Sunday swings' episode as well as attempting to measure the effect of O'Neill's new technocratic rhetoric on Labour's electoral support base.[246] The full extent of Labour's disastrous performance was not appreciated until six months later when Napier submitted his audit to the EC. His report summarised the NILP's difficulties:

> For us this election was the third in eighteen months, and it came just three months after the Northern Ireland election in which we lost two of the four seats at Stormont which we held. This Stormont election had been preceded by difficulties within the party, and all this had combined to lower the morale of the party members and to make the party less attractive than usual to the Labour voters.[247]

In the intervening period between November and March 1966 it became clear that the Protestant working class was undergoing fluctuations of a sectarian nature, which would prove to have long-term debilitating effects on the NILP's electoral fortunes. O'Neill's counter-attack had won his party back two seats but it nonetheless opened the floodgates to a tide of protest and reaction from both communities.

Notes

1 David Bleakley, speaking after his successful electoral bid in Belfast Victoria, *Belfast Telegraph*, 21 March 1958.
2 NILP, *Ulster Labour and the Sixties: Radical, Relevant, Realistic* (1962).
3 NILP, *Signposts to the New Ulster* (1964).
4 *Northern Whig*, 28 February 1958.
5 *Belfast Telegraph*, 28 February 1958.
6 *Belfast Telegraph*, 20 March 1958.
7 See the comments of the other NILP candidates in the *Belfast Telegraph*, 19 and 20 March 1958.
8 *The Round Table*, No. 191 (June 1958), p. 276.
9 See English, Richard, *Armed Struggle: A History of the IRA* (Basingstoke: Macmillan, 2003).
10 PRONI, D/2704/A14/2a–b, *NILP Documents*.
11 J.A.V. Graham notes that NILP candidates were instructed to play up their support for the B Specials. Arguably this was a tactic employed to fend off competition from Independent Unionists in the Woodvale and Shankill constituencies. It is debateable whether these instructions would have been given to NILP candidates in other outlying areas where IRA activity was more acute, as little NILP organisation was to be found in rural areas.

12 Paddy Devlin, writing in response to an article penned by David Bleakley in *Socialist Commentary*, May 1957. Devlin switched allegiance from the IrLP to the NILP the following year.

13 See Bleakley's rationale for socialists supporting partition in *Socialist Commentary*, April 1957.

14 See Graham, J.A.V., *The Consensus-Forming Strategy of the Northern Ireland Labour Party 1949–1968* (Unpublished MSc Thesis: Queen's University Belfast, 1972), p. 64.

15 *Irish News*, 14 February 1958.

16 Unless otherwise stated all figures are taken from Elliott, Sydney, *Northern Ireland Parliamentary Election Results, 1921–1972* (Chichester: Political Reference Publications, 1973).

17 *Belfast Telegraph*, 21 March 1958.

18 Interview with David Bleakley, 21 March 2006. For more on Sayers see Gailey, Andrew, *'Crying in the Wilderness' Jack Sayers: A Liberal Editor in Ulster, 1939–1969* (Belfast: Institute of Irish Studies, 1995).

19 The results for these four constituencies were as follows: Belfast, Oldpark – 6,307 (majority of 155); Belfast, Victoria – 7,198 (majority of 147); Belfast, Pottinger – 4,573 (majority of 1,333); and Belfast, Woodvale – 7,529 (majority of 80). One must bear in mind that some districts in Belfast had not succumbed to demographic change – as they were to in the late 1960s and early 1970s – and the segregation which existed was less overtly physical: Catholics and Protestants still walked up and down each other's streets, still lived side by side, and still worked together in relative harmony.

20 Walker, Graham, *A History of the Ulster Unionist Party: Protest, Pragmatism and Pessimism* (Manchester: Manchester University Press, 2004), p. 140.

21 Ibid., p. 139.

22 LPA, GS/12/NI, Report to the NEC on Northern Ireland by the General Secretary, 25 June 1958, Northern Ireland Correspondence and Statements, 1955–59. Hugh Gaitskell had visited Northern Ireland shortly before the election to show his support for the NILP's election campaign.

23 Ibid.

24 Ibid.

25 PRONI, D/2704/A14/25, *NILP Documents*, Tom Boyd to Norman Stronge, 26 March 1958.

26 PRONI, D/4276, *Tom Boyd Papers*.

27 The Nationalist Party refused to become Her Majesty's Loyal Opposition because it would have meant accepting the state. There is some debate over whether or not the decision not to accept the title was unilateral. Brendan Lynn points to the threat by some Nationalist politicians to resign if the party accepted the position. See his *Holding the Ground: The Nationalist Party in Northern Ireland, 1945–72* (Aldershot: Ashgate, 1997).

28 *Irish News*, 5 April 1958.

29 PRONI, D/3233/7/2, *Vivian Simpson Papers*.

30 Ibid.

31 NILP, Minute Book of the Woodvale Divisional Labour Party, privately held.

32 The strike ended on 16 May following a vote of 600 to 500 among those affected. Over 6,000 were rendered idle. See the *Irish News*, 17 May 1958.

33 Mulholland Marc, *'Stolen Thunder!': The Northern Ireland Labour Party in Context, 1958–1965* (Unpublished MA Thesis: Queen's University Belfast, 1994), p. 11.

34 Wichert, Sabine, *Northern Ireland since 1945* (Harlow: Longman, 1991), pp. 61–6. See also Harris, Richard, *Regional Economic Policy in Northern Ireland, 1945–1988* (Aldershot: Avebury, 1991).
35 Northern Ireland House of Commons Debates, Vol. 42, Col. 212–13, 22 April 1958.
36 Northern Ireland House of Commons Debates, Vol. 42, Col. 208–9, 22 April 1958.
37 Interview with Robert Bingham, 24 February 2005. AEU officials formed a canvassing team, with the Short and Harland Works Committee providing 60 workers and 15 cars. See Graham, *The Consensus-Forming Strategy of the Northern Ireland Labour Party*, p. 79.
38 Interview with Robert Bingham, 24 February 2005. Paddy Devlin, who eventually joined the Woodvale DLP in 1958, said of Boyd that, 'He held strong support throughout the constituency for his surgery work, looking after the social problems of the area. It has long been a fact of political life in Belfast that constituents turn to their elected representatives as a first resort when they hit a problem.' Devlin, Paddy, *Straight Left: An Autobiography* (Belfast: Blackstaff, 1993), p. 78.
39 See Chapter 1.
40 Graham, *The Consensus-Forming Strategy of the Northern Ireland Labour Party*, p. 73.
41 For a discussion of the British Labour Party and its interest groups see Ludlum, Steve, 'Too Much Pluralism, Not Enough Socialism: Interpreting the Unions–Party Link', in Callaghan, John, Steven Fielding and Steve Ludlam (eds), *Interpreting the Labour Party: Approaches to Labour Politics and History* (Manchester: Manchester University Press, 2003), pp. 150–65.
42 For a detailed analysis of the background to NIC recognition see Mulholland, Marc, '"One of the Most Difficult Hurdles": The Struggle for Recognition of the Northern Ireland Committee of the Irish Congress of Trade Unions, 1958–64', *Saothar* 22 (1997), pp. 81–94.
43 Purdie, Bob, *Politics in the Streets: The Origins of the Civil Rights Movement in Northern Ireland* (Belfast: Blackstaff, 1990), pp. 12–13.
44 See PRONI, D/3233/5/5, *Vivian Simpson Papers*, ICTU, Northern Ireland Committee, 'NI Labour Party – Sunday Opening of Children's Playgrounds', a statement issued by Billy Blease, 30 November 1964.
45 Graham, *The Consensus-Forming Strategy of the Northern Ireland Labour Party*, pp. 85–6.
46 This was established in 1961 on the joint recommendations of the PLP and the NIC. For an insight into this episode see Terry Cradden's interview with Lord Blease of Cromac in *Saothar* 19 (1994), pp. 145–57.
47 *Belfast Telegraph*, 18 March 1959. See also Graham, *The Consensus-Forming Strategy of the Northern Ireland Labour Party*, pp. 70–1.
48 Northern Ireland House of Commons Debates, Vol. 43, Col. 14–16, 19 November 1958.
49 PLP Report, 12 November 1958, cited in Graham, *The Consensus-Forming Strategy of the Northern Ireland Labour Party*, p. 74.
50 For a discussion of the parity issue in social service provision see Brett, Charles, 'The Lessons of Devolution in Northern Ireland', *Political Quarterly*, Vol. 41, No. 3 (July 1970), p. 264.
51 Purdie, *Politics in the Streets*, pp. 68–9.
52 Northern Ireland House of Commons Debates, Vol. 43, Col. 64, 21 October 1958.
53 Ibid., Col. 91, 21 October 1958.

54 Ibid., Col. 92, 21 October 1958.
55 Farrell, Michael, *Northern Ireland: The Orange State* (London: Pluto, 1976), p. 225.
56 NILP, *Ulster Labour and the Sixties* (1962).
57 According to the 1961 annual party conference all four MPs had voted for a review of the legislation throughout the previous parliamentary term. PRONI, D2704/A18/57a–c, *NILP Documents*.
58 LPA, GS12/NI, Northern Ireland Documents, 1960–62, Labour Party Research Department, *Civil Liberties and Administration of Justice*, 21 February 1962.
59 PRONI, CAB 4/1170.
60 Arnold Schofield served as a senator from 1961 to 1969.
61 PRONI, D/3233/1/5, *Vivian Simpson Papers*, Brookeborough to Simpson, 24 July 1962 and 14 August 1962.
62 Ibid. Brookeborough refuted any suggestion by the NILP that the government was being complacent on the economic front.
63 *Belfast Telegraph*, 5 March 1959.
64 See the arguments of Bew, Paul, Peter Gibbon and Henry Patterson, *Northern Ireland 1921–2001: Political Forces and Social Classes: Revised and Updated Version* (London: Serif, 2002), especially Chapter 2.
65 See Walker, *A History of the Ulster Unionist Party*, p. 139.
66 *Belfast Telegraph*, 12 February, 1959. Kerr was later to become a UUP Councillor in Woodvale between 1961 and 1964.
67 See Walker, *A History of the Ulster Unionist Party*, pp. 142–5.
68 Harbinson, John F., *The Ulster Unionist Party, 1882–1973: Its Development and Organisation* (Belfast: Blackstaff, 1973), pp. 109–110.
69 See Table 3.3 for the occupational backgrounds of party candidates at local government level.
70 This section draws heavily upon Edwards, Aaron, 'Social Democracy and Partition: The British Labour Party and Northern Ireland, 1951–64', *Journal of Contemporary History*, Vol. 42, No. 4 (October 2007), pp. 595–612.
71 LPA, GS12/NI/207i, Herbert Morrison to Morgan Phillips, 6 October 1959.
72 LPA, GS12/NI/208, Phillips to Morrison, 27 October 1959.
73 LPA, GS12/NI, *Northern Ireland Documents 1960–63*, Gaitskell to Seawright, 16 October 1963. Gaitskell said that 'the policies of both the Northern Ireland Labour Party and the British Labour Party have one common objective – to bring new vigour and justice to Northern Ireland as an integral part of a greater plan for the United Kingdom as a whole'.
74 British Governments and Elections since 1945: www.psr.keele.ac.uk/area/uk/ge59/results.htm.
75 Purdie, Bob, 'The Friends of Ireland: British Labour and Irish Nationalism, 1945–49', in Gallagher, Tom and James O'Connell (eds), *Contemporary Irish Studies* (Manchester: Manchester University Press, 1983), pp. 81–94.
76 See Rose, Peter, *How the Troubles Came to Northern Ireland* (Basingstoke: Palgrave Macmillan, 2001), pp. 20–8.
77 Ibid., particularly pp. 11–12.
78 Walker, Graham, *Intimate Strangers: Political and Cultural Interaction between Ulster and Scotland in Modern Times* (Edinburgh: John Donald, 1995), p. 141.
79 LPA, Northern Ireland Policy Box, Research Department Paper, Northern Ireland Liaison Committee: The Labour Party and Northern Ireland, *An Historical Account of the Relations between the Labour Party and the Northern Ireland Labour Party*.

80 LPA, GS12/NI/101–221, *Northern Ireland Papers* (NILP Correspondence). Transport House was the BLP's headquarters at the time.

81 LPA, GS12/NI/101–221.

82 Cradden, Terry, 'Labour in Britain and the Northern Ireland Labour Party, 1900–1970', in Catterall, Peter and Sean McDougal (eds), *The Northern Ireland Question in British Politics* (Basingstoke: Macmillan, 1996), p. 85.

83 David Bleakley speaking at the Centre for Contemporary British History (CCBH – now the Institute for Contemporary British History) Witness Seminar on 'British Policy in Northern Ireland, 1964–70' held on 14 January 1992 at the European Commission Offices, London.

84 Interview with George Chambers, 2 March 2005.

85 See Dixon, Paul, *The British Labour Party and Northern Ireland, 1959–74* (Unpublished PhD Thesis: Univeristy of Bradford, 1993), p. 63.

86 Ibid., p. 73.

87 Dixon (ibid., pp. 98–9) argues that these complaints contributed to the CDU's early success; see also Rose's argument that Wilson secretly planned to limit the power of the twelve Unionist MPs at Westminster in *How the Troubles Came to Northern Ireland*, p. 29.

88 Dixon, *The British Labour Party and Northern Ireland*, p. 188.

89 Ibid., Notes with Reference to Reg Sorenson's Letter, Re: Northern Ireland.

90 LPA, GS12/NI, *Northern Ireland Documents 1960–63*, National Agent and Deputy General Secretary to Mr L.W. Lonsinger, Secretary of the AEU (Islington Branch), 19 April 1961.

91 Ibid., Napier to Williams (National Agent and Deputy General Secretary of the Labour Party), 23 January 1961.

92 On the historical background to Catholic immigration in the Lancashire region (and Salford in particular) see Fielding, Steven, *Class and Ethnicity: Irish Catholics in England, 1880–1939* (Buckingham: Open University Press, 1993).

93 LPA, GS12/NI, *Northern Ireland Documents*, Letter from Harold Wilson to Morgan Phillips, 10 November 1958.

94 LPA, *Labour Party Report* (1963).

95 Interview with George Chambers, 2 March 2005.

96 LPA, GS12/NI, Report of the Fraternal Delegate to the NILP Annual Conference, Portadown, 18–19 April 1960, NEC, 25 May 1960.

97 Ibid.

98 Ibid.

99 Ibid.

100 Party activists like Secretary Sam Napier and Chairman Charles Brett came to the fore during this period in the party's evolution.

101 Bleakley, David, 'The Social and Industrial Effects of High Unemployment in Northern Ireland', *The Transactions of the Association of Industrial Medical Officers*, Vol. 11, No. 3 (1961), pp. 129–32.

102 PRONI, D/230/1/1, A Letter from Stormont – Electoral Communiqué from David Bleakley to his Constituents in Victoria, Spring 1962.

103 NILP, *Ulster Labour and the Sixties* (1962).

104 PRONI, D/230/1/1, A Letter from Stormont – Electoral Communiqué from David Bleakley to his Constituents in Victoria, Spring 1962.

105 Interview with Sir Charles Brett, 30 January 2004.

106 Bleakley, 'The Social and Industrial Effects of High Unemployment'; see also

Bleakley's book, *Beyond Work: Free to Be* (London: SCM, 1985).

107 Bleakley, 'The Social and Industrial Effects of High Unemployment', p. 132.

108 LPA, GS12/NI, Northern Ireland Documents, 1960–63, Memo prepared by Northern Ireland Labour Party for Submission to Rt. Hon. R.A. Butler, CH, MA, FRGS, MP, on 13 June 1961. The Committee was to be presided over by Sir Herbert Brittain.

109 See PRONI, D/2704/A18/83a&b, *NILP Documents*, for a reference to 'Agricultural Policy', 23 May 1962.

110 LPA, GS12/NI, Northern Ireland Documents, 1960–63, Memo prepared by Northern Ireland Labour Party for Submission to Rt. Hon. R.A. Butler.

111 Ibid.

112 *Belfast Telegraph*, 3 February 1962.

113 *Belfast Newsletter*, 3 March 1961.

114 The party gained two additional seats in Belfast and four in Newtownabbey in the May 1961 local government elections, but it lost its only seat in Portadown.

115 PRONI, D/2704/A, *NILP Documents*.

116 *Irish News*, 1 April 1965.

117 *Belfast Telegraph*, 27 April 1962.

118 Interview with Robert Bingham, 24 February 2005. Although Bingham never considered the NILP an exclusively 'Protestant party' its core support was pooled from majority Protestant districts.

119 *Belfast Telegraph*, 2 February 1962.

120 *Belfast Telegraph*, 5 February 1962.

121 Bell, J. Bowyer, *The Secret Army: The IRA, 1916–1979* (Dublin: Academy Press, 1979), p. 291.

122 *Belfast Telegraph*, 28 February 1962. See the interview with Brian Faulkner by W.D. Flackes in the *Belfast Telegraph*, 19 April 1962 and John Harbinson's profile of Faulkner in his *The Ulster Unionist Party*, pp. 159–65.

123 *Belfast Telegraph*, 28 February 1962.

124 *Belfast Telegraph*, 18 May 1962; Walker, *A History of the Ulster Unionist Party*, pp. 139, 142–3.

125 *Belfast Telegraph*, 17 May 1962.

126 *Belfast Telegraph*, 26 March 1962.

127 Graham, *The Consensus-Forming Strategy of the Northern Ireland Labour Party*, p. 95.

128 Elliott, *Northern Ireland Parliamentary Election Results, 1921–1972*, p. 94.

129 Graham, *The Consensus-Forming Strategy of the Northern Ireland Labour Party*, p. 96. The total opposition vote was 73,501 while the UUP vote was just 70,231. In effect the UUP lost Belfast.

130 *Belfast Telegraph*, 31 May 1962.

131 Interview with Sir Charles Brett, 30 January 2004.

132 Brett, C.E.B., *Long Shadows Cast Before: Nine Lives in Ulster, 1625–1977* (Edinburgh: John Bartholomew, 1978), pp. 85–7, 129–31, 133–4.

133 Report of the Joint Working Party on the Economy of Northern Ireland, *The Hall Report* (Belfast: HMSO, October 1962), Cmd. 446.

134 See PRONI, CAB 4/1200/7.

135 Graham, *The Consensus-Forming Strategy of the Northern Ireland Labour Party*, p. 100.

136 Bleakley, David, *Faulkner: Conflict and Consent in Irish Politics* (London: Mowbray, 1974), pp. 63–4.

137 Ibid., pp. 65–6.

138 Unionist leaders usually 'emerged' after consultation within the Parliamentary Party.

139 *Ulster Year Book, 1963–1965* (Belfast: HMSO, 1965), pp. xxxii–xxxiii.

140 Bew *et al.*, *Northern Ireland*, p. 125.

141 Graham, *The Consensus-Forming Strategy of the Northern Ireland Labour Party*, p. 100. Much to the Parliamentary Unionist Party's chagrin Bleakley had previously endorsed a motion on unemployment put forward by the backbench Unionist MP for Shankill Desmond Boal calling for government action on this pressing social issue. See the *Belfast Newsletter*, 3 March 1961. Interestingly the Shankill Labour Party (always dwarfed by the more successful Woodvale Labour Party) later took the decision not to oppose Boal in the 1962 Stormont election.

142 PRONI, D/2022/1/44, *John Kerr Papers*, Letter from Edmund Warnock to John Kerr, dated 12 October 1962. Apart from the four NILP MPs, Frank Hanna (Ind Lab), Gerry Fitt (IrLP) and Harry Diamond (RLP) held seats in Belfast Central, Dock and Falls respectively.

143 Walker, *A History of the Ulster Unionist Party*, p. 125.

144 O'Neill, Terence, *The Autobiography of Terence O'Neill: Prime Minister of Northern Ireland, 1963–1969* (London: Granada, 1972), pp. 52–3.

145 The Unionist Party election communiqués issued in May 1964 on behalf of local government candidates for Court Ward Billy Spence, Jack Bickerstaff, Billy Elliott and Johnny McQuade attacked Billy Boyd for advocating the opening of 'Sunday Band Concerts' and his support for 'the Nationalist cry of discrimination' and the candidacy of 'an ex-IRA internee' (Paddy Devlin). It even played up Charles Brett's statement that 'The beating of the Lambeg drums (by Loyalists) was reminiscent of savages in the jungle beating their tom-toms.' Significantly the Labour connection with Gerry Fitt's Connollyite RLP was also emphasised. See PRONI, D/2704/2.

146 Cochrane, Feargal, '"Meddling at the Crossroads": The Decline and Fall of Terence O'Neill Within the Unionist Community', in English, Richard and Graham Walker (eds), *Unionism in Modern Ireland: New Perspectives on Politics and Culture* (Dublin: Gill and Macmillan, 1996), pp. 148–68.

147 Bew, Paul, 'The Union: A Concept in Terminal Decay?' in Boyce, D. George and Alan O'Day (eds), *Defenders of the Union* (London: Routledge, 2001), p. 321.

148 Harris, *Regional Economic Policy in Northern Ireland, 1945–1988*, p. 31.

149 Edwards, Aaron, *Signposts to the New Ulster? Unionist Government Administration, the Labour Opposition and the Protestant Working Class in Northern Ireland, 1956–72* (Unpublished MA Thesis: Queen's University Belfast, 2002), p. 41.

150 For more on O'Neill's belief in 'self help' see Mulholland, Marc, *Northern Ireland at the Crossroads: Ulster Unionism in the O'Neill Years, 1960–9* (Basingstoke: Macmillan, 2000).

151 See Mulholland, 'One of the Most Difficult Hurdles', pp. 81–94.

152 *Belfast Telegraph*, 22 October 1963.

153 Graham, *The Consensus-Forming Strategy of the Northern Ireland Labour Party*, p. 114.

154 O'Neill, *The Autobiography of Terence O'Neill*, pp. 62–3.

155 LPA, Manifestoes and Policy Documents, *The New Britain* (1964).

156 Ibid.

157 See Fielding, Steven, '"White Heat" and White Collars: the Evolution of "Wilsonism"', in Coopey, Richard, Steven Fielding and Nick Tiratsoo (eds), *The Wilson Governments, 1964–1970* (London: Pinter, 1995), pp. 29–47.

158 NILP, *Signposts to the New Ulster* (1964).
159 LPA, *British Labour Party Parliamentary Labour Party Annual Report Session 1963–64*, p. 85.
160 Ibid., p. 85.
161 Ibid.
162 Wright, Frank, *Northern Ireland: A Comparative Analysis* (Dublin: Gill and Macmillan, 1992), p. 187.
163 PRONI, D/2704/1–6, *NILP Documents*, Enniskillen DLP election material for Borough Council candidates.
164 PRONI, D/3233/1/5, *Vivian Simpson Papers*, Draft Organisation Section: Executive Committee Report (1964). This was successful in Woodvale where branch membership reached almost 50:50 in gender terms by 1964.
165 *Belfast Telegraph*, 4, 6, 20 May 1964.
166 O'Neill, *The Autobiography of Terence O'Neill*, p. 62.
167 NAI, DFA/96/2/7, Letter from the Irish Ambassador, C.C. Cremin, to Hugh McCann, Dept of External Affairs, 5 February 1964 – 'Re: Visit of Nationalist group to London on 29 January to lobby MPs'.
168 In fact there had been no Nationalist Party representation in Belfast since the early 1950s.
169 See the comments on Wilson's Irish nationalist sympathies by his former press secretary and close confidant, Joe Haines, in Peter Rose's book *How the Troubles Came to Northern Ireland*, p. 13.
170 See LPA, GS12/NI, Northern Ireland Documents 1964, Napier to Williams, 26 October 1964; *Irish Times*, 15 October 1964; *Belfast Telegraph*, 19 October 1964.
171 *The Round Table*, No. 217 (December 1964), p. 61.
172 In scenes of jubilant triumphalism Paisleyites congregated outside Belfast City Hall, where the count was taking place, and chanted 'Here, Here, Paisley, here, where the hell is Billy Boyd'. Similarly, the NILP's North Belfast candidate John McDowell was prevented from speaking by cries of 'Lundy' and 'traitor'. *Belfast Telegraph*, 16 October and the *Irish Times*, 15, 17, October 1964.
173 PRONI, D/4127/5/1/2, *Kilfedder Papers*, 'Warning: Vote Kilfedder', UUP Election Leaflet (1964). Most of the republicans arrested attributed their involvement in the riots to Ian Paisley's intervention.
174 Ibid.
175 For an account of the riots see Garland, Roy, *Gusty Spence* (Belfast: Blackstaff, 2001), pp. 46–7.
176 *Belfast Telegraph*, 3 October 1964.
177 Interview with Billy Boyd, cited in Graham, *The Consensus-Forming Strategy of the Northern Ireland Labour Party*, pp. 132–3. It probably did not help matters much that the incumbent UUP MP, Jim Kilfedder, thanked Paisley for helping to secure his victory.
178 PRONI, D/4127/5/1/2, 'Warning: Vote Kilfedder', UUP Election Leaflet (1964).
179 Interview with Robert Bingham, 24 February 2005.
180 Interview with Beatrice Boyd, 21 February 2005.
181 PRONI, D/3233/5/5, *Vivian Simpson Papers*.
182 *Belfast Telegraph*, 30 November 1964.
183 PRONI D/3233/5/5, *Vivian Simpson Papers*, ICTU, Northern Ireland Committee, 'NI Labour Party – Sunday Opening of Children's Playgrounds', a statement issued by Billy Blease, 30 November 1964.

184 Ibid.

185 Ibid.

186 Interview with Sir Charles Brett, 30 January 2004.

187 *Irish News*, 4 March 1958.

188 Ibid.

189 Budge, Ian and Cornelius O'Leary, *Belfast: Approach to Crisis: A Study of Belfast Politics, 1613–1970* (Basingstoke, Macmillan, 1973), p. 294.

190 Interview with Erskine Holmes, 21 September 2005.

191 Graham, *The Consensus-Forming Strategy of the Northern Ireland Labour Party*, pp. 124–5.

192 Devlin, *Straight Left*, p. 79.

193 Budge and O'Leary, *Belfast*, p. 374.

194 Lynn, *Holding the Ground*, p. 171. See also the comments by the Belfast correspondent for *The Round Table*, No. 220 (September 1965), pp. 367–8.

195 Graham, *The Consensus-Forming Strategy of the Northern Ireland Labour Party*, pp. 141–2.

196 PRONI, D/3233/1/5, *Vivian Simpson Papers*, Simpson–Napier Correspondence 5, 6, 17 February 1965. It was agreed by a vote of three to two that Vivian Simpson would take over the role of PLP Secretary.

197 Napier was defeated in the Senate Election by the Nationalist Mr Mallon by 12 votes. Norman Kennedy was a powerful figure in the trade union movement. In 1961 he served as President of the ICTU.

198 David Bleakley and Billy Boyd were both Christian socialists. Charles Brett and Erskine Holmes were representative of the liberal and secular wing of the party.

199 PRONI, D/3702/C/8, *Sam Napier Papers*, Tom Boyd to Sam Napier, 24 October 1964.

200 PRONI, D/4276, *Tom Boyd Papers*, Tom Boyd to Sam Napier, 24 October 1964.

201 Ibid., Vivian Simpson to Tom Boyd, 6 January 1965.

202 Interview with Douglas McIldoon, 21 January 2004.

203 PRONI, D/3702/C/8, Napier to Gunning, 18 June 1965. Gunning was party chairman in 1965–66.

204 *Belfast Telegraph*, 21 June 1965.

205 Ibid.

206 *Belfast Newsletter*, 21 June 1965.

207 Ibid.

208 See Patterson, Henry, *Ireland Since 1939* (Oxford: Oxford University Press, 2002), p. 189.

209 Purdie, *Politics in the Streets*, p. 72.

210 LPA, GS12/NI, Northern Ireland Documents, 1960–63, Northern Ireland Constitutional Position, 21 February 1962.

211 Milliband, Ralph, *Parliamentary Socialism: A Study in the Politics of Labour* (London: Merlin, 1972).

212 Wilson, Harold, *The Wilson Government, 1964–70: A Personal Record* (Middlesex: Penguin, 1974), p. 140.

213 Ibid., p. 349.

214 See Warner, Geoffrey, 'Putting Pressure on O'Neill: The Wilson Government and Northern Ireland, 1964–69', *Irish Studies Review*, Vol. 13, No. 1 (February 2005), pp. 14–15.

215 PRONI, D/3702/C/1/12, *Sam Napier Papers*.

216 Garland, *Gusty Spence*, p. 45.

217 *The Round Table*, No. 224 (October 1966), p. 406.
218 Walker, *A History of the Ulster Unionist Party*, p. 159.
219 Graham, *The Consensus-Forming Strategy of the Northern Ireland Labour Party*, p. 138; see also the *Belfast Newsletter*, 4 January 1965.
220 Walker, *A History of the Ulster Unionist Party*, p. 139.
221 Bew *et al.*, *Northern Ireland*, pp. 130–1.
222 PRONI, PM/5/9/6, Northern Ireland General Election 25 November 1965, Speech made by O'Neill at Carrickfergus, 22 November 1965.
223 PRONI, PM/5/9/6, Captain O.W.J. Henderson to Captain Terence O'Neill, 27 October 1965.
224 PRONI, PM/5/9/6, Handwritten reply from O'Neill to Henderson, 28 October 1965.
225 PRONI, PM/5/9/6, O'Neill to Henderson, 29 October 1965.
226 Farrell, *Northern Ireland*, p. 229.
227 See Mulholland, *Northern Ireland at the Crossroads*, pp. 20–2.
228 Farrell, *Northern Ireland*, p. 229.
229 See De Baróid, Ciarán, *Ballymurphy and the Irish War* (London: Pluto, 2000).
230 Mulholland, *Northern Ireland at the Crossroads*, p. 32.
231 Ibid.
232 NILP, *Election Manifesto* (1965).
233 Graham, *The Consensus-Forming Strategy of the Northern Ireland Labour Party*, p. 121. The Bill was defeated on its fourth reading on 3 March 1964 by 27 votes to 13. Bill Craig referred to it as 'unworkable and an effort to solicit the Roman Catholic vote'. *Belfast Newsletter*, 4 March 1964.
234 NILP, *Memorandum on Northern Ireland's Future* (1966).
235 PRONI, PM/5/9/6, 'Northern Ireland General Election 25 November 1965', Speech made by O'Neill at Oldpark on Friday 19 November 1965.
236 O'Leary, Cornelius, 'Northern Ireland: The Politics of Illusion', *Political Quarterly*, Vol. 40, No. 3 (July 1969), p. 310.
237 Walker, *A History of the Ulster Unionist Party*, p. 152.
238 Cochrane, 'Meddling at the Crossroads', p. 149.
239 Interview with Bobby Cosgrove, 22 August 2005.
240 Interview with Jim McDonald, 4 May 2005.
241 Interview with Alan Carr, 3 August 2005.
242 Interview with George Chambers, 2 March 2005.
243 Simpson polled a clear majority of 1,989 votes, a reduction of 1,415. Tom Boyd had a tough time too and lost almost 1,000 votes from his 1962 majority of 1,852.
244 Sir John Milne Barbour had held the seat from 1929 until his death in 1951.
245 In 1965 the NILP's S.A. Stewart polled 4,113 votes, while the UUP's R.W.B. McConnell polled 14,491. The turnout in South Antrim was 54.1%. This was the first time the Stormont seat had ever been contested, at least since the abolition of PR in 1929. Elliott, *Northern Ireland Parliamentary Election Results, 1921–1972*, p. 59. David Bleakley lost Belfast, Victoria, by 147 votes and Boyd lost Belfast, Woodvale, by 1,724 votes in the 1965 Stormont Elections. Ibid., pp. 47, 50.
246 PRONI, D/3233/5/5, *Vivian Simpson Papers, Secretary's Report to the EC on the General Election*, March 1966.
247 Ibid.

4

The failure of the 'consensus-forming strategy', 1965–69

> Until the Government of Northern Ireland accepts the fundamental British principle of "one man, one vote" in elections of every kind; until it accepts that the citizens of Northern Ireland are entitled to enjoy equal rights with ... other British citizens; bodies representing Labour and the trade union movement in Northern Ireland will have a positive and over-riding duty to make known their views, and to press for their acceptance by every constitutional means at their disposal.[1]

Introduction: Unionist and Nationalist politics in the 1960s

The collapse of the IRA's armed irredentist campaign in February 1962 led to the cessation of its military activities against the Northern Ireland state. During its six year life-span this half-hearted offensive failed to gain 'any real momentum, or – significantly – any hold on popular Irish Nationalist imagination'.[2] Furthermore the republican threat was met by a stern counter-insurgency drive spearheaded by a resolute Unionist regime which acted swiftly to extract military and financial aid from the British government in order to quell the violence.[3] Moreover, security assessments made available to the Unionist government at the time spoke in terms of the calmness displayed by both communities and contrasted sharply this round of violence with that experienced in the 1920s: the 'life of the community', maintained the RUC, 'remains largely unaffected'.[4] By opting for a purely military campaign the IRA scrapped the option to politicise the wider Nationalist community, a course of action that would throw the organisation into disarray in later years and lead to a split in its ranks by the end of the decade.

By the early 1960s constitutionally-minded Nationalists had been embarrassed by the IRA's campaign and were forced to emerge from their political slumber to meet the calls by many working-class Catholics in Northern Ireland for the reinstatement of socio-economic rights.[5] It was generally recognised that the Nationalist Party's preoccupation with Irish reunification meant that it had neglected more pressing political issues. For most Nationalist politicians outstanding grievances like discrimination needed to be appropriately challenged via the constitutional route: the resort to 'armed struggle' would only serve to dissuade 'the government from radical initiatives and [help] prolong the life of traditional segregational Unionism'.[6] Conversely there were even some tentative signs that more and more Catholics had reconciled themselves to the idea that the Union might not be such a bad thing after all. But the difficulties facing those, like O'Neill, who attempted to accommodate Catholics under the Union, were multiple and included the prejudices of their ethnic-minded colleagues.[7]

Despite such explicit rumblings of discontent within the UUP Terence O'Neill remained undeterred in his quest to prise open the lines of political communication with the Irish Republic. His scheme eventually led to a meeting with the Irish Taoiseach, Sean Lemass, at Stormont in January 1965, reportedly without prior consultation with his cabinet.[8] The aim of the meeting was to discuss areas of 'common interest' and to enhance the rapport between both leaders, which would lead to further all-Ireland consultation and co-operation. A carefully worded joint statement issued shortly after the summit reinforced the point that the talks 'did not touch upon constitutional or political questions' but were focused much more on economic matters.[9] Historians are generally in agreement that O'Neill's rationale for instigating a thaw in the frosty relations between the states, while it certainly freed up inter-governmental diplomacy, was in part a response to the impending economic realities of a European Common Market. Additionally, the fact that the British Exchequer held on tightly to the province's purse strings was not something lost on O'Neill. In contrast to his predecessor O'Neill remained distinctly more circumspect. As Patterson has observed:

> He had ... got more directly involved in relations with Treasury officials than had been the case previously ... In essence it involved a shift away from Brookeborough's emphasis on the North's special circumstances and ad hoc responses to short-term crises of the local economy towards portraying Northern Ireland as a relatively backward region of the UK whose modernisation would contribute to the economic health of the kingdom as a whole.[10]

It could be argued that O'Neill's meeting with Lemass was a set piece in a much more ambitious plan designed to stir Unionism into accepting the economic realities of the Republic's break from autarky. By encouraging the emergence of a more sophisticated political response from Unionists on economics O'Neill was by no means placing inter-community harmonisation at the top of his agenda; instead his rapprochement with Lemass was a gesture made on the basis of sound economic advice which suggested a shift in attitudes among Northern business elites.[11]

Contemporary political observers were decidedly more upbeat, claiming that the gesture showed 'the reality of the political situation as Mr. Lemass's bold declaration for Anglo-Irish free trade was an acknowledgement of the reality of economic independence'.[12] Despite the praise heaped on O'Neill by progressive Unionist allies in the Belfast dailies a residual concern remained within some sections of the Protestant community about his attempted conciliation with the

Republic. Nevertheless within a few months the Ulster Unionist Council voted overwhelmingly in favour of a motion supporting the meeting.[13] One further, direct consequence of O'Neill's diplomatic efforts was Eddie McAteer's visit to Dublin for talks with the Taoiseach and other leading Irish politicians on the question of Nationalist Party acceptance of the Official Opposition whip at Stormont.[14]

However, to those reactionary elements lining themselves up against O'Neill's liberalising agenda the Prime Minister's conciliatory approach represented an imminent threat to the marginal socio-economic advantages they claimed Protestant workers held over their Catholic neighbours. The electoral threat posed by Paisley at this time was perhaps minuscule but his influence on members of the Unionist Parliamentary Party (UPP) should not be underestimated.[15] For David Gordon the 'secrecy surrounding the meeting certainly planted seeds of suspicion and mistrust about his intentions within the Unionist Party and the Protestant community'; it was this factor which hastened the resort to disobedient tactics by some in the UPP.[16] And it was O'Neill's plans to shake-up devolved arrangements – while actively encouraging Nationalist re-engagement in politics – that were to provide grist to the mill for his Paisleyite critics as the decade progressed.[17]

The emergence of civil rights

The tide of conciliation was now beginning to rise behind those who argued that Nationalism should take a more pro-active role in the political life of Northern Ireland. It can be argued with some degree of certainty that Catholics were opting out of tribal political choices and plumping instead for non-Nationalists at election time. Mulholland rather overstates the view that it 'is clear that Catholics were optimistic and happy with the direction in which politics was moving in the 1960s'.[18] The NILP's Organisation Committee chairman, Paddy Devlin, summed up the feelings of many Catholics when he said:

> For the first time in forty years there was a spirit of compromise in the air. People from the two communities were more prepared than ever to live together in harmony, and the old shibboleths that had for so long been sources of division were being closely questioned.[19]

The prior debarment of Catholics from entering the upper echelons of Ulster society undoubtedly contributed to the advent of a reticent mood among the minority community, but this was offset, to a large degree, by the social mobility afforded by favourable welfare state legislation, like, for instance, the Education Act of 1947.[20] In Patterson's view Catholics, as 'Children of the British welfare state ... were less interested in the national question than in the fact that post-war expansion had disproportionately benefited Protestants.'[21]

Although sectarian antagonism had not disappeared altogether, it did begin to dissipate as people became more affluent and moved out of mildly segregated inner-city areas and into new 'mixed' housing estates. Sam McAughtry, an NILP member who held executive rank in the Northern Ireland Civil Service, observed that:

> The reason for it was *work*. Because that's when the multinationals came pouring across here. And they were up and down the roads in the South. And they were in Ballymena and everywhere else ... It was just a wonderful time for the working classes ... But of course, when the multinationals started to do their books and found out that it was cheaper to go to other places, *bingo*, it was a wasteland. Here and in England ... Once that started, the job pressure started once again. We were back where we started.[22]

As Mulholland reminds us, even though Catholics were increasingly abandoning abstentionism and militancy, they still remained largely unwilling to ingratiate themselves with the Unionist bourgeoisie, which they viewed with incessant hostility.[23] It could be said that with the advent of O'Neillism some Catholics were beginning to probe the foundations upon which Unionist power was predicated.

The NILP and the Campaign for Social Justice

By early 1963 radical agenda-centric groupings had begun to spring up in rural areas typically dominated by Unionist local government machinery. The Campaign for Social Justice (CSJ), which grew out of the Dungannon-based Homeless Citizens League, was launched at a press conference in Belfast's Wellington Park Hotel on 17 January 1964,[24] and sought to highlight discrimination 'against the Catholic section'[25] in housing and jobs. Initially it found little time for romantic Nationalist notions of a United Ireland. Instead its emphasis was on practical agitation for change.[26] The rationale of the CSJ was thus: 'we lived in a part of the United Kingdom where the British remit ran, we should seek the ordinary rights of British Citizens which are so obviously denied us'.[27] The argument was strikingly familiar to what had hitherto been advocated by the NILP; the only difference was that while Labour chose to draw attention to such deficiencies in the parliamentary arena the CSJ at first resisted electoral politics and took to the streets.[28] Admittedly its activities attracted the attention of Northern Ireland's security apparatus and by late 1965 regular RUC briefings had begun to appear on O'Neill's desk warning of the CSJ's apparent republican agenda.[29] Retrospectively, the CSJ's co-architect, Conn McCluskey, claimed that its principal objective was to 'collect comprehensive and accurate data on all injustices done against all creeds and political opinions, including details of discrimination in jobs and houses and to bring them to the attention of as many socially minded people as possible'.[30]

The organisation's main programme was designed specifically with a British mainland audience in mind.[31] Yet the Unionist regime misinterpreted the CSJ's aims, confusing these with the kind of United Ireland concessions habitually sought by ardent republicans during the IRA's border campaign. Furthermore, the CSJ not only made Dungannon District Council a target in its campaign to

Failure of the 'consensus-forming strategy', 1965–69

expose the 'discriminatory practices of local government authorities'[32] but all Unionist-dominated local authorities across Northern Ireland. This sort of agitation aroused deep suspicion amongst many rural-based Unionists. Although the publicising of Unionist misdemeanours hardly constituted subversive activity, much of the CSJ's propaganda was invariably bellicose in its narrow focus on 'Catholic grievances'; it failed miserably in its bid to involve rural Protestants from an equally low income bracket who led a similar hand-to-mouth existence west of the Bann.[33]

It was not immediately obvious that the CSJ's agitation on discrimination was in any way incompatible with what Charles Brett and the NILP had been calling for since 1962. We now know, from the expert research undertaken by J.A.V. Graham, that the NILP's local government manifesto *Policy for Progress* (1963) displayed great concern for citizens' rights by advocating 'one man, one vote', the abolition of plural voting and the greater centralisation of education provision, amongst other demands.[34] In fact, if anything, policy documents produced by both organisations seemed suitable bedfellows in the sense that they greatly played up the parity deficit which existed between Westminster and Stormont legislation in terms of the local government franchise.[35] The main difference which existed between the groups, however, was not the principle of reform but the actual tactics to be deployed to combat perceived injustices, whilst implementing a rewarding social reform programme for impoverished communities. It could be argued that the methods used to spearhead a campaign for a return to British democracy made co-operation between the two groups unlikely. Without recourse to Stormont or the legal system Purdie argues that the CSJ's 'last prospect of advance by constitutional means' was eliminated.[36] Moreover, despite the retrospective praise heaped on Jack Hassard[37] and the Dungannon Labour Party by Conn McCluskey in his memoirs, the CSJ saw little profit in collaborating with the indigenous Labour Party and instead turned its attention directly to the BLP and its new leader Harold Wilson.[38]

Wilson's initial correspondence with Conn McCluskey and his wife Pat during his final months as Leader of the Opposition was certainly upbeat and enthusiastic. However Labour's return to power in October 1964 revealed his words to be little more than empty rhetoric designed specifically to erect a self-serving image of a great reformer.[39] Wilson may have had one eye on the descendants of Irish immigrants who made up a large proportion of his Huyton constituency. Later correspondence between Wilson and the McCluskeys is notable for the loss of temper by the latter over Labour's sluggish attitude towards reform.[40] The BLP's refusal to intervene, bemoaned the husband and wife team, 'shows how difficult absence of positive help from the Labour Party is making our attempt to field some anti-Unionist candidates at the next Westminster election'.[41] The Labour government was acutely aware of its position on 'internal Northern Ireland matters' vis-à-vis the Stormont Parliament because of the clauses built into the Government of Ireland Act (1920):

You will know that the legal position is that while the United Kingdom

Government is opposed to all forms of discrimination on religious or other grounds, most of the matters regarding which discrimination is alleged in Northern Ireland fall within the field of responsibility of the Northern Ireland Government.[42]

The tone of this riposte was typical of the bureaucratic replies sent to the McCluskeys at this time.

The fact that the BLP's General Secretary, Len Williams, passed correspondence on to the Home Secretary, who in turn brought his representations to O'Neill, probably sickened the CSJ even further. On the positive side it could be argued that, strategically at least, the Labour Party had been sticking to its guns about keeping Northern Ireland business at arm's length. There is also an implicit indication that not only was Wilson 'dealing personally with a number of Northern Ireland matters' but that he was still keeping track of the NILP's involvement in key civil rights debates at Stormont.[43] On the other hand, despite the provision allocated to the British government under the Government of Ireland Act, it may have chosen to shelter behind the so-called Northern Ireland 'convention' then operating at Westminster. Another point worth considering might also be that which was raised in private correspondence between Williams and Harold Wilson:

> Although Mrs. McCluskey claims that she and her husband are working very hard to have three anti-Tory members returned for Northern Ireland at the next Westminster election we have no evidence that they are co-operating in any constructive way with the Northern Ireland Labour Party.[44]

While Williams's thoughts provide a fairly accurate barometer reading of the frosty relations which existed between the NILP and Nationalist-orientated groups, like the CSJ, his correspondence tells us little about the gravitational pull now under way among the BLP's backbenchers for a more interventionist agenda.

The NILP and the Campaign for Democracy in Ulster

The formation of the backbench Labour Party pressure group the Campaign for Democracy in Ulster (CDU) in 1965 was a direct response to the perceived injustices being meted out to the minority community in Northern Ireland. Among its many objectives it sought to secure a full and impartial enquiry into the administration of local government in the region 'with particular reference to allegations of discrimination on religious or political grounds in the field of housing and employment, and into the continued existence of the Special Powers Act' – an Act which allowed the local administration to arrest and detain without trial those suspected of engaging in terrorist activity – and to 'bring electoral law in Northern Ireland at all levels into line with the rest of the United Kingdom'.[45] According to the CDU's constitution its membership books were open exclusively to individuals, and organisations, which were eligible for membership of the BLP, though as Geoff Bell has shown leading Liberals also flocked to its cause.[46] Its regular meetings were hosted by the Irish Club in

London, as well as in the parliamentary offices of its members in the House of Commons.

From the CDU's inception – until the resignation of Terence O'Neill in April 1969 – it held regular private meetings with the NILP, the CSJ and the Northern Ireland Civil Rights Association (NICRA).[47] Additionally, it organised and headlined large rallies in Hyde Park and Trafalgar Square in London. One of its main functions was to issue strong ultimatums to the Stormont regime on its civil rights record; and it was the major bugbear issue of gerrymandering which incurred the wrath of many CDU members. Most of the CDU's demands sought more than piecemeal change and it was committed to a complete overhaul of the relations between Northern Ireland and Great Britain. For the CDU, British standards of democracy had to apply to all British citizens without distinction.

For Cradden the 'NILP established fairly cordial relations with the CDU, since their ambitions coincided almost precisely';[48] however some important qualifications are needed here. The Queen's University of Belfast Labour Group (QUBLG) was the first NILP branch to request a more formal rapprochement with the CDU in an effort to harness the powerful resources of the British Labour movement for popular anti-Tory purposes. Indeed the first mention of the CDU cropped up in a Queen's Labour Group submission to the NILP's 1967 annual conference. It called on:

> The British Government to institute a public enquiry into allegations of religious discrimination and electoral gerrymandering in Northern Ireland. Conference instructs the Executive Committee to take all possible steps to publicise the Northern Ireland situation and the necessity for such an enquiry in Britain and especially in the British Labour movement. To this end Conference instructs the Executive Committee to support and co-operate closely with the Campaign for Democracy in Ulster.[49]

Yet the NILP's EC appeared reluctant to get too involved in the CDU's activities for a variety of reasons. As Cradden has suggested:

> The party's concerns, as they grew, were not of course about the CDU's agenda, but about the possible effects – certainly as more conservative NILP members saw them – on long-standing NILP voters of the CDU's seeming interference and its apparent siding with Irish Nationalism.[50]

Earlier analysis has concurred with Cradden's point about the attitudes of Protestant NILP supporters towards Wilson; equally it should be recognised that the thinking of some Labour backbenchers was gradually becoming coloured by a green tinge, i.e. an Irish Nationalist bias.

An important illustration of the frosty relations between the organisations can be found in the inaugural NILP–CDU meeting on 2 August 1967, when the latter's secretary Paddy Byrne met the former's Executive at its Waring Street offices in Belfast. Byrne did not attempt to hide his exasperation in his subsequent report at the discourteous attitude of NILP party officers towards him. Moreover, it seems that the NILP wanted the CDU to take a more pro-Ulster approach in its criticisms of Unionist rule and to desist from 'always indulging in carping criticism'. In the party's opinion the CDU should be above all 'friends of Ulster'. The loaded comparison with the 'Friends of Ireland' (the perceived precursor to the CDU) is difficult to downplay.[51] Nevertheless, the NILP Executive thought that the backbench pressure group could press for a 'fair shares for Ulster' scheme at Westminster which would benefit the region in terms of factory allocation. 'Ulster is a depressed area, like parts of Scotland or Wales, and should get, as part of the United Kingdom, a fairer share of any relief measures that are going.'[52]

The NILP's commitment to regionalism was much in evidence during this meeting, as too was its reprimand that the CDU 'must not appear to be attacking the constitutional position'.[53] On this occasion the NILP's cautious pro-Unionist attitude inevitably jarred with the ambitions of openly anti-partitionist elements within the BLP. However, the party's tentative reproach should not to be confused with inertia; nor should it be reduced to simply a clash of personalities.[54] An NILP statement, published in the CDU's newsletter in October 1967, revealed the party's policy on discrimination to be beyond question:

> The Northern Ireland Labour Party has always been opposed to discrimination on religious and political grounds and particularly since 1959 has included statements against such discrimination in all its policy proposals ... Resolutions opposing discrimination have been adopted by successive Annual Party Conferences and Northern Ireland Labour Members of Parliament have both sponsored and supported anti-discrimination legislation in the Northern Ireland Parliament.[55]

The fact was indisputable. Inside and outside parliament the NILP was exposing the glaring disparities in the minority's dubious socio-political and economic position.

The election of Gerry Fitt in 1966 magnified the issues of gerrymandering and discrimination even further. Fitt's involvement in civil rights marches meant that he could draw attention to the injustices in a more high-profile manner than the NILP, which had no MPs returned to Westminster. Dixon's observation is telling:

> The establishment of the CDU, not to mention the CSJ, represented a firm challenge to the influence of the NILP on the British Labour Party. Unlike the NILP, the CDU had MPs at Westminster to lobby for it within the Labour Party, and was close at hand to give guidance.[56]

At a time when Wilson was making moves to curb the voting rights of the solid bloc of Unionists who traditionally sided tactically, if not ideologically, with their Conservative allies, Fitt's election represented a welcome addition to the BLP's backbenches.[57] However, it would be wrong, as Rose points out, to claim that Fitt's return to Westminster brought the Irish question firmly back onto the British agenda: 'While Fitt galvanised the CDU and raised the profile of Northern Ireland in mainland Britain,' writes Rose, 'there is no evidence that Wilson's policy of non-intervention in the province was affected.'[58] Nevertheless Fitt was instrumental in organising a key fact-finding mission for three CDU MPs (Paul Rose, Maurice Miller and Stan Orme) in April 1967. The delegation 'met the executive of the NILP, shop stewards from Harland and Wolff, the officers of the Belfast trades council, the CSJ, and representatives of the Ulster Liberal Party, the Derry branch of the NILP, the RLP, and the NDP'.[59] The visit raised eyebrows among many NILP members who saw Fitt's influence growing steadily among Labour's backbenches.[60]

Invariably the close relationship between the CSJ and CDU was compromised by the presence of right-of-centre individuals involved in the Dungannon-based organisation. In 1967 Conn McCluskey wrote to Byrne to formally turn down an open invitation for him to attend the 1967 Labour Party conference because, he claimed, the CSJ's membership was essentially 'non-political, indeed one or two are right-wing, so if it became known that we were attending what is essentially a Labour enclave unfavourable comment might occur'.[61] The uneasy coalition of people from across the political spectrum which made up the bulk of the CSJ's membership is revealing because, even though it presented itself as a progressive social force, catering for a broad base of deprived Catholic support, most of its membership remained avowedly conservative Catholic Nationalists. Even more surprising perhaps is the attitude adopted by the Labour government towards Nationalist-based civil rights groupings in the wake of Wilson's return to power with an increased majority in 1966. In a letter to Paddy Byrne, Patricia McCluskey asked, 'Why has the National Executive of the BLP up till now, not included any resolutions on Northern Ireland on the final Agenda at Party Conference?'[62] Her hopes that the CDU could influence a radical new departure in BLP policy towards Ulster were further dashed when such demands were repeatedly turned down flat by Wilson's private secretary because such matters affecting the province quite clearly came under the remit of the Stormont government.[63]

The next available opportunity for the CSJ to raise the hardy annual of discrimination came in early October 1968 at the BLP conference in Blackpool. Between 1964 and 1968 thousands of CSJ newsletters had been circulated at Labour Party conferences drawing attention to the plight of the Catholic minority. By 1968 the CSJ recognised that even though incremental changes were now under way, 'the suspension of Londonderry City Council, while an improvement on control by a Unionist majority, is no substitute for ordinary, democratic rule, according to standards ruling in Britain'.[64] It was clear that calls for Wilson and his cabinet to take a firm grip on the Stormont government were falling largely on deaf ears.

There has been much debate among historians over the intentions of the Labour government at this time. As argued above it was initially concerned with prompting the Unionist regime into introducing reforms without having to resort to the imposition of sanctions. Patterson points to the reliance by Wilson and Jenkins 'on the advice of senior Home Office officials traditionally sympathetic to the Stormont Government' to explain the absence of confrontation on discrimination allegations.[65] However, if Warner's interpretation of recently released evidence is to be accepted (and there are strong reasons to do so) then we should perhaps view the British government as exerting increasing pressure on O'Neill from 1966 when Wilson was returned on an increased mandate.[66] In private correspondence between the BLP's general secretary, Harry Nicholas, and grass-roots activists it was commonly reiterated that the party in government would 'continue to keep a close watch on events in Northern Ireland'.[67] Nevertheless the fact remained that parliamentary 'convention' at the time prevented any discussion of Northern Ireland affairs from being aired. In 1965 when one Labour MP attempted to raise the issue of Northern Ireland in the House he was overruled by the deputy speaker.[68]

Warner is the latest historian to query Wilson's supposed favouritism of O'Neill's reform programme in the late 1960s. Although his argument is grounded in the idiosyncratic nature of inter-governmental dialogue between Whitehall and Stormont during Wilson's first and second terms in office, he does offer a more nuanced interpretation of Rose's earlier conjecture about Wilson's insulationist approach.[69] Perhaps more importantly he uncovered contravening evidence to suggest that the British government had not only formulated contingency plans in the event of having to deploy troops in support of the civil power, but also assessed the prospects in the event of Stormont's dissolution and the imposition of direct rule.[70] Interestingly, Warner reminds us that the 'Wilson government was forced to take a tougher line'[71] towards Northern Ireland only after the events of 5 October 1968 in Derry. He accepts the view that prior to 1968 the Labour government abdicated its responsibilities in relation to Northern Ireland because of the isolationist gloss provided by *Government of Ireland* legislation.[72] Although Warner does not alert us to it, O'Neill had been using the NILP's trumpeting of its fraternal relationship with the BLP to twist the knife into the body of the party's local Protestant working-class electoral core. Matters were not helped by Wilson's tendency to parade his anti-partitionist sympathies in public. Thus, right-wing Unionists could taint British socialism with a communist *and* a republican brush. McCarthyism had its converts in Ulster too – most obviously in the form of Ian Paisley – who spearheaded attacks on popery and godless communism with equal venom.

The NILP and citizens' rights

The publication of *Electoral Reform Now* (1965) represented the culmination of over three years' consistent lobbying by the NILP on the issues of electoral malpractice and discrimination in jobs and housing. The central argument of this document was unambiguous:

> It is time the Unionist Government, which glories in the fact that Ulster is British, accorded to British citizens in Northern Ireland the common democracy which they receive as of right in all other parts of the United Kingdom. There are a number of respects in which the present law is thoroughly objectionable.[73]

The party returned to a theme it had consistently lobbied over since the early 1950s, when it called for 'British Rights for British Citizens'. NILP attempts to

Failure of the 'consensus-forming strategy', 1965–69

play up the 'parity' issue were continually hamstrung by the Unionist regime which introduced social welfare legislation on a 'step-by-step' basis. These benefits were considered the inalienable rights of citizens of Northern Ireland regardless of their religious convictions or constitutional orientation. One high-profile activist at the time, Erskine Holmes, gave his retrospective view of the party's political objectives at this time:

> The Northern Ireland Labour Party had obviously on an intellectual basis arrived at a policy document – well in advance of the Northern Ireland Civil Rights Association – which articulated the campaign issues relating to civil rights in Northern Ireland about the need to have the electoral system brought up to date with UK standards and issues about allocating housing on points [and so on].[74]

Significantly, the NILP had already turned its attention to explicit discussion of civil liberties in several of its election manifestos. *Ulster Labour and the Sixties* (1962) was explicit in its attacks of the sectarian *realpolitik* underpinning Ulster's politics:

> For forty years the Unionists and Nationalists have based their appeal to the electorate on the border issue, thereby distracting attention from their failures in the economic field. Their method of doing so has encouraged the survival of sectarian bitterness, and has discouraged the creation of a more unified community and a friendlier co-operation between Protestant and Roman Catholic. Even in the Sixties the Unionist Party, by refusing to accept Roman Catholics as members (with the inescapable inference that it considers them untrustworthy citizens) has aroused new, and justified, resentment.[75]

In its Westminster election manifesto two years later, *Signposts to the New Ulster* (1964), the party again challenged electoral malpractice and religious discrimination. The main thrust of its political discourse may have been on 'bread and butter' issues but the party was not beyond plugging away 'at many of the issues that were taken up by the civil rights movement'.[76]

NILP policy documents such as *Electoral Reform Now* and *Citizens' Rights* (1966–67) poured scorn on the malformed sectarian underbelly of the local state. *Electoral Reform Now* outlined in great detail the party's calls for the revision of parliamentary boundaries (which had been left unchanged since the early 1930s when corresponding legislation was passed to amend those in Great Britain) and for future local authority elections to be based on the principle of 'one man, one vote'. In December 1967 the NILP – together with the ICTU – made a representation to the Northern Ireland government on the cardinal issue of citizens' rights. The cross-community delegation from the NILP comprised party leader Tom Boyd and leading party officers Charles Brett, Erskine Holmes, Michael Farrell and Paddy Devlin. Their ultimatum was telling:

> Until the Government of Northern Ireland accepts the fundamental British principle of 'one man, one vote' in elections of every kind; until it accepts that the citizens of Northern Ireland are entitled to enjoy equal rights with ... other British citizens; bodies representing Labour and the Trade Union Movement in Northern Ireland

will have a positive and over-riding duty to make known their views, and to press for their acceptance by every constitutional means at their disposal.[77]

Holmes revealed how O'Neill approached the Labour delegation and claimed that he would have instigated reforms had it not been 'for that man up there', gesticulating in the general direction of the Minister for Home Affairs Bill Craig.[78] He thought that, in many ways, O'Neill was a prisoner of his own cabinet and was prevented from acting on his liberal instincts because of the tight leash placed around him by his colleagues.[79] The critique presented by the joint delegation was publicly rebuked by O'Neill, and the NILP resolved to make direct overtures to the British Labour government.[80]

It is difficult to disconnect party policy at this time from the forceful personality of chief scribe Charles Brett.[81] In April 1963, during his outgoing speech as NILP chairman, Brett made clear his wish for the party to pursue a more liberal and inclusive agenda by challenging those politicians who fermented socio-economic stagnation among the working classes to rethink their narrow political vision:

> In the past ten years, Labour has fought elections in Protestant seats with Protestant candidates, but its beliefs and reputation for integrity have earned us much Catholic support. The first and paramount battle has been with the Unionists, the party in power representing what I might perhaps call the Protestant vested interests. I believe that the time has come when we must challenge the Catholic vested interests as well as the Protestant ones.[82]

In light of his sterling superintendence of the party through the consolidation of its initial victories over the previous 12 months Brett was re-confirmed as head of the party's Policy Sub-Committee and given further creative licence to pursue his behind-the-scenes social justice interests. Brett's involvement in strategising can be traced to his early years in the NILP when Napier and other leading figures recognised that he could usefully 'turn a phrase', having just served an apprenticeship in journalism in continental Europe.[83] He had been much influenced by the radical leftist ideas gripping the imaginations of countless young intellectuals in the immediate post-war period, and in many ways Brett shared personality traits with other privileged liberals, turned socialist activists, like the former British Labour leader Clement Attlee.[84]

In many respects Brett's political involvement played second fiddle to his more venerable full-time employment in his family's long-established law practice in Belfast. Brett's promise to his father, who remained concerned at the prospect of his son's political activism, was that he would not run for public office; a promise he was to keep until his eventual resignation from the NILP Executive in 1969.[85] Yet it would be wrong to suggest that Brett was totally confined to the backrooms of Labour headquarters. On sporadic occasions he was to engage in street-level canvassing and often spoke on behalf of NILP candidates. Contrary to Graham's characterisation of him as a 'party ideologue', the task of drafting policy documents did not absolve him of the 'more down-to-earth obligations of party membership'.[86]

Failure of the 'consensus-forming strategy', 1965–69   129

Like his parliamentary colleagues Brett also exuded charm and charisma. His intellectual reach extended into the realm of public relations and he made frequent appearances on television talk shows, spoke regularly on radio programmes and contributed numerous articles to newspapers. Unlike the four Labour MPs, though, he lacked the colourful Belfast vernacular spoken by the NILP's working-class constituents. In many respects his accent clearly reflected his bourgeois upbringing. Although not at all ill at ease with working people, he undoubtedly represented the middle-class intellectuals who had been drawn to the party in the 1950s. And his metropolitan liberal demeanour and pronounced atheism made him popular with many of those Catholic-born radicals who had found a political home in Labour. As Paul Arthur recalls:

> One of the influences that made me join the NILP was actually watching Charles Brett on local radio and television programmes. I just found him very impressive. And I found him urbane. And I said that if we are going to move out of our sectarian politics it's going to be people like him [who will lead us]. I saw Labour as an opportunity to move away from sectarianism, both Green and Orange, and I was very influenced by that.[87]

Brett's conciliatory moves towards the Catholic minority were above all sincere and well placed. Nevertheless he continued to view organised religion with disdain. In one visit to the Roman Catholic Bishop of Down and Connor, Dr William J. Philbin, in 1963, Brett used the occasion 'to convey to him the message that not all non-Catholics were bigots; that there existed a non-sectarian party with much sympathy for Catholic grievances against the Unionist State; and that the time was ripe for a coming-together of reasonable and civilised Ulstermen of both traditions'.[88]

In a series of articles he penned for the *Manchester Guardian* in March 1964[89] Brett set out his position on discrimination and wrestled directly with the prevailing sectarian social, cultural and political 'norms' in Ulster society. It was not empty criticism for he rebuked discrimination and saw it as abhorrent, something to be condemned. Brett's critique of clerical Catholic influence is in evidence throughout his first article. Moreover, his synopsis of the socialisation of segregation is startling. It is surely misguided then to claim that the NILP steered away from attacking Catholic- or Protestant-vested interests, as some commentators have presumed.[90] In terms of local government appointments both Unionists and Nationalists were lambasted for their tolerance of an anachronistic patronage system:

> The difficulties in the way of effective legislation are tremendous. A widespread change of attitude could be brought about only if the Unionist, Protestant, Nationalist and Catholic leaders were all to appeal to employers throughout Ulster to make appointments on grounds of merit alone.[91]

Brett also targeted the local government franchise system, which he found antiquated. The fact that most leeway was given to those who were fortunate to own business property represented a weighting of the entire system in favour of the prosperous few and against the working-class many – irrespective of religion.

What can be extrapolated beyond Brett's run of articles is his personal angst towards the segregationist nature of Northern Ireland society and political culture. His analysis focuses on religious incommensurability as it existed between Catholics and Protestants, though Brett was writing at a time when ecumenicalism had begun to break down orthodox barriers between the two communities. The Second Vatican Council (1962–65) made profound concessions in this regard by recognising the existence – if not the legitimacy – of other faiths. The impact of this on mainstream religious preaching was in many ways positive but there were still those, like the leader of the Free Presbyterian Church, Ian Paisley, who continued to protest virulently against attempts by the main churches to reconcile their differences.

Paisleyite attacks on community relations proposals tabled at the so-called 'Orange–Green talks' in August 1962 were unrelenting; though both sides, it seemed, appeared more focused on stalling discussions over outstanding national identity issues than grappling with practical suggestions for improving the lot of the working classes. Brett was scathing. 'Both Nationalists and Unionists are now under the control of their own extremists,' he said; 'either the moderates have not the power or they have not the courage to bring about any change in the traditional attitudes!'[92] Even calls by the Minister for Home Affairs, Bill Craig, for those with influence to discourage discrimination, failed to wash with Brett. Not in the main because they may have been hollow, but because they were empty words in the absence of Unionist government action – action, not rhetoric, was the watchword for the NILP's critique of O'Neillism.[93]

While it could be said that Brett was less of a utopian visionary and more of a political pragmatist, his challenge to the Unionist Party was not without its consequences. Brett's agitation for a switch in focus towards the needs of the Catholic community, to a large degree put an immediate strain on sitting Woodvale MP Billy Boyd, who was becoming increasingly more susceptible to grass-roots Protestant populism. Brett's publicised attendance at the London conference of the National Council for Civil Liberties (NCCL) in 1965 established him as the NILP's principal speaker on civil rights issues. Indeed, on that occasion Brett called for a cross-community tribunal to be appointed to investigate housing and employment allegations.[94] Yet to Labour activists at the working-class coalface a hardening in attitudes was now detectable. Robert Bingham, a former EC member and NILP councillor in Castlereagh during the 1960s, explains:

> The kind of Protestant–Catholic thing was beginning to rear its head. David Bleakley losing Victoria was disgraceful in the sense that he had been a very very good MP. I may not have agreed with him on policy and that kind of thing, in a Labour sense, but one could not have disagreed with his service as a Member of Parliament. And yet there was something around there that he lost his seat. The two who held on were Tom Boyd and Vivian Simpson. And that again goes back to the 50:50 Protestant–Catholic thing. So I think that the thing of losing seats was the slippery slope.[95]

One could certainly make the argument that Brett was unhindered in his attempts to reconcile Labour to the Catholic working class because he had little

Failure of the 'consensus-forming strategy', 1965–69   131

political capital to lose; in other words he never sought nomination or election for public office and therefore did not depend on a particular local constituency base to install him in the party's hierarchy. With this diminished lack of responsibility Brett was jeopardising little in pushing a liberal agenda.

'Step by step with Labour Britain'

By 1966 heightened tensions had returned to the streets of Northern Ireland after nearly two years of détente. The pending Golden Jubilee celebrations of the Easter Rising transmitted confusing signals to many Protestants. Additionally the British government's decision to return the bones of Roger Casement – together with the tricolour which had been unfurled above the Dublin GPO during the 1916 rebellion – left Unionists aghast.[96] The capture in Dublin of a secret IRA plan detailing the IRA's inventory and likely strategy in the event of an attack by loyalists or state forces on Easter Rising commemorations further alarmed Ulster Unionists.[97] Although the plan was essentially a paper exercise (penned principally by the militarist Sean Garland) it did contain comprehensive details of an IRA scheme designed to infiltrate trade unions and other pressure groups and to agitate on a socio-economic basis.[98] For now political ends were to be pursued by political means and this meant getting out the vote for republican candidates in the March 1966 British general election. Five republican candidates contested the election, including Tom Mitchell who came extremely close (by 2,560 votes) to winning Mid-Ulster.[99]

The NILP also polled extremely well in the March election, considering it only contested four out of the 12 Westminster constituencies. In the previous election in 1964 the party fielded an impressive 10 candidates in 12 constituencies. This time round the party contested North, South and East Belfast and South Antrim. In a private communiqué to the BLP's Chief Whip, Vivian Simpson proudly reported the good news: 'four seats secured 72,620 votes and by doing so ... reduced the Unionist majorities by 31,362 over the four'.[100] Yet the party made perhaps its biggest tactical faux pas by allowing the West Belfast Federation (incorporating Woodvale, Shankill and Falls) to stand aside, thereby facilitating Gerry Fitt's triumphant return to Westminster. Rather than risk splitting the vote three or four ways the NILP resolved to back Fitt's campaign to unseat the UUP's Jim Kilfedder.[101] Although Fitt's election had been fought on the basis of securing greater social justice for the Belfast working class, his narrow Connollyite stance sat incongruously with the non-sectarian programme advocated by the NILP. Simpson warned his opposite number:

> It may be that the new Republican Labour Member for West Belfast – Mr. Gerald Fitt – will be in touch with you regarding taking the Labour Whip at Westminster. We would esteem it a favour if you would discuss this matter with us before any decisions are taken. It could involve both sides in some considerable difficulties.[102]

It is unclear from Simpson's letter whether the 'difficulties' he referred to would have become more pronounced had Fitt been appointed to the post. What is clear from the available evidence is that some NILP activists clearly had reservations about what Graham Walker has rather harshly called Fitt's 'Catholic tribalism'.[103]

Elsewhere Sydney Stewart, the 28-year-old teacher from Lisburn and the youngest candidate in the election,[104] once again contested South Antrim and confidently increased his share of the vote. As his election agent confirmed:

> It was the third or fourth largest swing in the United Kingdom. It was about an eight and a half per cent swing, which in those days was regarded as a very large swing. And it was a very enjoyable election, I must say, because we got the vote out well.[105]

Stewart polled an impressive 22,679 (35.70%) votes – an improvement of 6,148 votes on his 1964 total – in an election which not only witnessed the ebbing away of the huge majority held by the UUP but also the political retreat of republicanism in South Antrim.[106] In North Belfast David Overend challenged the Unionist solicitor Stratton Mills for his seat and polled a respectable 19,927 (42.56%) votes: Mills won 26,891 (57.44%) votes – a battered majority of 6,964.[107] Disappointingly for some activists the NILP found it difficult to connect to the broader working-class constituency in the north of the city. One activist remembers how:

> We had an MP in North Belfast – Stratton Mills. If you wanted Stratton Mills you would have had to go to the Bahamas or somewhere to see him. But I mean that was the type of person people voted in. That's what you were up against.[108]

Despite the rumblings of sectarian discontent in Belfast the results showed that a sizeable majority of people were still willing to vote on 'bread and butter' issues.

However, the electoral results disguise the profound angst which the Easter Rising commemorations stirred up among the Protestant grass-roots. The rejuvenation of the Ulster Volunteer Force (UVF) in late 1965 brought the promise of further militancy; sporadic attacks against Catholic residences in South East Antrim and West Belfast quickly followed.[109] Yet it was the mortal wounding of John Scullion, the firebombing of the home of Matilda Gould and the slaying of Peter Ward in Malvern Street in the Summer of 1966 which brought the organisation most notoriety in the public mind.[110] Following the Malvern Street shootings Tom Boyd and Vivian Simpson met with the secretary to the cabinet, Harold Black, to express their reservations at what had taken place. They issued a joint statement urging the '100,000 electors' they represented to 'co-operate with all those striving to bring about improved relationships'.[111]

The UVF was a small but vicious organisation. Initially raised by middle-class Unionists,[112] it served two interlocking purposes: as a clandestine praetorian guard reconstituted to meet the perceived threat of IRA violence over the Easter Rising commemorations and as a tool to bring down O'Neill.[113] The fear of a resurgent IRA campaign was played upon by Paisley, who was intimately involved in fuelling many hard-line attitudes harboured by those loyalists who took up arms at the time.[114] In an emergency meeting between the Northern

Ireland cabinet, the Inspector General of the RUC and the British Army's General Officer Commanding (GOC), recent UVF violence was considered to have been a short-lived rupture in otherwise good inter-community relations.[115] Conversely, they were wary about advocating a heavy-handed policing approach against the extremists because it would only serve to 'give the outside world an exaggerated impression of the situation in Northern Ireland, by suggesting that it had been necessary to impose something close to Martial Law'.[116] Despite the Unionist government's feeble attempts to create the impression that tranquility reigned in inter-community relations 'the killings sent a tremor through Northern Ireland. It was a clear and ugly manifestation of the often respectable sectarianism that flowed through the veins of Protestant society.'[117] By their brinkmanship both the IRA and the UVF exposed the shadowy subculture of violence that existed, albeit bridled, in Ulster. It is difficult to picture a more discouraging set of circumstances in which the emerging civil rights agenda could thrive.

This was a difficult time for Labour and for many non-Unionists who had pointed towards a future free from Unionist Party rule. Moreover, the NILP's close ties to the BLP were used by O'Neill as a stick with which to beat the local party in the 1966 election.[118] Yet there is little evidence to suggest that it had any great impact on the NILP's morale because, as Brett pointed out, 'we saw every advantage for the party and the people of Northern Ireland to be closely aligned with GB and the British Labour Party'.[119] Brett's sentiment was shared by many rank-and-file members. Evidence of this support can be found if we examine the resolutions submitted and passed by both the 1965 and 1966 NILP conferences which called for more intimate relations with the BLP. Bleakley's Victoria branch was the most vocal in this respect.

In contrast Michael Farrell's QUBLG called for the convening of a Council of Labour in Ireland,[120] 'in co-operation with the Irish Labour Party and the Irish Congress of Trade Unions', with the option to consult British Labour left open-ended.[121] Regular trilateral meetings between the IrLP, NILP and BLP, it was thought, would facilitate an enhanced archipelagic-wide strengthening of North–South and East–West relationships. Initially, correspondence between the IrLP and NILP in 1966 was amiable and sought to enhance discussion on 'matters of mutual interest'.[122] Economic and social co-operation between both parts of Ireland was the broader framework within which the IrLP's leader Brendan Corish chose to frame his party's approach.[123] The decision was affirmed at the IrLP's annual conference in October 1966 by 187 votes to four.[124] Both wings of the Northern Labour movement (including the ETU and NUSWC trade unions and the Oldpark, Newry, Shankill and Clifton Labour Parties) supported the motion[125] and it was passed unanimously at conference.[126] The envisioned framework would serve to add much-needed pluralism to the cause of Labour in Northern Ireland and appeal more conceivably across the ethno-religious divide by accommodating those with differing pro-Irish and pro-British aspirations. This might have worked well in theory but it showed little appreciation of political realities.

Since Fitt's election in 1966 relations between Republican Labour and the NILP had deteriorated. Conversely, it was made expressly clear in joint meetings of the NILP and IrLP that partition would not be on the agenda. Moreover the IrLP had obviously pushed the idea of the Council of Labour as an 'alliance' of parties (that would include the RLP) but this was rejected outright by the NILP's conference which set the strict parameters within which discussions could take place.[127] The inclusion of the RLP on the Council of Labour was a move guaranteed to raise further questions from pro-Ulster British ranks in the NILP.[128] In reality trade union organisation in the South 'operated within a self-sufficient and protected economy'[129] and Fianna Fail had successfully incorporated much Labour support into its hegemonic domination of that state's political culture, squeezing out IrLP support in the few industrial districts. In addition, the Council of Labour idea coincided with half-hearted moves by the IrLP to formalise links with the ICTU: however, as Gallagher notes, 'little had been either attempted or achieved'.[130]

On 27 April 1967 the PLP met with its comrades from the party's ruling EC at Stormont to endorse the conference's decision to set up a Council of Labour in Ireland.[131] The previous month an NILP delegation had met IrLP TDs (Dáil members) on 23 March in Leinster House.[132] However, the decision to include the BLP in the proposed framework allayed fears that it would lead to electoral pacts or agreements of any kind.[133] As the year progressed the reality of Fitt's popularity finally began to sink in, thus weakening NILP enthusiasm for the deal. Farrell's speech to the Irish Association of Labour Students' Organisation (IALSO) saw him publicly bemoan the fragmentation of Labour in Ulster whilst also recognising the potential for growth in Republican Labour.[134] His hope that the proposed arrangement would 'eradicate the legacies of the past' by fusing the NILP rank-and-file with 'the more radical attitudes and policies of Republican Labour' won him few plaudits from Billy Boyd and David Bleakley, who had both been returned to the EC at conference. With a change-over in its leadership the NILP's enthusiasm for implementing a working Council of Labour waned. Privately, those representing Protestant districts would have been wary of cutting their losses with a firmly pro-Unionist support-base and plumping instead for a retrogressive step towards an Irish Republic, especially with Fitt as figurehead.

Although the party remained firm in its commitment to maintain the constitutional position of Northern Ireland as long as the majority wished it, there was considerable leeway within its democratic structures to tolerate differing views on the future of the border. In many respects this was also due to the fact that many of the anti-partitionist members who had previously crossed over from the IrLP in the late 1950s were now accommodated by the NILP. Such flexibility partially explains why Paddy Devlin could quite happily sit on the NILP's EC (1963–69) while privately harbouring anti-partitionist aspirations. The management of these incommensurable national identity aspirations was vital for the maintenance of party discipline. With the onset of sectarian tensions in 1966 and the radicalisation of many younger members of the party who became radicalised by 'green' Marxist influences, the fragility of the NILP's centrist position became apparent. Militants like Farrell and others with a penchant for radical Trotskyite Marxism used their affiliations to the Young Socialist Alliance (YSA), the IALSO and the Irish Workers' Group (IWG) 'to move the NILP in a leftward and anti-partitionist direction'.[135] By attacking his party in 1967 for 'parading their "Loyalty"',[136] as well as trumpeting the merits of Irish republicanism, Farrell paved the way for his own expulsion.

The NILP and the Northern Ireland Civil Rights Association

The Northern Ireland Civil Rights Association (NICRA) was formed in Belfast on 1 February 1967. It originated from a meeting of the Wolfe Tone Society in the house of a leading republican in Maghera in August 1966.[137] By January 1967 a draft constitution had formally brought the organisation into existence and made provision for the formation of an Executive. Among those elected to this body was NILP stalwart Paddy Devlin.[138] NICRA's initial objectives were to lobby for the reinstatement of individual rights and freedoms where abuses of power occurred. According to Bob Purdie, however, these objectives 'said nothing about concrete grievances over discrimination in housing, employment and the electoral franchise'.[139] Despite its republican origins NICRA did not pose a militant threat. That said, as the organisation grew so too did its supporters' expectations for reform. Following the reconstitution of the organisation in 1968 it made key demands for reform in local government franchise, the redrawing of electoral boundaries, anti-discrimination legislation, a compulsory points system for housing, the disbanding of the Ulster Special Constabulary and the termination of the Special Powers Act.[140] By the Summer NICRA's leadership was open to proposals for protest action.[141]

Purdie has contended that it is important to draw an important distinction between the civil rights movement before 5 October 1968 and the mass civil disobedience-led organisation which emerged out of the violence of that day.[142] Those operating under the NICRA umbrella before 5 October 1968 were a diverse coalition of pressure groups and oppositional political parties. Although they may not have necessarily been controlled by an IRA conspiracy, the general perception of broad sections of grass-roots Protestants in the late 1960s was that the civil rights movement was motivated by the imperative to reinstate 'civil rights for Catholics'.[143] This view is supported, to an extent, by some historians of the period, who argue that 'NICRA underestimated the problems which its slight republican taint would cause'.[144] In the eyes of many Protestants NICRA's republican taint was anything but 'slight'. Even opinion among many liberal socialists was divided over whether the association's methodology of civil disobedience placed in jeopardy the fragile cross-cutting cleavage underpinning the NILP's goal of creating an inclusive socio-political culture in which respect for human rights reigned supreme.

It could be strongly argued that some leading NILP members had alr empted the unfurling of a civil rights banner. Apart from the oc journalism of Charles Brett and NILP documents like *Electoral Reform Now*, resolutions on human rights had been habitually appearing on party conference agendas since the late 1950s. This new wave of civil rights protest opened the floodgates for more explicit calls for intervention by non-Unionists. In the words of the Falls Labour Party, for instance:

> this conference expresses the view that the issue of Human Rights in Northern Ireland is the most important political question to be solved by this Party today. Thus, it recognises that, where common ground exists, co-operation with other political parties in an all-out drive to bring about these urgent social and political reforms is necessary.[145]

Human Rights legislation had been constantly scrutinised by the NILP's parliamentary team over the preceding nine years. Yet outside of parliament the NILP confined its calls for action to seeking rectification on anomalies through the vehicle of the Northern Ireland branch of the Society of Labour Lawyers, a London-based organisation affiliated to the party.

In 1968 the Society published perhaps one of the most socially progressive documents to emanate from Labour ranks since the publication of *Citizens' Rights* in 1966. *Discrimination: Pride or Prejudice* (1968) was a remarkable example of what legalistic prowess could deliver. One of its principal authors, Brian Garrett, recalls:

> We didn't have parity in relation to local government. We didn't ... have parity in relation to trade union rights; we didn't have parity in a variety of other areas. What we did have parity in (I suppose) was in relation to social security issues where Northern Ireland was on a par with the rest of the UK.[146]

The NILP membership placed its collective trust in its politicians to spearhead political opposition to Unionist conservativism. Its calls for reform of these outstanding socio-economic grievances placed it in the vanguard of citizens' rights as a means of accomplishing its stated objectives of full 'British rights for British citizens'.[147]

Senior liberal-leaning individuals within the NILP were broadly supportive of the decision by Falls to become more involved in civil rights agitation. In a speech to Falls members at the newly opened Labour Club in Waring Street in May 1968 Garrett attacked the Nationalist Party for its failure to oppose the UUP on behalf of its constituents – a large proportion of whom were the very rural Catholics who had been hit hardest by social injustices.[148] Garrett claimed that 'People of all persuasions in Northern Ireland must be asked "Do you want an opposition that can be an alternative to the present Unionist Party?"' He asserted that 'for people to find their way out of the straightjacket they must vote Labour'. It was the NILP which would legislate to ensure freedom of choice in housing and education.[149] Perhaps he was mindful of his audience on this occasion but there can be no doubting the prescience of debate and discussion over the civil rights issue within the NILP at this time. By the end of the year Paddy Devlin tabled a newly formulated civil rights motion at branch level:

Failure of the 'consensus-forming strategy', 1965–69

> That this conference commits itself to full support for the programme of civil rights as expressed by the Civil Rights Association and that individual members of the Labour Party should support the civil rights movement and their activities.[150]

The motion was seconded by the NILP's newest councillor in Falls, Harry Donaghy, and agreed by the remainder of attending members. It was clear that NICRA had now bedded down firm roots in Catholic working-class areas.[151]

Yet by and large the party remained cautious of this new mass movement. As argued below, NILP grandees had forecast the potential for civil disobedience just as their predecessors had done in the 1930s. Indeed, the first civil rights protest march which left Coalisland for Dungannon on 24 August 1968 effectively announced NICRA as an activist-led organisation in which strategic policy dictated little of the actual physical action unfolding on the streets. Erskine Homes, who sat on both the NICRA and NILP Executives in the late 1960s, recalls how the Dungannon march was called specifically:

> to highlight some of the issues there, for example, housing, education and employment. So that particular march was one that was discussed by the NILP Executive and it was proposed – possibly by me – that we agree to take part in it and we would provide a speaker for the platform. I was the speaker.[152]

In any event the rally was halted by the police and a meeting took place illegally. The march organisers thought that 'there was great potential for pressure on the Unionists to recognise this emerging tactic, similar to marches in the USA, or CND'.[153] The Dungannon march is important because it set the precedent for future protests by drawing loyalist counter-demonstrators and the state's law enforcement agencies into the frame. The potential for violence was troubling for the NILP.

Constitutional politics and civil disobedience

Charles Brett's admission that the NILP found itself marginalised by its commitment to the democratic process is an argument couched in a lawyer's intuition about what constitutes lawful and unlawful activity.[154] For many of those congregated under the NICRA umbrella there was no such contradiction in their actions. The call to escalate the marching tactic was being openly advocated by many civil rights leaders from August 1968 because of what they perceived to be the futile and unimaginative implementation of reforms by the Unionist government. Brendan Mackin was a leading member of the Falls Labour Party when that local branch first proposed NILP involvement in the civil rights movement. He recalls one meeting with Sam Napier, at which the party's overall position was made clear to him:

> I remember having a discussion with Sam Napier about it. He said he supported civil rights and the concept of civil rights but was concerned that the party would be sectarianised by it at a time when the party was attracting support from both communities. Even the party Executive reflected both traditions.[155] So many people supported civil rights but opposed the party taking a position on the issue as it

could be construed as anti-Union, pro-United Ireland. So Sam, etc. were not against civil rights, only wary of the impact on the party, indeed they feared a split within the party.[156]

This correlates well with Brett's comments that 'we were all for civil rights'[157] as well as leading Derry Labour Party activist Eamonn McCann's admission that:

> The whole civil rights thing alarmed many people in the NILP. I mean ... the party had supported civil rights in 1966, 1967, 1968 and so forth. It had in principle been progressive. Even before that – in the early 1960s – the Northern Ireland Labour Party was sending delegations to London ... about fair allocation of housing, one person one vote, about the Special Powers Act and so on ... [They] took a progressive view in relation to the sectarian setup here. But it is true that once violence started, I remember meetings in Belfast of the Executive of the NILP in which you could see that people were frightened; they were alarmed. Not that this was going to be a civil war zone, but just about the idea that they might be associated with people who were in conflict with the cops. There were a number of people I remember who couldn't tolerate that; they couldn't fit that into their minds, because they believed in law and order.[158]

The NILP initially remained flexible on the issue, allowing individual members to become involved in NICRA activities, but the party itself eschewed direct involvement because of fears about the potential for civil rights protests to spill over into violent confrontations on the streets. The province's long history of marching and its mixed tribal symbolism of triumphalism and provocation kept the NILP spectating on the sidelines. Arguably, its pro-civil rights stance gave the party the shelter needed to weather the storm whipped up by those younger members who harboured more radical convictions.

On looking back at this period it is not uncommon for some of those leading NILP and civil rights activists to view their involvement not so much as a personal failing but as a collective one. For instance, Alan Carr, one of the most high-profile NILP–NICRA activists, is markedly critical about the leadership at this juncture:

> I think the leadership of the NILP were petrified of getting involved in street demonstrations. I think they thought that it was something to be achieved by political lobbying at Westminster and basically by bringing legislation into line with the rest of the United Kingdom and they saw that as the primary means of achieving [civil rights]. They were petrified about getting involved in street protests because they thought that would lead (as indeed it did) to sectarian confrontation. Some of us didn't take that view, including Erskine Holmes who was the first chairman of the Civil Rights Association. I was actively involved in it.[159]

With the benefit of hindsight it is certainly possible to view party leader Tom Boyd as a fickle and over-cautious optimist in terms of his firm belief in parliamentary democracy. However there is a surprising historical echo in the travails he faced and those that faced his predecessor Harry Midgley who led the party in the 1930s. Walker writes that, 'Midgley believed devoutly in the processes of parliamentary democracy, and on one occasion warned the government that if

Failure of the 'consensus-forming strategy', 1965–69

it did not listen to other points of view, people might turn to groups who were opposed to parliamentary institutions.'[160] No such onus was placed on Boyd, for the forces of opposition mounting against O'Neill were in plain sight. They had after all taken to the streets as a means of impressing upon the embattled premier that they existed and were prepared to air their grievances in public.

That said, the NILP has suffered almost irreparably from pseudo-historical judgement since the 1970s and this makes it difficult to get a holistic impression of its activism. Many contemporary civil rights activists privately and publicly criticised the NILP for not getting involved, though this criticism has been magnified in the years since the explosion of literature on the 'troubles'. One could argue quite convincingly that the NILP's tactics were misguided, given the intransigent attitude displayed by many of O'Neill's cabinet towards civil rights demands. However this is only partly true. The NILP did rally against Unionist policies, especially after the trouble in Londonderry in October 1968, and called on the regime to 'recognise the integrity of the civil rights movement'[161] in a bid to alleviate inter-communal tension. The party's long cross-sectarian lineage meant that it was better placed to know the impact that confrontation between marchers and the state's security forces would arouse in the divided working class it traditionally represented. In his analysis of the sectarian violence of 1935 Walker writes that, 'The NILP had to make its appeal across the community divide and to attempt, however despairingly to harness energies and passions to class rather than ethnic politics.'[162] Almost 35 years later the party once again faced the same stark options.

It is impossible to argue that these individuals had foreknowledge of the violence which would transform the face of the province irreparably. However, Carr understood the restrictions the NILP had placed itself under by continually backing the parliamentary process:

> I have a fair degree of sympathy with the leadership of the NILP at the time in being cautious about getting involved. I think ... [they were] politically cautious on everything. They were basically right-wing social democrats completely hung up on parliamentary processes regarding any form of street protests.[163]

Nevertheless, the determination by Labour and trade union leaders to prevent sectarian tensions boiling over into violence was changed utterly by the events in Derry on 5 October 1968. Admittedly the closing months of 1968 were the most difficult for the party since the patriotic fervour whipped up by the Unionists at the time of the Ireland Act in 1949. Douglas McIldoon, who took over from Napier as party secretary in 1969, thought that the NILP lacked a coherent damage limitation strategy:

> 1968 was, of course, the beginning of the civil rights. 5 October was the Duke Street march which was when Gerry Fitt and lots of other people got their heads battered in by the police. And I suppose that was the time when things started to unravel. And in fact Sam Napier wrote a very perceptive minute to the first meeting of the party Executive immediately after the Duke Street riot – if that was the word – it wasn't really a riot it was just a march that got beaten up by the police. They would

polarise in sectarian terms and the Labour and trade union movement would be just pushed aside [he wrote]. That is basically what happened. It took slightly longer and I was presiding over the corpse as it were.[164]

Charles Brett thought that Tom Boyd faced an uphill struggle in weaning people away from new and emerging popular slogans. He maintained that although he had the 'utmost respect' for Boyd as party leader his decision-making process was weighed down heavily by the nightmare of 'opening that can of worms' and the explosion in sectarian warfare that might potentially follow suit.[165]

While Boyd may have had measured success in stressing this point to the ordinary rank-and-file – which was by and large a 'fairly disciplined body'[166] – it proved a little more difficult with the younger membership. Like the entryists in the British Labour Party the NILP had its own Young Turks eager to force change via extra-parliamentary activities. However, they were precluded from shifting the party's politics onto the streets by Napier and Tom Boyd who held a tight grip on the levers of power within the party's Waring Street offices throughout 1968 and 1969.[167] The NILP's constitutional commitment to working within democratic parameters had been an integral component of its political programme since its formation in 1924. The fear of reopening old sectarian wounds dictated much of the party's strategic imperatives during the late 1960s. As Erskine Holmes explained:

> Quite a number of Northern Ireland Labour Party people, including Tom Boyd out in East Belfast, had experience of the riots and pogroms of the Twenties and the Thirties. And they could see that these tactics were going to produce heightened sectarian tensions and could possibly even lead to a civil war condition. So you had a division within the party between those who thought that you should support the civil rights movement and those who thought you shouldn't because it was going in the wrong direction. It would end up being taken over by Nationalists, the community would be split and divided by it. So who was right in the end? Obviously the more conservative and cautious people who had first-hand experience of Belfast sectarianism.[168]

Of course there was always a danger that the NILP would alienate its hard-earned working-class support-base and this almost certainly contributed to the party's ambiguity on the matter.[169]

Bob Purdie has suggested that the NILP was ill-equipped to become the political vanguard of the civil rights movement because it was 'a party which was orientated to parliamentary methods, it was not a suitable instrument for creating a mass extra-parliamentary movement, indeed most of its leaders were incapable of engaging in such a course of action'.[170] Erskine Holmes, who addressed the protest march at Dungannon, gave this analysis:

> Certainly the Northern Ireland Labour Party had no difficulty setting out civil rights demands. But they were by-passed by the advent of street politics because the Northern Ireland Labour Party was never going to lead street politics.[171]

This is a little oversimplified. The problem was not about the NILP involving itself with the civil rights campaign per se, as much as it was the party's decision

Failure of the 'consensus-forming strategy', 1965–69

to retain its impartiality in the face of growing attempts by the Unionists to taint NICRA with a republican and communist brush. The NILP had absolutely no problem endorsing NICRA's objectives whilst it was led by moderates.[172] Only when militants were seen to have publicly taken over NICRA did the NILP fall back on its exclusive commitment to supporting the parliamentary process.

By the opening months of 1969 NICRA's objectives had altered to take into consideration the rapid mushrooming in its ranks. It now sought 'to bring to Northern Ireland effective democracy, and to end all the forms of injustice, intimidation, discrimination and deprivation, which result from the partisan rule of the Stormont regime'.[173] NICRA's *Ultimatum to Stormont* (1969) demanded action from the government by asking for no less than a timetable giving firm dates for the implementation of further reforms.[174] The Electoral Law Act (1968) and the setting up of a Parliamentary Ombudsman failed to placate those who had undergone a radical transformation over the previous six months chiefly because 'one man, one vote' had still not been conceded.[175] NICRA now became a huge populist campaign with a broad spectrum of supporters (including students, workers and professionals) using mass methods of protest in the struggle for civil rights.[176] The effects that NICRA's radicalism was having on the NILP was significant, as Brian Garrett points out:

> What we wanted to do was to deal with it on its own terms. Not as part of an agenda which people would be suspicious about, but they were going to be suspicious anyway you could say. So there were concerns, I think, among sections of the Labour Party about the pursuit of single issue civil rights campaigns and that it might get a green tinge. Historically we were right but I think we were more fearful than we should have been. Of course various members of the Northern Ireland Labour Party played a major role in relation to civil rights. There was Eamonn McCann, there was Erskine Holmes, there was Paddy Devlin, there was Michael Farrell. There was a variety of other people I could name who were all deeply involved. But the actual party kept its distance from the individuals' campaigns. You might say wrongly but that is a matter of historical judgement.[177]

By now it was obvious that events on the streets had shifted focus away from the parliamentary arena and onto the streets.

The political machinations of Unionist and Nationalist parties may have dictated whether or not the party's political fortunes stayed afloat but it was in developments within the ethno-religiously mixed constituencies that most of the significant work took place. Those branches which did weigh in behind Charles Brett's cross-sectarian vision most loyally – Ballynafeigh, South Antrim, Falls and the radical QUBLG – almost certainly did this knowing full well the complexities of open co-operation between Protestants and Catholics at grass-roots level. The question about the NILP's attempt to put clear blue water between itself and NICRA is a structural one which must include an appreciation of the NILP's local democratic structures. As Brendan Mackin suggested:

> No. Nobody wanted to take it to a vote, not even to take it to that level. There was enough flexibility within the party to allow individual support/constituency level support in civil rights. There is no evidence I am aware of that any NILP branch

opposed civil rights. There was benign support, some active support – much of the leadership of civil rights came from that radical Presbyterian background, for example, John D. Stewart. There were people who were shop stewards, for example, Andy Barr and Jimmy Graham. There was enough cover for the Protestant branches to give civil rights tacit support but not maybe to come out and actively support it. There was active engagement on one side of the NILP but not active rejection from the other side.[178]

Individual members from these aforementioned branches typically became more involved in civil rights because of the domineering political influence of Ulster Unionism in local electoral constituencies. The Newtownabbey branch, for instance, frequently invited along Young Turks such as Eamonn McCann and Inez McCormick to address Labour meetings and believed strongly in the principle of civil disobedience.[179] However in contrast to the personal convictions of these speakers they were also firmly wedded to the ideological principles of the BLP.

The British Labour government must also share some of the blame at this juncture. Notwithstanding claims made by senior ministers in subsequent years that they received no prior warning of the inflammatory social and political issues in Northern Ireland,[180] the fact remains that Napier and other NILP leaders had been updating their comrades in the BLP since the 1940s. Yet that is not to dismiss the very perceptive point made by Purdie that British Labour made 'the will-o'-the-wisp of an NILP electoral breakthrough a precondition for action by the Labour Government. This was a safe way of putting off any action whatsoever.'[181] As noted above O'Neill had long regarded Northern Ireland's treatment under Attlee to have been fair and generous, though by the summer of 1968 events saw London put increasing pressure on him to placate the Catholic minority. In Stormont he pondered the potential for Labour intervention: 'Today's circumstances are possibly different and to some extent less favourable to Northern Ireland than they were in the immediate post-war years.'[182] However, it was not until later in the year that he brought himself to publicly criticise the Labour government. After all Wilson had offered an invaluable economic crutch which enabled the Harland and Wolff shipyard and Shorts Aircraft manufacturers to stay afloat, thus preventing them from going into liquidation.[183]

In light of these economic reprieves O'Neill thought it best to keep harsh criticisms behind closed doors.[184] Conversely, the NILP had no intention of keeping its views on British Labour silent. Regarding Wilson's interference, the party still preferred to view it through the prism of a broader fraternal commitment to transforming the fortunes of the embattled proletariat residing in the regional industrial centres of Belfast, Clydeside and Merseyside. Tom Boyd reminded the Prime Minister that the good-humoured spirit with which Labour grandees like Attlee and Morrison had treated the province sprang from the terrible catastrophic events endured by the British working class during the Second World War. It was incumbent upon the post-war Labour government to see a New Jerusalem built upon sure socio-economic foundations.[185]

Underpinning this desire lay a determination that British citizens would have access to the full fruits of British democracy. This could not be done by supporting legislative discrepancies between Great Britain and Northern Ireland. As Boyd put it:

> It seems rather strange that after almost a quarter of a century we in Northern Ireland should still be debating questions such as 'one man, one vote' ... The Prime Minister has been in power for nearly six years. Can we say that in those six years there have been fundamental changes in legislation that would encourage confidence in many people? We all talk of minorities in Northern Ireland other than the one referred to by the Prime Minister and the Nationalist Opposition. Do they not also deserve better treatment than has been afforded to them in the past?[186]

From most parliamentary speeches delivered by Boyd and Simpson in this period it can be ascertained that they considered their suggestions for bringing legislation on social, economic, political and legal concerns into line with the rest of the UK to be falling on deaf ears. Indeed they felt a keen sense that all of the progressive legislation that they had proposed during the 1958–65 period had been in vain.

Even speeches by Senator Norman Kennedy gave the impression that the NILP considered the province to have enjoyed only a fraction of the social welfare legislation that parity promised. In a speech on the occasion of the second reading of the Electoral Law Bill he pointed to the unresolved anomalies in current voting legislation, including age and residence qualifications and the archaic postal voting mechanisms. For Kennedy 'we should bring ourselves into line with the situation at Westminster'. Moreover:

> In this modern world it is becoming more and more unrealistic and it will soon become impossible to conduct the affairs of this province of 1.5 million people in isolation from Britain and ignore the necessity to bring about major changes that would bring us into conformity with Britain. I am sorry to say that today Northern Ireland presents to the world and particularly to the people of Britain the image of a community still rooted in the sectarianism of the past, struggling to modernise its economy but not its social set-up. For this image nobody can be held responsible but the Government of the day.[187]

The focus of much criticism was still O'Neill's regime. The removal of Billy Boyd and Bleakley may have lessened the party's impact on parliamentary proceedings; however, it did not lessen the remaining parliamentarians' resolve in speaking out about social and political injustice.

Paul Dixon has argued that 'the contribution of the NILP to the civil rights movement has been airbrushed from history by some nationalist writers who were perhaps a little too keen to paint a black and white story of the civil rights period'.[188] The arguments made by some Nationalist-leaning writers that most Protestants were inherently reactionary towards Catholic socio-economic grievances cannot be fully justified in light of the contravening empirical evidence. Many Protestant NILP activists did hold radical socialist convictions which encompassed civil rights grievances. Cursory glances over the party's discourse from this period would indicate that it had been highlighting discrimination in jobs and housing, and instances of electoral malpractice, long before the formation of the CSJ or NICRA. Indeed, even when the civil rights movement resorted to the tactic of protest marches to draw attention to their grievances some NILP members opted to play a logistical role: according to one former high-profile activist, 'the Derry Labour Party was by far the most involved'.[189]

Ostensibly, therefore, the NILP's undistinguished role in the civil rights movement had more to do with its inability to take a clear and unambiguous stance on the issue. In large part this was due to a genuine belief that it would re-open old enmities between Protestants and Catholics, than intra-party wrangling over strategy, although the autonomy of local Constituency Labour Parties (tied to upholding party policy ratified at annual conference) did ultimately have an impact on its discipline and morale. It could be said in the party's defence that the civil rights movement itself failed to counter the Unionist Party's propaganda which claimed that it was a 'republican or Communist conspiracy'; or to challenge prevailing stereotypes about the Protestant working class. Thus, it missed a fundamental opportunity to broaden its cross-sectarian base and instead became, indirectly, a campaign for 'civil rights for Catholics' as many Protestants at the time perceived it. As David Boulton puts it:

> To fight discrimination in housing was to demand that Catholics be given houses which, under the prevailing system would go to Protestants. To fight discrimination in employment was to demand that Catholics move into jobs currently held by Protestants. NICRA was later to switch its emphasis to demanding *more* houses and *more* jobs, rightly recognising that discrimination breeds on scarcity.[190]

Of course the NILP could well have avoided being brushed to the side by the civil rights movement had three ingredients remained consistent in the six months after August 1968. First, had the NILP emerged to expose the political calculation of Nationalist politicians attaching themselves to the agenda for narrow political purposes it might well have copper-bottomed the loss of those Catholic supporters who were now flocking to the beat of a tribal drum. Second, had the party actually come out in support of those individual members who led marches and addressed rallies on the firm basis of *officially endorsed* NILP policy then it might well have been in a much better position when jockeying for votes in those inner-city areas where newly formed Nationalist parties had emerged. Lastly, and in chorus with Walker, if the BLP had actually 'responded to the promptings of the NILP in the 1960s it might have applied the necessary pressure on O'Neill to carry out reforms speedily'[191] thus averting the disaster which was about to engulf the province. As it stood the British Labour government held firm to its non-interference agenda.

Following a crisis meeting with Wilson and Callaghan on 4 November 1968, O'Neill, Faulkner and Craig were forced to begrudgingly agree to a five-point plan of reform. Even though the Northern Ireland delegation played up Unionist moves to improve the lot of the Catholic community the die had been cast by Wilson who remained unconvinced about the pace of reform. In an

Failure of the 'consensus-forming strategy', 1965–69

'embarrassing sign of weakness at a critical juncture' by the Unionist delegation, Wilson and Callaghan steadfastly called for nothing less that the immediate introduction of 'one man, one vote' at local elections.[192] Over the next two weeks Unionism was thrown into crisis as several members of the cabinet refused to be pushed on Wilson's demands. When the five-point plan was announced by O'Neill on 22 November it left out 'one man, one vote', but did include the introduction of a points system for public housing allocation (though this was not to be mandatory), the creation of a Parliamentary Commissioner for Administration, reform of local government including the abolition of the company vote, revision of the Special Powers Act to conform to international obligations and the replacement of Londonderry Corporation with a non-elected Development Commission.[193] It could be said that Craig's insistence that NICRA was infiltrated by the IRA – and his 'playing the role of the only – or nearly the only – man in the cabinet who could "save Ulster"'[194] animated his stern refusal to bow to the demands of the civil rights leaders. In any event Unionist dogmatism served only to give greater impetus to NICRA's demands.

In its first year and a half of existence, NICRA had achieved very little.[195] If the NILP had actually trumpeted its parliamentary record of exposing how the Stormont government departed from the rest of the UK on key legislative matters, instead of merely drawing Stormont's attention to how 'the present law is thoroughly objectionable'[196] then it might have been more successful in discouraging some sections of the Catholic working class from taking to the streets. Consequently, a programme which gave the strong impression that both Catholic and Protestant working-class interests were being safeguarded by Labour politicians at Stormont might have won over more moderate Protestant and Catholic opinion, thereby forming a democratic socialist non-sectarian 'British rights for British citizens' campaign. As it stood the dynamic driving the civil rights agenda took on a different meaning for both participants and their opponents. As Patterson argues, 'despite the non-sectarian language of the march organisers, many of the marchers and their opponents defined "civil rights" in terms of traditional aspirations and antagonisms'.[197]

The re-awakening of Nationalist political consciousness in Belfast may have found an appropriate outlet in the Nationalist Democratic Party (NDP) by 1967 but it had been absorbed through a variety of candidates in the local government elections of that year. Yet support for the NILP at a local level was still strong. In 1958 it was 21%, but by 1967 it had reached 24%; what was left of moderate opinion was soaked up by O'Neill's rallying call in December 1968. The NILP's constitutional movements were further restricted by the departure of several prominent Catholic-born members of the party – Michael Farrell, Eamonn McCann and Paddy Devlin – for radical new vistas, thus exposing the fragility of the party's cross-sectarian political programme. Arguably, the NILP was ill-equipped to meet the challenges posed by the transformation of politics in the late 1960s, not because it was tethered to a narrow middle of the road agenda but because it was deeply wedded to the process and fundamentals of

146 A history of the Northern Ireland Labour Party

British parliamentary democracy. As such, it could not (and would not) fathom or condone a turn to street politics or civil disobedience.

The 'Crossroads Election' and the failure of conciliation

Faced with mounting civil disobedience and the promise of inter-communal discord O'Neill made a direct appeal to moderates of all shades in a televised broadcast on 9 December 1968:

> What kind of Ulster do you want? A happy and respected province, in good standing with the rest of the United Kingdom? Or a place continually torn apart by riots and demonstrations, and regarded by the rest of Britain as a political outcast? As always in a democracy, the choice is yours. I will accept whatever your verdict might be.[198]

There was little ambiguity in O'Neill's words. They were above all conciliatory in tone and moderate in outlook. He remained essentially committed to the implementation of reforms; appealing both to civil rights activists and the right of his party to draw back from the brink: 'Your voice has been heard, and clearly heard. Your duty now is to play your part in taking the heat out of the situation before blood is shed.'[199] O'Neill's grip over the UPP had now loosened but that did not prevent moderate opinion from rallying behind their ill-fated premier. The *Belfast Telegraph* collected over 150,000 letters and telegrams, while another 120,000 newspaper coupons were returned supporting O'Neill's political line.[200] When released the pro-O'Neill manifesto trumpeted the progressiveness of its leader:

> The party acknowledges and proclaims the right of all citizens to equal treatment under the law, to full equality in the enjoyment of health, education and other social benefits, and to the protection of authority against every kind of injustice.[201]

Although the *Belfast Telegraph* suggested that Catholics were prepared to vote for O'Neill there were still those already caught up in civil rights activism who would accept nothing less than unconditional reforms.[202] 'In many respects,' writes Mulholland, 'the civil rights movement was actually calculated to counteract O'Neill's assimilationism.'[203]

The NILP's response was vitriolic: its EC issued a blistering attack on the premier accusing him of an arrogant disregard for public opinion, a contemptuous attitude towards criticism and an obsequious attitude towards extremists. Moreover, it described his public announcements of an imminent reform programme as 'feeble gestures'.[204] The statement ended with a call for immediate action in three areas:

1. Rid the Unionist Party of sectarian and extremist individuals and organisations;
2. Recognise the integrity of the civil rights movement;
3. Accept publicly the fundamental principle that British citizens should enjoy the same rights in every part of the United Kingdom.[205]

However, there were practical constraints on O'Neill's position, which the NILP chose to mention only briefly, but which Geoffrey Bing, a long-standing back-bench critic of British Labour's procrastination on Northern Ireland, articulated more fully:

> It is unbelievably naïve to suppose that such a tribal-based party, however willing its leaders might be, can in fact carry out reforms which would in themselves destroy the basis upon which it is built.[206]

Bing claimed in private meetings with Irish government officials that they might wish to consider taking allegations about British 'colonialism' in Ireland to the United Nations, though he failed to excite the interests of Southern bureaucrats.[207] This sort of tactic might have drawn international attention to the peculiar legislative mechanisms binding Stormont to Westminster but it was ludicrous in light of the presence of Ulster MPs at Westminster who fed into the British political system, albeit in a semi-detached and unconvincing manner. It served to highlight that many civil rights activists saw the overthrow of the Unionist regime as a necessary precursor to the full implementation of reforms.

The caution observed by the NILP leadership was not shared by those who went on to become involved in the People's Democracy (PD). Formed at Queen's University Belfast following an unsuccessful march by civil rights activists in the autumn of 1968, the PD contained a bulky student membership.[208] In many ways the PD captured the essence of the global age. Just as other student-based protest movements had done elsewhere the PD rode on the crest of a wave of radicalism which sought to challenge the virulent anti-communism and war-mongering of many Western liberal democratic states.[209] Proxy wars between the two great nuclear superpowers of the United States and the Soviet Union were a recurrent feature of an age which saw rock 'n' roll music, radicalism and disposable incomes shake off the cobwebs of conservative social norms.[210]

The decision by the PD to hold a 'long march' from Belfast to Londonderry in the New Year was a fateful one. On 4 January 1969, at Burntollet, loyalist protestors attacked the marchers in an action 'which plunged the province back into a political maelstrom'.[211] Burntollet gave the first major reaction to the cause of civil rights. Many of the leading PD activists had crossed to the radical student body from the Labour Group at Queen's. Michael Farrell, Eamonn McCann, Cyril Toman and Paul Arthur had all been members of the NILP. McCann and Toman were candidates for the party in the 1967 local government elections. Although McCann held dual membership until the latter months of 1970, Farrell was abruptly expelled in 1968 for stirring up trouble among the NILP rank-and-file. Rumours were rife that he had been a card-carrying member of the Communist Party, which was still considered a proscribed organisation by the NILP.[212] Farrell's radicalism found little in the way of reciprocal enthusiasm from Catholic NILP members, particularly those living in what soon became the ghettoised communities of West Belfast.[213]

As a further means of maximising the groundswell in moderate support for his conciliatory appeal, O'Neill called a snap general election for 24 February 1969. It provoked the first major public split within the UUP since its foundation in the early twentieth century. Occasional fissures had certainly been in evidence before, but these were small-scale affairs in comparison to the dichotomous division now discernable along pro- and anti-O'Neill lines. The NILP was caught completely off guard. Wilson's dependency on O'Neill to push reform through in the face of a critical mass of opposition within his party was ill-fated. Paddy Devlin's involvement with NICRA had hitherto proven relatively compatible with his NILP convictions and his party's commitment to see the implementation of 'Full British Rights for British Citizens'. In fact it was this very slogan which returned him as Stormont MP for Falls. His electoral communiqué further asserted:

> Only a party which can unite Protestant and Catholic and has the support of the trade union movement can hope to form a government in opposition to the Unionist Party. The *only* party which has this appeal and this support is the NILP.[214]

Devlin's term as NILP chairman (1968–69) was to prove productive and decisive, not only for his own political career but also for the future of Belfast politics generally.

For Vivian Simpson, the incumbent MP for Oldpark, campaigning proved a little more delicate in light of the raw nerves touched upon during recent street disturbances. Nevertheless, in an area of mixed religious affiliation, Simpson sought re-election on Labour's generic platform of citizens' rights:

> Northern Ireland needs above all a constructive, non-sectarian, constitutional and reforming alternative to the Unionists. Northern Ireland Labour stands uncompromisingly for full Citizens' Rights and full British standards of living in earnings, jobs, housing and social services.[215]

Simpson signed off his electoral address by reiterating his pledge to 'continue to serve the entire community to the best of my ability'.[216] In late February he was returned on a slightly battered majority of 434 votes. In other parts of Belfast Erskine Holmes, the former Labour Group stalwart, failed for the second time to unseat the Unionist Party's Ivan Neill, who had held his ground since 1949. NILP candidates in Bloomfield, Clifton, Cromac, Pottinger, St Annes, Shankill, Victoria and Willowfield polled much better than candidates outside the city, throwing the party's urban character into sharp relief. Eamonn McCann ran as the first NILP candidate in Foyle since the 1940s, though he was defeated in a two-horse contest between the old Nationalism of Eddie McAteer and the new civil rights-based nationalism personified by the Independent politician John Hume. Overall, the 1969 election showed a marked increase in voter turnout. Interestingly constitutional Nationalist politicians came under heavy flak for leaving their constituents exposed to loyalist counter-demonstrations. In the simmering heat of sectarian violence caused by a summer of discontent in 1969 Protestants and Catholics began to drift further apart. Large parts of Belfast and

Failure of the 'consensus-forming strategy', 1965–69   **149**

Londonderry would soon become segregated along ethno-religious lines, effectively ghettoising the working classes.

In the wake of the NILP's diminished performance at the 'Crossroads Election' the party had retained two seats in the House of Commons. Vivian Simpson and the new MP for Falls, Paddy Devlin, were returned in a faction-ridden contest, which not only threw up a dazzling range of candidates but also emphasised the divisions within Unionism.[217] The departure of Senator Arnold Schofield left Norman Kennedy as the party's only member in the Upper House. More significantly, Tom Boyd announced his retirement from politics thus signalling the temporary retreat of Labour in the east of the city. Boyd's nominated successor, the former party chairman, Martin McBirney[218] trailed in behind his Unionist opponent on 2,744 votes, narrowing the gap by 716 votes to only 158. The party suffered a downturn in what was to be the last ever election to the Stormont Parliament; its share of the vote dwindled from 20.4% to 8.1%. However, it is difficult to take an accurate barometer reading of the popularity of the NILP at a time when elections were fast becoming personality-driven contests with little focus placed on 'bread and butter' policies. Electoral competition in Belfast up until that point had been between Official Unionism, Independent Unionism and Northern Ireland Labour. This would soon change as new priorities came to the forefront.

Conclusion

The clandestine bombing campaign initiated by the Ulster Protestant Volunteers (UPV) and UVF in April 1969 was designed to give the impression that an imminent IRA threat looked likely. In reality the specific aim was to engineer the destabilisation of O'Neill's authority.[219] It might even be argued that these attacks were the physical manifestation of the failure of O'Neillism's conciliatory politics to minimise sectarian tensions in Northern Ireland.[220] On 28 April 1969 O'Neill tendered his resignation with the Governor of Northern Ireland and left the political stage: not before persuading his reluctant administration to vote through 'one man, one vote'.[221] His cousin, Major James Chichester Clark, who had previously resigned over the granting of universal suffrage, narrowly defeated Brian Faulkner to take over the reigns of power. Arguably, O'Neill's capitulation was due mainly to his 'inability to win sufficient Catholic backing to balance defections from the intransigent Unionists who were distrustful of his conciliatory approach'.[222] The divisions within the UUP led to a more deliberate campaign to win over the hearts and minds of those floating voters who had previously opted for the NILP but who were now living in the grip of renewed sectarian tension. Nevertheless, it was to be a few more tortuous years before the NILP found itself squeezed out electorally. The impact of ethnically exclusive groups vying for a stake in Northern Ireland's rapidly changing socio-political environment had not yet come to pass.

Overall the late 1960s witnessed the emergence of a revitalised sectarian brinkmanship on the streets of Northern Ireland, as progressive and reactionary forces simultaneously mobilised and converged with deadly consequences. Forcible demographic change and widespread sectarian segregation took root within these years. While one side, led from the front by middle-class Catholics, agitated for reform of the system, the other – Protestant followers of Ian Paisley and his allies within O'Neill's parliamentary team – sought to entrench the traditional Unionist rhetoric of 'this we will maintain'. Perhaps the most salient feature of these conflicting trends was that they took place largely through the conduit of angry confrontations on the streets, not in the conventional arena of parliamentary politics. One direct response to the escalation of violence was the re-emergence of paramilitary groupings such as the UVF and IRA. Since the formation of the Northern Ireland state these forces had periodically emerged from the shadows at times of civil strife and contributed to the brisk descent into sectarian violence and murder. Ulster's working classes would soon share in the effects of an aborted attempt by their leaders to tinker with the ethno-religious dichotomy underpinning the province's society and political culture. By the close of the decade Northern Ireland's socio-political landscape would be utterly transformed.

Notes

1 PRONI, D/2704, *NILP Documents*, NILP–NIC ICTU, *Joint Memorandum on Citizens' Rights in Northern Ireland* (1966).
2 English, Richard, *Armed Struggle: A History of the IRA* (Basingstoke: Macmillan, 2003), p. 75.
3 Patterson, Henry, *Ireland since 1939* (Oxford: Oxford University Press, 2002), p. 138.
4 PRONI, HA/32/1/1317, *Activities of the IRA*, August 1957. A briefing paper prepared by for the Unionist government by the RUC revealed that ' ... the present IRA Campaign has evoked no reprisals. This is due in no small degree to the influence of the Northern Ireland Prime Minister and his colleagues who have consistently urged upon Government supporters the need to exercise restraint in the face of provocative attacks'.
5 Murray, Gerard and Jonathan Tonge, *Sinn Féin and the SDLP: From Alienation to Participation* (Dublin: O'Brien, 2005), pp. 6–7.
6 Mulholland, Marc, *Northern Ireland at the Crossroads: Ulster Unionism in the O'Neill Years, 1960–9* (Basingstoke: Macmillan, 2000), p. 9.
7 Patterson, *Ireland since 1939*, pp. 181–2.
8 According to O'Neill, the day before the Lemass visit he informed 'the next most senior member of the cabinet, the Minister of Finance, and had already received the approval of the Governor of Northern Ireland, Lord Erskine. The next day I told the other Ministers and the Chairman of the UUP and the British Home Office.' O'Neill, Terence, *The Autobiography of Terence O'Neill* (London: Granada, 1972), pp. 70–1.
9 *Belfast Newsletter*, 15 January 1965.
10 Patterson, *Ireland since 1939*, p. 187.
11 Patterson, Henry, 'Seán Lemass and the Ulster Question, 1959–65', *Journal of Contemporary History*, Vol. 34, No. 1 (January 1999), p. 152.

12 *The Round Table*, No. 220 (September 1965), p. 366.

13 *Belfast Newsletter*, 8 April 1965.

14 O'Neill, *The Autobiography of Terence O'Neill*, p. 73.

15 Garland, Roy, *Negotiating History: The Ulster Volunteer Force* (Unpublished MA Thesis: Queen's University Belfast, 1991), p. 30; see also Gordon, David, *The O'Neill Years: Unionist Politics, 1963–1969* (Belfast: Athol Street, 1989), pp. 36–7.

16 Gordon, *The O'Neill Years*, p. 37.

17 By the following summer many journalists were suggesting that 'internal divisions within the Cabinet may give the Paisley movement much of its cutting edge', *Belfast Telegraph*, 17 June 1966. A month later it was reported that on Belfast Corporation 'at least twelve of the forty councillors are acknowledged Paisleyites, while within the Parliamentary Party eighteen of the thirty six are doubtful', *Belfast Telegraph*, 22 July 1966.

18 Mulholland, *Northern Ireland at the Crossroads*, p. 2.

19 Devlin, Paddy, *Straight Left: An Autobiography* (Belfast: Blackstaff, 1993), p. 80.

20 See Simpson, Kirk and Peter Daly, 'Politics and Education in Northern Ireland: An Analytical History', *Irish Studies Review*, Vol. 12, No. 2 (2004), pp. 163–74.

21 Patterson, *Ireland since 1939*, p. 201.

22 Interview with Sam McAughtry, 27 April 2006.

23 Mulholland, *Northern Ireland at the Crossroads*, pp. 3–4.

24 Purdie, Bob, *Politics in the Streets: The Origins of the Civil Rights Movement in Northern Ireland* (Belfast: Blackstaff, 1990), p. 94.

25 CSJ, *Why Justice Cannot be Done: The Douglas Home Correspondence* (1964).

26 McCluskey, Conn, *Up Off Their Knees* (ROI: Conn McCluskey and Associates, 1989), p. 17.

27 Ibid., p. 16.

28 Interview with Sir Charles Brett, 30 January 2004.

29 PRONI, CAB/9N/4118.

30 McCluskey, *Up Off Their Knees*, p. 17.

31 Purdie, *Politics in the Streets*, pp. 95–6.

32 PRONI CAB/9N/4118, 4 August 1965.

33 See the seminal study by John Whyte 'How much Discrimination was there under the Stormont Regime?', in Gallagher, Tom and James O'Connell (eds), *Contemporary Irish Studies* (Manchester: Manchester University Press, 1983), pp. 1–35.

34 Graham, J.A.V., *The Consensus-Forming Strategy of the Northern Ireland Labour Party 1949–1968* (Unpublished MSc Thesis: Queen's University Belfast, 1972), p. 123.

35 Compare, for instance, the policy documents *The Plain Truth* (1964) and *Electoral Reform Now* (1965).

36 Purdie, *Politics in the Streets*, pp. 102–3.

37 Jack Hassard was a prominent NILP councillor on Dungannon Urban District Council in the 1960s and was also active in the civil rights movement.

38 McCluskey, *Up Off Their Knees*, pp. 16–17.

39 For more on Wilson and British policy in this period see Bew Paul, Peter Gibbon and Henry Patterson, *Northern Ireland 1921–2001: Political Forces and Social Classes: Revised and Updated Version* (London: Serif, 2002), pp. 150–7.

40 LPA, GS12/NI, Northern Ireland Documents 1966, Pat McCluskey to A.L. Williams, 13 February 1966.

41 Ibid., Conn McCluskey to A.L. Williams, 21 February 1966.

42 Ibid., A.L. Williams to Pat McCluskey, 14 March 1966.
43 LPA, GS12/NI, Northern Ireland Documents 1966, Williams to Wilson, 28 February 1966.
44 LPA, GS12/NI, Northern Ireland Documents 1966, Williams to Wilson, 28 February 1966.
45 PRONI D/3026, *CDU Papers*, Constitution of CDU.
46 PRONI D/3026, *CDU Papers*, Constitution of CDU; see also Bell, Geoffrey, *Troublesome Business: The Labour Party and the Irish Question* (London: Pluto, 1982), pp. 103–4.
47 PRONI D/3026, *CDU Papers*, Minutes of Meeting between Byrne and the NILP Executive Committee, 17 September 1967.
48 Cradden, Terry, 'Labour in Britain and the Northern Ireland Labour Party, 1900–70', in Catterall, Peter and Sean McDougall (eds), *The Northern Ireland Question in British Politics* (Basingstoke: Macmillan, 1996), p. 83.
49 NIPC, Draft Agenda for the 44th Annual NILP Conference (1967).
50 Cradden, 'Labour in Britain and the Northern Ireland Labour Party', p. 84.
51 See Purdie, Bob, 'The Friends of Ireland: British Labour and Irish Nationalism, 1945–49', in Gallagher, Tom and James O'Connell (eds), *Contemporary Irish Studies* (Manchester: Manchester University Press, 1983), pp. 81–94.
52 PRONI D/3026, *CDU Papers*, CDU Secretary's Notes on a Meeting with the NILP Executive, 2 August 1967; see also the correspondence between Byrne and the McCluskeys, 13 August 1967.
53 Ibid.
54 Purdie informs his readership that Tom Boyd was a long-standing personal friend of Paddy Byrne since their political activities in support of anti-Fascist fighters in the Spanish Civil War. See his *Politics in the Streets*, p. 70.
55 PRONI D/3026, *CDU Papers*, Statement from the Northern Ireland Labour Party
56 Dixon, Paul, *The British Labour Party and Northern Ireland, 1959–74* (Unpublished PhD Thesis: University of Bradford, 1993), p. 102.
57 Ibid., p. 138; Rose, Peter, *How the Troubles Came to Northern Ireland* (Basingstoke: Palgrave Macmillan, 2001), p. 29.
58 Rose, *How the Troubles Came to Northern Ireland*, p. 35.
59 Purdie, *Politics in the Streets*, p. 111.
60 Interview with George Chambers, 14 February 2006.
61 PRONI, D/3026, *CDU Papers*, Conn McCluskey to Paddy Byrne, 25 August 1967.
62 Ibid., Pat McCluskey to Paddy Byrne, 25 August 1967.
63 Ibid., Private Secretary to Smyth, 8 January 1968.
64 PRONI, D/3026, *CDU Papers*, CSJ Campaign Newsletter, No. 8; Patricia McCluskey to Paddy Byrne, 27 December 1968.
65 Patterson, *Ireland Since 1939*, p. 197.
66 Warner, Geoffrey, 'Putting Pressure on O'Neill: The Wilson Government and Northern Ireland, 1964–69', *Irish Studies Review*, Vol. 13, No. 1 (2005), pp. 15–16.
67 LPA, GS12/NI, Northern Ireland Documents, 1970, Harry Nicholas to Frank Ing, North Hammersmith Labour Party, 29 January 1969.
68 Bing, Geoffrey, 'What Westminster Left to Another Debate', *Irish Times*, 17 October 1969.
69 Warner, 'Putting Pressure on O'Neill', pp. 13–31.
70 Ibid., pp. 24–5.
71 Ibid., p. 28.

Failure of the 'consensus-forming strategy', 1965–69

72 Ibid., p. 14.
73 NILP, *Electoral Reform Now* (1965).
74 Interview with Erskine Holmes, 21 September 2005.
75 NILP, *Ulster Labour and the Sixties: Radical, Relevant, Realistic* (1962).
76 Purdie, *Politics in the Streets*, p. 69. The point about the NILP's integrative agenda is also stressed in Dixon, Paul, 'Explaining Antagonism: The Politics of McGarry and O'Leary', *Irish Political Studies*, Vol. 11 (1996), p. 134.
77 PRONI D/2704, *NILP Documents, Joint Memorandum on Citizens' Rights in Northern Ireland* (1967).
78 Interview with Erskine Holmes, 21 September 2005.
79 Ibid.
80 Interview with Sir Charles Brett, 30 January 2004; interview with Brian Garrett, 30 September 2003.
81 Interview with Brian Garrett, 30 September 2003.
82 Brett, C.E.B. *Long Shadows Cast Before: Nine Lives in Ulster, 1625–1977* (Edinburgh: John Bartholomew, 1978), p. 85.
83 Interview with Sir Charles Brett, 30 January 2004.
84 Brett, *Long Shadows Cast Before*, pp. 62–3, 101–3.
85 Interview with Sir Charles Brett, 30 January 2004.
86 Brett, *Long Shadows Cast Before*, p. 128; interview with Sir Charles Brett, 30 January 2004.
87 Interview with Paul Arthur, 7 December 2004.
88 Brett, *Long Shadows Cast Before*, p. 105.
89 Brett, C.E.B., *Manchester Guardian*, 3, 4, 5 March 1964.
90 Brett, C.E.B., 'Religious Apartheid', *Manchester Guardian*, 4 March 1964.
91 Ibid.
92 Ibid.
93 NILP, *Election Manifesto* (1965).
94 NILP EC Minutes, 16 March 1965, cited in Graham, *The Consensus-Forming Strategy of the Northern Ireland Labour Party*, p. 173.
95 nterview with Robert Bingham, 24 February 2005.
96 Rose, *How the Troubles Came to Northern Ireland*, p. 16.
97 Edwards, Aaron, *Signposts to the New Ulster? Unionist Government Administration, the Labour Opposition and the Protestant Working Class in Northern Ireland, 1956–72* (Unpublished MA Thesis: Queen's University Belfast, 2002), pp. 21–6.
98 NIPC, NIO Cuttings Files on the IRA in 1966, *Secret IRA Inventory* (1966).
99 Mitchell had previously contested and won the Westminster seat in 1955 but was disqualified because he was serving 10 years' imprisonment for IRA activities.
100 PRONI, D/3233/1/2, *Vivian Simpson Papers*, Simpson to Short, 2 April 1966.
101 Kilfedder's election address to his constituents contained 14 extracts from his recent speeches. All of them, apart from two, plagiarised NILP policies on socio-economic issues and flagged up Kilfedder's wish not to 'slavishly vote' with his Tory allies on legislation harmful to working class interests. See PRONI, D/4127/5/2/4, *Kilfedder Papers*, 'Vote Unionist, Vote Kilfedder' (1966).
102 PRONI, D/3233/1/2, *Vivian Simpson Papers*, Simpson to Short, 2 April 1966.
103 Walker, Graham, *A History of the Ulster Unionist Party: Protest, Pragmatism and Pessimism* (Manchester: Manchester University Press, 2004), p. 164.
104 Stewart was Head of Religious Studies at 'Friends' School in Lisburn, a Quaker maintained school.

105 Interview with Douglas McIldoon, 21 January 2004.

106 A republican candidate would not run again in South Antrim until 1979.

107 Craig, F.W.S., *British Parliamentary Election Statistics, 1918–1970* (Chichester: Political Reference Publications, 1971).

108 Interview with Jim McDonald, 4 May 2005.

109 See the comments by Republican Labour MP Harry Diamond in Northern Ireland House of Commons Debates, Vol. 64, Col. 652–3. For a more rounded picture of events during this period see David Boulton's *The UVF 1966–73: Anatomy of Loyalist Rebellion* (Dublin: Torc Books, 1973).

110 *Belfast Telegraph*, 27 June 1966.

111 Ibid.

112 See Garland, Roy, *Gusty Spence* (Belfast: Blackstaff, 2001), pp. 48–9, 53–4; also interview with Billy Mitchell, 27 September 2005.

113 Interview with Billy Mitchell, 27 September 2005.

114 Boulton, *The UVF, 1966–73*, pp. 51–2; see also O'Callaghan, Margaret and Catherine O'Donnell, 'The Northern Ireland Government, the "Paisleyite Movement" and Ulster Unionism in 1966', *Irish Political Studies*, Vol. 21, No. 2 (2006), pp. 203–22.

115 PRONI, CAB 4/1336, Meeting held between Cabinet and RUC leadership at Stormont Castle on 25 July 1966.

116 Ibid.

117 Hennessey, Thomas, *Northern Ireland: The Origins of the Troubles* (Dublin: Gill and Macmillan, 2005), p. 57.

118 Purdie, *Politics in the Streets*, p. 73.

119 Interview with Sir Charles Brett, 30 January 2004.

120 For a more detailed analysis of the influence of the QUB Labour Group see Arthur, Paul, *The People's Democracy, 1968–1973* (Belfast: Blackstaff, 1974), pp. 24–5.

121 NILP, Final Agenda for the 43rd Annual Conference, Holywood, County Down, 17–18 June 1966.

122 PRONI, D/3233/5/8, Record of Correspondence between the NILP and IrLP, 17 May 1966.

123 Ibid., Corish to NILP, 20 June 1966.

124 PRONI, D/3233/5/8, Text of Resolution adopted by 1966 IrLP Conference, October 1966.

125 NILP, Final Agenda for the 43rd Annual Conference, Holywood, County Down, 17–18 June 1966.

126 NILP, Resolution 25 (Composite 6) submitted to the 43rd Annual Conference, 17–18 June 1966.

127 PRONI, D/3233/5/8, Record of Correspondence between the NILP and IrLP, 'Council of Labour for Ireland'. Charles Brett drafted many of the 'non-committal and lawyer-like communiqués'. See his *Long Shadows Cast Before*, pp. 136–7.

128 Ibid., NILP to Corish, 27 June 1966; see also the document 'Council of Labour for Ireland'.

129 Bew, Paul, Henry Patterson and Ellen Hazelkorn, *The Dynamics of Irish Politics* (London: Lawrence and Wishart, 1989), p. 168.

130 Gallagher, Michael, *The Irish Labour Party in Transition, 1957–82* (Manchester: Manchester University Press, 1982), p. 64.

131 PRONI, D/3233/5/8, 'Decision of Executive Committee – Re: Attendance at Meeting at Stormont on 27 April 1967'.

Failure of the 'consensus-forming strategy', 1965–69

132 PRONI, D/3233/5/8, Record of Correspondence between the NILP and IrLP, IrLP to Norman Kennedy, 2 March 1967.
133 PRONI, D/3233/5/8, 'Decision of Executive Committee – Re: Attendance at Meeting at Stormont on 27 April 1967'.
134 Farrell, Michael, *Labour in Northern Ireland: An Historical Sketch*, Paper delivered at the IALSO weekend school, 24–26 November 1967, pp. 6–7.
135 Arthur, *The People's Democracy, 1968–1973*, p. 24.
136 Farrell, *Labour in Northern Ireland: An Historical Sketch*, p. 7.
137 Patterson, *Ireland Since 1939*, p. 200.
138 Adams, Gerry, 'A Republican in the Civil Rights Campaign' in Farrell, Michael (ed.), *Twenty Years On* (Dingle: Brandon, 1988), pp. 39–53.
139 Purdie, *Politics in the Streets*, p. 133.
140 NIPC, *Ann Hope Papers*, NICRA Constitution.
141 *Disturbances in Northern Ireland The Cameron Commission* (Belfast: HMSO, September 1969), Cmd. 532, p. 78; see also Purdie, *Politics in the Streets*, p. 135.
142 Purdie, *Politics in the Streets*, pp. 155–6.
143 Interview with Billy Mitchell, 4 May 2001. Mitchell was a leading Paisleyite in the mid-1960s, a member of the UPV and later a senior UVF officer in the 1970s.
144 Purdie, *Politics in the Streets*, p. 248.
145 NILP, Final Agenda for the 44th Annual Conference (1967).
146 Interview with Brian Garrett, 30 September 2003.
147 Ibid.
148 NIPC, *NILP Box 1*, Minute Book of the Falls DLP, 19 May 1968.
149 Ibid., 19 May 1968.
150 Ibid., 15 December 1968.
151 Bew *et al.*, *Northern Ireland*, p. 141.
152 Interview with Erskine Holmes, 21 September 2005.
153 Ibid. CND (Campaign for Nuclear Disarmament) was a British non-party political organisation formed in 1958 and it held many marches throughout London and the British Isles.
154 Interview with Sir Charles Brett, 30 January 2004.
155 Members of the NILP's EC in 1967 included Tom Boyd, Vivian Simpson, Michael Farrell, Paddy Devlin and Erskine Holmes.
156 Interview with Brendan Mackin, 10 January 2006.
157 Interview with Sir Charles Brett, 30 January 2004.
158 Interview with Eamonn McCann, 21 December 2007.
159 Interview with Alan Carr, 3 August 2005. Carr was a founding member of the Labour Club at the New University of Ulster at Coleraine. He served on the NILP EC in 1970–71.
160 Walker, Graham, *The Politics of Frustration: Harry Midgley and the Failure of Labour in Northern Ireland* (Manchester: Manchester University Press, 1985), p. 71.
161 *Belfast Telegraph*, 23 December 1968.
162 Walker, *The Politics of Frustration*, p. 71.
163 Interview with Alan Carr, 3 August 2005.
164 Interview with Douglas McIldoon, 21 January 2004.
165 Interview with Sir Charles Brett, 30 January 2004.
166 Ibid.
167 Confirmed in an interview with former Newtownabbey Labour Party activist Anne Foster, 16 August 2005.

168 Interview with Erskine Holmes, 21 September 2005.
169 Interview with Alan Carr, 3 August 2005.
170 Purdie, *Politics in the Streets*, pp. 71–2; see also Cradden, 'Labour in Britain and the Northern Ireland Labour Party', p. 82; Dixon, Paul, *Northern Ireland: The Politics of War and Peace* (Basingstoke: Palgrave, 2001), p. 272.
171 Interview with Erskine Holmes, 21 September 2005; see also Dixon, *Northern Ireland*, p. 136.
172 In fact the Party's EC endorsed the civil rights movement in December 1968 and again at its annual conference in May 1969; see also the *Belfast Telegraph*, 22 November 1969.
173 NIPC, Civil Rights Material: *Ann Hope Papers*, 'Explanatory Memorandum on Proposed New Constitution', 5 January 1969.
174 Ibid., NICRA 'Ultimatum to Stormont' (June 1969).
175 'One man, one vote' was eventually conceded shortly before Terence O'Neill's resignation in April 1969.
176 NIPC, Civil Rights Material: *Ann Hope Papers*, 'Explanatory Memorandum on Proposed New Constitution', 5 January 1969.
177 Interview with Brian Garrett, 30 September 2003. Garrett was opposed to the tactic of 'direct action'.
178 Interview with Brendan Mackin, 10 January 2006.
179 Interview with Anne Foster, 16 August 2005.
180 See Brett, *Long Shadows Cast Before*, p. 139.
181 Purdie, *Politics in the Streets*, p. 105.
182 Northern Ireland House of Commons Debates, Vol. 70, Col. 910, 24 July 1968.
183 Northern Ireland House of Commons Debates, Vol. 70, Col. 910, 24 July 1968. Between 1967 and 1975 the British government was to invest about £80 million in Harland and Wolff. See letter from Joel Barnett, Chief Secretary to the Treasury, to Merlyn Rees, Secretary of State for Northern Ireland, 20 January 1975, National Archives of the United Kingdom (NAUK), PREM 16/490.
184 Northern Ireland House of Commons Debates, Vol. 70, Col. 910, 24 July 1968.
185 Walker, Graham, 'Loyalist Culture, Unionist Politics: A Response to Stephen Howe', *Open Democracy*, 11 October 2005.
186 Northern Ireland House of Commons Debates, Vol. 70, Col. 915–16, 24 July 1968.
187 Northern Ireland Senate Debates, Vol. 51, Col. 1724, 29 October 1968.
188 Dixon, *Northern Ireland*, p. 272.
189 Interview with Eamonn McCann, 21 December 2007. According to Bew and Gillespie among the first people arrested on 5 October 1968 in Derry were three NILP members stopped in a van with loudspeakers. Bew, Paul and Gordon Gillespie, *Northern Ireland: A Chronology of the Troubles 1968–1999* (Dublin: Gill and Macmillan, 1999), p. 3.
190 Boulton, *The UVF 1966–73*, pp. 66–7.
191 Walker, Graham, *Intimate Strangers: Political and Cultural Interaction between Ulster and Scotland in Modern Times* (Edinburgh: John Donald, 1995), p. 143.
192 Walker, *A History of the Ulster Unionist Party*, p. 166; see also the report of the meeting in PRONI, CAB 4/1413.
193 Walker, *A History of the Ulster Unionist Party*, p. 168; Cunningham, Michael *British Government Policy in Northern Ireland, 1969–2000* (Manchester: Manchester University Press, 2001), p. 5.
194 O'Neill, *The Autobiography of Terence O'Neill*, p. 106.

195 Patterson, *Ireland since 1939*, p. 202; see also Purdie, *Politics in the Streets*, pp. 133–4.
196 NILP, *Electoral Reform Now* (1965).
197 Patterson, *Ireland since 1939*, p. 203.
198 O'Neill, *The Autobiography of Terence O'Neill*, p. 149.
199 Ibid., p. 148.
200 Bew *et al.*, *Northern Ireland*, p. 171.
201 UUP, *Ulster at the Crossroads* (1969).
202 *Belfast Telegraph*, 13 February 1969.
203 Mulholland, Marc, 'Assimilation versus Segregation: Unionist Strategy in the 1960s', *Twentieth Century British History*, Vol. 11, No. 3 (2000), p. 305.
204 *Belfast Telegraph*, 23 December 1968.
205 Ibid.
206 *Irish Times*, 17 October 1969.
207 NAI, DFA, 2000/5/14.
208 See Arthur, *The People's Democracy 1968–1973*.
209 See Prince, Simon, *Northern Ireland's '68* (Dublin: Irish Academic Press, 2007).
210 Interview with Bobby Cosgrove, 22 August 2005.
211 Walker, *A History of the Ulster Unionist Party*, p. 168.
212 NILP, *Constitution* (1964).
213 See NIPC, *NILP Box 1*, Minute Book of the Falls DLP, 'Michael Farrell Addresses the Monthly Meeting of the Falls Labour Party', 13 May 1971.
214 NILP, *British Rights for British Citizens* (1969) - Stormont Electoral Manifesto for Falls.
215 PRONI, D3233/5/9, *Vivian Simpson Papers*, 'Vivian Simpson for Oldpark' electoral pledge-card.
216 Ibid.
217 Bew and Gillespie, *Northern Ireland*, pp. 13–14.
218 Martin McBirney QC was a member of the NILP's EC (1964–67), party chairman in 1966–67 and a leading figure of the Northern Ireland branch of the Society of Labour Lawyers. He was later appointed as a Resident Magistrate, a post he occupied until he was murdered by the Provisional IRA at his home on the Belmont Road on 16 September 1974.
219 Interview with Billy Mitchell, 4 May 2001.
220 Bew, Paul and Henry Patterson, *The British State and the Ulster Crisis* (London: Verso, 1985), p. 12.
221 Walker, *A History of the Ulster Unionist Party*, pp. 172–3.
222 McAllister, Ian, *The Northern Ireland Social Democratic and Labour Party: Political Opposition in a Divided Society* (Basingstoke: Macmillan, 1970), p. 19.

5

The NILP in retreat, 1969–72

Introduction

By the opening months of 1969 the storm whipped up by those congregated under the umbrella of the Northern Ireland Civil Rights Association (NICRA) had broken over the province's streets with great ferocity. Arguably Terence O'Neill's Unionist regime had been anticipating the need for concessions on local government electoral reform and discrimination in jobs and housing for some time. In his own unique way O'Neill had even made gestures (albeit symbolic) to pave the way for these as far back as 1965 – by encouraging closer North–South relations and, later, by promoting his highly altruistic 'Civic Weeks' agenda.[1] In December 1968 he had announced a package of reforms to take the sting out of the civil rights movement's accusations about the tardiness of improvement in the socio-economic and political standing of Roman Catholics.

In return for O'Neill's compliance Wilson invested his full support in the Ulster Premier, whom he admired for carrying through 'a remarkable programme of easement' on the reform issue, despite mounting opposition from Protestant ultras.[2] However it could be argued that Wilson fundamentally misinterpreted O'Neill's ability to implement a cast-iron reform programme because of the strength of feeling in the local cabinet against British government interference in the affairs of Northern Ireland.[3] This was recognised somewhat belatedly – and exaggeratedly – by Wilson in his memoirs when he revealed how 'progress [in reforms] had aroused open hostility on the part of his atavistic grass-roots supporters and many of his backbenchers, to say nothing of a black reactionary group in his Cabinet'.[4]

However, the intentions of the British government at this critical juncture were still unclear. Officially, Whitehall's attitude was best summed up by the Home Secretary, James Callaghan, who said in debate: 'we believe that it is our responsibility to use our maximum influence on the institutions which exist in Ireland to secure the same standards in that country as exist here'.[5] In however, as Bew and Patterson suggest, both Wilson and Callaghan 'had

The NILP in retreat, 1969–72

no conception' of the underlying dynamics shaping the Northern Ireland state and therefore their decision to resist attempts to 'embroil'[6] themselves directly lacked a firmness of conviction.[7] One casualty in British Labour's decision to prop up O'Neill's weakened authority was the NILP, which was finding it ever more difficult to find a receptive audience for its political outlook in British ministerial circles.[8]

Whatever the recriminations from his opponents O'Neill was viewed rather sympathetically by some like-minded liberals in the NILP – including Charles Brett – as a 'well meaning man' who tried and failed to break up the stagnant sectarian politics of right-wing Unionism and Nationalism.[9] Brett's rose-tinted view is surprising given O'Neill's personal campaign to oust Labour from Protestant working-class districts.[10] It could be convincingly argued that O'Neill's rhetoric of 'transforming the face of Ulster' only proposed cosmetic alterations to the deep sectarian dichotomy underpinning the state.[11] That material prosperity would ultimately truncate tribal sentiment has now been discredited as fanciful but in the 1960s there was a real belief that ethnic antagonism would dissipate once money was thrown at it.[12] As the dawn of a new decade broke the modernisation project which had temporarily gripped the imaginations of British politicians fell into terminal decline across the United Kingdom.[13]

Following O'Neill's capitulation on 28 April 1969 – and his replacement by his cousin Major James Chichester-Clark – Callaghan held firm to his private belief that his comrades in the NILP possessed the level-headedness and political acumen necessary to administer the final *coup de grâce* to an ailing Unionist regime.[14] But the NILP had been irreparably damaged on two fronts: by O'Neill's skilful theft of its 'technocratic clothes' during the 1960s and by Wilson's obsession with propping up O'Neillism in lieu of any real policy formulation on Ireland.[15] British Labour's lack of coherent policy on Northern Ireland was an obstacle the NILP could have successfully traversed if only the BLP had listened attentively to its comrades in Ulster prior to the return of Edward Heath in June 1970.

What made matters so intolerable for the NILP at this time was the attitude of the Labour Party whilst in government, which preferred to take the platitudinous course of believing that 'the unionists were never really as bad as they were painted'.[16] The reality, as Brendan O'Leary has argued, was that 'Statements they [Wilson and Callaghan] made before or after their premierships showed they had formulated preferences substantively different from the status quo, but in office did nothing that significantly advanced these goals.'[17] Under the strain of such conditions the NILP could be forgiven for travelling unwittingly 'down a blind alley',[18] as one former leading activist described his party's latest attempt to affiliate to its British sister party in 1970. These merger talks collapsed prematurely, partly due to a failure of nerve on the British side, and partly because of the return to office of the Tories, an event which was unlikely to herald any significant departure from the new spirit of bi-partisanship.[19] As this chapter will show the NILP was left to face the impending crisis alone.

Politics in the streets: the Labour movement and the return to violence

Purdie's claim that the NILP was ill-equipped to become the political vanguard of the civil rights movement[20] did not prevent its membership, individually or collectively, from becoming involved in joining in the chorus of calls for a reinstatement of 'British rights for British citizens'.[21] Nor did it prevent the party from calling on the Unionist Government to 'recognise the integrity of the civil rights movement'[22] or voting with a large majority to support its individual members in their contribution to the civil rights campaign.[23] Unfortunately for those NILP activists willing to raise their heads above the parapet, sectarian violence would soon be reignited among broad sections of the population. Consequently, working-class areas – forever bearing the brunt of antagonism – became ghettoised for the first time since the inter-war period.

However, it is important to stress here that Protestants and Catholics had, generally speaking, lived in harmony for over a generation. The lull in sectarian conflict gave the NILP enough leeway to put down firm roots in the community and build up its membership and organisation among skilled manual workers in urban areas. Moreover, the party was well suited to embrace the changes ushered in with the dawn of a radical new era by soaking up support from a newly created class of upwardly mobile Protestant and Catholic workers in the 1960s. Such 'embourgeoisement' was beginning to make its presence felt as these more affluent workers dispersed into the new suburban hinterlands surrounding Belfast.

One of the areas beyond greater Belfast which benefited from the influx of new multi-national companies was East Antrim, which contained many of the major industries enticed into the province in the early 1960s. Firms such as General Electric Company (GEC), Standard Telephones and Cables (STC), Courtaulds, Imperial Chemical Industries (ICI), Michelin and Carreras Rothmans (NI) Ltd could be found in relatively close proximity to one another. This inevitably led to calls 'west of the Bann' that the Unionist regime was carrying out a process of geographical discrimination in the siting of the province's new manufacturing base. Indeed it has subsequently been taken up as a clarion call in the literature.[24] Anti-colonialist commentators, for instance, have argued that O'Neill's modernisation programme 'reinforced the Protestant privileges he ostensibly deplored by pouring foreign investment into Protestant areas'.[25] However, this is a matter of political speculation, fuelled by the fallacies of hindsight. Bew et al. have maintained a sceptical stance on the issue, instead articulating the view that new industry did not substantially alter the inner-mechanics of the local state. Their interpretation centres on the fact that Stormont's bonanza pay-out to 'new projects' did not automatically lead to the dissolution of old industries, for 'in 1970 some 60 per cent of the manufacturing and 86 per cent of the total workforce were still employed outside the new

ably safe to assume that the motivations animating the boardrooms
ng multinationals were fixated more on the relative closeness which

north-east Ulster gave them to British and global markets.[27] Put simply, it made better business sense to situate factories in an area where considerable non-unionised manual workers could be pooled, where communications were better and where lower transport costs and rival competitive ventures could be dealt with on a level economic playing field. Capital, historically transnational, drew little except profit from risking such ventures in the well-subsidised near-periphery of the Anglo-Irish free trade arena. As the pre-eminent Marxist historian Eric Hobsbawm reminds us, 'The most convenient world for multinational giants is one populated by dwarf states or no states at all.'[28] In the free-trade arena little would be lost by exploiting these favourable conditions. In another sense the influx matched the pressing priorities of the Unionist regime, which had sought to expand Northern Ireland's industrial base through diversification since the 1950s.[29] By and large this was motivated by the reality of a contracting staple industrial base in a changing global marketplace.[30] One fact remains, though, that as increasing numbers of Protestant and Catholic workers became unionised they flocked to the burgeoning ranks of the NILP.

Traditionally, the NILP had been propped up by two key pillars in Northern Irish society: materially, in its structural agreement with several of the largest British-based trade unions operating in Northern Ireland, and spiritually by the leadership and support exercised by those churchmen (mostly Protestant) who peppered its ranks. In many instances these actors dedicated the amenities under their stewardship to the social and cultural development of local community infrastructure. The minute books of the Woodvale and Falls Labour Parties frequently reported the success of fundraising activities – such as jumble sales, fêtes, games competitions, dances and other working-class recreational pursuits – and signalled a strengthening of a Labour culture in and around Belfast.[31] Many of these leisure pursuits, especially those involving youth, took place free from sectarian antagonism.[32]

The gathering storm of violence threatened the very foundations on which this Labour culture rested. It was feared that not only would the recreational and leisure pursuits of workers be affected but, more importantly, the actual industries needed to sustain the livelihoods of dependent wage earners. 'Riots,' noted Victor Blease at the time, 'drive away investment.'[33] The Labour movement was therefore either in the worst position imaginable or, on the other hand, well placed to hold the line against trouble. If it faltered the whole fabric of post-war working-class society would be jeopardised.

As violence unfolded in 1969 the Labour movement found itself in an unenviable position; how it managed its response, however, depended largely on the interplay of two factors: its position in relation to the state and the attitudes adopted towards physical force by its mass (and very diverse) membership. From August 1969 the ICTU's Northern Ireland Committee issued regular statements calling for 'the introduction of full democratic and civil rights for all citizens'. It unreservedly condemned the violence, stating that had trade union proposals been implemented in the past the present tragedy could have been avoided.[34] After the introduction of direct rule it became clear that the British government was still prepared to invest in the maintenance of this 'moderate centre ground', as much for its restraining cross-sectarian influence, as its tendency to think beyond the zero-sum arguments of Unionist and Nationalist political forces.

The promotion of the 'silent majority' vis-à-vis the 'troublesome minority' mythology gave British ministers the opportunity to bolster the position of civil society in the face of some of the most horrendous acts of violence witnessed in post-war Europe. By encouraging people to stay off the streets and out of trouble the moderates were performing a useful service in the bid to return Northern Ireland to a state of civility. It would therefore be simply disingenuous to portray leading trade union figureheads, like Billy Blease, Sandy Scott and Norman Kennedy, as quiescent about violence – as some scholars have tried to do.[35] Publicly trade union leaders had no qualms about forcefully condemning the

> rable-rousing utterances or doctrinaire theories of office seekers and political opportunists who sought to exploit the present political situation ... the social needs and the political allegiance of different sections of the working class people.[36]

The threat of violence spilling over onto the shop floor was not lost on Blease or his colleagues because, for them, 'Strife, hatred and civil commotion can only turn Northern Ireland into an industrial wasteland.'[37]

In many respects the way forward was clear. The sectarian violence which had blighted the workforce in the shipyard and other workplaces in Belfast in the 1920s would not be permitted to happen again.[38] It was therefore incumbent upon all trade union leaders to face down any turn towards rampant blood-thirsty mob rule, whilst – and this point is crucial for explaining the weakness of the NILP by 1975 – needing to appear impartial in the eyes of a divided working class. The latter point was especially important for those holding dual leadership positions in the trade unions and their political wing. For Blease – who owed his allegiance to trade unionism first and foremost – all that was needed to restore goodwill among men was an injection of level-headedness and sincerity on the part of politicians: 'The light of reforms is now beginning to shine through the blanket of political bigotry, arrogance and stupidity, which has hampered progress and development in the province.'[39] Blease's own disillusionment with extremist politicians led him to urge his fellow trade unionists to support only those candidates who were known to stand for non-sectarian political objectives and who 'have worked with the trade union movement in pursuit of peace, full employment, prosperity and social justice'.[40]

David Bleakley's *Peace in Ulster* (1972) was the first book to actually analyse the uphill struggle facing those trade unionists who 'met the challenge head on' and is consequently an important contribution to our understanding of the response of civil society to quell the first orchestrated attacks between Protestant and Catholic workers from 1969.[41] At a mass outdoor meeting at the Harland and Wolff shipyard on 15 August, following the worst day of sectarian rioting since 1935, churchmen and shop stewards addressed an estimated crowd of 8,000[42] and appealed for calm in the workplace:

This mass meeting of shipyard workers calls on the people of Northern Ireland for the immediate restoration of peace throughout the community. We recognise that the continuation of the present civil disorder can only end in economic disaster. We appeal to all responsible people to join with us in giving a lead to break the cycle of mutual recrimination arising from day to day incidents.[43]

Arguably, the decisive action taken by trade unionists gave the British government an exaggerated picture of what could actually be accomplished in keeping violence off the shop floor. As Dixon argues, this may well have 'misled observers into believing they had more of a "moderating" influence over their members than was the case'.[44] The violence visited on working-class areas in August had a short incubation time of only a matter of months. Its immediate origins – stemming from the recent young hooligan riots in Derry and the reciprocal brutality meted out by ill-disciplined sections of the RUC and B Specials – certainly fanned the flames of communal discord, though NICRA must share in part of the blame for its 'decision to hold protest marches and not to recognise the legitimacy of sectarian territorial divisions'.[45]

The Falls Labour Party and the burning of Bombay Street

Significantly, important changes were now gripping the NILP too as Charles Brett had declined to allow his name go forward for re-election to the EC earlier in the spring, leaving Brian Garrett as the principal liberalising force on the party's Executive.[46] Garrett recalled how by this stage the eruption of sectarian violence challenged the personal and political convictions of many members: 'If you live in a society like Northern Ireland. We all had homes and backgrounds. There were conflicts within the Labour Party; there was no question about that.'[47] Nevertheless, by the mid-1960s the NILP had successfully straddled the deep cavernous ethnic, national and religious gulf which separated the two traditions in Ulster, recruiting both Protestants and Catholics to its membership in relatively high numbers.[48]

The return of Paddy Devlin as MP for Falls in the February 1969 Stormont election was a turning point for the NILP and pointed to a consolidation of its support in Catholic working-class areas. His defeat of the sitting Republican Labour MP Harry Diamond was certainly a victory for the NILP's brand of non-sectarian democratic socialism but in overall strategic terms the party had done quite badly in its bid to secure more seats, or even to win back those which it had lost in 1965. Again the distinction between total votes actually cast for Labour and the number of seats finally won masked its modest electoral performance. The party polled 45,113 votes (8.1% of the total vote) and was knocked into third place by the Anti-O'Neillite Unionists. The Nationalists had gained only 26,009 votes, retaining only six of their original eight seats, while a plethora of new civil rights-linked parties returned such dominating personalities as John Hume, Paddy O'Hanlon and Ivan Cooper, who later went on to form the nucleus of the Social Democratic and Labour Party (SDLP) in August 1970.[49] Consequently, the NILP once again found its politics excluded from the mainstream of political life. Yet there was little the NILP could have done at this point. It was obvious that the main electoral issue centred on the future political direction of Unionism, not on socio-economic issues or the mediocre leadership provided by Unionist MPs at Westminster. In the end it was an unpropitious context for the NILP to plump for a settlement based on shared communal grievances.

Interestingly, Devlin's maiden speech provides us with only a small glimpse into his socialism (as it concentrates heavily on law and order) and it would be unfair to interpret this as suggestive of his overall ideological prospectus. In committee rooms he was a far more formidable opponent. For example, when the Public Order (Amendment) Bill came under scrutiny, Devlin took centre stage. While Hume articulated concerns from a narrow Derry nationalist perspective,[50] Devlin brought a broader socialist appreciation of the plight of Ulster's working class. Conversely, his internationalist outlook meant that he was equally at home deploying the language of the European Convention for the Protection of Human Rights and Fundamental Freedoms (1950) to justify the ringing endorsement of public protest, as he was in condemning the rampant inequalities in Northern Irish society. As he saw it the civil rights agenda had a moral dimension that went beyond political point-scoring:

> The whole range of civil rights issues has brought people on to the streets particularly over the past six months, in order first of all to get attention and secondly, to get redress for the things they morally believe to be right.[51]

His casual flaunting of procedural undertakings in favour of an intensely plebeian agenda earned him a fearsome reputation and led to much handwringing amongst his opponents.

Table 5.1 Falls Labour Party in the 1960s

Constituency of residence	Males	Females	Total
North Belfast	24	2	26
West Belfast	101	11	112
East Belfast	10	0	10
South Belfast	4	1	5
Miscellaneous	43	3	46[a]
Total	182	17	199

Source: The data shown in this table were compiled by comparing the membership list in the Woodvale minute book with the Belfast and Northern Ireland Street Directories for the years 1958 and 1964 the dates when the first and last entries were made.

[a] Most of these individuals lived outside the Belfast municipal boundary in the catchment area of Lisburn Rural District Council.

The NILP in retreat, 1969–72 165

Table 5.2 Religious breakdown of the population in Falls (1961)

Religion	Male	Female	Total
Roman Catholic	14,966	16,713	31,679
Protestant	1,885	910	2,795
Other	634	662	1,296
Total	17,485	18,285	35,770

Source: Census of Population, 1961: Belfast County Borough (Belfast: HMSO, 1963), p. 33.

Significantly, it could also be argued that Devlin's cavalier attitude in Stormont left his parliamentary colleague, Vivian Simpson, as an onlooker rather than as a cheerleader in his assaults on Unionist political stubbornness. Devlin was certainly not a stickler for protocol and he often preferred to hold firm to his Labour convictions, preferring to side-step parliamentary procedure in favour of verbal sparring with his opponents. At times he punctuated his debates with real-life illustrations from his constituency-level work; a trademark of all Labour parliamentarians who had served in the House since the 1920s. In many respects he possessed admirable qualities, not least in holding firm to the steely socialist conviction of 'from each according to his abilities, to each according to his needs', a trait shared by other agnostic socialists in his party.[52] On one occasion he kept debate fired up at Stormont throughout the night on the issue of public order, purely out of an acute awareness of how such legislation would eventually play out on the streets.[53] The hitherto part-time administration had not witnessed anything like it since Labour held four seats in the 1958–62 and 1962–65 parliaments.

Devlin's abilities as a street-wise politician were equally impressive. Along with Hume and Cooper in Derry, Devlin and Paddy Kennedy frequently claimed to be in the thick of demonstrations and violence in Belfast during 1969–70.[54] This ground-level perspective gave the Falls MP an authority and respect from his constituents few other Northern Ireland politicians could command. As a consequence, however, Devlin could not be in two places at once and while Simpson felt more at home in the debating chamber his Falls comrade preferred to work at the coalface. There is certainly much evidence that Devlin spoke sporadically on important political and socio-economic issues such as electoral law and housing matters[55] but these almost pale into insignificance when compared to Simpson's incessant speeches on official NILP policy issues.

The NILP's presence features frequently in parliamentary debates in the three years between March 1969 and the prorogation of Stormont in March 1972. However, there is a clear disparity in terms of the contribution made by Devlin and Simpson. Arguably Devlin just does not feature as often in parliamentary proceedings and when he does his speeches are brief, single-issue orientated and somewhat out of sync with those made by his PLP colleague. This could easily be explained by Devlin's lack of experience in the debating chamber (after all Simpson had been there for over a decade plugging away on the NILP's behalf) but that cannot account for the very exhaustive contributions he made on public order and discrimination issues.

In fact one might generalise further by making the point that Devlin was so concerned with the dynamics of political life in Northern Ireland more generally that he sometimes neglected the necessary clientalist management of his own constituency base, something that could not be said about Hume, Fitt or, indeed, Simpson. Devlin's maiden speech came a full week after Simpson's. Greeted with cheers as he rose, the Falls MP chose to make it an abrupt (it lasted only a few minutes) and abrasive attack on the government's proposed Public Order Bill. While Simpson spoke eloquently about the socio-economic fabric of his constituency and the province at large,[56] Devlin chose to focus on the heavy-handed tactics of successive Ministers of Home Affairs. During the Bill's second reading Devlin's adherence to the hypothetical constraints of this legislation could not mask his penchant for how such issues affected the ordinary man on the street. Nevertheless, both Devlin and Simpson did co-operate on profoundly ethical socialist matters: perhaps the most significant collective action culminated in the Private Members' motion on World Poverty, moved by Simpson and championed by both men.[57]

Reflecting on recent events in his inaugural speech at Stormont, Simpson made the point that the February elections had been fought on the basis of 'personalities and personality cults'. The Unionists, he angrily concluded, 'were washing their dirty linen in public'.[58] Simpson reserved his main attack for the outgoing Minister for Health and Social Services, Robert Porter, whom he quizzed for omitting any mention of the future of the Mater Hospital in his opening address to Parliament. Catering for the whole province, the Mater was held up by Simpson as a model of modern health care delivery and he hoped the Unionists would soon admit it into the NHS system.[59] Equally important were the knock-on effects of street disturbances on the tourist industry and the question over increases in the capacity of ferry services between Northern Ireland and Scotland. He commended the involvement of youth in the election, although remained somewhat reticent about their revolutionary zeal and vitality. Rarely patronising or patriarchal, Simpson struck the right balance between the party's Christian right and its liberal soft centre-left. As Brett had said of him: he was 'somewhere in the middle' as far as the party spectrum was concerned.[60]

Simpson often looked to the future in his speeches and for a reversal in the province's unfortunate economic fortunes. He held firm to the gradualist belief (like his predecessor as leader, Tom Boyd) that a turnaround in the atmosphere in the House would inevitably seep out in society.[61] The following excerpt encapsulates his ethical socialist thinking:

> It is perhaps apposite that such comments should be made by one of the opposition parties and especially when over a period of 20 years at least that party has striven to present a constructive political programme to the Government and people. It does not matter whether it was along the line of economic well-being or of cures for our urgent social ills and continuing unhappy community relations, the party I

represent, the Northern Ireland Labour Party, speaks for a very wide cross-section of the electorate. We are still the second largest political force in this country, and will continue, I hope, to fulfil our role with a due sense of responsibility.[62]

Despite Simpson's attempts to keep politics on a realistic footing it was clear that others outside the House believed passionately that their legal and political channels were blocked, taking 'to the streets as a substitute for the constitutional battle'.[63] Northern Ireland was moving closer to all-out conflict.

The summer months of 1969 saw the worst sectarian violence in Belfast since the 1964 Divis Street riots. Following confrontations in Derry nightly rioting spread to the Ardoyne area of North Belfast, situated in the heart of Vivian Simpson's constituency. Four Catholics and one Protestant were killed as a result of sectarian clashes. Significantly, trouble centred on Divis Street, the site of Paisley's uncouth intervention five years earlier. In response local NILP branches became hubs for activity as a flurry of statements emerged condemning the violence. By early August the Newtownabbey Labour Party was engaging in a civil disobedience campaign to draw attention to the material hardship suffered by striking council workers while also calling for the RUC to be placed under British control and the accelerated disbandment of the B Specials.[64] Meanwhile, Vivian Simpson made an emotional plea for calm from Stormont and the Shankill Labour Party spokesman David Overend issued a press statement condemning 'any acts of physical violence from any quarter' and calling on residents to 'exercise all possible restraint in the coming week'.[65]

Two days later a further two civilians had lost their lives and the mainly Catholic Bombay Street was razed to the ground. The following day James Callaghan endorsed the Inspector General's call for military aid to the civil power and troops were ordered onto the streets. The NILP soon came face to face with its nemesis. For the Chairman of the Falls Labour Party (FLP), Brendan Mackin:

> Bombay Street was a catalyst for everything. The NILP practically did not exist from 1970. There were structures ... [though] the vast majority of people who were active members left, dropped out. The party was not able to handle the schism, the fall out when both communities felt under attack. If that dies down and you move towards a political compromise then people start to emerge; but what emerged was the like of the Provos. They started their 'armed struggle' and then there was the reaction to that. So that left no room for the NILP. Some from the NILP joined the Republican Clubs, etc., but there was a few that held on. But the party ceased to exist in electoral terms, post-1970. There were no electoral campaigns.[66]

At a special meeting of the FLP a few weeks later Mackin made clear that he 'felt that there had been a lack of communication between the Executive of the NILP and the Falls division immediately after these riots had commenced'.[67] Although the main point of the meeting was to determine whether Devlin ought to continue to attend Stormont there could be no mistaking the general feeling of malaise now setting in amongst local party members.

In a pre-emptive move aimed at alleviating Catholic fears Callaghan made a diplomatic visit to Northern Ireland on 27 August 1969, touring many of those areas in Belfast and Derry blighted by disturbances. His decision to authorise the deployment of troops meant that he could not easily shake off the incessant vilification emanating from both Unionists and Nationalists who accused him of 'escalating the conflict'. He fell further out of favour with Protestants when he commissioned the Hunt Report, which recommended the permanent holstering of RUC firearms and the disbandment of the B Specials. Callaghan's popularity waned dramatically in the eyes of a minority in the Shankill who took to the streets to vent their anger. Ironically their actions culminated in the death of the first police officer in the conflict.[68] Meanwhile, working-class Catholics remained disparaging of his political contributions after their resolute challenge to the British Army during the Ballymurphy riots of April 1970.

It was becoming increasingly obvious after September 1969 that sectarian confrontation on the streets was furthering the entrenchment of ethno-national divisions between the working classes. Some NILP activists jumped ship from the party because they thought that the increasing polarisation of the two communities would lead to them eventually finding their own 'tribal camp'.[69] Others tended to concur with the argument put forward by the newly elected MP for Mid-Ulster at Westminster, Bernadette Devlin, who claimed in her maiden speech that:

> Since 5th October, it has been the unashamed and deliberate policy of the Unionist Government to try to force an image on the civil rights movement that it is nothing more than a Catholic uprising.[70]

The perception was enough for many NILP activists to retract from the NICRA radar, although many like the liberal Erskine Holmes remained loyal to the ideal. In fact the incoming NICRA Executive commissioned another NILP member, the Belfast broadcaster and former colonial civil servant John D. Stewart,[71] to raise a standing committee to enquire into the current working of NICRA's constitution.[72]

For many Catholics forced to vacate their homes loyalist attacks only served to increase the feeling of isolation. Several community leaders representing Catholic areas in Belfast – including Paddy Devlin and Gerry Fitt – banded together under the Central Citizens' Defence Committee (CCDC) as a means of providing a stop-gap against loyalist incursions. Very quickly it became necessary to search out allies beyond local areas and the decision was taken to ask the Fianna Fáil government in the South to provide assistance to help protect vulnerable communities. Material aid was filtered through the open channels created by community leaders. There were even suggestions that the Dublin government had financed the setting up of a civil rights office in Monaghan and the publication of the newssheet *Voice of the North*. These allegations emanated chiefly from Cathal Goulding's Marxist-inspired Official IRA and met with strong repudiation in the Dáil. However, there was a feeling that the Republic was operating a cloak-and-dagger policy in the North which only served to heighten the tensions between Stormont and Leinster House.[73]

As the violence worsened Paddy Devlin, Paddy O'Hanlon and Paddy Kennedy travelled south to seek help for the Catholic community in Belfast. According to Hennessey all three men sought an audience with the Taoiseach 'for the purpose of obtaining arms for Catholics in the Falls Road'.[74] When news broke of Devlin's diplomatic mission Sam Napier quickly issued a statement from the NILP's Waring Street offices affirming that a 'statement made by Mr Devlin was made in a personal capacity and not on behalf of the party'.[75] In subsequent weeks the NILP Executive publicly reprimanded him for temporarily boycotting Stormont because of, in Devlin's words, 'the inadequacy of the unionist government responses to the crisis'.[76] By the end of the year Devlin's association with the NILP had all but elapsed, although he would still officially remain the NILP's MP for Falls until he was eventually expelled by the party's EC on 19 August 1970.[77] In the meantime things were going from bad to worse on the streets as the British Army flooded ghettoised areas to arrest IRA personnel and disrupt their activities. As Devlin remarked in his autobiography:

> Overnight the population turned from neutral or even sympathetic support for the military to outright hatred of everything related to the security forces. As the self styled generals and godfathers took over in the face of this regime, Gerry Fitt and I witnessed voters and workers in Dock and Falls constituencies turn against us to join the Provisionals.[78]

The situation worsened with the discovery of a plot by Fianna Fáil government ministers to smuggle 800 automatic pistols and 80,000 rounds of ammunition into the hands of the Provisional IRA; as a direct result two of the most powerful politicians in the South, Charles Haughey and Neil Blaney, were sacked in disgrace.[79]

When Paddy Devlin appeared at the acquittal of Newry civil rights leader Samuel Dowling, who had been caught in possession of arms and explosives in Dundalk in November 1970, it confirmed just how far some members of the Catholic working class had drifted towards militancy.[80] Arguably, Devlin's demand for guns was to Eoghan Harris 'a passing moment of weakness for which he never forgave himself',[81] though as Richard English has remarked, following Bombay Street, 'Sectarianism had been intensified, and the need for Catholic ghetto defenders now seemed unchallengeable.'[82] The issue of the procurement of illegal arms would continue to fuel hard-line attitudes, to the detriment of Labour interests, particularly in Derry and Belfast.

Meanwhile, significant changes were ongoing within NICRA. It had become increasingly obvious throughout the summer of 1969 that Betty Sinclair's star had begun to wane in the civil rights movement. The influx of radicals into the National Executive precipitated her downfall. Sinclair's biographer, Hazel Morrissey, wrote that as chairperson of NICRA the Belfast communist 'was in a very strong position to block the more militant tactics advocated by other members of the Executive'.[83] However with the continual groundswell in support of the more extreme Catholic Nationalist leadership one might speculate that Sinclair's Stalinist convictions were used against her by radical young

Trotskyites in the PD. In a letter written to a NICRA sympathiser in Canada shortly before he replaced Sinclair, Frank Gogarty, a committed Nationalist member of the NICRA Executive, claimed condescendingly that 'Betty Sinclair is not the Maud Gonne of C. Rights. She is one great reactionary bitch who is holding up the revolution'.[84] Sinclair became the main obstacle to his more militant revolutionary ambitions.

Even though Gogarty initially dismissed PD calls for him to take over from Sinclair in the summer months of 1969, his support for Michael Farrell would not have gone unnoticed. In any event it took less of a push and more of a shove to displace Sinclair from her chair. Four committee members (including Sinclair) resigned from the National Executive in protest in September.[85] Former Executive member Raymond Shearer angrily protested in a press statement that:

> We have been infiltrated by an extreme socialist group which is using us for political ends which have nothing to do with civil rights. They have split the movement down the middle.[86]

The departure of the NICRA 'old guard' had corresponded inexorably with a further shift towards a policy of 'complete civil disobedience'.[87]

With Sinclair's demise and the fusion of socialist and Nationalist ideas on NICRA's Executive 'the Labour Movement lost its capacity to influence the organisation and as a result the republican movement grew in authority and influence'.[88] Nevertheless, it must be acknowledged that Sinclair continued to play a significant leadership role on the NICRA Executive despite the influx of radical new members.[89] In Patterson's opinion:

> Unlike many of the ultra-left student elements of the burgeoning protest movement, she knew from her personal experience during the 1930s of the terrible danger of exacerbating traditional animosities. However, it was those who criticized her for 'reformism' and 'Stalinism' who had their way, with disastrous results.[90]

Inevitably the switch in control of NICRA spoken about by Unionists – from the moderates, who were 'anti-Protestant', to the extremists who were 'even more anti-Protestant'[91] – would soon scupper its commitment to non-sectarianism in the eyes of even liberal Protestants. Granted, it might well be counter-intuitive to write the civil rights movement off as a republican plot – brought about more through design than accident – but one should not discount how it furnished right-wing Protestants with the ammunition needed to check any future advances by the NILP.[92] In retrospect, the former 'token' communist appointed to replace Sinclair, Edwina Stewart, thought that the change in personnel was too much for the Protestant community.[93] Predictably this 'Catholic image' would have reflected very badly on the NILP's broad cross-sectarian front had it linked itself to what was fast becoming an unstable coalition of anti-state forces.

Despite the electoral setbacks the NILP hierarchy continued to proffer the progressiveness of their socialist ideology as a way out of the chaos which was erupting on the province's streets. As a means of strengthening the party's non-sectarian image the South Antrim Labour Party proposed a motion at the April 1969 conference calling on the EC to vigorously pursue a firming up of fraternal relations with the BLP. Before the end of the year Harry Nicholas (BLP secretary) was in Belfast on a fact-finding mission to ascertain how the local membership felt about bringing the parties closer together.[94] On arrival Nicholas was greeted by the NILP's new secretary Douglas McIldoon, who had taken over from Sam Napier at the annual party conference. Napier had held the NILP together for 20 years, often with considerable detriment to his personal life, though he had ensured that sturdy processes had been bedded down within the party which would last beyond his tenure: an integral component being, of course, the close ties with British Labour.[95] In a press statement McIldoon revealed that proposals for a closer liaison were actively being sought and that favourable reactions had been forthcoming from among the party's rank-and-file.[96] On 6 December McIldoon announced publicly that the NILP would be holding a special meeting in the New Year to decide whether affiliation ought to be the way forward.[97] A 200-strong delegation would decide by a card vote (which represented the 29,600-strong individual and affiliated members) whether or not to proceed with plans for the merger. Farrell condemned the move as a 'shoddy little manoeuvre'[98] while Devlin and the Falls Labour delegation considered it a move in the wrong direction.[99]

Interestingly, British Labour's 1969 conference was 'the first time for nearly fifty years that the Labour Party had debated Ireland, yet the atmosphere was headily optimistic'.[100] Bell attributes this to the personal interest taken in Northern Ireland by Callaghan,[101] who had succeeded Roy Jenkins as Home Secretary in 1967. Nevertheless the chance to reshape BLP policy towards the province was missed. Although a more intimate relationship would have presented the electorate with a non-sectarian alternative, the BLP continued to believe that 'the Unionists were never really as bad as they were painted'.[102] That said, the decision to reinvigorate the link between the two parties would not only lead to more direct access, through Transport House, to Harold Wilson and his cabinet, but it would also add a lucrative financial dimension to the relationship. It was thought by many in the party that its Waring Street headquarters could be expanded and a deposit insurance scheme drawn up to give the NILP more financial security in order to contest more Westminster constituencies. Nicholas indicated that he would like to see the NILP contest all 12 Westminster seats in the forthcoming British general election – a marked increase in the four previously contested in 1966.

The Derry Labour Party and the Catholic working class

Outside Stormont events on the streets moved quickly. The 'honeymoon period' in relations between the British Army and sections of the minority Catholic community was all but at an end by Easter 1970. Indeed some historians have argued that in Derry at least this relationship began to break down within weeks of the army's arrival.[103] Peace-rings, totally different than the peace-lines of Belfast, ensured that the majority Catholic Bogside and Creggan estates rapidly became no-go areas for the RUC, B Specials and recently arrived troops, who were accused by republicans and Nationalists of propping up the local regime. Many civil rights activists – from a multiplicity of smaller pressure groups – coalesced under the banner of the Derry Housing Action Committee (DHAC). Its leading lights were drawn largely from the Londonderry Labour Party (LLP) and the Republican Clubs,[104] though it did include several affluent members of Derry's Catholic community. All were united in campaigning to improve the way of life for local people.

In many ways Derry was historically quite different from Belfast in socio-economic and political composition. Its industrial base was less solid and fluctuated uncontrollably whenever a credit squeeze was initiated from the centre. The textile industry – and the shirt-making factories in particular – formed the basis of employment in the city. It employed mostly female workers and therefore the main challenge for many of the city's trade union activists in the 1960s was the development of opportunities for male labour.[105] Politically, Unionists had dominated the city's local government machinery for decades. Catholics suffered most from the gerrymandering in the local electoral wards; instigated by the landowning and mercantile Unionist elites in the 1930s, the electoral boundaries effectively kept most non-Unionists out of virtually all aspects of political life. In her maiden speech Bernadette Devlin indicted the Unionist MP for Londonderry for failing to alleviate the abject poverty and deprivation visited on the divided working class in the city's Bogside, Creggan and Fountain estates.[106]

The fact that some kind of gerrymandering did exist has since been proven.[107] But it often worked both ways and more often to the detriment of non-Unionists – a group which, contrary to popular belief, also included socialists, liberals, labourists and non-conformists of varying religious and political hues.[108] Not all Protestants were as affluent as Michael MacDonald has disingenuously claimed.[109] Moreover, it is a matter of political caricature to claim that the NILP could not challenge these grievances because this 'was potentially to jeopardise the socio-economic and political privileges which defined what it meant to be Protestant'.[110] Unemployment, inadequate housing and the antiquated local government franchise operated to the disadvantage of Protestants too. Tom Boyd, for instance, had been taunted by Terence O'Neill on many occasions when his party challenged the Unionists on this very issue because he had for many years lived with his elderly mother and therefore – as a 'lodger' – was ineligible to vote in local government elections.[111]

It could be strongly argued that all creeds in the north-west of the province suffered diminishing economic fortunes throughout the post-war period. The loss of the proposed New University of Ulster to Coleraine in 1968 and the subsequent all-party mobilisation that this occasioned was well stocked with people from both communities and those who belonged to none. Thus a critical mass of Protestants and Catholics were left disillusioned by the tide of reaction blowing from the progressive east of the province. Alarmingly, the impact on Catholic employment prospects in particular was predictable. As Barritt and Carter observed:

> Since a great many workers do not manage to rise above the occupational class of their parents, a group which is confined to unskilled labour in one generation will produce many unskilled labourers in the next.[112]

It is therefore no surprise then that the cutting edge of the civil rights movement in Londonderry quickly became the Derry Young Hooligans after 5 October 1968. Overwhelmingly, the Young Hooligans were unskilled, long-term unemployed males who habitually vented their anger and frustration with the local Unionist authorities in a tirade of violence.[113]

Insofar as the LLP tabled motions for annual NILP conferences these were aimed at specific grievances acute to the north-west region. For instance, at the 1970 conference in Newry the LLP injected a west of the Bann flavour into proceedings, with calls for 'a working party to make a study of the feasibility of public enterprise industry as a solution to high unemployment west of the Bann'.[114] Ballynafeigh Labour Party thought that the costs of maintaining the newly formed Ulster Defence Regiment (UDR) would be better spent on increasing the provision of houses and jobs. Peculiarly, and as a sign of its growing Marxist-inspired radicalism, Newtownabbey Labour demanded that the party seize control of shop floors and establish 'co-operative collectives'.[115] For Derry Labour the bottom line was that the infrastructural deficit in their region would need to be tackled first and foremost without recourse to dogmatic Marxist flights of fancy. Its proposals sought the immediate expansion of further and higher education in Derry and more jobs and housing as a basic human necessity.

As the one-time secretary of the LLP (and now a well-respected Irish writer) Nell McCafferty later said of her branch: 'We weren't looking for much, really – jobs, universal franchise, and housing. Our demands were for nothing more or less than full civil rights such as were enjoyed over in Britain.'[116] McCafferty had joined the ranks of the LLP in the 1960s, captivated by the lucid oratorical skills of the young firebrand socialist Eamonn McCann. Both McCafferty and McCann depict the incessant hostility displayed by the Roman Catholic Church towards the Derry Labour Party, in which labourism was equated with 'communism' and 'atheism'.[117] The Catholic clergy tended to flock to the traditional conservative politics of the Nationalist Party and republicanism rather than to the ecumenical strands which ran through Labour circles. At election times the Nationalists, as much as the Unionists, were content to drive a wedge between the working classes by emphasising the dangers of cross-sectarian co-operation.[118]

What is interesting about the local party's contribution to conference proceedings is that for the first time since its formation it became totally immersed in the most pressing matters of the day. Formed in 1965 by Willie Breslin, Ivan Cooper and Dermie McClenaghan,[119] the Derry Labour Party included young radicals like McCann and McCafferty in its ranks. By 1968 it had approximately one hundred members on its books and had stood successfully in Unionist- and Nationalist-dominated wards in the 1967 local government election, picking up almost 30% of the vote without winning any seats.[120] The LLP was also successful in soaking up the pockets of independent labourism formerly represented by older trade union hands like Stephen McGonagle.[121] Derry trade unionism centred on the shirt-making industry and garment trade, which consisted of 23,000 men and women in the late 1960s.[122] In the wake of the Duke Street dispersals one would have expected the party to go into virtual hibernation, yet it emerged confident (if slightly shaken) in its democratic socialist convictions and more willing than ever before to represent the interests of working people. Even though it had previously resolved to defy Craig's ban and support the planned march it did not push a militant communist or republican line. Its commitment to radical activity rather than socialist pontificating alarmed the NILP hierarchy in Belfast,[123] yet it nevertheless cut a reasonable voice amidst the heated political exchanges that followed the clashes between civil rights marchers and the security forces in Londonderry.

Out of the five emergency resolutions appended to the Final Agenda for the 1970 NILP conference, three emanated from the LLP and two from Newtownabbey.[124] The LLP condemned recent calls for a coalition government to achieve peace in Northern Ireland. It thought that 'this would be a coalition of the Horse and Rider – with the Labour movement as the Horse – as the example of other coalition Governments on the island show'.[125] The Derry Party's resolution calling for a withdrawal of American troops from South East Asia was typical of McCann's internationalist views at this time. But it was the LLP's concern over the news from the Irish Republic that a section of Fianna Fáil had been secretly importing arms for use by their supporters in the North, which seemed to most alarm Derry Labour activists. For many, the Unionist regime was on a par with its Fianna Fáil counterpart – stoic, and politically bankrupt:

> We reiterate our belief that no section of the working class in Northern Ireland would gain anything from the extension over the whole island of their type of society represented by Messrs. Haughey, Blaney and Boland. We believe it is necessary to fight both green and orange Toryism and to be seen to be doing so.[126]

By now Derry had become a front line for pitched battles between the Young Hooligans and what was widely perceived to be a Unionist police force. The LLP was to the fore in calling for leadership to be exercised over the city's youth 'by people who can talk to them' and not by those who sought to exploit them.[127]

Perhaps the biggest blow to the LLP came not from without but from within. Following his continued support for Bernadette Devlin, McCann was expelled from the NILP Executive by the remainder of the EC.[128] It was also clear that beneath the surface McCann's resistance to party attempts to merge with the BLP raised more questions than it resolved.[129] In any normal circumstances expelling one member might have been relatively easy. The problem here was that McCann was Derry Labour Party chairman and a high-profile figure in his own right. Almost immediately speculation spread like wild-fire that he would

The NILP in retreat, 1969–72 175

form a breakaway faction.[130] NILP secretary Douglas McIldoon warned that McCann would be thrown out of the party altogether 'if he continues to violate our standing orders'. In defiance of central party orders supporters of the expelled chairman met in Newtownabbey to discuss his expulsion.[131] Not long after this meeting McCann left Northern Ireland for a research post at the London School of Economics.

The Falls Road curfew and aftermath

Despite their best efforts the party hierarchy could not contain the sectarian cancer from spreading throughout some of its local branches. McIldoon admitted that, 'It was at the margins, but there were always people within the party who would [allow] their tribal neuroses [to] appear. I wouldn't say it was a majority thing but it was there.'[132] Matters were worsened on 3 July 1970 when the British Army imposed a 33-hour curfew on the Lower Falls while it searched for illegal arms and ammunition. It was to take nearly six months for a press statement to emerge from the FLP condemning the outrage, due mainly to the arrest and detention of some of its members. The statement read:

> Logically, all the monstrous acts of injustice covered by the curfew could be called illegal, but a biased judiciary has made it evident that it is prepared to uphold all actions committed by the military on that infamous occasion ... if by accident of birth one happened to be born in the Lower Falls area, one was not only suspect, one was downright criminal on the nod from anyone in uniform.[133]

Paddy Devlin denounced the Army's heavy-handed tactics in November 1970 when he called on the government to reimburse loss of earnings for the 400–500 workers estimated to have been prevented from going to work.[134]

Despite such provocation the local party soldiered on in a bid to 'continue to look for good employment, better housing and true Christian charity for our community'.[135] Several academic commentators view the Falls Road curfew as a

> 'turning point' in relations between the Catholic working-class community in Belfast and the British army, in that the operation so soured relations that the army would no longer be seen as the protectors of the Catholic community.[136]

Brendan Mackin left the party not long after the curfew. He was disappointed that more could not be done to reconnect the embattled people of the Falls community to the cause of Labour:

> Yes, that's when the back was broken. Effectively in 1970 the areas where most trouble happened [Oldpark and Falls] were both represented by the NILP. To some extent the party split along sectarian lines. It was a time of fear, when common sense can go out the window. You could look at events which colour people's life-long perspectives; people who had worked within the Unionist community to build a non-sectarian party, who then thought Northern Ireland was under attack. [It was the] same as in the 1914–18 war when many people in the South, who opposed British rule in the South, joined the British Army thinking that by showing loyalty you could achieve your goals back home.[137]

The indiscriminate use of CS gas during the curfew hastened the Catholic community's alienation from the army and led directly to the swelling of the IRA's ranks in the autumn of 1970.[138]

However, the security forces were not the only factor at play here. What probably accelerated the demise of the Falls Party even further was not so much the jackboot of the British Army as the fanatical reaction of some IRA activists to the local Labour Party and its supporters. Devlin recalled in his memoirs how entire areas transferred loyalty to either the Official IRA or to the newer Provisional IRA. The Lower Falls, the nerve centre of the FLP, 'broke about even'.[139] As both wings of the IRA set about consolidating their control over territory and people there is strong evidence to suggest that the homes of NILP supporters were attacked by some republicans who feared an adverse reaction from those civilians who disagreed with the return to the physical force tradition.[140]

Notwithstanding the difficulties involved in fighting elections with a reduced campaign capacity, the NILP launched into the June 1970 British general election with a dogged determination to reverse 'the lurch to extremism'.[141] The party lambasted 'sectarian blends' for fermenting violence[142] while also pledging 'to heal the internal divisions within our community'.[143] By now the dove of peace (or 'the pregnant pigeon' as some members preferred to call it in private) was beginning to appear against a red background on all party literature. Together with the NILP's symbol of the flaming torch of socialism the dove of peace came to symbolise how most members felt about their party's stance on the sectarian disturbances.[144] Impressively, and despite mounting pressures within its traditional support-bases, Labour polled a magnificent 98,194 votes (12.6% of total votes cast). Paisley's Protestant Unionists captured only 35,303.[145] The NILP came second in three of the four Belfast constituencies – and it once again gave Gerry Fitt a monopoly in the race against his Unionist opponent. Certainly cracks began to appear along the sectarian fault-lines of the party system and these were brought out into the open in the wake of the election. However, press statements emanating from some Protestant EC members praised the civil rights movement for continuing to focus the attention of the world onto 'the real enemy of the people of Northern Ireland which is the social, political, economic and religious privilege as personified by the Unionist Party'.[146]

The NILP failed to carry its broader cross-sectarian support-base with it after the election for three main reasons. First, the party's hesitant public stance on law and order allowed its ethnic Protestant rivals in the Democratic Unionist Party (DUP) and Vanguard Unionist Progressive Party (VUPP) to supersede its strong opposition to terrorist activity (arguably a political stabilising mechanism for the NILP during the previous IRA campaign of 1956–62) making it appear soft on the issue. Second, that the IRA and loyalist paramilitaries had begun to explode no-warning bombs in Belfast pubs and shops (traditionally places where most working-class activity was concentrated on a daily basis) eroded the temptation to socialise or mix on a cross-sectarian basis. Even neutral haunts such as the Waring Street Labour Club or Lavery's Bar, close to the Queen's University campus, in the city centre, became dangerous places to frequent.[147] Furthermore, it could be added that this was also a time when even the daily task of travelling to – and home from – work became an arduous and risky activity leading many people to change their jobs. Third, the attitude of the British state turned ever increasingly towards a strong military containment of the conflict as evidenced by the Falls curfew in July.

From this point on more repressive measures aimed at routing the IRA from working-class areas were serving only to alienate moderate opinion in the Catholic community. As Frank Burton has shown, broader community support for the IRA was a 'see-saw relationship'; what really tilted the balance away from localised support for armed republicanism was not continued repressive activity by Crown forces but 'the various activities of the British Army, protestant paramilitary groups and the Provos' own military profile'.[148] Traditional patterns of living were irreparably damaged by the biggest population shift since the Second World War. In 1974 the Northern Ireland Community Relations Commission recorded a minimum of 8,000 households moving between 1969 and 1973 due to intimidation.[149] While a high degree of residential segregation existed between Catholics and Protestants in 1969, as Boal *et al.* later pointed out, the 'sharpening of the conflict since has resulted in a further dramatic increase in segregation'.[150] Accompanying such high levels of segregation in Belfast were low levels of social interaction. Street barricades and vigilante squads patrolled areas on a nightly basis, filling the vacuum created by the breakdown in law and order and central government authority in working-class areas.

Politically, matters were worsened for the NILP during the summer of 1970 when a matter of days after his expulsion from the party Paddy Devlin joined forces with Gerry Fitt, John Hume, Ivan Cooper, Paddy O'Hanlon and Austin Currie to officially launch the SDLP.[151] The entry into the political arena of this new party caused multiple problems for the NILP. Not only did it emerge as a contender for the NILP's share of support amongst the Catholic community but it drew on the skills, organisational and creative abilities of former Labour figures like Devlin and Cooper. Just as the PD had benefited from the abilities of Farrell, McCann, Arthur and Toman so the SDLP threatened to poach invaluable personnel and electoral support away from the NILP.

In an extensive analysis of the birth of the SDLP the chairman of the NILP's Policy Sub-Committee (and Brett's replacement) Brian Garrett observed that it was 'unlikely' that the new party's emergence would 'rank as a spectacular event in the eyes of an outsider to Irish politics'.[152] He based his claims on the relative failure of other Catholic groupings to successfully engage with the Labour movement or indeed to band together and speak from a coherent and unified political platform. To an extent Garrett was justified in his assumption. In its bid to distinguish its programme from the 'Catholic bourgeoisie'[153] involved in leading NICRA, the PD had sacrificed organisation on material issues for single agenda-centric calls for 'one man, one job' and 'one family, one house'. Like the emergent SDLP the PD had also made the mistake of failing to build up a genuine non-sectarian movement.[154] As McCann admitted in the wake of the Burntollet march:

> We were to [sic] busy shouting 'One man-One job' and keeping our mass audience, that when a real concrete material issue came up on which it might have been possible to prove to Protestant workers that what we are demanding is in their material interests, we were running around the streets in the Civil Rights movement. We have failed to give a socialist perspective because we have failed to create any socialist organisation.[155]

The comparison was a tenuous one given the PD's revolutionary socialist credentials. In concluding his analysis Garrett concentrated his attack on uncloaking what he saw as the SDLP's narrow sectarian political agenda:

> For the Northern Ireland Labour Party (and, I feel sure, the Liberals too) the new group represents further entrenchment of the politically divided within the community. Bereft of any legitimate Socialist philosophy the SDLP group, however well intentioned, merely matches a "moderate" Unionist or Alliance type approach, with the obvious underlying emphasis on the constitutional issue rather than the urgent social and economic problems of Northern Ireland.[156]

As policy chief Garrett recognised that the NILP would need to place its policies 'in sharp relief' to ensure that its political message was easily distinguishable from the emerging Alliance Party and SDLP. However, he greatly misunderstood the challenge, preferring to see the SDLP as the NILP's main electoral opponent. As the SDLP became more politically 'green' than 'red' it adopted a place in the party system in the Catholic bloc, not the political centre. Consequently, Alliance was permitted a clear run by liberal NILP members sympathetic to its non-sectarian ethos but totally unaware of the new political realities.

Throughout the closing months of 1970 gunfire and explosions became daily occurrences in Northern Ireland. At the end of October riots in Ardoyne lasted for three nights and witnessed serious confrontation between local people and the security forces. The IRA had murdered 15 people by December 1970. All of them (apart from one IRA member who blew up himself and his family in a premature explosion in Derry's Creggan estate) were Protestant civilians. Meanwhile loyalist paramilitaries killed two, one of whom was a member of the IRA, during separate rioting incidents.[157] In a bid to ease the remainder of reforms through, the NILP proposed the immediate abolition of all local councils and the creation of new commissions, although it left little impression on an under-fire Unionist Party.[158] Perhaps the one significant coup for the NILP was the beginning of talks with representatives of the BLP. A high-ranking NILP delegation met privately with Sir Harry Nicholas and former Home Secretary James Callaghan.[159] The outcome was positive but measured. Impressed by the NILP's contributions Callaghan was non-plussed at the failure of a strong political Opposition to deal with the Unionist government, admitting publicly that 'as long as opposition forces are disunited in the province, the Unionists will continue to run the country'.[160]

Internment and the move towards 'Community Government'

Between the burning of Bombay Street in August 1969 and the introduction of internment two years later events moved quickly on the streets of West Belfast. Morale within the FLP had been seriously deteriorating since the Falls curfew. The countless riots, bombings and shootings took their toll even on the most ardent opponents of violence in this small community. Although events had taken a turn for the worse by the New Year, the report of the *Review Body on Local Government in Northern Ireland* (1970), or Macrory report, paved the way for the introduction of the Housing Executive Act (NI) on 25 February 1971, ensuring that the future allocation of public authority houses would be fairer and more transparent.[161] The Parliamentary Commission also guaranteed that the civil rights demands would be met, though the fate of the Special Powers Act and the B Specials was less than clear.

The NILP should have had reason to be proud of these reforms; after all it had originally instigated discussion over them in countless parliamentary debates since 1958. Sadly, it soon became a cold fact of political life that the party could not take full credit for their implementation in light of the pressure exerted by the British government on the Unionists to find a political accommodation with the Nationalist minority. The new Prime Minster, Brian Faulkner, had been given the task of floating the proposals for 'minority participation' in an enhanced committee system.[162] Ironically, these proposals were first mooted by the NILP 13 years previously. Had a deal been done to safeguard Opposition participation in the locally devolved system then it is plausible that the SDLP could have negotiated on behalf of their Catholic support-base from a much stronger position. Arguably, the SDLP's combative rhetoric masked its genuine willingness to compromise with Chichester-Clark's replacement.[163]

Nevertheless, Faulkner finally recognised the NILP as a non-sectarian centrist party when he appointed David Bleakley as Minister of Community Relations in March 1971. Bleakley recalls how Faulkner asked:

> How about you stop talking about power-sharing and how about doing something about it? And the two of us together, I remember saying at the time you know 'life will never be the same again politically, because when you get a bright idea, it's one thing, it's doing something about it' and ... we gave the impression (the impression was there) that he was bringing me in for a variety of reasons. Between ourselves, the two of us ... also saw the bigger dimension ... I never had the slightest difficulty, nor did Faulkner with me, in co-operation. And we only made – we were making a surprising gesture then to something that nowadays would be taken for granted ... And ... that's why the Faulkner episode in my life I regard it as important. Not only as helping Faulkner, but as promoting the idea which we [the NILP] had always promoted. And do remember that at the Labour Party conference after I was appointed I got an overwhelming (overwhelming) majority of people in support of me at the idea. At that time it was only for six months ... I resigned over the difficult issue of internment.[164]

Bleakley had been heavily criticised for joining the Unionist team. Recently released Home Office correspondence reveals that they too forecast internal problems for the NILP over the issue. In a briefing paper prepared for Reginald Maudling shortly before he met an NILP delegation, Brian Garrett's continued support for the policy indicated further turbulence in the issue beyond Bleakley's resignation.[165]

Bleakley's tenure as Minister for Community Relations marked a high point in his party's agitation on the theme of reconciliation between the two communities. However, his appointment sat uncomfortably with those in the party who viewed the shift towards a repressive security policy by Faulkner as inimical to the safety and security of the working classes.[166] In a key speech to the Victoria Labour Party, on the eve of Faulkner's announcement, Bleakley lost little time in mourning the political passing of Chichester-Clark, hoping that something could be rescued from the ashes of his caretaker regime. What he wanted to see was the emergence of 'a Unionist leader who would be prepared to put province before party – someone who will pick the best team from all those committed to a peaceful and prosperous Ulster within the United Kingdom'.[167] Interestingly, several of Bleakley's critics drew the comparison with Harry Midgley, the former NILP Chairman (turned Commonwealth Labour Party leader) who accepted Basil Brooke's invitation to join the Unionist Cabinet in May 1943.[168] Like his predecessor Bleakley was jeered loudly by those in the party who lost no time in making their views known at the annual conference the following month.

In policy-making terms the NILP turned its attention towards working up constitutional solutions as a means of truncating the violence now manifest on the streets of Northern Ireland. In May the party's chairman Brian Anderson was realistic in his conference address. His analysis was that the 'ordinary decent people were being stranded high and dry above the high water of sectarian politics'; the party to rescue them, he said, was the NILP.[169] One proposal was for the introduction of the List System of Proportional Representation for Stormont elections. Brian Garrett illustrated his talk by using the Scandinavian and Belgium models to show how – by increasing the Stormont seats from 52 to 100, with multi-party constituencies of six and nine – tensions could be potentially diffused.[170] The party resolved to embark on a co-ordinated campaign to highlight the possible benefits of the PR List System, stressing the importance of now rejecting the PR Single Transferable Vote as the only way to ensure adequate representation of those who did not wish to vote for 'tribal' politicians. Elections in 1973 soon disproved this overly optimistic view.

Despite the forward-thinking tone set at the beginning of the conference the remainder of proceedings were to be overshadowed by two significant disputes between delegates. The first rupture occurred in the NILP–ICTU relationship as the Young Socialists succeeded in pushing through a motion condemning the trade union movement for accepting £10,000 in funding from the Unionist government. The slender majority exposed latent tensions within the wider movement.[171] The air was further poisoned by a resolution from Woodvale Labour Party asking the party to reaffirm its commitment to its 1949 declaration

The NILP in retreat, 1969–72

in favour of partition. Surprisingly, the Young Socialists came across as the honest broker on this occasion by successfully including an amendment stating clearly that the party's first loyalty was to the working class of Northern Ireland. A card vote carried the amendment by 13,200 to 10,200.[172] Internal rifts reflected the diversity of opinion within the party which had been steadily building up since the influx of new Catholic members in the early 1960s. Jack Hassard perfectly summed up the atmosphere by claiming, bitterly, 'that in whipping this constitutional issue to death they were also whipping the party to death'.[173]

An attempt by the NILP's so-called 'left-wing' to have Bleakley expelled from the party had the kibosh put on it by a powerful trade union block vote of 13,000 to 2,000.[174] South Antrim had been simmering about Bleakley's appointment since March[175] though it had been prevented from taking its grievances any further when the EC flatly rejected its bid to throw Bleakley out by 13 votes to 2.[176] As a consequence the two party officers who voted to expel Bleakley, Alan Carr, chairman of the New University of Ulster Labour Club, and Desmond Bromley, a former chairman of South Antrim Labour Party, resigned in protest.[177] Rubbing salt into the wounds Victoria Labour, in a follow-up meeting, gave the new Minister of Community Relations a resounding vote of confidence.[178] The acrimony generated by the fallout led the *Newsletter*'s correspondent to suggest that 'the rift between left and right wing factions within the party ... could hint at difficulties in the future'.[179] Callaghan's personal fraternal greetings on behalf of his party cut little ice with those delegates clearly alienated by the political direction in which their own party was now travelling.

Despite the adverse press attention the remainder of the summer saw the party's spokesmen emerge energetically to concentrate attention on poverty, which still remained 'enemy number one', and away from discussion on the ongoing security problem.[180] McIldoon embarked on a round-trip to brief all NILP branches on how the party's proposed reforms to the electoral system would operate in practice.[181] He explained that he favoured a PR List system and wanted electoral reform to reflect preferences for parties, not personalities. This would ensure that politics would be rescued from the religious quagmire into which it had sunk.[182]

That Hume had led his fellow SDLP MPs out of Stormont in July in response to the British Army killings of two of his constituents played into the NILP's hands.[183] 'Under pressure from the wider Republican community, the SDLP had to take this action,' argue Murray and Tonge, but it was nonetheless, 'an outward manifestation of constitutional nationalism withdrawing consent from the system of government in Northern Ireland.'[184] As the secretary of the newly formed Newry Labour Party, Bill Moyna, perceptively argued, Irish unity would eventually come about, but abstentionism had failed in the past, and it would fail again.[185] By remaining inside governmental institutions Simpson could draw further attention to his party's electoral reform proposals. Although he was set against the walkout, Simpson even called for a meeting of all Opposition MPs to discuss the implications of their move but his call was rebuffed.[186] In response, three Protestant Unionists crossed the floor of the House to join

Simpson as Her Majesty's 'loyal' Opposition to ensure that Stormont still functioned as a parliamentary government.[187]

If the split in NILP ranks occasioned by the conference was not bad enough a second body blow was delivered with the introduction of internment on 9 August. The party split even further over this emotive issue, as predominantly Protestant branches such as Woodvale supported it, while predominantly Catholic ones, like Falls, unequivocally opposed it. The reason was fairly straightforward: it was a blunt instrument used exclusively, in the first instance, against the minority population.[188] At one point the Falls Labour Party had issued a statement attacking Billy Boyd's support for the policy: what made the statement significant was that it came over a week before Faulkner had even officially approved the policy.[189] For Brendan Mackin, who had now gravitated towards republican politics:

> Internment was the biggest recruiting tool for the Provos and how it was handled made it even worse because about 70% of those arrested were not involved at all. The records were too old. They arrested the guy who bought my house from seven months previous and he was interned for two or three months. The politicisation arising from all that meant they were queuing up to join the Provos at a time when the Stickies were arguing about cease fires, etc. The Provos were saying, 'Let's shoot the Prods'.[190]

In direct response to internment Willie Breslin and the LLP spearheaded calls for people to join in a mass rents and rates strike.[191] Despite the prevailing scholarly view that the SDLP led the way in promoting a civil disobedience campaign,[192] the programme actually originated from the (now largely independent) Derry Labour Party.[193] It was hoped that this disobedient action would hit hard at the pockets of the Unionist Government, thereby reducing it to the role of 'debt collector'. Adding to the momentum NICRA and John Hume 'saw the potential for this mass mobilisation of oppositional opinion and soon endorsed the action',[194] calling for people to withdraw their savings from government-sponsored schemes and instead to place them in Credit Unions, co-ops and private banks while also initiating a leaflet drop calling for an escalation of the civil disobedience campaign.[195] This strategy jarred with the NILP's official stance on civil disobedience, which still held firm to its conviction of parliamentary socialism as the only true way out of the quagmire. Two NILP councillors in Newry, Thomas Markey and Gerard Sloan, immediately resigned in response to the first swoops on 9 August. It could be said that the party was left numbed by the experience.

The massive publicity generated by internment overshadowed the publication of *Community Government* (1971), the NILP's most ambitious policy document to date. Since the annual conference in May the party's policy committee had been busy fleshing out proposals for a future settlement for Northern Ireland. Briefly it sought to transform the political situation into something more conducive to inter-communal co-operation and had a form of power sharing as its touchstone.[196] Although Faulkner had rejected the

Community Government proposal as being 'unrealistic' he did welcome its other ideas on PR.[197] In a deputation to Whitehall the NILP presented its case to the Home Secretary, Reginald Maudling, who, together with Wilson, had arguably lacked any Irish policy up until that point.[198]

The meeting between the NILP and Maudling took place in London on 15 September 1971 and was led by the party's only remaining MP at Stormont, Vivian Simpson. It included two of the party's prominent Catholic members, Archie McArdle and Pat McHugh, who outlined the severity of the situation in the province. The delegation put forward some hypothetical political solutions (including ambitious proposals for a 'Government for Social Reconstruction') and called decisively for an end of internment without trial. McArdle, a long-time Labour activist in Falls, called for further round table talks as a way out of the violence: 'Time is running out for us in Northern Ireland,' he said. Similarly, McHugh, the party's vice-chairman, talked tough on the lack of empathy in Downing Street for those living under the psychological trauma being exacerbated by daily bombs. His pessimism was unmistakable: 'We are going to have 2,000 dead in Northern Ireland as a result of the disturbances if we don't take action soon.'[199] The vice-chairman's remarks remained consistent on these issues long before the summer, often criticising the SDLP for failing to represent its constituency base.[200]

Although it is difficult to appreciate that the NILP remained the third largest party in electoral voting terms at this time, the fact remains that it could still muster 8.1% of the total share of the votes at the 1969 Stormont election. Moreover, in the 1970 Westminster contest it polled almost 100,000 votes (26%), a point which party officers continually re-emphasised to government ministers.[201] The benefit of hindsight should not cloud our judgement of the party in these years. It was a major political player and could seek an audience with government ministers when required. Civil servants working within the Home Office were still apt to write in their briefing papers that, 'The Northern Ireland Labour Party is not identified with either community, and is therefore well placed to press ideas for reform within the context of the continuance of Northern Ireland as part of the United Kingdom.'[202] Although recognising its smallness (in relative comparison with the Official Unionist Party) the Conservatives were keen to see the dissipation of violence and would therefore talk to whichever group could exert influence on the grass-roots of both communities. The NILP was unique in the sense that it commanded 'considerable support from Catholics and Protestants, particularly in the towns, but also in the country' according to Simpson.[203] His re-election to represent the Oldpark constituency was evidence that the party was still having some success in presenting itself as a cross-sectarian force, especially in districts where the twin social evils of poverty and terrorism held sway.

Simpson was at pains to stress the destabilising effects such socio-political upheaval was having on local businesses and consequentially the local economy as a whole. As a grass-roots-based party the NILP's strategy at this time was aimed at gaining consensus on 'a Government of Social Reconstruction which would command the support of the majority of the people and isolate the extremists on both sides'.[204] However, it still incorporated the party's long-term ideological aims; that is to say 'the preservation of the border, a regional assembly and the principles of democracy'.[205] Northern Ireland's devolved character was to be preserved but substantive changes were lobbied for in terms of making the electoral system more representative. The party also hoped that bi-partisanship would remain intact at Westminster. Perhaps the most innovative initiative announced by Ulster Labour was its wish to see a conference convened to try to work through the present constitutional impasse. These ideas were a year ahead of their time; they would come to pass in the NILP's submissions at Darlington in late 1972 but for now they remained in draft format.

Maudling's meetings at the time with the NILP, the NIC and the newly formed Alliance Party had concentrated on finding a way out of the protracted inter-communal conflict. They also pointed to the British government's willingness to buoy up the 'moderate centre ground' in Northern Ireland politics.[206] The reluctance of the SDLP to become involved in consultations at this stage contributed to the feeling that grass-roots Catholics were unreachable. Maudling's statement released just after the talks was nevertheless upbeat:

> I trust that the decision of these bodies will have an influence on others in Northern Ireland. I naturally regret the initial reaction of the Social Democratic Labour Party and I hope that in the light in particular of the attitude of the trade unions and the Labour Party in Northern Ireland, they will reconsider their position.[207]

The disengagement of Catholic political representatives from high-ranking political teach-ins nevertheless pointed to the retreat of that community to a situation almost comparable to the late 1950s, though it was a scenario which the NILP sought to rectify. Over the next 12 months the party began to present a more cross-sectarian face in its negotiations with senior British officials. Furthermore, the continued alienation of Catholics from the army meant that Unionists had by now claimed them as their defenders against the IRA. McHugh spoke at length about how the British Army was losing the 'propaganda war' as far as working-class Catholics were concerned;[208] about how 40 people had been killed in the space of the five weeks since internment was introduced and how this blunt tactic was seen as 'a partial option' that would not lead to the isolation of extremists. To an extent the party was generally apprehensive about internment. Within a matter of weeks it became evident that most of the new Provisional IRA leadership had evaded capture and that many ordinary Catholic civilians had been arrested in their stead.

What made life more difficult for Bleakley was that he had not received prior consultation on the policy of internment from Faulkner. Added to the mounting opposition facing him within his own party over internment,[209] Bleakley was left with no other option than to resign as Minister of Community Relations.[210] In his resignation letter to Faulkner, Bleakley conveyed his belief that the policy would do little except provoke further bitterness amongst a bitterly divided community:

The NILP in retreat, 1969–72   185

> I cannot accept that the policy of internment is assisting the cause of law and order. On the contrary I believe that internment is wrong; that this aspect of our policy is a tragic mistake which has made matters worse; further I believe that the terrorists welcome internment for it gives the IRA and other militant groups a sympathy and a hearing on a world-wide scale which otherwise they could not get. In addition the internment controversy handicaps those who are presenting the Northern Ireland case against the campaign of violence.[211]

Several contemporary political commentators interpreted Faulkner's appointment of a Minister for Community Relations as a 'gimmick and no personality under the sun would have made it less so'.[212] With Bleakley's authority diminished in the eyes of both his own party and the wider community, resignation gave him the opportunity to make the honourable choice, but it failed to heal the intra-party rifts occasioned by his initial appointment.

Meanwhile another controversy was brewing as several newspapers reported unofficial meetings between BLP officials and the SDLP[213] at a time when the latter 'wanted to see the end of the Stormont regime'.[214] This caused something of a stir in NILP ranks, prompting a spokesman to reveal that 'It's well known that certain sections of the British party are sympathetic towards the SDLP – but that is as far as it goes.'[215] In NILP eyes, for relations to be anything more than cordial was unthinkable. At a previous meeting of the four main Labour parties (the NILP, BLP, IrLP and SDLP) in Belfast and Dublin the NILP had threatened to withdraw because there was disagreement over the wording of a joint statement. Relations since then, said the spokesman, were practically 'non-existent'. In a further housekeeping matter the three Irish parties met in Dublin to hammer out a new constitution for the Council of Labour, instigated principally because of a highly publicised dialogue entered into between Paddy Kennedy and the Provisional IRA.[216] The NILP directly criticised the Provos in the aftermath of the bombing of the Co-operative building in Belfast in late 1971.

By now it was clear that the Protestant working class had grown tired of the BLP's duplicity. On a fact-finding visit to the province in November 1971 James Callaghan and newly elected BLP chairman Tony Benn were greeted by silence as an estimated 20,000 Protestant workers stayed away from work as a protest against the rumoured decisive shift in British Labour's Irish policy.[217] The protest ran in parallel with traditional Remembrance Day commemorations, giving it the bearing of a dignified and defiant display of British patriotism.[218] As O'Leary has written, 'Wilson's fifteen point programme effectively saw private radicalism on Ireland seep through into his public attempts at solving the problem.'[219] Further deliberations by Wilson on finding a way out of the Ulster quagmire put an immediate strain on the NILP at a time when it was trying to reassure its Protestant supporters that involvement in paramilitarism was not the way forward. In a statement issued on behalf of the Woodvale Labour Party, George Chambers responded to Wilson's recent anti-partitionist remarks by alleging that 'to put it bluntly, Wilson and Callaghan have sold the NILP down the river'.[220] Retrospectively, Chambers thought that British Labour had made life increasingly difficult for the NILP by their hostile attitude:

The main reason for that [increasingly poor relations] was the popularity in England of Gerry Fitt. He was popular till he died. And it was understood that he was a character, was easy to get on with and a popular person at Westminster ... Wilson's Huyton constituency ... had a huge Irish population and whether or not Harold Wilson and people like him played to that I don't know but it certainly came across as if they were playing to that audience. I'll tell you a thing that happened: I was standing in some sort of an election (doesn't matter which) and got no help or support from the British Labour Party. Gerry Fitt received telegrams that were widely spread ... wishing him all the best. That was the type of thing you were up against. Some people like McNamara and other people ... they were openly republican in the Irish sense ... They were definitely more hostile than they could ... [have been] towards us.[221]

When set against the backdrop of unofficial talks with the SDLP this signalled the beginning of debilitating strains on the fraternal relationship.

Notes

1 See Mulholland, Marc, *Northern Ireland at the Crossroads: Ulster Unionism in the O'Neill Years, 1960–9* (Basingstoke: Macmillan, 2000), pp. 128–33.

2 Wilson, Harold, *The Labour Government, 1964–70: A Personal Record* (London: Pelican, 1974), p. 140.

3 Bew, Paul and Henry Patterson, *The British State and the Ulster Crisis: From Wilson to Thatcher* (London: Verso, 1985), p. 13.

4 Wilson, *The Labour Government*, p. 349.

5 United Kingdom House of Commons Debates, Vol. 782, Col. 323, 22 April 1969.

6 The word was used by Callaghan in debate, United Kingdom House of Commons Debates, Vol. 782, Col. 323, 22 April 1969.

7 Bew and Patterson, *The British State and the Ulster Crisis*, p. 26.

8 The leading Labour grandee Richard Crossman made it clear in his diaries that 'the wall of silence around Northern Ireland which was to be so manifest in British politics in the 1970s was laid in the 1960s'. For further discussion see Bell, Geoffrey, *Troublesome Business: The Labour Party and the Irish Question* (London: Pluto, 1982), p. 106.

9 Interview with Sir Charles Brett, 30 January 2004. Some activists were not so certain that O'Neill's motivations were as well intentioned. Interview with Alan Carr, 3 August 2005.

10 Bew and Patterson, *The British State and the Ulster Crisis*, p. 13.

11 Cochrane, Feargal, '"Meddling at the Crossroads": The Decline and Fall of Terence O'Neill Within the Unionist Community', in English, Richard and Graham Walker (eds), *Unionism in Modern Ireland: New Perspectives on Politics and Culture* (Dublin: Gill and Macmillan, 1996), pp. 148–68.

12 Paul Dixon is one political scientist who has cast serious doubt on the credibility of modernisation theory; see his *Northern Ireland: The Politics of War and Peace* (Basingstoke: Palgrave, 2001), Chapter 3, for a fuller analysis.

13 Bew and Patterson, *The British State and the Ulster Crisis*, p. 20.

14 Callaghan, James, *A House Divided Cannot Stand: The Dilemma of Northern Ireland* (London: Collins, 1973), pp. 152, 157, 161.

15 A similar argument can be found in Bew and Patterson, *The British State and the Ulster Crisis*, p. 20.

16 Cradden, Terry, 'Labour in Britain and the Northern Ireland Labour Party, 1900–1970', in Catterall, Peter and Sean McDougal (eds) *The Northern Ireland Question in British Politics* (Basingstoke: Macmillan, 1996), p. 85.

17 O'Leary, Brendan, 'The Labour Government and Northern Ireland', in McGarry, John and Brendan O'Leary (eds), *The Northern Ireland Conflict: Consociational Engagements* (Oxford: Oxford University Press, 2004), p. 196.

18 Interview with Erskine Holmes, 21 September 2005.

19 Cunningham, Michael, *British Government Policy in Northern Ireland, 1969–2000* (Manchester: Manchester University Press, 2001), p. 8.

20 Purdie, Bob, *Politics in the Streets: The Origins of the Civil Rights Movement in Northern Ireland* (Belfast: Blackstaff, 1990), pp. 71–2.

21 Interview with Erskine Holmes, 21 September 2005.

22 *Belfast Telegraph*, 23 December 1968.

23 McAllister, Ian, *The Northern Ireland Social Democratic and Labour Party: Political Opposition in a Divided Society* (Basingstoke: Macmillan, 1977), p. 27.

24 MacDonald, Michael, *Children of Wrath: Political Violence in Northern Ireland* (Cambridge: Polity, 1986), pp. 72–3. Anti-colonialists, like MacDonald, tend to root their analysis in caricature and parody rather than in sound empirical analysis. For a more sophisticated 'green' Marxist analysis of the 'west of the Bann' deficiency in Northern Ireland's economy see McCann, Eamonn, *War in an Irish Town* (London: Pluto, 1993), pp. 284–9.

25 MacDonald, *Children of Wrath*, p. 73.

26 Bew, Paul, Peter Gibbon and Henry Patterson, *Northern Ireland 1921–2001: Political Forces and Social Classes: Revised and Updated Version* (London: Serif, 2002), p. 165.

27 For an insider's point of view see the comments made by the former Northern Ireland Cabinet Secretary Kenneth Bloomfield in his book *Stormont in Crisis: A Memoir* (Belfast: Blackstaff, 1994), p. 65.

28 Hobsbawm, Eric, *The Age of Extremes: A History of the World, 1914–1991* (New York: Vintage Books, 1996), p. 281.

29 *Report of the Joint Working Party on the Economy of Northern Ireland: The Hall Report* (Belfast: HMSO, October 1962), Cmd. 446; *Belfast Regional Survey and Plan: Recommendations and Conclusions: The Matthew Plan* (Belfast: HMSO, 1963), Cmd. 451; *Economic Development in Northern Ireland: The Wilson Report* (Belfast: HMSO, 1965), Cmd. 479.

30 *Ulster Year Book 1969* (HMSO: Belfast, 1968), p. 117; For an informed historical analysis of the global economy in the 1960s see also Hobsbawm, *The Age of Extremes*, pp. 278–86.

31 Minute books of the Woodvale and Falls DLPs.

32 Barritt, Denis P. and Charles F. Carter, *The Northern Ireland Problem: A Study in Group Relations* (Oxford: Oxford University Press, 1962), p. 146.

33 Victor Blease, 'Community News Extra: An Appeal to the Ulster Rioters', *Sunday News*, 28 June 1970.

34 *Belfast Telegraph*, 19 August 1969.

35 Rolston, Bill, 'The Limits of Trade Unionism', in O'Dowd, Liam, Bill Rolston and Mike Tomlinson, *Northern Ireland: Between Civil Rights and Civil War* (London: CSE Books, 1980), pp. 68–94.

36 Speech delivered by Billy Blease, NI Officer, ICTU, to a meeting of trade unions at the City Hotel, Derry, 26 May 1970, The Private Papers of Lord Blease of Cromac.

37 Ibid.

38 *Belfast Telegraph*, 19 August 1969.
39 Speech delivered by Billy Blease, at the City Hotel, Derry, 26 May 1970.
40 Ibid.
41 Bleakley, David, *Peace in Ulster* (London: Mowbray, 1972), p. 72.
42 *Belfast Telegraph*, 16 August 1969.
43 Bleakley, *Peace in Ulster*, p. 73.
44 Dixon, *Northern Ireland*, p. 152.
45 Bew and Patterson, *The British State and the Ulster Crisis*, p. 16.
46 Brett, C.E.B., *Long Shadows Cast Before: Nine Lives in Ulster, 1625–1977* (Edinburgh: John Bartholomew, 1978), p. 139.
47 Interview with Brian Garrett, 30 September 2003.
48 See Simpson's comments in the *Belfast Telegraph*, 1 April 1965. The Falls Labour Party had approximately 200 members on its books by the late 1960s.
49 Murray, Gerard and Jonathan Tonge, *Sinn Féin and the SDLP: From Alienation to Participation* (Dublin: O'Brien, 2005), pp. 10–11.
50 Northern Ireland House of Commons Debates, Vol. 72, Col. 858–9, 2 April 1969.
51 Ibid., Col. 89, 2 April 1969.
52 Interview with Anne Foster, 16 August 2005.
53 Northern Ireland House of Commons Debates, Vol. 72, Col. 1053–4, 2 April 1969.
54 Ibid., Col. 1456, 23 April 1969.
55 See, for instance, Northern Ireland House of Commons Debates, Vol. 72, Col. 1701–3, 29 April 1969.
56 Ibid., Col. 142, 6 March 1969.
57 Ibid., Col. 1619, 17 June 1969.
58 Ibid., Col. 101–2, 6 March 1969.
59 Ibid., Col. 142, 6 March 1969.
60 Interview with Sir Charles Brett, 30 January 2004; for an example of Simpson's ethical socialism see Northern Ireland House of Commons Debates, Vol. 72, Col. 254–6, 12 March 1969.
61 Northern Ireland House of Commons Debates, Vol. 72, Col. 1746–7, 30 April 1969.
62 Ibid., Col. 1746, 30 April 1969.
63 Purdie, *Politics in the Streets*, p. 245.
64 *Belfast Telegraph*, 5 August 1969.
65 *Belfast Telegraph*, 12 August 1969.
66 Interview with Brendan Mackin, 10 January 2006. This has to be qualified in light of the historical evidence, however, as candidates were fielded in the local government and Assembly elections in May and June respectively. In the February and October 1974 elections the West Belfast Federation of Labour Parties went into organisational flux with decisions increasingly being taken by the party's EC without local autonomous consultation.
67 NIPC, NILP Box 1, Minute Book of the Falls DLP, Special Meeting of the Falls Labour Party, 29 September 1969.
68 The Sutton Index. Archived at http://cain.ulst.ac.uk/sutton/chron/1969.html (accessed 7 March 2006).
69 Interview with Bobby Cosgrove, 22 August 2005.
70 United Kingdom House of Commons Debates, Vol. 782, Col. 282, 22 April 1969.
71 John D. Stewart was proposed by the NILP to be its latest Senator at a future election to the Stormont Upper House in the 1970s. Disappointingly the Stormont Parliament was prorogued before an election could be held. However, there can be

The NILP in retreat, 1969–72   189

no question that both Simpson and Devlin held Stewart in high regard and would have succeeded in getting him elected had direct rule not been imposed.

72 *Belfast Telegraph*, 3 November 1969.
73 Northern Ireland House of Commons Debates, Vol. 76, Col. 564–8, 20 May 1970.
74 Hennessey, Thomas, *Northern Ireland: The Origins of the Troubles* (Dublin: Gill and Macmillan, 2005), p. 344.
75 *Belfast Telegraph*, 19 August 1969.
76 Devlin, Paddy, *Straight Left: An Autobiography* (Belfast: Blackstaff, 1993), p. 133.
77 Ibid., p. 139.
78 Ibid., p. 134.
79 MacAonghusa, Proinsias, 'Dublin's Curious Crisis', *New Statesman*, 15 May 1970.
80 *Irish Times*, 8 January 1971.
81 Eoghan Harris writing in the *Sunday Times*, 22 August 1999.
82 English, Richard, *Armed Struggle: A History of the IRA* (Basingstoke: Macmillan, 2003), pp. 103–4.
83 Morrissey, Hazel, *Betty Sinclair: A Woman's Fight for Socialism* (Belfast: John Freeman, 1983), p. 17.
84 PRONI, D/3253, *Frank Gogarty Papers*, Gogarty to George (n.d.).
85 They were: Betty Sinclair (former chair), John McAnerney (former secretary), Fred Heatley (former treasurer) and Dr Raymond Shearer, who had been at the forefront of treating injuries sustained by rioters in their clashes with police in Belfast.
86 *Sunday Telegraph*, 7 September 1969.
87 *Irish News*, 1 November 1969.
88 Morrissey, *Betty Sinclair*, p. 18.
89 *Irish News*, 7 November 1969.
90 Henry Patterson, 'Sinclair, Elizabeth Margaret [Betty] (1910–1981)', *Oxford Dictionary of National Biography*. Archived at www.oxforddnb.com/view/article /92407 (accessed 10 March 2006).
91 McCann, *War in an Irish Town*, p. 297.
92 See Purdie, Bob, 'Was the Civil Rights Movement a Republican/Communist Conspiracy?', *Irish Political Studies*, Vol. 3 (1988), pp. 33–41. Purdie's view that the civil rights movement was 'not a republican/communist conspiracy' is regarded as the generally accepted analysis by most historians of the period.
93 Interview with Edwina Stewart, 31 January 2006.
94 *Belfast Telegraph*, 22 November 1969.
95 See Edwards, Aaron, 'Social Democracy and Partition: The British Labour Party and Northern Ireland, 1951–64', *Journal of Contemporary History*, Vol. 42, No. 4 (October 2007), pp. 595–612.
96 *Belfast Telegraph*, 22 November 1969.
97 *Guardian*, 7 December 1969.
98 *Irish News*, 17 December 1969.
99 Devlin, *Straight Left*, p. 133.
100 Bell, *Troublesome Business*, p. 110.
101 Ibid., p. 110.
102 Cradden, 'Labour in Britain and the Northern Ireland Labour Party', p. 85.
103 Ó'Dochartaigh, Niall, *From Civil Rights to Armalites: Derry and the Birth of the Irish Troubles* (Cork: Cork University Press, 1997), p. 154.
104 McCann, *War in an Irish Town*, p. 83. Republican Clubs were banned by the then Minister for Home Affairs, Bill Craig, in 1967.

105 PRONI, D/3702/C/1/2, Sam Napier 'Report on Meeting with Derry Trades Council held on 18 October 1961'.
106 United Kingdom House of Commons Debates, Vol. 782, Col. 282, 22 April 1969.
107 See Whyte, John Henry, 'How Much Discrimination Was There Under the Stormont Regime?', in Gallagher, Tom and James O'Connell (eds), *Contemporary Irish Studies* (Manchester: Manchester University Press, 1983), pp. 1–35.
108 In Rose's 1968 Loyalty survey (see Rose, Richard, *Governing Without Consensus: An Irish Perspective* (London: Faber, 1971), p. 235) 49% of respondents thought of themselves as Unionist, 21% as Nationalist, 18% as NILP and 9% didn't know. The 2005 Northern Ireland Life and Times Survey found that 40% regarded themselves as Unionist, 22% Nationalist, 35% Neither, 1% Other and 2% didn't know. Archived at www.ark.ac.uk/nilt/2005/Political_Attitudes/UNINATID.html (accessed 5 January 2006).
109 MacDonald, *Children of Wrath*, p. 8.
110 Ibid., p. 74.
111 Interview with Sir Charles Brett, 30 January 2004.
112 Barritt and Carter, *The Northern Ireland Problem*, p. 146.
113 *Irish Times*, 11 December 1969.
114 Final Agenda for the Annual NILP Conference, May 1970 – Emergency Resolutions.
115 Ibid.
116 McCafferty, Nell, *Nell: A Disorderly Woman* (London: Penguin, 2005), pp. 126–7.
117 Ibid., pp. 115–16 ; McCann, *War in an Irish Town*, pp. 68–9.
118 See McCann, *War in an Irish Town*, pp. 68–9.
119 Written Statement submitted to the Bloody Sunday Inquiry by William J. Breslin, 30 January 2002. Archived at www.bloody-sunday-inquiry.org/index2.asp?p=3 (accessed 5 March 2006).
120 McCann, Eamonn, 'The Roots of Revolt', *Socialist Review*, No. 114 (1988).
121 See McCann, *War in an Irish Town*, p. 68.
122 *Ulster Year Book* (1969), p. 117.
123 Interview with Eamonn McCann, 21 December 2007.
124 There were close links between the Derry and Newtownabbey Labour Parties, not only in terms of a shared agnostic socialist ethos but also in the willingness to countenance militant tactics to highlight socio-economic grievances at a localised level. Interview with Anne Foster, 16 August 2005.
125 Final Agenda for the Annual NILP Conference (May 1970).
126 Ibid.
127 *Irish Times*, 16 October 1970.
128 *Belfast Telegraph*, 21 November 1970.
129 Andrew Boyd writing in the *New Statesman*, 4 December 1970; see also Devlin, *Straight Left*, p. 133.
130 *Belfast Telegraph*, 21 November 1970.
131 *Irish News*, 25 November 1970.
132 Interview with Douglas McIldoon, 21 January 2004.
133 *Irish News*, 25 January 1971.
134 Northern Ireland House of Commons Debates, Vol. 77, Col. 997, 11 November 1970.
135 *Irish News*, 26 January 1971.
136 Bew, Paul and Gordon Gillespie, *Northern Ireland: A Chronology of the Troubles 1968–1999* (Dublin: Gill and Macmillan, 1999), p. 29.

137 Interview with Brendan Mackin, 10 January 2006.
138 Dixon, *Northern Ireland*, p. 117.
139 Devlin, *Straight Left*, p. 123.
140 *Irish News*, 26 January 1971; see also Paddy Devlin's memoirs in which he recalls how he had to move from the Lower Falls community to a new home in the Oldpark area of North Belfast.
141 NILP, *British General Election Manifesto* (1970).
142 Interview with Brian Garrett, 30 September 2003; the phrase is Garrett's.
143 NILP, *British General Election Manifesto* (1970).
144 Interview with Douglas McIldoon, 21 January 2004.
145 Archived at www.psr.keele.ac.uk/area/uk/ge70/partycand.htm (accessed 5 March 2006).
146 *Irish News*, 22 October 1970.
147 A number of my respondents stressed that the Labour Club was something of a refuge from what was going on outside on the streets.
148 Burton, Frank, *The Politics of Legitimacy: Struggles in a Belfast Community* (London: Routledge and Kegan Paul, 1978), p. 85.
149 CRC, *Intimidation in Housing* (Belfast: Northern Ireland Community Relations Commission, 1974).
150 Boal, Frederick W., Russell C. Murray and Michael A. Poole, 'Belfast: The Urban Encapsulation of a National Conflict', in Clarke, Susan E. and Jeffrey L. Obler (eds), *Urban Ethnic Conflict: A Comparative Perspective* (North Carolina: Institute for Research in Social Science, 1976), p. 121.
151 Murray and Tonge, *Sinn Féin and the SDLP*, pp. 10–11. Murray and Tonge remind us that the initial decision to form the SDLP came in May 1970 at a meeting of the six MPs in Bunbeg, Donegal.
152 Brian Garrett, 'Enter a New Party: Social Democratic but not Labour', *Irish Times*, 15 September 1970.
153 See Farrell's comments in Baxter *et al.*, 'PD Militants Discuss Strategy', *New Left Review* 55 (1969), p. 9.
154 *Disturbances in Northern Ireland: The Cameron Commission* (Belfast: HMSO, 1969), Cmd. 532, paragraph 197.
155 Baxter *et al.*, 'PD Militants Discuss Strategy', p. 13.
156 Garrett, 'Enter a New Party', *Irish Times*, 15 September 1970.
157 Sutton Index, archived at http://cain.ulst.ac.uk/sutton/chron/1970.html.
158 *Belfast Telegraph*, 24 October 1970.
159 *Belfast Telegraph*, 26 November 1970.
160 *Daily Mirror*, 22 November 1970.
161 Bew and Gillespie, *Northern Ireland*, p. 33.
162 McAllister, *The Northern Ireland Social Democratic and Labour Party*, p. 87.
163 Ibid., pp. 88–9.
164 Interview with Rt. Hon. David Bleakley, 21 March 2006.
165 NAUK, CJ4/313, NILP: Ministerial and Official Contacts (Administrative Papers), 15 January 1970–13 March 1973. For the background on these meetings see *Irish Press*, 10 May 1971.
166 See Dixon, *Northern Ireland*, p. 127.
167 *Irish Times*, 22 March 1971.
168 Walker, Graham, *The Politics of Frustration: Harry Midgley and the Failure of Labour in Northern Ireland* (Manchester: Manchester University Press, 1985), pp. 147–8.

Midgley became the first ever non-Unionist to enter the cabinet, taking up the post of Minister of Public Security.

169 *Irish News*, 8 May 1971.

170 Ibid. As we know from hindsight communalism still persists in a proportional system.

171 *Belfast Newsletter*, 10 May 1971.

172 Ibid.

173 *Irish News*, 8 May 1971.

174 *Belfast Newsletter*, 10 May 1971.

175 *Irish Independent*, 26 March 1971.

176 *Belfast Telegraph*, 2 April 1971.

177 *Belfast Telegraph*, 3 April 1971.

178 *Belfast Telegraph*, 2 April 1971.

179 *Belfast Newsletter*, 10 May 1971.

180 Erskine Holmes press statement, *Irish Times*, 1 June 1971.

181 *Irish News*, 21 May 1971.

182 Ibid.

183 *Derry Journal*, 1 June 1971. The SDLP's leader, Gerry Fitt, was reluctant to walk out of Stormont.

184 Murray and Tonge, *Sinn Féin and the SDLP*, p. 26. See also Buckland, Patrick, *A History of Northern Ireland* (Dublin: Gill and Macmillan, 1981), p. 151, for a similar argument.

185 *Irish News*, 15 July 1971.

186 *Irish News*, 16 July 1971.

187 McAllister, *The Northern Ireland Social Democratic and Labour Party*, p. 94. The three were Ian Paisley, Desmond Boal and William Beattie.

188 Cunningham, *British Government Policy in Northern Ireland*, p. 9. Faulkner claimed in private a number of weeks later that, 'There has certainly been evidence over the past few days that the terrorists have lost many sympathisers, but it remains to be seen whether there will be a worthwhile intelligence follow-up which is, of course, the key to the whole security problem.' Brian Faulkner to Reginald Mauldling, 6 September 1971, PRONI, CAB 9R/238.

189 *Irish News*, 29 July 1971.

190 Interview with Brendan Mackin, 10 January 2006.

191 Murray and Tonge, *Sinn Féin and the SDLP*, p. 26.

192 McAllister, *The Northern Ireland Social Democratic and Labour Party*, pp. 100–2; Murray and Tonge, *Sinn Féin and the SDLP*, p. 26.

193 Interview with Willie Breslin, 17 February 2006.

194 Ibid.

195 NIPC, *Ann Hope Papers*, NICRA, 'Civil Disobedience'.

196 *Belfast Telegraph*, 26 August 1971.

197 NAUK, CJ4/313, The Northern Ireland Labour Party and its Present Attitudes, Home Office briefing paper for Home Secretary, Reginald Maudling, 14 September 1971.

198 Bew and Patterson, *The British State and the Ulster Crisis*, p. 42.

199 *Belfast Newsletter*, 16 September 1971.

200 *Irish News*, 27 May 1971; *Belfast Newsletter*, 11 September 1971.

201 NAUK, CJ4/313, Note of a Meeting between the Home Secretary and the Northern Ireland Labour Party, 15 September 1971.

202 NAUK, CJ4/313, The Northern Ireland Labour Party and Its Present Attitudes.
203 NAUK, CJ4/313, Note of a Meeting between the Home Secretary and the Northern Ireland Labour Party, 15 September 1971. It is difficult to quantify just how extensive NILP organisation was in country areas.
204 Ibid.
205 Ibid.
206 Dixon, *Northern Ireland*, p. 133.
207 NAUK, CJ4/313, Northern Ireland Office Files, Draft Statement of the Home Secretary's Statement, 15 September 1971.
208 Ibid.
209 Bleakley was holidaying in Cornwall at the time. Interview with Rt. Hon. David Bleakley, 21 March 2006.
210 Bew and Gillespie, *Northern Ireland*, p. 40; Interview with Rt. Hon. David Bleakley, 21 March 2006.
211 Bleakley, David, *Faulkner: Conflict and Consent in Irish Politics* (London: Mowbray, 1974), p. 104.
212 Kelly, Henry, *How Stormont Fell* (Dublin: Gill and Macmillan, 1972), p. 21.
213 *Belfast Newsletter*, 31 December 1971.
214 Murray and Tonge, *Sinn Féin and the SDLP*, p. 29.
215 *Belfast Newsletter*, 31 December 1971.
216 *Sunday News*, 2 January 1972.
217 Dixon, Paul, *The British Labour Party and Northern Ireland, 1959–74* (Unpublished PhD Thesis: University of Bradford, 1993), p. 280.
218 *Guardian*, 12 November 1971.
219 O'Leary, 'The Labour Government and Northern Ireland', pp. 196–7.
220 Letter from the George Chambers to the *Belfast Telegraph*, 14 February 1972.
221 Interview with George Chambers, 14 February 2006.

6
The fall of the NILP, 1972–75

In the party's favour it can be said that it has tried to fight Northern elections, not on the border or associated issues, but on more 'bread-and-butter' questions. That it has failed to make an impression is a commentary as much on the electorate as on itself.[1]

Introduction

In a bid to repair the damage wrought on its fraternal relationship with the British Labour Party (BLP) the Northern Ireland Labour Party (NILP) changed tack and openly repudiated Brian Faulkner's attack on Harold Wilson for the latter's anti-partitionist speech in Dublin. The NILP argued that although 'Partition cannot be ended without the consent of the majority of people of Northern Ireland' a radical alternative to internment was still badly needed.[2] Side-stepping the BLP's hostility towards the Unionist position, the NILP recommended additional heavy investment from the British Exchequer as one tangible way to alleviate unemployment and to develop the province's ravaged economic base.[3] Behind the scenes the party was formulating a comprehensive constitutional settlement that would enable a return to socio-economic priorities. The holding of fresh elections to a substantively reorganised Stormont would continue to remain high on the party's agenda over the next few years.[4] All these initiatives would regrettably be overshadowed by the threat of terrorism on law and order – clearly now being exploited by emerging political parties as a potential vote-winner in any future elections. In any event Faulkner's failure to concede security powers to Whitehall led directly to his resignation and the eventual prorogation of Stormont in late March 1972.

Direct rule was imposed by Edward Heath on 24 March 1972. Wilson immediately supported it as one means of enticing the Conservatives into a bi-partisan line on all-party talks.[5] Outside Westminster the NILP responded positively to Wilson's calls for dialogue, claiming it as necessary to get local government up and running in Northern Ireland. That said, Northern Ireland Labour repudiated any suggestions that this would mean the participation of

The fall of the NILP, 1972–75   195

'terrorists in the talks'.[6] Vivian Simpson reiterated his preference for an immediate plebiscite on partition so that a level playing field could be made available for non-sectarian politics to be given a contest free from the hardy annuals of the border and security.[7] Significantly, Wilson had begun secret exploratory talks with the Provisional IRA. When details of these meetings were leaked the NILP publicly criticised him for his actions.[8]

The NILP as third-party arbitrator

Despite its revulsion for paramilitary violence the NILP was being less than candid in its public attitude towards how best to deal with its root causes. There were those in the party's ranks, from its leader Vivian Simpson down to community activists like the Reverend John Stewart, who were intimately involved in top secret behind-the-scenes discussions aimed at bringing an end to hostilities. Simpson's position as MP for Oldpark placed him at the epicentre of the sectarian maelstrom and he frequently made clandestine visits to Crumlin Road prison for discussions with its Assistant Governor, Robert Gibson, and the leaders of loyalist and republican prisoners. On several occasions in May 1972 he met both the UVF's Gusty Spence and the Provisional IRA's Frank Kard for exploratory talks aimed at brokering a truce between warring factions.[9] During these meetings various issues were discussed including political status for prisoners, access to ordinary privileges and what was termed 'current affairs'. On this occasion Billy McKee's weak condition due to his hunger strike was given as the reason why he could not meet personally with Simpson.

Prior to these meetings it was 'decided by prisoners that Vivian Simpson, MP (Oldpark) could be trusted!' as an intermediary.[10] There was a three-pronged aim behind the meetings:

    a. To urge a 3 months' truce – to commence at the earliest possible date and thus secure a hasty end to violence.
       During the Truce – an urgent review of Internment, and, if possible, the release of all detainees who are NOT being charged with offences against the State.
    b. Release of Detainees and Internees.
    c. Amnesty for Political Prisoners – to include ALL SIDES, and to embrace entire United Kingdom, The Republic of Ireland, and Northern Ireland.[11]

Confidential correspondence revealed that 'the above points are reflected down from the I.R.A. Army Council in Dublin'. The Provos even recognised that public reaction might militate against the Secretary of State for Northern Ireland, William Whitelaw in the event of the dialogue being publicly exposed. On a more serious level it was thought that the proposed truce would immediately result in:

    a. Greatly reduced activity by Troops.
       Reduction of Military presence, if Truce agreed, could automatically follow.
    b. No further arrests – unless known crimes involved.

c. Increase in Army involvement in Community Welfare Activities.
d. Intelligence Depts. could keep close watch on any breach of Truce by any groups on any side.
e. Very prompt action if Truce broken in any area.[12]

Both Gibson and Simpson made clear in their meeting with Whitelaw, on 8 May 1972, that their involvement – 'which MUST BE KEPT IN THE STRICTEST CONFIDENCE – is outside their normal function; but their actions, jointly or severally, can hasten peace, they will serve to the best of their ability'.[13] Indeed there is strong evidence to suggest that Simpson continued to represent the interests of his constituents imprisoned in both Crumlin Road and Long Kesh prisons, and their families, at this time.[14]

Previously, in a delegation to Whitelaw on May Day 1972, the Labour representatives admitted that even though 'it could not be conclusively [argued] that PR would produce favourable results for the Labour Party' it was argued 'that the present system would produce a perpetuation of sectarian politics'.[15] Apart from introducing PR into local government elections the NILP hoped that a renewed political initiative would be met by an overhaul in the government's economic strategy in Northern Ireland.[16] Despite the courageous efforts of Simpson and his colleagues it was clear that the intensification in violence and atrocities was engineering the NILP's electoral decline, as the 1973 elections would soon prove.

Since its last conference the killings had escalated and it was making it difficult for Labour candidates to speak on political platforms. As the EC's report admitted:

> The mounting violence has made political work much more difficult. It has made people unwilling to leave their homes to attend meetings and cynical as to the value of normal political activities.[17]

Nevertheless the introduction of PR into provisions for future local government elections was noted and commended.[18] Significantly, Erskine Holmes later championed it as a possible way out of the stasis generated by confessional party competition for (now) minor parties like the NILP. Reflecting upon his year as party chairman Holmes conceded that Callaghan had made genuine efforts to help out the NILP and that interestingly, 'he [Callaghan] did of course at that time approach Maurice Hayes to play an active part in the NILP but Hayes either had the good sense to recognise that the NILP did not have a future, or he had other fish to fry'.[19] Within months Brian Garrett had taken over as chairman, choosing to focus the party's attention on tackling the electoral threat posed by the SDLP while also calling for the prorogation of Stormont.[20]

The Darlington Conference and aftermath

The NILP was among the Northern Ireland delegation which met in Darlington on 25–27 September 1972 for round table discussions on the way forward for

The fall of the NILP, 1972–75

the province. Initially the party's high-ranking talks team was to include the NIC's Officer Billy Blease but he declined the invitation, citing the misrepresentation which might be caused by his appearance. It was clear that Blease was finding it 'extremely difficult to publicly differentiate my party political associations from my official trade union work'.[21] In any event the invitation was not extended to the ICTU to join the NILP delegation and Blease concluded, somewhat ambiguously, that 'My own view is that the human issues involved transcend all party political or personal differences.'[22] Despite Blease's absence the party's advisers included Erskine Holmes, Archie McArdle, Brian Garrett, Billy Boyd, Pat McHugh and the British Labour Party's Roland Moyle, MP for Lewisham North and a Barrister at Law.[23] All delegates, apart from the latter, were members of the NILP Executive.

In a press statement at the close of the conference the NILP said 'it will be regarded as an important stage in the process by which future institutions for the government of Northern Ireland will be arrived at'.[24] Looking to the future, Labour hoped that Darlington 'will have shortened the timetable for the return of devolved government in Northern Ireland', reiterating its belief that it would provide the people of Northern Ireland with 'a legislative assembly by which they can set about the social and economic reconstruction of their own community'.[25] Brian Garrett recalls how the NILP was pushing for what it termed 'community government', which effectively meant the Unionist Party accepting that it had to enter into a voluntary coalition with some of its opponents. While Brian Faulkner turned it down flat, William Whitelaw did give it a huge amount of publicity. Unfortunately for the NILP, as Garrett later observed, 'we were doing that almost as spectators, rather than as participants by that stage'.[26]

In response to the round table discussions at Darlington the British government published its Green Paper The Future of Northern Ireland: A Paper for Discussion at the end of October 1972. Although it reaffirmed the constitutional guarantee that 'The view of HM Government has always been that no change should be made in the constitutional status of Northern Ireland without Northern Ireland's free agreement',[27] considerable leeway was given to the parties to interpret how such sovereignty could be exercised locally. Moreover, the British government recognised the strength of feeling among Nationalists that the Irish government should play a consultative role in Ulster's affairs. The NILP's submission included provision for 'A consultative and deliberative Council of Ireland to be established.'[28] This sat incongruously with the decision of the Alliance Party of Northern Ireland (APNI) that the Republic should not be represented at talks; an uncompromising position for a purportedly non-sectarian party but one that adequately captured the essence of its liberal unionist ethos.[29] Bew et al. have argued that Alliance's origins lie precisely in the collapse of the Unionist Party's 'centre' from 1969,[30] while later scholars point to its 'unrepresentative class base'[31] that eventually contributed to the APNI's failure to stabilise the moderate centre ground. From the latter's early policy documents it is evident how dependent it actually was on middle-class unionists of a liberal-leaning disposition.

One important point to make about the NILP's submissions to the newly formed Northern Ireland Office (NIO) was that these included content dealing with social justice, which the other parties (including the SDLP) had neglected to put forward. It was a reflection perhaps of the priorities of security that the NILP's recommendation was overlooked in later discussions about the *future* of Northern Ireland:

> A Bill of Rights to give statutory expression to the Downing Street Declaration of August 1969 and acknowledge the Westminster Parliament's role as guarantor of civil, religious and political liberty in Northern Ireland. The position in Northern Ireland on such matters as the death penalty, race relations, homosexual practices, termination of pregnancy and divorce to be brought into line with that in the rest of the United Kingdom; all future legislation in the field of civil (and individual citizens') rights enacted at Westminster to be applied to Northern Ireland unless the Westminster Parliament determines otherwise; and the Westminster Parliament to reserve expressly the right to annul any provision made by the Northern Ireland Assembly which it resolves to affect adversely citizens' rights.[32]

The NILP's pledge to implement its quintessential social reconstruction programme slightly overshadowed its staunch commitment to maintaining Northern Ireland's constitutional position at a time when the new parties concentrated on single issues as the key mobilising force behind their successful political inaugurations.

In an NILP Memorandum to Whitelaw in December 1972 the party was generally positive about what had been accomplished at Darlington.[33] However the length of the 'Post Darlington Vacuum' still alarmed those who saw the slow pace of political progress as a 'further opportunity for violence and destruction'. Its advice that a plebiscite should follow the government's publication of a White Paper fell on deaf ears: 'The Government must think again about the dangers of a strategy which permits the referendum to take place in a political vacuum.' With regards to the 'checks and balances' for any new administration, Labour reiterated its proposals for a local legislative assembly 'based on the need to create social harmony and avoiding the inherent pitfalls of inbuilt sectarian devices'. It did so by placing the overriding sovereignty of the British Parliament at the apex of any legislature to avoid the abuse of powers. Perhaps its most important point was on power sharing:

> We believe power sharing can best be achieved by freely arrived at coalitions or alliances with membership of departmental executive committees allocated on a proportionate basis to the parties represented in the Assembly. We feel that it would be unwise to have a form of power sharing which ignores the legitimate right of a Socialist Party such as the N.I.L.P. to refuse to serve in government on ideological grounds with right-wing parties which will not carry out our programme. Equally it would be unwise to have a structure which could be undermined at the first test if Ultra-loyalists or republican groups refused to participate.[34]

Earlier Nationalist political withdrawals from Stormont were recounted as frustrating episodes and it was hoped that such behaviour would be prevented in any future dispensation.

Other areas covered by the document included recognition of an Irish dimension as 'an important instrument for developing harmony throughout the island as well as a means of satisfying the aspirations of those who look to eventual Irish unity'[35] and the all-important economic field in which the injection of an increased subvention would tackle unemployment. It was clear that NILP proposals had taken into account the ethno-national aspirations of the minority community despite SDLP claims to the contrary.[36] Since September 1971 the NILP had consistently warned that 'while a military solution without a political strategy would be insufficient to end the violence both together would also be inadequate without a comprehensive social component as well'.[37] All these suggestions were made in the context of reinstating 'normal conditions in those areas which have suffered most since 1969'.[38]

Before the proposals were included in the Government White Paper a referendum was called on the constitutional position of Northern Ireland.[39] The border poll was held on 8 March 1973 but was of limited value in that Nationalists and republicans boycotted it. The result was in favour of maintaining the link by 591,820 votes to 6,463.[40] The White Paper, Northern Ireland Constitutional Proposals (1973), was published in March and included the three key ingredients for any future settlement: devolved government, power sharing between Protestants and Catholics and an Irish dimension.[41] On a practical level the NILP expressed concern about 'the background to the poll, the results and the methods used', including the excessive long distances travelled by many voters and the 'serious complaints ... made in many areas of names being omitted from the Register'.[42] It was hoped that these logistical inconsistencies could be ironed out in time for the two forthcoming elections.

The 1973 local government election

Matters were made worse for the party in the May 1973 local government election when it got just four candidates elected out of a possible 519 seats while its SDLP rival won an impressive 82.[43] It later emerged that the NILP was prevented from making an election broadcast because the BBC said it had not fielded enough candidates.[44] One candidate justified its absence in rural areas by conceding that it was 'basically an urban party'.[45] In direct contrast to its clandestine attempts to facilitate a truce between warring factions, Labour made little headway in its overt calls for calm. It even made several fruitless attempts to appear robust on the security issue by publicly calling on the Provos to stop their violence, even sending a telegram to Sean MacStiofain demanding 'the complete standing down now of [the] Provo campaign as totally discredited, politically inexcusable and [a] horrific slur on the Irish people at home and abroad'.[46] This latest dialogue with the deaf provided a signal of what was in store for moderates across the board in the June Assembly elections.

The NILP came out in public support of power sharing at the beginning of the summer[47] when it launched its assembly manifesto *Peace through Partnership* on 15 June 1973, making it clear that the 'wreckers' should be shunned by the electorate.[48] It set out its stall firmly and unambiguously by again reaffirming its commitment to the existing constitution, though calling for a 'New partnership within Northern Ireland' based on a power-sharing arrangement arrived at by PR. Essentially it was building on its earlier proposals at Darlington and the memorandum sent to Whitelaw in December 1972. The NILP remained totally opposed to ultra-loyalist calls for a Unilateral Declaration of Independence (UDI) and said that it would 'be prepared to work with any group prepared to accept the basic principles of the White Paper and who reject violence as a means of promoting political change and who are pledged to the service of all the people of Northern Ireland'. Calling for the creation of two new ministries, for the Environment, and Sport and Leisure, it reiterated a previous commitment to work with the Southern government to improve cross-border relations, though it urged the South 'to give full recognition to the Northern Ireland state and to make whatever amendments necessary in the Constitution of the Republic to enable them to do so'.[49] In closing Labour called on the people of Northern Ireland to reject private armies.

The *Irish Times* carried the favourable editorial 'Labouring' and provided a thoughtful analysis of the NILP's once distinguished strategic position on the political landscape. It highlighted 'a certain vigour in the party's election manifesto' and said that it would be 'easy, too, to forget that in the last British general election, the NILP polled more than 100,000 votes. That made it the closest vote-gatherer to the Unionists.'[50] Noting its extensive organisational base the editorial praised the party for fighting the electoral campaign not on the border issue but on 'bread-and-butter questions'.[51]

The attempts by some anti-White Paper Unionists to introduce UDI into the mix found few champions among the NILP's Assembly election candidates. Announcing his candidacy, David Bleakley warned that a successful wrecking campaign against the White Paper and the Assembly would lead directly to what he called 'the disaster of UDI'.[52] A total of 16 high-profile candidates were fielded for the Assembly elections. Among them were: Pat McHugh (North Antrim), Sandy Scott, Deirdre Byrne and Councillor Bob Kidd (South Antrim), Reverend John Stewart (North Belfast), Billy Boyd and Paddy Doherty (West Belfast), Erskine Holmes (South Belfast), Tommy Newell (Armagh) and Delap Stevenson (Londonderry). Significantly the party appointed former BLP member Paddy McGarvey as its campaign publicity director. In any event the party only polled 18,675 votes (2.6%), trailing in behind the Alliance's impressive 66,541 votes (9.2%).[53] That only Bleakley was returned, for East Belfast, shattered the British government's hopes that the so-called 'moderate silent majority' would finally make its voice heard and reject the extreme loyalist parties. As Paul Dixon argues, the hopes for a 'moderate power-sharing executive composed of the NILP, APNI and liberal Unionists' was at an end; the 'strong showing of the hardline VUPP and the DUP was likely to constrain Faulkner's room for manoeuvre'.[54]

In November 1973 the composition of the power-sharing executive was finally announced and it formally took office in January 1974. Amidst the flames

The fall of the NILP, 1972–75

and smoke-filled streets of January 1974 emerged a new animosity among the working classes. The sheer scale of violence led some NILP members to doubt whether power sharing would be enough to tackle the law and order problem. Erskine Holmes, like other sceptics in the party, wavered on the issue.[55] In a sworn affidavit to the High Court of Justice in Northern Ireland SDLP Leader Gerry Fitt lodged a complaint about the disproportionate number of Catholics interned since 1971.[56] The British Conservative government was unmoved and instead pressed on with the macro-level government initiatives to see the constitutional issue resolved. With 'elections out of the way', as Dixon has argued, 'the government now attempted to coerce the parties towards the centre ground'.[57]

Dixon has made the convincing argument that the British government took the deliberate decision to bolster the 'moderate centre ground' in Northern Ireland politics in the weeks and months leading up to the Sunningdale Conference – an attempt to establish a power-sharing devolved executive in Northern Ireland – of 6–9 December 1973.[58] Unlike the Darlington Conference the NILP had no representation present, nor was it consulted to the extent that it had been 12 months previously. It was now becoming apparent that the APNI was beginning to eclipse the NILP as the main centrist party.[59] With an agreement hammered out between the constitutional political parties at Sunningdale in December the British government now turned its attention to the paramilitaries. Encouraged by recent UVF statements,[60] it lifted the ban on the group in February 1974, along with Provisional Sinn Féin.[61] The group was courted by many suitors who often whisked them off to country retreats for extensive talks on the possibilities of peace. As Sarah Nelson's early research showed, 'Northern Ireland Labour Party members were often present on these parties, for the NILP had joined the queue of suitors'.[62]

The NILP announced in February 1974 that although it supported power sharing it did not support the reinforcement of a sectarian *realpolitik*.[63] Officially it did not align itself with the pro-Sunningdale parties, though a later EC Report revealed that it thought the electorate had done so. The party's 1974 manifesto made clear that NILP MPs at Westminster would introduce legislation aimed at urging the government to increase the number of MPs in the province from 12 to 18 in line with its new policy of supporting direct rule.[64] Meanwhile Billy Boyd entered into a verbal sparring match with Gerry Fitt, accusing him of 'trying to make the election campaign into an old sectarian clash between him and his Unionist opponent Johnny McQuade'.[65] Overall the February election 'caught the NILP unprepared'. While its East, South and North Belfast constituency parties decided to contest the election and select candidates, West Belfast procrastinated, eventually leading the EC to nominate Boyd as its official candidate. However unstable the party was organisationally, it still remained electorally relevant.[66] In North and East Belfast its vote share actually rose by 6.1% and 1.4% respectively, while in South Belfast it fell slightly by 0.3%. The party had resorted to contesting the three parliamentary constituencies where it had traditionally gained strong support throughout the post-war period. As the party's secretary Douglas McIldoon concluded:

Subsequently people would have realised that a party with, say, four or five per cent of the support of the electorate was actually quite a significant force. That's what level of support the Alliance Party has now, and the Alliance Party really doesn't exist outside Belfast, or in the greater Belfast area now, and it only exists by virtue of the strength of its incumbents who stand clearly on a strong personal base. So when we declined to those four or five per cent support which we did in the mid-1970's we are still maintaining that kind of figure in the Belfast area even facing moderates going to the Alliance Party – because that was the other factor.[67]

Perhaps the greatest test of electoral viability came in the wake of the strike by the Ulster Workers' Council (UWC) when the Protestant working class revolted against a Labour government, thereby initiating the most successful political strike in modern British industrial history.

Figure 6.1 UUP–NILP local government electoral competition in Belfast, 1946–73

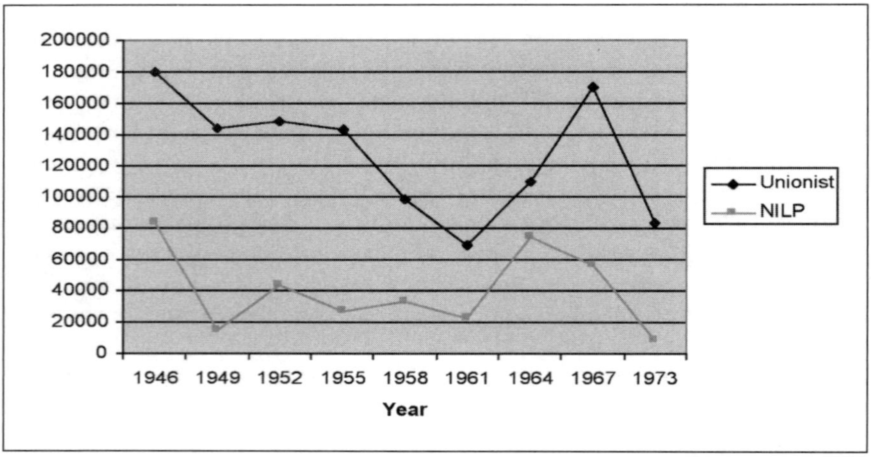

Source: Compiled from data in the *Belfast Telegraph*, 1946–73. Figures based on total votes cast.

The UWC strike

In May 1974 the UWC strike united Protestant politicians and paramilitaries in opposition against the new power-sharing government. The NILP opposed strike action but, like its comrades in the NIC, was powerless to stop the popular mobilisation of workers in the key industries. The crippling effect on the province's infrastructure was enforced by the might of loyalist paramilitary muscle and superintended by plebeian leaders who had emerged to take autocratic control of the political direction of the strike. Although the strike lasted only two weeks it resulted in the fall of the power-sharing executive and with it the prospects of political settlement between the moderates.[68] Meanwhile the political ripple effects of the strike led to the serious deterioration in relations between the NILP and Labour government; although arguably this had been on the cards since it emerged that they had been in unofficial talks with the SDLP, by now a clear political rival in majority Catholic working-class areas. However, a climatic change had generally been averted in the past due to the NILP indecision over whether to take a collective decision to sever its links with the BLP.

In the wake of the UWC strike Douglas McIldoon wrote a strongly worded letter to the *Guardian*, the left's main liberal-leaning daily in England, in which he criticised Labour's 'inability to cope' with the strike.[69] Not only did he publicly indict the political credibility of the power-sharing executive (which had in any event already been discredited in the eyes of both loyalists and republicans) but he pondered the intelligence of Labour's decision not to enter into dialogue with the strike leaders directly, thus feeding Protestant disgruntlement and alienation. Arguably, Harold Wilson's televised broadcast labelling Northern Ireland citizens 'spongers' only played into the hands of extremists and led to the final dilution of the NILP's restraining influence on certain sections of the Protestant working class. Predictably, McIldoon placed all of the blame at the door of the Labour government, thereby weakening any remaining goodwill between the parties.[70] In closing he warned that although the 'Protestant working class today is less likely to go Fascist than it was two years ago ... it is not by any means inevitable' and he appealed directly to the British Labour movement to:

> realise what an enormous failure of will, imagination and nerve the Labour government's handling of this crisis represents for all democratic socialists and the credibility of democratic socialism as a political philosophy relevant to the needs of ordinary people in slightly extraordinary situations.[71]

McIldoon's comments were greeted with surprise by Labour officials in Transport House. Immediately the British party sought clarification on the NILP's official position. In a letter to his counterpart Ron Hayward wrote that:

> Our two parties have had a long a history of close liaison and co-operation and we have done our best to assist your party both financially and in a physical sense. We would therefore have thought that any views which your party may have would be best channelled through me as General Secretary so that our own National Executive Committee could be informed.[72]

McIldoon issued an unsatisfactory reply that glaringly omitted any explanation for his *Guardian* letter.[73] Naturally this incurred the wrath of several BLP officials and led to the immediate breakdown in communications between the parties.[74] Hayward asked for a meeting to clear the air but as the year progressed none was forthcoming.

The problem for the NILP was that Labour ministers had bungled their way through the first few weeks of their return to office, preferring to carry on where Whitelaw and Heath had left off and exploring few new avenues in the search for peace. Adding insult to injury the BLP now began to actively court the SDLP.[75] The closeness reflected the absence of a suitable electoral challenger from the minority community which could act as an ethno-national counterweight to moderate Unionism. As the reporter Robert Fisk wrote at the time, Merlyn Rees, Secretary of State for Northern Ireland, was 'trying to graft someone else's ideas onto someone else's government in someone else's country'.[76] Moreover, one might also point to the British Labour government's failure to understand the complex multi-faceted character of Northern Ireland's Labour movement as a means of explaining why McIldoon's criticisms of Wilson and his ministers in the wake of the UWC strike in May 1974 were so badly misconstrued.[77] McIldoon was unapologetic about the bad feeling now poisoning relations between the two parties. 'Frankly,' he said in retrospect, 'the British Labour Party pulled the rug from under us. There was no point really appealing to the Protestant working-class if the British Labour Party was Republican.'[78]

Events on the streets throughout the previous months signalled a major sea change in Protestant working-class opinion towards the Wilson government. There now emerged a clear demarcation between those trade unionists committed to a British style of labourism and those loyal to a localised regional variant of working-class solidarity. As Nelson observed, 'One of the major and most visible effects of direct rule was that it stirred a new class consciousness, both among members of Protestant paramilitary and workers' groups, and among residents of loyalist working class areas.'[79] The very fact that a new label, 'loyalist', had come into play around this time and was used as shorthand to describe those who had mobilised on a purely sectarian (as opposed to cross-sectarian) basis, signalled a weakening in inter-communal relations. Whether class consciousness was 'stirred' or not is a moot point for it would not have benefited the NILP, even in those staunch working-class heartlands like Woodvale and Falls. The reason was simple: although the plebeian outgrowth of loyalism had left the Vanguard alliance inherently unstable it had nonetheless successfully siphoned off from local NILP branches those who under normal circumstances (i.e. in the absence of physical force republicanism) would have been involved in non-sectarian class politics.

Internal dissatisfaction over the NILP's role in the UWC strike had reached its zenith and led to the breaking away of Newtownabbey Labour Party, ironically, to a position broadly supportive of the British Labour Party's outlook.[80] Individual party members and associates of an agnostic hue (incidentally representing strongly cross-sectarian branches) clamoured together to harangue the party's liberal-leaning EC for its failure to inject a proper 'socialist' outlook into Northern Irish politics. In an anti-EC document *Why the NILP?* the rebels regarded the NILP's recent moves to be 'damaging the labour ideal to an intolerable degree'.[81] The document accepted that while the NILP could have plausibly claimed to be non-sectarian in the mid-1960s it had now adopted a wholly Protestant standpoint.

Officially of course nothing could have been further from the truth. As the party's only Assembly Representative, David Bleakley had even proposed a non-sectarian amendment to replace the resolution of the United Ulster Unionist Council (UUUC) to collapse power sharing:

> The NILP welcomes the success to date of powersharing in Northern Ireland and believes it to be in the best interests of the province that the present arrangements

The fall of the NILP, 1972–75   205

should be developed and that elected leaders representing a significant section of the community should be encouraged and enabled to participate, notes the differences which have arisen over the meaning and implementation of the Sunningdale Agreement particularly the ruling in the Dublin High Court that it is not possible under the present Constitution of the Republic to give full legal recognition to Northern Ireland; and believes that until such difficulties can be resolved to the satisfaction of both North and South, it is desirable, possible and urgent that the two administrations should co-operate on mutually vital matters and effective cooperation to stamp out the campaign of violence which at present constitutes the greatest threat facing the people of Ireland both North and South.[82]

Nevertheless, the author of the damming *Why the NILP?* document Roger Byrne acknowledged how far the party had drifted from left to right in the previous decade from adopting 'a social democratic position on the Civil Rights question' to a point where the 'duplicity, dishonesty and sectarianism of the party leadership have fatally damaged the party' and it 'cannot be reformed from within'.[83] Byrne intimated that the NILP by 1974 was 'no longer a socialist organisation. On the contrary it has identified itself with right-wing Loyalist groups.'[84] At a meeting of several dissidents it was resolved to seek the removal of those individuals at the helm who sought to bring the party into disrepute.[85] At this point it is perhaps worth analysing just how the NILP co-existed alongside Protestant paramilitaries at this particular time in a bid to answer these charges.

Holding the line: Reverend John Stewart and loyalist paramilitarism

Between 1969 and 1974 there occurred a mass mobilisation of grass-roots Protestants in response to what many perceived to be a threat to Northern Ireland's constitutional position within the United Kingdom. Various vigilante defence associations sprung up in loyalist areas across the province and were finally brought together under the umbrella grouping Ulster Defence Association (UDA) in 1971.[86] Meanwhile, the UVF, which had lain in almost suspended animation since the incarceration of its leading lights in 1966 (except for the occasional bombing run in 1969), continued to recruit new members. In late 1970 the UVF emerged from the shadows much stronger and more militarily astute than it had been in 1965–67, due in the main to the influx of ex-servicemen to its ranks.[87] These UVF men:

> Believed there was a sell out, there was a rebellion which had to be stopped. Whether you were from the Shankill or East Antrim you had the one enemy – the IRA, indeed the nationalist community, as most UVF volunteers didn't distinguish between the IRA and those they fought for.[88]

According to Billy Mitchell, who was a leading UVF officer at the time, 'the UVF saw itself as a military machine ... it was [about getting] your retaliation in first, defence of working class areas, retaliation for republican activities'.[89] Inevitably this led to the targeting of Catholic civilians as much as known republican activists. In what was fast becoming a tit-for-tat escalation of the conflict Protestants and Catholics began to intimidate out of 'their' areas those who were not co-religionists. As McDonald and Cusack have observed, 'although this period is portrayed as a one-sided pogrom against Catholics the blame goes both ways, and Protestants were also burned out in significant numbers in the surrounding Catholic areas'.[90] This is important because of the calamitous impact it had on those local NILP branches containing relatively mixed cadres.

Not all Protestants became militants overnight, nor did they become recalcitrant in the face of intimidation either. For a few years the Woodvale Labour Party continued to co-exist alongside Protestant paramilitarism, enjoying what could be described as a protean relationship with working-class militants. Nonetheless it issued statements condemning the violence of paramilitants of both hues. In January 1971, for instance, Woodvale DLP issued a strongly worded statement denouncing rioting from whichever quarter: 'Any subversive groups which may be at work in these areas depend on the continued animosity of the public to the police and Army.'[91] Woodvale Labour relied heavily on its grass-roots membership to forge or maintain relations with those who operated in the shadows, for a number of key reasons. Firstly, the NILP's priority at the local political level was to offset the potential for violence. Secondly, it was recognised by local members that Labour's support-base needed to be managed at what was a very vulnerable time for its socially radical message and, lastly, it was vital for many of those in the Woodvale DLP to maintain a degree of civility in the face of adversity from political opponents as well as those competing for active support from loyalists sympathetic to paramilitarism.[92] In all this the NILP relied on several key charismatic figures to soothe the fears of its core support-base.

One of these charismatic figures was the Reverend John Stewart, Minister of Woodvale Methodist Church in the heart of the West Belfast interface, and member of the NILP Executive in the mid-1970s. Stewart was a down-to-earth character with deep democratic socialist convictions. As one former party colleague recalls:

> I mean John – he was an 'odds on' guy. This was at a time when the district was just hiving with street confrontations. Where I lived (still live), it was directly opposite Hooker Street. I mean John was right there in the thick of it and was there for the people. He didn't look at it from an ivory tower. He was in there amongst the people.[93]

Notwithstanding the attempt to dissuade the NILP's core support-base away from violence, a mobilisation of a critical mass of working-class Protestants under the auspices of loyalist paramilitary organisations did take place. Even though many loyalists still remained committed trade unionists they rejected the NILP's moderate influence. Instead support was soon channelled towards the hard-line populist politics of Bill Craig's Vanguard Unionism and Ian Paisley's fledgling DUP. On the whole loyalist paramilitary political thinking remained in a foetal state until the late 1970s when the ties binding it to mainstream Unionism began to loosen as many became disenchanted with the broken promises of middle-class politicians.

The efforts of the British government to wean people away from violence were greeted by many loyalists with a lukewarm response and it was initially thought of as a uniquely highbrowed utilitarian intervention in troubled communities. Principally it was about being able to hold people back from colliding on ethno-national grounds. In the Northern Ireland context there were many front-runners who have been lauded throughout the years for their remarkable tenacity and courage in the face of adversity. One could name a handful of prominent Christian peace-makers at this time, such as the leading NILP member Sadie Patterson,[94] who opted to confront the ugly face of tribal violence along the battlefronts of West Belfast. Others, such as the devout atheist and Communist Party member Betty Sinclair, worked tirelessly to police the lines of their working-class areas which had begun to degenerate into ritual killing fields. However steadfast and sanguine these grass-roots activists became in their opposition to violence, the hard-men of loyalist paramilitarism were only open to advice from those who dared to confront them on their own turf and more precisely in the back rooms of smoky shebeens.

The Reverend John Stewart was certainly one of those brave individuals willing to enter into dialogue with the gunmen and bombers. For Billy Mitchell – who was a key UVF leader in the 1970s – the NILP's influence was being felt across the ranks of his organisation, which was beginning to explore political alternatives to its military campaign:

> A lot of the UVF at that time were old NILP. It shows our naivety – on the one hand we were trying to get away from the Communist accusations, on the other hand the Reverend John Stewart was taking us through working class politics. John was a member of the NILP.[95]

Elsewhere Mitchell has further divulged details of the impact of Stewart's political leadership style and ideas on the UVF:

> During late 1972 a number of key figures within the UVF began to engage in dialogue with members of the Northern Ireland Labour Party. One of the NILP members was the late Rev. John Stewart, then Minister of Woodvale Methodist Church in the Greater Shankill area. Rev. Stewart met regularly with senior members of the UVF during the next few years and encouraged them to think in terms of bread and butter politics as well as the constitutional issue. He also encouraged them to respond to republicanism through non-violence and dialogue. A number of the UVF members who met with Stewart had a labour or trade union background and were open to both the working class politics and to the moderate unionism that he espoused.[96]

At this time there had been little love lost between the NILP and loyalist para-militaries as each tolerated the other, accepting that both were germane components of working-class society. Nevertheless, on numerous occasions, Labour leaders displayed their disgust at the 'butchering' of Catholic workers by loyalist terrorists.[97]

Stewart's peace-making activities serve as a stark reminder that there were NILP members prepared to take risks for peace. Although Simpson's attempts to broker a truce between warring factions would eventually aid the facilitation of ceasefires by both the UVF and IRA, these would soon prove short-lived. That they had occurred at all ought to serve as a potent reminder that the middle ground still held a restraining influence over the extremes. NILP leaders such as Simpson and Stewart were the real 'unsung heroes'[98] of the conflict who were willing to risk their lives in a bid to return these battle-scared areas to normality.

Conversely, it would also later transpire that some NILP members who had left the party were drifting into the ranks of the UDA and UVF.[99] One of those trade unionists who broke ranks with the NILP after the arrival of troops on the streets in August 1969 was Billy Hull, convenor of the engineering shop stewards at Harland and Wolff, who apparently 'resigned from the NILP in protest at the British Labour government's intervention, and led a sizable group with him into the Workers' Committee for the Defence of the Constitution'.[100] This group subsequently became the Loyalist Association of Workers (LAW), an organisation which would later play a central role in the UWC strike in 1974.[101] LAW mirrored an earlier organisation led by Ian Paisley; Ulster Protestant Action – which called for the unity of Protestant labour in the face of Catholic (and supposed 'IRA') incursions in the late 1950s – was synonymous with ethnic exclusiveness and patriotic bombast. It made minor inroads into the Protestant working-class consciousness at a time when the IRA launched its so-called 'border campaign'. What made LAW distinct from the earlier UPA incarnation was that it co-existed with local neighbourhood vigilante groupings born out of the sectarian rioting.

Rumpf and Hepburn have been a little overzealous in describing the sectarianised nature of Protestant working-class politics at this juncture. Having said that, their failure to grasp the salience between Unionist and loyalist politics in the early 1970s did not prevent them from making fairly accurate assertions such as:

> Although the NILP was not formally associated with its British counterpart, the distinction was too subtle for the average loyalist. In the minds of many Protestants, a Labour government at Westminster meant alarms about the future of the border, which in turn reduced a climate of opinion in which the NILP could not thrive.[102]

However, even here one should tread carefully, especially because they seem to make this point when referring to the entire period from Wilson's arrival in Downing Street, via his spell in Opposition to a position where he prioritised Catholic interests above those of Protestants. This is simply not the case, as the NILP itself did not formally break its links with the BLP until 1974, and even then the British party had to sever those links.[103] There were those in the party, like Bleakley, who wished to see a closer relationship between the two parties but also, invariably, those who did not want any part of 'an unconsummated marriage'. The latter group were made up predominantly of Catholics, and they found an ally in the form of Paddy Devlin and the Falls Labour Party which had categorically opposed the proposed merger in 1970.[104] The problem was not so

The fall of the NILP, 1972–75

much the Labour government's Irish policy per se as Wilson's calls for Irish unity while in Opposition. O'Leary has been more critical, characterising Labour's conduct during the UWC strike as 'abject spinelessness'.[105]

In Opposition Wilson had frequently called for 'the virtually total disarmament of the province – excluding the security forces and limited licenses for self-protection, for example, in limited areas such as those near the border'[106] – a demand which set alarm bells ringing for Protestant civilians who possessed either legally or illegally held weapons. The BLP's rationale was that although all premises could be searched with impunity it would cease to feed the perception that it was selective or partial. This is evidence of some of Wilson's practical thinking on law and order in Northern Ireland but there can be little doubt that he tired of what he constantly called the 'un-British situation', wherein millions of pounds of tax-payers' money was being wasted on those who held nothing but contempt for Britain. While Wilson's condemnation of the principle of UDI chipped away at the credibility of Vanguard Unionism it made little difference to the UVF, Pro-White Paper Unionists or the NILP who all wished Northern Ireland to remain an integral part of the UK. By grouping all of the people of Northern Ireland into one homogeneous constituency to be talked down to like a child, Wilson – 'the most interventionist British Prime Minister in Ireland since Lloyd George'[107] – made little headway in resolving this 'troublesome business' in his third term in office.

Conclusion

The NILP was left with few committed friends in the British Labour Party by the mid-1970s; even Callaghan had publicly sought to distance himself from the party's requests for financial and organisational support.[108] However, a definite rupture in the fraternal relationship was narrowly averted by a meeting of both parties in London on 8 May 1975. For the most part the delegation was received with pleasantries, though discussion did centre round Douglas McIldoon's departure from the post of NILP secretary, especially because of his earlier criticism of Labour ministers in the press. In McIldoon's defence the NILP's continued close association with the BLP raised the difficulties of communicating with the Protestant working class, particularly in light of Labour government policy towards Northern Ireland.[109] In a letter to Ron Hayward, Brian Garrett observed how for 'our part you recognised that the right to be critical was a corollary of being independent. But all criticism (if any) must be as between fraternal parties.'[110] The meeting repaired some of the damage wrought over the previous year, though the failure by the NEC to support the NILP financially in its immediate aftermath is considerably telling. It was only a matter of time before the relationship between the two parties fully disintegrated.

Notes

1 'Labouring', *Irish Times* editorial, 16 June 1973.
2 *Irish News*, 16 March 1972.
3 *Irish Times*, 20 March 1972.
4 Interview with Brian Garrett, 30 September 2003.
5 United Kingdom House of Commons Debates, Vol. 833, Col. 1865, 24 March 1972.
6 *Irish Times*, 28 April 1972.
7 *Belfast Telegraph*, 27 April 1972.
8 *Belfast Telegraph*, 19 July 1972.
9 PRONI, D/3233/2/1/1, *Vivian Simpson Papers*, Visit to Crumlin Road Prison, 21 May 1972. The important role played by Simpson at this time was corroborated by Gusty Spence, in a conversation with the author, on 8 April 2006.
10 PRONI, D/3233/2/1/1, *Vivian Simpson Papers*, Strictly Confidential: Assistant Governor Robert Gibson and Vivian Simpson, MP – Approach to Secretary of State for NI, RE: Continuing discussions at Crumlin Road Prison with Political Prisoners, 8 May 1972.
11 Ibid. Emphasis in original.
12 Ibid.
13 Ibid. Emphasis in original.
14 PRONI, D/3233/2/1/1, *Vivian Simpson Papers*, Minister of State, Lord Windlesham to Vivian Simpson, MP, 19 October 1972 in reply to letter from Simpson to Whitelaw, 10 October 1972 – RE: Events which took place in Maze Prison on 22 September.
15 NAUK, CJ4/313, Meeting between the Secretary of State for Northern Ireland and the NILP, 1 May 1972.
16 See comments by McIldoon in NAUK, CJ 4/313, Meeting between the Secretary of State for Northern Ireland and the NILP, 1 May 1972.
17 NILP, Executive Committee Report to the 49th Annual Conference, 30 September-1 October 1972.
18 See also PRONI, D/3233/2/1/1 for Whitelaw's reply to Simpson on PR, 2 June 1972.
19 Interview with Erskine Holmes, 21 September 2005.
20 Interview with Brian Garrett, 30 September 2003.
21 PRONI, D/3233/2/2/1, *Vivian Simpson Papers*, Blease to Simpson, 28 August 1972.
22 Ibid.
23 Moyle held many posts in the Gas and Electricity Industries. He was also Chief Secretary to the Treasury (1966–69), Chief Secretary to the Home Secretary (1969–70), Secretary to the Committee on Race Relations and recognised as someone close to the trade union movement. See PRONI, D/3233/2/2/1.
24 PRONI, D/3233/2/2/1, *Vivian Simpson Papers*, NILP Press Statement at the end of the Darlington Conference.
25 Ibid.
26 Interview with Brian Garrett, 30 September 2003.
27 *The Future of Northern Ireland: A Paper for Discussion* (Belfast: HMSO, 1972), p. 17.
28 Ibid., p. 13.
29 Ibid., p. 12.
30 Bew, Paul, Peter Gibbon and Henry Patterson, *Northern Ireland 1921–2001: Political Forces and Social Classes: Revised and Updated Version* (London: Serif, 2002), p. 174.
31 Tonge, Jonathan, *The New Northern Irish Politics* (Basingstoke: Palgrave, 2005), p. 90.

The fall of the NILP, 1972–75   211

32 *The Future of Northern Ireland*, p. 13.
33 PRONI, D/3233/2/1/1, *Vivian Simpson Papers*, NILP Memorandum for the Secretary of State, 11 December 1972.
34 Ibid.
35 Ibid.
36 SDLP, *Towards a New Ireland*, p. 4. Having said that the SDLP's critique of the Alliance Party was justified as the party wanted no interference from the Irish Republic and stressed the merits only of an Anglo-Irish mechanism.
37 PRONI, D/3233/2/1/1, *Vivian Simpson Papers*, NILP Memorandum for the Secretary of State, 11 December 1972.
38 PRONI, D/3233/2/1/1, *Vivian Simpson Papers*, NILP Public Security: Points to be put to the Secretary of State by NILP, 11 December 1972.
39 Cunningham, Michael, *British Government Policy in Northern Ireland, 1969–2000* (Manchester: Manchester University Press, 2001), p. 13.
40 Ibid., pp. 13–14.
41 *Northern Ireland Constitutional Proposals* (Belfast: HMSO, 1973), Cmd. 5259, pp. 2–3, 13–14.
42 PRONI, D/3233/2/1/1, *Vivian Simpson Papers*, Vivian Simpson, Leader of the NILP, to Professor R.J. Lawrence, Queen's University Belfast – RE: Border Poll, 30 March 1973.
43 Unless otherwise indicated all data are taken from the *Belfast Telegraph*, 1 and 2 June 1973.
44 Letter from George Chambers to the *Belfast Telegraph*, 19 May 1973.
45 Ibid.
46 *Irish Independent*, 14 June 1973.
47 *Belfast Newsletter*, 16 June 1973.
48 *Irish Times*, 16 June 1973.
49 NILP, *Peace Through Partnership* (1973).
50 *Irish Times*, 16 June 1973.
51 Ibid.
52 *Belfast Newsletter*, 26 May 1973.
53 Northern Ireland Assembly Results 1973, archived at www.ark.ac.uk /elections/fa73.htm (accessed 14 March 2006).
54 Dixon, Paul, *Northern Ireland: The Politics of War and Peace* (Basingstoke: Palgrave, 2001), p. 139.
55 *Belfast Newsletter*, 17 August 1973.
56 NAI, DFA/2003/17/416, Affidavit of Gerard Fitt, 5 September 1973, Intimidation Reports.
57 Dixon, *Northern Ireland*, p. 140.
58 Ibid., pp. 131–8.
59 During the 'second peace process', as Coakley has observed, 'many would see the Alliance Party as heir not so much to the Ulster Liberal Party as to the Northern Ireland Labour Party (NILP)'. Coakley, John, 'Conclusion: New Strains of Unionism and Nationalism', in Coakley, John (ed.), *Changing Shades of Orange and Green: Redefining the Union and the Nation in Contemporary Ireland* (Dublin: UCD Press, 2002), p. 140.
60 *Sunday News*, 4 February 1974.
61 Nelson, Sarah, *Ulster's Uncertain Defenders: Protestant Political, Paramilitary, and Community Groups and the Northern Ireland Conflict* (Belfast: Appletree, 1984), p. 173.

62 Ibid.

63 *Belfast Telegraph*, 22 February 1974.

64 For the reasons behind this shift away from devolution in favour of Direct Rule see the interview with the party's chairman Brian Garrett in the *Irish Times*, 23 February 1974.

65 *Irish Times*, 26 February 1974.

66 Executive Committee Report to the 51st Annual Conference of the NILP (1974), Private Papers of Lord Blease of Cromac.

67 Interview with Douglas McIldoon, 21 January 2004.

68 Arguably the fate of the moderates had been sealed with the resignation of Brian Faulkner from the Unionist Party in January 1974 and his setting up of the Unionist Party of Northern Ireland (UPNI), which later polled dismally.

69 See Douglas McIldoon's letter ' . . . and the sad failures of will of the Labour men in office' in the *Guardian*, 1 June 1974.

70 See Ron Hayward's letter to Vivian Simpson on 2 April 1973 confirming the NEC's decision to give the NILP a grant of £2,000 for 1973, PRONI, D/3233/2/1/1.

71 Douglas McIldoon letter in the *Guardian*, 1 June 1974.

72 LPA, GS12/NI, Northern Ireland Documents, 1974, Hayward to McIldoon, 11 June 1974.

73 Ibid., McIldoon to Hayward, 28 June 1974.

74 Ibid., Hayward to McIldoon, 22 July 1974.

75 See the comments on Northern Ireland in the memoirs of Wilson's special adviser at the time: Donoughue, Bernard, *Downing Street Diary, With Harold Wilson in No. 10* (London: Pimlico, 2006).

76 Fisk, Robert, *The Point of No Return: The Strike which Broke the British in Ulster* (London: Andre Deutsch, 1975), p. 241.

77 *Guardian*, 30 May 1974; Brendan O'Leary maintains that 'the collapse of the Sunningdale experiment of 1974 was the decisive event of the Labour Government and it haunted the rest of Labour's term of management and it is the event by which Labour ministers should be judged'. O'Leary, Brendan, 'The Labour Government and Northern Ireland, 1974–9', in McGarry, John and Brendan O'Leary (eds), *The Northern Ireland Conflict: Consociational Engagements* (Oxford: Oxford University Press, 2004), p. 210.

78 Interview with Douglas McIldoon, 21 January 2004.

79 Nelson, *Ulster's Uncertain Defenders*, p. 128.

80 The NILP's full-time organiser Erskine Holmes, elected to Belfast City Council in 1973, launched a bitter attack on the BLP claiming that, 'We cannot place the future safety of Ulster, or either of her communities, in the hands of these timorous Englishmen.' *Belfast Telegraph*, 24 July 1974.

81 Roger Byrne, *Why the NILP? A Dossier on the Northern Ireland Labour Party*, December 1974.

82 Northern Ireland Assembly Debates, Vol. 3, Col. 843–4, 14 May 1974.

83 Byrne, *Why the NILP?*

84 Ibid.

85 *Irish Times*, 27 August 1974.

86 Wood, Ian S., *Crimes of Loyalty: A History of the UDA* (Edinburgh: Edinburgh University Press, 2006).

87 *Observer*, 18 April 1971; Bell, Geoffrey, 'Looking for the UVF', *Irish Times*, 22 April 1971.

88 Interview with Billy Mitchell, 27 September 2005.

89 Ibid.

90 McDonald, Henry and Jim Cusack, *UDA: Inside the Heart of Loyalist Terror* (Dublin: Penguin, 2005), p. 12.

91 *Belfast Newsletter*, 29 January 1971.

92 See PRONI, D/3233/2/1/1, Public Security: Points to be Put to the Secretary of State by the NILP, 11 December 1972 and the reply by Whitelaw to the letter by Oldpark DLP on 7 February 1973, PRONI, D/3233/2/1/1.

93 Interview with Jim McDonald, 4 May 2005.

94 See Bleakley, David, *Sadie Patterson: Irish Peacemaker* (Belfast: Blackstaff, 1980).

95 Interview with Billy Mitchell, 27 September 2005.

96 Mitchell, Billy, *The Principles of Loyalism: An Internal Discussion Paper* (Belfast, 2002), pp. 65–6.

97 Sandy Scott statement in the *Belfast Telegraph*, 14 February 1974.

98 See the generalised points about the NILP made in Howe, Stephen, 'Mad Dogs and Ulstermen: The Crisis of Loyalism: Part One', *Open Democracy*, 28 September 2005. Archived at: www.opendemocracy.net/globalization-protest/loyalism_2876.jsp (accessed 15 October 2005). See also Walker, Graham, 'Loyalist Culture, Unionist Politics: A Response to Stephen Howe', *Open Democracy*, 11 October 2005. Archived at: www.opendemocracy.net/democracy-protest/protestant_2910.jsp (accessed 15 October 2005).

99 Interview with George Chambers, 14 February 2006.

100 Rumpf, Erhard and Anthony C. Hepburn, *Nationalism and Socialism in Twentieth Century Ireland* (Liverpool: Liverpool University Press, 1977), p. 207.

101 LAW Enrolment Form, September 1969.

102 Rumpf and Hepburn, *Nationalism and Socialism in Twentieth Century Ireland*, p. 207.

103 LPA, Northern Ireland Policy Box, 1980–1990, Northern Ireland Liaison Committee: The Labour Party and Northern Ireland: An Historical Account of the Relations between the Labour Party and the Northern Ireland Labour Party (Labour Research Department, February 1984).

104 Devlin, Paddy, *Straight Left: An Autobiography* (Belfast: Blackstaff, 1993), pp. 133–4. Devlin claims that the other two in the Falls delegation, his daughter Anne and the Judge Turlough O'Donnell, were set against what they viewed as an attempt to consolidate 'the Act of Union' (1801).

105 O'Leary, 'The Labour Government and Northern Ireland, 1974–9', p. 196.

106 NAI, DFA 2002/19/379, 'Speech by Harold Wilson at the Cantril Farm Labour Club, Huyton, 2 December 1972', contained in Visit to Dublin by Mr Harold Wilson MP, leader of the British Labour Party, 1971–78.

107 Hennessey, Thomas, *Northern Ireland: The Origins of the Troubles* (Dublin: Gill and Macmillan, 2005), p. 387.

108 LPA, GS12/NI, Northern Ireland Documents, 1975, James Callaghan to Brian Garrett, 19 May 1975.

109 LPA, GS12/NI, Northern Ireland Documents, 1975, Handwritten Notes of a Meeting between representatives of the NILP and the Labour Party's NEC, Transport House, London, 8 May 1975.

110 LPA, GS12/NI, Northern Ireland Documents, 1975, Brian Garrett to Ron Hayward, 13 May 1975.

7

Squeezing the moderates, 1975–87

> The conclusion that many of us reached, certainly by the 1970s, was that the only conceivable way in which viable labour politics could be developed here was by getting the British Labour Party to organise here; either by absorbing the NILP or simply disbanding it and replacing it.[1]

Introduction: the Constitutional Convention election

It was an unfortunate fact of political life that for the third consecutive election the NILP presented a disunited front to the electorate. It was at one on policy, though it could not agree on the endorsement of its highest-profile politician David Bleakley. Jealousies and animosities raged and had been brought to a head when Newtownabbey Labour disaffiliated from the party in the aftermath of the Ulster Workers' Council (UWC) strike of May 1974.[2] Newtownabbey's reaction was an inevitable consequence of the NILP's rejection of power sharing with an Irish dimension,[3] which saw the party now plump for Direct Rule. The NILP claimed that:

> The Agreement placed the party in some difficulty in that while we welcomed the spirit of inter-communal reconciliation it was supposed to enshrine we had strong reservations about the methods to achieve that – having always opposed a Council of Ireland having Executive Powers – and grave doubts as to whether or not, setting aside our own reservations – the entire package did not go as far as to be totally unrelated to what was acceptable to the population.[4]

In Brian Garrett's address to his party's annual conference in December 1974 he recognised that 'this movement has paid dearly in electoral terms for the violence'; however he remained hopeful that a unified stance could be taken by the Labour movement. His analysis was that 'the British Government and Parliament are increasingly under pressure from the electorate in Britain to find some way to end the drip-drip of the blood of British soldiers on the streets and villages of Northern Ireland'.[5] In the end Garrett regarded it as the NILP's duty to enter the forthcoming Convention election 'with a clear powerful message. It is – "Confrontation spells disaster" – our duty is to paint the picture of the true meaning of UUUC/SDLP confrontation.'[6]

Hoping to bolster the political standing of two of its most well-known figures in North and West Belfast, the Reverend John Stewart and Billy Boyd, the Woodvale party endorsed them as their chosen candidates for the May 1975 Constitutional Convention election. This was in keeping with Woodvale's earlier controversial decision in 1974 not to contest West Belfast. Jim McDonald recalls the reason for nominating Stewart as the North Belfast candidate:

> We proposed John and got John put forward as a candidate, albeit with very little success. But if anybody wouldn't have voted for John Stewart then I don't know what they were looking for; cos he was a down-to-earth guy. A very very capable guy. Lived in the community. Worked for the community. Toured bombings with me. John and I were in the rubble of the Mountainview bomb.[7] [He] went to the hospital with me. Seen victims of the Mountainview bombing. John was something else. But John died at a very early age of 44 (I think he was when he died of cancer). A huge huge loss to the community and to everybody – working-class people. John was a brilliant guy and a big influence on my early thinking.[8]

McDonald's characterisation of Stewart as a charismatic and deeply revered preacher tallies well with George Chambers's recollections of him too. It appears that Stewart was willing to risk entering into negotiation, dialogue and debate with armed loyalist paramilitaries who held court in the back-street social clubs of North and West Belfast.[9] On most occasions he wore his Methodist collar openly and could be found in the thick of the violence – along what later became known as the so-called 'peace-line' separating Protestants and Catholics – actively trying to prevent loss of life. Stewart was one NILP politician who gave hope to those living in squalid, segregated conditions, yet he could not exercise his calming influence in every corner. By now violence was beginning to take its toll on even dyed-in-the-wool Labour supporters, with many leaving the party amidst an extremely busy campaign trail.

The NILP's Constitutional Convention manifesto made clear the party's belief in the British connection. It gave three reasons why the link was vital:

1. As part of the United Kingdom Northern Ireland people enjoy the advantage of living in one of the most advanced and progressive countries in the world;
2. As part of the United Kingdom the people of Northern Ireland secure all the advantages – such as the Health Service and the Welfare State – which the British Labour and Trade Union Movement have won since the war;
3. Northern Ireland is part of the British economy. Over eighty per cent of our trade is with Britain and being part of a much larger, richer state has provided Northern Ireland over the years with the extra money needed to modernise our economy and stand up to terrorist attack.[10]

Surprisingly, the NILP advocated a strong local Executive presiding over departmental committees in which Protestants and Catholics would 'share responsibility'. It marked the final salvo in the NILP's class-based appeal to the Northern Ireland electorate. Although Bleakley was once again returned for East

Belfast the party polled only 9,102 votes (1.4%).[11] McIldoon's recollection was that:

> I think the sort of things that the Labour Party was primarily on about were just irrelevant to most people, which were things like survival and not getting burnt out of your house – and getting home from work without being blown up by a car bomb.[12]

Bleakley's election to the Convention certainly confirmed his personal popularity among a section of the electorate in East Belfast. Operating from the same political base for over a generation, Bleakley had cultivated long-term loyalty from Labour activists and supporters alike. Despite his success, a question mark still hung over the political careers of his NILP colleagues, many of whom polled dismally in the politically crowded constituencies in other parts of Belfast. The only exception was Billy Boyd in North Belfast who came within one thousand votes of being elected. In electoral terms the Convention election marked the NILP's last high tide, as the Alliance Party began to take over the reigns as the principal moderate centrist party in Northern Irish politics. The election also saw the return of various Nationalist and republican political forces to the city from which they had been banished thirty years earlier.

The NILP at the sectarian interface: beating the retreat?

In the years immediately following the UWC strike, relations between the NILP and BLP deteriorated to an all-time low. Recriminations were rife about which partner had consequently made life more difficult for the other in terms of domestic political issues. Nevertheless the NILP resolved to ensure that 'persistent disagreement should not disrupt the fraternal relationship and the common[alities] which exist over a wide range of policies'.[13] The party's chairman in 1975–76, George Chambers, was an unrepentant critic of the British party and laid the blame squarely on it for not doing enough to help the NILP in its hour of need. Yet, as Rumpf and Hepburn state:

> While it is unlikely that this was the sole cause of the NILP's near-collapse – it would of course be very comforting to place all the blame on an external factor over which the party had no control – the party certainly had cause to reflect somewhat bitterly that whenever British Labour has won power it has placed its confidence not in its socialist comrades of the NILP, but in the Unionist government – in the case of the Attlee administration – and, more recently, in the predominantly Catholic and anti-partitionist Social Democratic and Labour Party.[14]

Arguably, these scholars offer little or no evidence why the NILP should have faltered in light of its association with the British party. As demonstrated in previous chapters the British Labour tradition was of pivotal importance in determining the political allegiance of most NILP activists after 1949. It was not necessarily the BLP as a political party which many NILP activists found attractive, but the opportunity to satisfy their ideological needs in the same way as

Squeezing the moderates, 1975–87

other regional and ethnic minorities (with sectional class interests) were doing elsewhere in Scotland, England and Wales.

In terms of what later transpired the NILP was correct in initially advocating a devolved power-sharing government with a limited Irish dimension; however it was hasty in abandoning this to the liberal integrationist whims of those who favoured the authority of a Westminster Parliament above a locally devolved settlement. Commentators writing about the Sunningdale Agreement are often divided over the relative merits of British intentions. Brendan O'Leary, for instance, has argued that the collapse of the Sunningdale arrangement 'did not break the will of the British to stay in Northern Ireland, what it broke was the London Government to have a significant Irish dimension in addressing the conflict'.[15] On the other hand, and with the benefit of hindsight, 1973–74 may well have marked the beginning of a British policy-learning process which, according to Jonathan Tonge, 'after Sunningdale eventually moved towards Anglo-Irish intergovernmentalism, bypassing Northern Ireland's political parties'.[16]

Undoubtedly the NILP still had a political message to transmit to the electorate but it was an electorate that needed something more tribally comforting when deep-rooted ethnic quarrels threatened not just a particular set of principles and convictions, but human survival itself. In war-torn Northern Ireland this injection of realism only dawned on individual NILP members at a time when it was too late to rein in events on the streets. As McIldoon put it:

> It was not the sort of world where people were thinking: "ah yes, I've got to vote Labour because I am not happy with the council's policy on changing the rent rebate system", or whatever [were] the sort of things that normally ... drove people to vote for Labour.[17]

By this time new social and political forces had risen from the ashes of working-class areas, like the Bogside and the Fountain in Derry, and Oldpark and Ardoyne in Belfast, to preside over a mutation of socialist politics across the province. The NILP, a party that had attracted both Protestants and Catholics to its ranks, finally succumbed to the fragmentation and party proliferation of the local political scene.[18] Ironically, the introduction of PR hastened, rather than stabilised, the party's decline. Speaking retrospectively former NILP Chairman, Brian Garrett, said:

> I mean I think the Alliance Party, the DUP, the SDLP – all of which are new organisations. There was a new politics of frustration and defensiveness. This was pretty macho politics we are now into. It was highly sectarianised. It ran against all the ethos of the Labour Party, which had come up in the fifties to say well the border is settled. We'll try and have an inter-community party. We will try and make everything as if this is not an issue. So therefore don't push on the constitutional issue sort of line, if you like. People thought that that was a sort of boyscout attitude. And it wasn't realistic. Certainly on the doorstep that's what we were being told by electors, many of whom would have said 'well, I'll get round to voting for you, but I'd like to sort this out first', they would say. So that was a great disappointment. What

happened in '68 onwards ran absolutely head-bang into the ethic of the Northern Ireland Labour Party ... We were finished by that stage. The show was over.[19]

Difficulties abounded for the party as it increasingly fell back on its core Protestant working-class support base. Some scholars have argued that this 'suggested that the party's only hope in retaining a political base lay in promoting its loyalism at the expense of its bi-confessionalism'.[20] The only problem with this analysis is that it is disingenuous to the NILP's own reasoning for courting its working-class Protestant support-base, albeit unsuccessfully. Above all it was a last-ditch effort to preserve its membership. In policy terms the NILP had not abandoned the political centre and, despite much criticism, it continued to maintain a non-sectarian labourist outlook.

The Labour vote fractures

By the mid-1970s the NILP's political fortunes had taken a dramatic downswing. Its membership had dwindled to several hundred and it finally resolved itself, unhappily, to punching above its weight in the Constitutional Convention. More worryingly the trade union movement had been steadily distancing itself from its political partners since 1970. This came to a head on the annual May Day parade in 1976, in the main because the ICTU had prevented the NILP from forming up and walking with its own distinct political identity. Some senior members of the party thought that 'it was foolish'[21] and it certainly reflected extremely badly on the Labour movement as a whole, especially since the NILP insisted on holding its own counter-demonstration in the Cornmarket area of the city centre. This drew heavy criticism from the Belfast press, which thought that it 'highlighted a split' in the NILP.[22]

What served to distance the party from the British Labour mainstream even further was the trenchant criticism of the BLP by NILP activists, which sealed the fate for the latter financially. The second instalment of the annual maintenance grant for 1974 – 'regarded by the NILP as getting their own money back'[23] – was only paid, after considerable lobbying, in 1976. In many ways it served as the party's severance pay; a fact that left, in one member's opinion, 'massive bitterness against the Labour Party when the grant was withdrawn in the 1970s'.[24] Nevertheless, the NILP continued to court the British party. In a jovial letter to Labour's National Organiser George Chambers reported, somewhat over-optimistically, a steady improvement in his party's fortunes. The letter also highlighted the impending crisis facing the NILP with regard to its relationship with the ICTU:

> Since our meeting in Transport House last January the fortunes of the NI Labour Party have maintained a steady improvement – membership, party activities and Publicity have all been stepped up – and a meeting with the NI Committee of the ICTU is scheduled for next month. We issued full support for the ICTU 'Better Life for all' campaign but so far have failed to persuade them to abandon their 'non-political' stance and join with us in presenting a united Labour Alternative to the people of Northern Ireland ... It is most disappointing that our relationship with

Squeezing the moderates, 1975–87

the British Labour Party is still unresolved but we appreciate the pressure of business on the NEC agenda over recent months and hope that the matter will soon reach a mutually satisfactory conclusion.[25]

The NILP also reported how it was seeking out ways to tackle sectarianism. In particular, the party had organised a rally in the wake of the May Day fiasco – at which several local councillors, including Independent Unionist Hugh Smyth and the SDLP's Tom Donnelly, shared a platform with Billy Boyd – as a means of pushing forward a concerted inter-ethnic response to remedy working-class division:

> As you can see we are determined to continue our struggle to raise the standard of political debate in Northern Ireland above the level of our traditional sectarian squabble and so advance the cause of socialism throughout the Province. Any support you can give us would be most welcome.[26]

Notwithstanding these upbeat reports it soon became obvious that the NILP was being given the cold shoulder by its 'sister' party. British Labour had tired of carping criticisms and some of its members even began to align themselves more openly with Gerry Fitt and the SDLP. Ironically Fitt soon became a casualty of the continuing 'greening' of the SDLP.

Electorally speaking, the squeezing of the moderate vote at this time came initially from within the bi-confessional bloc itself, as the NILP and APNI clashed over the exact panacea for solving the violent conflict. Alan Carr, who was a prominent leader of the party in the late 1970s and 1980s, felt that there were two distinct strands co-existing in the NILP at this time:

> There was the sort of middle-class liberal strand, who were in it almost in spite of the fact that it called itself a Labour Party. And there were those who saw it as being basically the equivalent of the British Labour Party in Northern Ireland.[27]

After 1970, with the departure of Paddy Devlin and other members who resisted internal moves to make the NILP a region of the BLP, these two strands became more entangled over strategy, to such an extent that several disgruntled members left the party for a plethora of new political parties and pressure groups.

For those who wished to concentrate their efforts more on building up a non-liberal political party in Protestant working-class districts there were plenty of opportunities. In 1977 two prominent NILP activists from the Shankill area, David Overend and Jim McDonald, left the party to join with Independent Unionist councillor Hugh Smyth to form the Independent Unionist Group, later to become the Progressive Unionist Party (PUP) in 1979. Smyth became its first leader and Jackie Hewitt its first secretary. Indeed, Overend was responsible for drafting many of the party's early documents. Incidentally, throughout its existence the PUP has consistently played up the fact that it was formed by ex-NILP members, former Ulster Volunteer Force and Red Hand Commando prisoners and Independent Unionists.[28]

The campaign for Labour representation

Another offshoot of the NILP – which did have considerable influence from the late 1970s onwards – was the Campaign for Labour Representation (CLR). It was established in the wake of the abortive United Unionist Action Council strike of May 1977, which was intended as an instrument by which to force the British government to get tough with the IRA. The 1977 strike was led by the DUP's Reverend Ian Paisley, and backed by paramilitary muscle provided by the Ulster Defence Association (UDA), although the organisation 'itself went divided into the strike action'.[29] Indeed, much like the 1974 strike, tensions between Paisley and the UDA had again become manifest.[30] NILP members who channelled their energies into the CLR included Derek Peters, David Morrison, Boyd Black and Cecil Allen. Morrison, who later became its secretary, had been an active member of the Newtownabbey Labour Party in the late 1960s and early 1970s. He remembers how the CLR

> started in 1977 ... We had some involvement with working-class Protestants who were of a general labour disposition [and] who had been in and around the Ulster Workers' Council Strike, and the subsequent one. And we tried to find some framework in which people of a labour disposition could function in politics. And by that time the NILP was on its last legs and, well, it occurred to us that there was this great anomaly in Northern Ireland. Here we were nominally part of the United Kingdom but excluded from the politics of the United Kingdom and how could you possibly develop non-sectarian politics in those circumstances when a great motivating factor for bringing about dissolving these two peoples was access to governmental politics.[31]

The CLR consistently lobbied the BLP to organise in Northern Ireland. In an early letter to Labour's National Agent, Reg Underhill, the CLR was at pains to stress how it 'exists for the sole purpose of persuading the Labour Party to organise in Northern Ireland'. Indeed in the most succinct explanation of its reason for existence it stated:

> We would emphasise that we are not a political party, that our views on the matter are not coloured by anticipation of our electoral fortunes being either jeopardised or enhanced by the Labour Party establishing here. Our sole purpose is in hastening the development of Labour politics and the end of the sectarian politics of the past, a process which, in our view, can only be accomplished through the Labour Party operating in Northern Ireland and in so doing bringing the great social and economic questions of United Kingdom politics to the forefront of politics in the province.[32]

The organisation emerged at a time when there were few choices open to those of a labour or democratic socialist disposition. As Boyd Black remarked, 'you couldn't join the Labour Party, there was no NILP, and I mean what we did was to campaign for the right to join the Labour Party'.[33]

The mainstay of the group's argument was that if 'normal politics' could be extended to Northern Ireland it would usher in a new spirit of co-operation between Protestants and Catholics; eventually, it was argued, this would lead to

Squeezing the moderates, 1975–87

an eradication of 'sectarian politics'. As Morrison went on to explain:

> We kept playing up things like the Protestant–Catholic antagonism in Glasgow and Liverpool – and places like that – had melted away in part at least because of their involvement in politics that was governmental. It was about ruling the state, not about local issues where majorities and minorities rub up against one another and end up squabbling. So it came from that.[34]

Another CLR member, Mark Langhammer, reiterated the point that the organisation

> was never conceived as an electoral thing. It was about civil rights. Here we were being governed (potentially) by a party that didn't have one vote to its name. Not one vote! And it was prepared to take our taxes and govern us![35]

Morrison was at pains to stress that the grouping, although accepting what would later be known as the 'principle of consent', was never

> primarily a unionist enterprise. It's about finding circumstances in which the working-class Protestant and Catholic can participate together in the Labour movement of the state in which they currently live. And that was definitely the framework in which we set it and we just argued for it continuously.[36]

The CLR emerged at a time when the left was in the ascendancy within the Labour Party:

> It started at a time when the Labour Party was in Troops Out mode and the Bennites were on the up and up and it was greeted with hostility from a wide range of people in the Labour Party. So it was a pretty massive task to turn the Labour Party around on the issue.[37]

Even though James Callaghan had given overwhelming backing to the NILP in the early 1970s, his spell as Prime Minister between 1976 and 1979 revealed that he had little time for Northern Irish affairs and the CLR case gained little ground.

Presiding over the 'corpse': the NILP's final years

The Labour government lost the 1979 Westminster election to Margaret Thatcher's Conservative Party, which was returned with a 44-seat majority. Locally, the NILP polled only 4,411 votes and all three of its candidates forfeited their deposits.[38] It was the worst result for the party in decades and in many ways it confirmed its electoral passing at a national level. Interestingly, even though the NILP did not contest the first European Parliamentary elections the following month, David Bleakley managed to poll 9,383 (1.6%) first preference votes on an Independent United Community ticket, placing him eighth overall and several thousand votes ahead of Paddy Devlin who stood as a United Labour Party candidate.[39] Whatever possibility remained of the British Labour Party coming to the aid of the NILP was lost by this stage, especially since the former was now dogged by its own internal fluctuations, as Diane Hayter explains:

At the time the Labour Party, reeling from its 1979 defeat, faced disillusion from unions and party activists, infiltration from the Trotskyist Militant Tendency, a dysfunctional party apparatus, policy divides (especially over Europe) and a campaign to rewrite the party's constitution to transfer power from the Parliamentary Labour Party (PLP) to the conference and constituencies. Meanwhile the left-controlled National Executive Committee (NEC) appeared at war with the record of the last Labour government, vindictive towards MPs, tolerant over Militant and unable to turn the party's infantry or big guns on its opponents in the House of Commons.[40]

Whatever sympathy Labour now had for its comrades in Ulster was strangled by the left's dominance over policy. Furthermore, those who had previously held moderate anti-partitionist convictions were now being eclipsed by outwardly republican sympathisers in the BLP's front-ranks.

Despite limited – and increasingly hostile – support from the BLP several senior NILP activists continued to carry the mantle of the party even after its inter-community support-base had been polarised and siphoned off in more ethnically-exclusive ways. By the end of the 1970s the Provisional IRA had dug in for its 'long war' and the province continued to be greeted by daily news bulletins of death and destruction. Wading through the rubble on the streets to reach their place of work became the humdrum reality for many working-class people. The working classes became further polarised when an IRA hunger striker, Bobby Sands, was returned to the vacant Westminster seat of Fermanagh and South Tyrone in a 1981 by-election. The hunger strikes had touched a raw nerve with the Catholic working class, so much so that the SDLP opted to stand aside in the poll to allow Sands a clear run. After 66 days on hunger strike Sands died, nightly rioting broke out across the province and working-class areas once again returned to a war-footing.

Within weeks a local government election was called. There was much hope among moderates that the poll would heal the battle scars between the two communities, as the *Belfast Telegraph* pointed out in an unrealistic eve of poll leader:

> Meanwhile, Alliance battles to hold the balance of power, which its 14.4% vote in 1977 gave it. Thanks to PR, there is no prospect of an overall majority in more than a handful of councils, and it is a proven fact that where Alliance is a significant force, as in Belfast, sectarian bickering is reduced to a minimum.[41]

All three of the NILP's candidates were unsuccessful. Contrary to media speculation that the election would buoy up the moderate centre ground, bitterness remained endemic between Protestants and Catholics during the poll, as the more extreme parties benefited while the centre was further squeezed.[42] Tellingly the *Belfast Telegraph* rescinded on its previous optimism and now claimed that:

> In a polarised situation, people vote in a polarised manner. That is the obvious conclusion to be drawn from the election result, which proved the extent to which the two communities have moved apart.[43]

Squeezing the moderates, 1975–87   223

The NILP was not the only loser. Gerry Fitt lost his council seat and Paddy
Devlin only just got elected. The local media considered this 'the penalty for
abandoning a tribal position'. Devlin was later expelled from his home by the
Provisional IRA.[44]

The NILP's poor showing meant that by now 'it was clear that there was no
basis for the party continuing'[45] and in Carr's opinion:

> It ceased to exist effectively in 1982 or thereabouts I would put it. It was shortly
> after our failure to make the slightest impact in the 1981 local government elec-
> tions. I mean there was one councillor elected in the whole of Northern Ireland. It
> was a fellow called Eddie Gaw in Newtownards and I mean he could have stood
> describing himself as anything and got elected. It was simply a personal vote. It
> wasn't a party vote.[46]

In a meeting between an NILP delegation and Michael Foot in February 1982,
the Labour leader refused to repudiate what Alan Carr referred to as 'the idiotic
and undemocratic policy of "rolling republicanism" which was adopted at the
last party conference'. Leaving the meeting amidst acrimonious dispute, Carr
said, it 'marked a watershed in relations between the Labour movement in the
province and the leadership of the British Labour Party'.[47] The fraternal relationship between the two parties had ended. In a newspaper article written
several weeks later Sam Napier estimated that the party's membership was 'now
put less than 200'. He attributed its difficulties to the BLP's declaration in favour
of reunification of Ireland and said that recent events 'have combined to indicate that the obituary of the NILP can soon be written'.[48] His words soon proved
prophetic.

In the run-up to the 1983 Westminster election the serving party chairman
Bob Clarke resigned, citing the fact that 'the executive had neither the will nor
the finance to enter the fray'.[49] Hot on his heels the party's serving secretary Bill
Whitley also left, complaining bitterly about the prevalence of 'antagonism' in
the NILP executive and 'a structure which derives from the days of much larger
membership, representation and interest'. He stated that if the executive 'feels it
is unable to accept this challenge, then the only honourable thing to do is give a
decent burial to a party that has an admirable past'.[50] At a special conference at
the end of May 1982, which only 40 delegates attended, some members
attempted to force a two-thirds majority to disband the party. The move was
unsuccessful and the NILP soldiered on divided, with several branches winding
up and lacking clear leadership.[51] Although three candidates ran on an NILP
ticket in Castlereagh East in the 1985 local government election there was no
formal party mechanism behind their campaign. In effect the party existed only
on the electoral communiqués of these candidates. Disastrously they won only
129 votes collectively, a minuscule fraction of what the NILP could easily
command in the same area in its heyday of the 1960s.[52]

Following the NILP's electoral demise the Labour vote retracted even further.
Soon Bob Kidd became the most electorally successful Labour politician at the
local level. Kidd had been an NILP councillor from the early 1960s, until

Newtownabbey Labour broke away in 1974. In 1985 and 1987 he contested the local government elections, along with his running mate, Tommy Davidson, who had at one time served on the NILP Executive. Newtownabbey had always been a relative hot-bed for labourism. In fact, one of the most successful Labour councillors, apart from Kidd, was Mark Langhammer, who served on Newtownabbey Borough Council between 1993 and 2005. Reflecting on his years spent as a Labour councillor, Langhammer said that he 'came out of the remnants of the NILP'.[53] In his words:

> The Northern Ireland Labour Party was quite strong in Newtownabbey, partly because it was a strong blue-collar area. It had a lot of manufacturing industry, engineering industry. A lot of people moved there who would have worked in the shipyard, Sirocco, Mackies, and so on. So there was a trade union ethos in Newtownabbey, which was perhaps stronger than in most other places. So there was the natural element prepared to vote for somebody standing up for Labour and trade union things. The other thing was that there were quite a number of councillors at one stage. I mean at one stage in the 1960s there were six Newtownabbey Labour councillors on the old Newtownabbey Urban District Council, which was quite a lot. They weren't all superbly progressive councillors – some were 'Sunday swings' types – but it was a Labour element that was there. It was active.[54]

Nonetheless, while the Labour tradition remained strong and politically healthy in certain local districts throughout the 1980s, it could not muster the resources that once marked it out as a worthy challenger to its confessional-based rivals. At a special conference on 14 March 1987 a unanimous motion was carried which stated that 'This special conference agrees that the Northern Ireland Labour Party shall disband and that all existing members shall transfer to the new broad based "Labour 1987".'

Conclusion

Even though the NILP did not officially wind up its operations until as late as 1987 it had effectively ceased to exist with every new plume of smoke that bellowed over the Belfast skyline in the 1970s. The political space the NILP occupied has since been taken up by a multitude of parties, all of which have inherited several of its genetic features. In a polarised political atmosphere the NILP's electoral support-base certainly did scatter when presented with confessional-based rivals in the form of the DUP and SDLP (not to mention the fragmentation of Unionism along extremist–moderate lines) and the comparative successes of its bi-confessional 'successor' in the form of the Alliance Party.[55] Labour had once again failed in its bid to break the sectarian dichotomy of Northern Irish politics.

Notes

1 Interview with Alan Carr, 3 August 2005.
2 Newtownabbey Labour Party members were appalled by the NILP's support for the

Squeezing the moderates, 1975–87   225

UWC strike and used this grievance as a basis for attacking the party in later years. See the correspondence between Alan Carr of the NILP and Vincent McCormack of Newtownabbey Labour in the *Belfast Telegraph*, 13 and 18 March 1976.

3 See the interview with the party's Chairman Brian Garrett in the *Irish Times*, 23 February 1974.

4 Private Papers of Lord Blease of Cromac, Executive Committee Report to the 51st Annual Conference of the Northern Ireland Labour Party (December 1974).

5 NILP, Chairman's Address to the 51st Annual Conference of the NILP (1974).

6 Ibid.

7 Five Protestant civilians were killed when a no-warning Provisional IRA bomb went off in the Mountainview Tavern on the Shankill Road on 5 April 1975.

8 Interview with Jim McDonald, 4 May 2005.

9 Interview with George Chambers, 2 March 2005. Stewart served on the NILP's EC from 1976 until his death in 1977.

10 NILP, *Constitutional Convention Election Manifesto* (1975).

11 Results obtained at: www.ark.ac.uk/elections/cnb.htm (accessed 5 November 2007).

12 Interview with Douglas McIldoon, 21 January 2004.

13 NILP, Executive Committee Report to the 51st Annual Conference of the NILP (1974).

14 Rumpf, Erhard and Anthony C. Hepburn, *Nationalism and Socialism in Twentieth Century Ireland* (Liverpool: Liverpool University Press, 1977), p. 208.

15 O'Leary, Brendan, 'The Labour Government and Northern Ireland, 1974–9', in McGarry, John and Brendan O'Leary (eds), *The Northern Ireland Conflict: Consociational Engagements* (Oxford: Oxford University Press, 2004), p. 214.

16 Tonge, Jonathan, 'From Sunningdale to the Good Friday Agreement: Creating Devolved Government in Northern Ireland', *Contemporary British History*, Vol. 14, No. 3 (2000), p. 41.

17 Interview with Douglas McIldoon, 21 January 2004.

18 Mitchell, Paul, 'The Party System and Party Competition', in Mitchell, Paul and Rick Wilford (eds), *Politics in Northern Ireland* (Boulder: Westview Press, 1999), p. 96.

19 Interview with Brian Garrett, 30 September 2003.

20 McAllister, Ian and Sarah Nelson, 'Modern Developments in the Northern Ireland Party System', *Parliamentary Affairs*, Vol. 23, No. 3 (1979), p. 295.

21 Interview with Brian Garrett, 30 September 2003.

22 *Sunday News*, 2 May 1976.

23 Interview with Alan Carr, 3 August 2005.

24 Ibid. Later, in a letter to Transport House from John Chalmers, General Secretary of the Amalgamated Society of Boilermakers, Shipwrights, Blacksmiths and Structural Workers, it was pointed out that the local membership in the province harboured 'a strong sense of grievance and not without justification' about the BLP's handling of the situation. Indeed Chalmers went on to say that 'we should take steps to immediately restore the grant to the NILP'. The appeal to his party's hierarchy fell on deaf ears. LPA, GS12/NI, Northern Ireland Documents, 1978, Letter from John Chalmers to Reg Underhill, National Agent, 15 December 1978.

25 LPA, GS12/NI, Northern Ireland Documents, 1976, Letter from George Chambers to Reg Underhill, National Agent, 21 April 1976.

26 Ibid.

27 Interview with Alan Carr, 3 August 2005.

28 See Edwards, Aaron, 'Democratic Socialism and Sectarianism: The Northern Ireland Labour Party and Progressive Unionist Party Compared', *Politics*, Vol. 27, No. 1 (February 2007), pp. 24–31.

29 Wood, Ian S., *Crimes of Loyalty: A History of the UDA* (Edinburgh: Edinburgh University Press, 2006), p. 66.

30 Taylor, Peter, *Loyalists* (London: Bloomsbury, 1999), pp. 134–5; Wood, *Crimes of Loyalty*, p. 67.

31 Interview with David Morrison, 13 December 2007.

32 LPA, GS12/NI, Northern Ireland Documents, 1978, Letter from Derek Peters to Reg Underhill, National Agent, 3 December 1978.

33 Interview with Boyd Black, 18 December 2007.

34 Interview with David Morrison, 13 December 2007.

35 Interview with Mark Langhammer, 3 December 2007.

36 Interview with David Morrison, 13 December 2007.

37 Interview with Boyd Black, 18 December 2007.

38 Results obtained at: www.psr.keele.ac.uk/area/uk/ge79/partycand.htm (accessed 5 November 2007).

39 Results obtained at www.ark.ac.uk/elections/fe79.htm (accessed 5 November 2007).

40 Hayter, Diane, *Fightback! Labour's Traditional Right in the 1970s and 1980s* (Manchester: Manchester University Press, 2005), p. 3.

41 *Belfast Telegraph*, 19 May 1981.

42 Bew, Paul and Gordon Gillespie, *Northern Ireland: A Chronology of the Troubles 1968–1999* (Dublin: Gill and Macmillan, 1999), p. 151. In 1982 Brian Garrett openly stated that the 'public frankly do not understand why there has not been the closest possible relations between Alliance and ourselves as the obvious moderate parties when there can be coalitions by other groupings'. *Belfast Newsletter*, 31 May 1982.

43 *Belfast Telegraph*, 22 May 1981.

44 Ibid.

45 Interview with Alan Carr, 3 August 2005.

46 Ibid.

47 *Belfast Newsletter*, 4 February, 1982

48 Napier, Sam, 'The Demise of Northern Ireland Labour', *Sunday News*, 23 May 1982.

49 *Belfast Newsletter*, 15 October 1982.

50 *Belfast Telegraph*, 25 November 1982.

51 *Belfast Newsletter*, 31 May 1982.

52 Results obtained from: www.ark.ac.uk/elections/85–89lgcastlereagh.htm (accessed 5 November 2007). The three candidates were W.J. Gunning, W.T. Copley and J.M. Bate. Gunning and Copley were well-known NILP activists who had stood unsuccessfully for the party in the 1960s and 1970s.

53 Langhammer, Mark, *What Next for the Labour Party in Northern Ireland?*, Speech to the Tom Johnson Summer School, Galway, 13–15 July 2007.

54 Interview with Mark Langhammer, 3 December 2007.

55 See McAllister, Ian and Brian Wilson, *Bi-Confessionalism in a Confessional Party System: The Northern Ireland Alliance Party* (Glasgow: University of Strathclyde, 1977).

Conclusion

> The older you get the more you regret the opportunities you failed to take. You do
> your best: some you win, some you lose. But I would say that the NILP is one of the
> most significant developments in the history of Northern Ireland, not only because
> of what it did, but also because ... it made unionism much more conscious of its
> social obligations and it also made people realise that parliament could work.[1]

Just over half a century after its formation the NILP had become rudderless.
Graham's deterministic analysis of the party's so-called 'consensus-forming strategy' emphasised its abysmal failure to cut across the dominant ethno-national
cleavage and unite Protestants and Catholics in a single 'socialist overlordship' at
Stormont. However, as this book has shown, Graham was over-pessimistic in
claiming that the party had all but wound up its political organisation in 1967.[2]
Indeed, it could be said that those commentators who have prematurely written
the party off before the ashes had even settled on Bombay Street in August 1969
overemphasised the NILP's meteoric political decline.[3] Arguably, the NILP persevered beyond Graham's terminal date, shaking off individual members (and in
some cases whole branches – Derry and Newtownabbey being the two principal
losses) as the years progressed. Nonetheless, the party maintained a pragmatic
stance in the face of violent provocation from paramilitary and state forces and
held firm to its commitment to the path towards parliamentary socialism even
after the prorogation of the locally devolved parliament.

The retirement of long-term leader Tom Boyd in late 1968 – closely followed
by the exit of Charles Brett and Sam Napier in 1969 – heralded the eclipse of
those leading moderates who had built up the party from a tiny Protestant rump
in 1949 to a formidable inter-ethnic political force in the 1960s. Admittedly,
these individuals misread the mood of their constituents, hoping that the party's
working-class support-base could remain insulated from the clash of re-entrenched ethno-national identities in Northern Irish society. Ironically, in the
fluid electoral system created by Proportional Representation (reintroduced in
1973) ethno-national rivals could build up their electoral blocs with just as
much ease as had been the case under the 'first-past-the-post' system. While
inter-communal strife certainly made Labour politics 'irrelevant in most

peoples' minds'[4] it was an irrelevancy reinforced by a complex web of electoral bad luck, inept decision-making at leadership level, and a global economic recession[5] which hastened the NILP's political decline in the 1970s. How far 'community as opposed to party imperatives absorbed attention'[6] depended largely on the attitudes of individual grass-roots activists, and not necessarily on the ambitions of the party's central bureaucracy being continually thwarted amidst a 'tribal' party system.[7]

Furthermore, there was nothing predetermined about the NILP's demise. By late 1969 the party was certainly sending out the common distress signals one would expect from a sinking ship but most of its activists soldiered on, holding firm to the conviction that politics would return to 'normal'. As one senior NILP politician put it, 'we all believed Northern Ireland would eventually get normal politics and that the NILP would emerge as a party capable of winning marginal seats like East Belfast'.[8] Unfortunately, what probably crippled morale even further among the rank-and-file was the blundering attitude of the British Labour Party, whilst in power and in Opposition. In his role as Home Secretary James Callaghan had ordered the introduction of troops onto the province's streets in August 1969; once out of office both Callaghan and Harold Wilson did little to reverse this decision – even entering into a bi-partisan line on security with Edward Heath and the Conservative Party.

The NILP, although 'always very deeply committed to the link with the British Labour Party', suffered in the early 1970s because of 'the incautious speeches of Harold Wilson and other people from time-to-time – the famous "spongers" speech and that sort of thing'.[9] The British government's robust security policy – later encompassing internment and Operation Motorman, the military drive to dismantle so-called no-go areas in republican strongholds across Belfast and Londonderry – set the army's counter-insurgency policy on a collision course with those activists who had previously held some semblance of authority in Catholic working-class areas. Arguably, the Falls Road curfew had already served to alienate those Catholics who had previously only advocated the reform of the Northern Ireland state. As Douglas McIldoon observed, the 1970s saw a splintering of the NILP's support-base, with

> Moderate Nationalists going to the SDLP [and] Unionist working-class supporters being scared off by Paisley, and the increasing republican flow within British Labour destroying the *raison d'être* of the Labour Party. Even in those circumstances we were actually stronger than we realised. But it looked bad because we were coming down from a position of greater numbers. And, I suppose, it was just a continuous downward spiral with uncertainty as to where you go. I suppose the thing to do would have been to draw in our horns and wait for a better time. But I don't think there were enough people around to put in that kind of long-term commitment.[10]

In 1972 the NILP still remained a key political player. It took a lead role at Darlington and was involved in all-party discussions well into the autumn of 1973 aimed at restoring locally devolved government to Northern Ireland.[11]

Conclusion

However, with the fall of the power-sharing executive in May 1974 the NILP again fractured, this time into opposing pro-Direct Rule and pro-devolution factions, in a similar fashion to the later integrationist–devolutionist debate within Ulster Unionism.[12] Significantly, the divisions now dogging the NILP were later to continue to affect the Social Democratic and Labour Party (SDLP) as the decade progressed. After its initial flirtation with social democracy the SDLP became more 'green' than 'red' in its politics, an inevitable result of the party's jettisoning of its well-respected labour politicians Gerry Fitt and Paddy Devlin.[13]

In the 1960s the NILP won between 16% and 26% of the total vote in Northern Ireland parliamentary elections and, according to O'Leary and McGarry, 'posed a straightforward threat to the UUP's electoral hegemony, especially in the Belfast urban area'.[14] By 1970 the party's political fortunes had peaked at an impressive 98,194 votes in that year's Westminster election, after which it entered a period of protracted electoral decline. Despite its decline the NILP remained at the forefront of attempts to broker a truce between warring paramilitary factions at the height of the 'troubles' in 1972. The facilitation of this 'bottom-up' peace initiative was greatly hampered by a lack of resources and by the fact that after 1973 the British government favoured a 'top-down' arbitration approach in which Official Unionists and the SDLP were pressured into embracing a power-sharing or consociational settlement.[15]

At a time when the newly formed Alliance Party was challenging the NILP for the cross-community vote, competition between these two centrist parties became inevitable. Thereafter a squeezing of the political centre in Northern Irish politics originated, not from competition *between* ethnic and centre parties per se, but from competition *within* the centrist non-confessional bloc. The NILP's political fortunes took a further downswing at the Constitutional Convention election in 1975 when its overall vote dipped to an all-time low of 1.4%. Despite Bleakley's re-election it became increasingly obvious that the electorate had consigned his party's inter-ethnic agenda to atrophy. Yet at a time of severe polarisation, a significant portion of the electorate were willing to cast their votes for a centre ground which some theorists would have us believe collapsed much earlier. Such empirical evidence, it could be argued, poses a significant analytical conundrum for scholars like Donald Horowitz and Paul Mitchell who have dismissed the possibility of a third political tradition operating outside Northern Ireland's 'ethnic dual party system'.[16]

The NILP's fraternal relationship with the BLP had been the ideological linchpin for many labourists in Northern Ireland throughout the twentieth century. In practical political terms though, the latter's popularity among local activists became somewhat inflated during election times. During Labour's second term in office, for instance, Callaghan recalled how 'if the Home Office officials had thought there was any chance of the Northern Ireland Labour Party or anybody else winning the election they would have cultivated them in order to continue with their quiet life'.[17] Somewhat decisively, the UWC strike, the largest mobilisation of Ulster Protestants against British policy in Ireland since the third Home Rule crisis, plunged the NILP into an internal crisis and broke Protestant working-class sympathy with the BLP.[18]

Throughout the late 1970s the NILP continued to court an unwilling partner in a stormy unconsummated relationship. Despite the fact that several high-ranking BLP members 'had a soft spot in their heart for us'[19] the impression generated from reading the British party's own records on Northern Ireland is of a party willing to examine the possibilities of aiding its comrades in the NILP through minimalist gestures. However, in a complicated three-way institutional structure (Labour Party Head Office–PLP–NEC) Transport House was increasingly sidelined in its official policy-making role following the deaths of its secretary Morgan Phillips and its leader Hugh Gaitskell; whatever chances remained of a closer affiliation between the two parties died with both men in 1963.[20] The rejuvenation in green feeling among Labour's backbenches heralded a more vexed relationship, coinciding with the elevation of Wilson to the Labour leadership in 1963. Arguably, Wilson's search for a lasting legacy as the British Prime Minster responsible for solving the 'Irish Question' is something which also preoccupied his successor Tony Blair from the time New Labour came to power in 1997 until his departure from Downing Street a decade later.

The NILP's failure to row back from successive electoral defeats in 1973–75 to its previous significant high point of 98,194 (21.29%) votes in June 1970 could be easily attributed to the emergence of a highly polarised electorate unresponsive to conventional politics; yet things were doubly compounded for the party by the BLP's continuing refusal to throw it a political lifeline. Some senior NILP activists, including Erskine Holmes, the party's chairman in 1971–72, recognised the importance of Callaghan's personal intervention as Labour's Northern Ireland spokesman (until December 1971) in which 'he threw his personal weight behind the NILP and gave it a boost'.[21]

Unfortunately, Holmes, like so many other former NILP politicians, concluded negatively that the 'course of events were against you at that time, it would not have mattered who was your leading spokesman ... Northern Ireland politics were going down a road which would make the NILP irrelevant'.[22] In a sense Graham Walker is not far off the mark when he apportions blame for the NILP's political misfortune to its failure to concretise its links with British Labour:

> Perhaps if the NILP had succeeded in its attempts in the early and mid-1960s to get proper backing from the British Labour Party and to become affiliated to it, then the advances which the NILP had made by the early 1960s would not have so rapidly eroded.[23]

Yet it remains debateable whether it was the BLP's obstinacy about helping the NILP – or the split within the NILP itself over closer integration with the British Labour movement – which precipitated the latter's electoral decline in the early 1970s. Wilson's later disastrous handling of the UWC strike in May 1974 certainly pointed to a major miscalculation, on his part, about the level of polit-

Conclusion 231

ical alienation felt by the Protestant community towards power sharing with an Irish dimension. Between 1975 and the end of the decade the BLP moved tentatively towards a flaccid endorsement of the SDLP and a United Ireland endgame.

Despite a valiant attempt by several leading members to revive its ailing fortunes, the NILP became consigned to minority party status by the time it contested the 1981 local government election. During the 1980s the NILP's core constituency dispersed into a wide range of parties which had been formed in the 1970s, including the Alliance Party, Workers' Party, Democratic Unionist Party, SDLP and Progressive Unionist Party. The Campaign for Labour Representation continued to seek full rights for Northern Ireland's citizens to become full members of the British Labour Party. Regrettably, for many of its activists, it was to take a generation before the BLP finally rescinded in its steadfast refusal to grant membership rights. Indeed, many of those who were previously active in the NILP – including several prominent leaders – have since become members of the BLP. However, even among some of these individuals, there is a realisation that the future prospects for the reincarnation of the NILP may be bleak, especially if ethnicity and national identity continue to maintain their relevance in the province's politics. In the words of one former NILP member, 'I think the reality is that while the national conflict continues to be the predominant politics of Northern Ireland, Labour politics will be a very fragile creation and will tend to be disrupted by it.'[24]

Notes

1 Interview with David Bleakley, 21 March 2006.
2 Graham, J.A.V., *The Consensus-Forming Strategy of the Northern Ireland Labour Party, 1949–1968* (Unpublished MSc Thesis: Queen's University Belfast, 1972), p. 289.
3 See Mitchell, Paul, 'The Party System and Party Competition', in Mitchell, Paul and Rick Wilford (eds), *Politics in Northern Ireland* (Boulder: Westview Press, 1999), pp. 91–116; McGarry, John and Brendan O'Leary, *Explaining Northern Ireland: Broken Images* (Oxford: Blackwell, 1995) and Rumpf, Erhard and Anthony C. Hepburn, *Nationalism and Socialism in Twentieth Century Ireland* (Liverpool: Liverpool University Press, 1977).
4 Interview with Douglas McIldoon, 21 January 2004.
5 Bew, Paul, Henry Patterson and Paul Teague, *Between War and Peace: The Political Future of Northern Ireland* (London: Lawrence and Wishart, 1997), p. 88. NB: The issuing of redundancies brought with it the diminishing threat from unionised workers on the shop floor.
6 Graham, *The Consensus-Forming Strategy of the Northern Ireland Labour Party*, p. 289.
7 Ibid., pp. 189, 286, 333, 336.
8 Interview with Erskine Holmes, 21 September 2005.
9 David Bleakley speaking at the CCBH Witness Seminar on 'British Policy in Northern Ireland, 1964–70' held on 14 January 1992 at the European Commission Offices, London.

10 Interview with Douglas McIldoon, 21 January 2004.
11 Rumpf and Hepburn, *Nationalism and Socialism in Twentieth Century Ireland*, p. 211.
12 Aughey, Arthur, *Under Siege: Ulster Unionism and the Anglo-Irish Agreement* (Belfast: Blackstaff, 1989), Chapter 5.
13 Murray, Gerard and Jonathan Tonge, *Sinn Féin and the SDLP: From Alienation to Participation* (Dublin: O'Brien, 2005), pp. 59–60, 62–4.
14 O'Leary, Brendan and John McGarry, *The Politics of Antagonism: Understanding Northern Ireland, Second Edition* (London: Athlone, 1996), p. 162.
15 Dixon, Paul, *Northern Ireland: The Politics of War and Peace* (Basingstoke: Palgrave, 2001), pp. 156–7; for an opposing interpretation see O'Leary and McGarry, *The Politics of Antagonism*, p. 197.
16 Horowitz, Donald L., *Ethnic Groups in Conflict* (California: University of California Press, 2000), p. 338; Mitchell, 'The Party System and Party Competition', pp. 91–116.
17 James Callaghan speaking at the CCBH Witness Seminar on 'British Policy in Northern Ireland, 1964–70' held on 14 January 1992 at the European Commission Offices, London.
18 See Patterson, Henry, 'British Governments and the Protestant Backlash', in Alexander, Yonah and Alan O'Day (eds), *Ireland's Terrorist Dilemma* (Lancaster: Martinus Nijhoff, 1986), pp. 231–47.
19 Interview with David Bleakley, 21 March 2006.
20 See Edwards, Aaron, 'Social Democracy and Partition: The British Labour Party and Northern Ireland, 1951–64', *Journal of Contemporary History*, Vol. 42, No. 4 (October 2007), pp. 595–612.
21 Interview with Erskine Holmes, 21 September 2005.
22 Ibid.
23 Walker, Graham, *A History of the Ulster Unionist Party: Protest, Pragmatism and Pessimism* (Manchester: Manchester University Press, 2004), p. 162.
24 Interview with Alan Carr, 3 August 2005.

Index

abstentionism 181
Agnew, Paddy 20
Allaun, Frank 81–2
Allen, Cecil 220
Alliance Party of Northern Ireland
(APNI) 178, 184, 197, 201–2,
216–19, 222, 224, 229
Amalgamated Transport and General
Workers Union (ATGWU) 46
Anderson, Brian 180
Andrews, John Miller 21–3
Anomalies Act 18
Anti-Partition League (APL) 33, 41–2,
82
arms procurement 169, 174
Arthur, Paul 129, 147, 177
Attlee, Clement 40, 77, 128, 142

B Specials 163, 167–8, 171–2, 179
Barr, Andy 142
Barritt, Dennis P. 173
Barton, Brian 21
Beattie, Jack 15, 18, 23–4, 45
Belfast 11–13, 16, 19–21, 24, 33–4, 42,
46, 50, 52, 58, 60, 71–4, 79, 85, 88,
92–3, 98, 101–3, 106, 148–9, 161,
167, 169, 179, 202, 216, 228
Belfast Newsletter 102
Belfast Telegraph 36, 40–1, 51, 71–2,
85–6, 95, 99–100, 146, 222
Belgium 4

Bell, Geoffrey 40, 122, 171
Benn, Tony 185
Bew, Paul 3, 8–9, 87, 89, 102, 158–60,
197
Bing, Geoffrey 36–7, 147
Bingham, Robert 75, 94, 130
bi-partisanship 80, 159, 184, 194
Black, Boyd 20–1, 220
Black, Harold 132
Black, John 95
Blair, Tony 230
Blakiston-Houston, Charles 17–18
Blaney, Neil 169
Bleakley, David 31, 39, 50, 58–9, 70–84,
87, 96–101, 106, 130, 134, 143,
162, 179–81, 184–5, 200, 204, 208,
214–16, 221, 228–9
Blease, Billy 76, 95–6, 162, 197
Blease, Victor 161
Boal, Frederick W. 177
Boulton, David 144
Bourne, Joan 80
Boyd, Beatrice 94
Boyd, Billy 56–9, 74–6, 93–8, 101, 104,
106, 130, 134, 143, 182, 197,
200–1, 215–16, 219
Boyd, Tom 50, 73, 98–9, 104, 106, 127,
130, 132, 138–43, 149, 166, 172,
228
Boyd, William 14
Braddock, Bessie 82

Bradford, Roy 106
Breslin, Willie 173, 182
Brett, Charles 46–50, 57, 84–6, 96–7, 121, 127–41, 159, 163, 166, 177, 228
British Army presence in Ulster 168–72, 175–8, 181, 184, 228
British Broadcasting Corporation (BBC) 199
British Labour Party (BLP) 11, 30, 34, 39–42, 45, 55, 70, 73, 76–82, 89–92, 100, 121–5, 133–4, 142–4, 159, 171, 174, 178, 185–6, 194, 203, 208–9, 214–23, 228–31
Brittain, Sir Herbert 84
Bromley, Desmond 181
Brooke, Sir Basil (later Lord Brookeborough) 23–4, 30–42, 51, 56–60, 76, 84–9, 105, 118, 180
Brookeborough, Lady 78
Budge, Ian 12, 96–7
Burntollet march (1969) 35, 147
Burton, Frank 177
Butler, R.A. 84
Byrne, Deirdre 200
Byrne, Paddy 123, 125
Byrne, Roger 205

Callaghan, Frank 16–17
Callaghan, James 144–5, 158–9, 167–8, 171, 178, 181, 185, 196, 209, 221, 228–30
Campaign for Democracy in Ulster (CDU) 122–5
Campaign for Labour Representation (CLR) 220–1
Campaign for Social Justice (CSJ) 92, 120–5
Campbell, Sir David 47
capital punishment 78
Carr, Alan 106, 138–9, 181, 219, 223, 231
Carter, Charles F. 173
Carson, Sir Edward 12
Casement, Roger 131

Catholic Church 19–20, 33, 173
Catholic community in Ulster 19, 119–21, 129–30, 137, 144–50, 163, 169, 172–9, 184, 205–6
Central Citizens' Defence Committee 168
Chambers, George 106, 185, 215–19
Chichester-Clark, James 87, 149, 159, 179–80
Christian socialism 20, 83, 98–9
Churchill, Sir Winston 45
civil disobedience 135, 137, 142, 146, 167, 170, 182
civil rights activism 80, 127, 137–47, 158, 160, 164, 168, 172–8, 205, 221
Clarke, Bob 223
Clifford, Angela 35, 61
Cochrane, Feargal 105
Confederation of Shipbuilding and Engineering Unions 85
Connellan, Joe 77
Connolly, James 11, 37–8
Conservative Party 45, 60, 72–3, 194, 221, 228
Cooper, Ivan 163, 173, 177
Corish, Brendan 133
Corrigan, Joseph 46
Costello, John A. 36
Council of Ireland proposal 133–4, 197, 214
Council of Labour 185
Cradden, Terry 37, 80, 123
Craig, Bill 87, 128, 130, 144–5, 174, 206
Craig, Sir James 9–15
Craigavon, Lord 19, 22, 32
Crumlin Road prison 77, 195–6
Currie, Austin 177
Cusack, Jim 206
Cuthbert, Norman 84
Cyprus 4

Darlington Conference (1972) 196–200, 228

Index

Davidson, Tommy 224
Davison, Sir Joseph 14
De Valera, Eamonn 19
Democratic Unionist Party (DUP) 176, 200, 206, 217, 224
Derry *see* Londonderry
detention without trial 81, 122
  see also internment
Development Corporation proposals 55, 58–9, 84
Devlin, Bernadette 168, 172, 174
Devlin, Paddy 14, 44, 71, 97, 119, 127, 134–6, 141, 145, 148–9, 163–71, 175–7, 208, 219–23, 229
Diamond, Harry 52, 98, 163
Direct Rule 194, 204, 214, 229
Dixon, Paul 80, 124, 143, 163, 200–1
Doherty, Paddy 200
Donaghy, Harry 137
Donnelly, Tom 219
Dowling, Samuel 169
Downey, Hugh 21, 34, 85
Duffy, Luke 37
Dungannon 120–1, 137

Easter Rising commemoration (1966) 132
Eden, Anthony 45
election results 9, 12–19, 22, 33–4, 42–5, 71–2, 86, 131–2, 148–9, 163, 176, 199–202, 221–2
  for European Parliament 221
  in Great Britain 79, 93, 125–6, 221
electoral system 2, 12–15, 34, 127, 143, 145, 172, 180–1, 184, 228
  see also proportional representation
emigration from Ulster 53, 83
English, Richard 169
ethnic divisions and ethno-nationalism 3–5, 8, 10, 24, 168, 207, 228
European Common Market 118

Falls Labour Party 11, 92, 136-8, 141, 148-9, 161, 163–9, 171, 175-7, 182–3, 208

Farrell, Michael 52, 78, 103, 127, 133–5, 141, 145, 147, 170–1, 177
Faulkner, Brian 85, 87, 144, 149, 179–85, 194, 197, 200
Fianna Fail 134, 168–9, 174
First World War 7–8, 175
Fisk, Robert 203–4
Fitt, Gerry 45, 52, 98, 124–5, 131–4, 166–9, 176–7, 186, 201, 219, 223, 229
Follis, Brian 8
Foot, Michael 223

Gaitskell, Hugh 79, 89, 230
Gallagher, Michael 134
Garland, Sean 131
Garrett, Brian 136, 141, 163, 177–80, 196–7, 209, 214–18
Gaw, Eddie 223
Gemmell, Hugh 11
George VI, King 35
Germany 8
gerrymandering 2, 18, 123–4, 172
Getgood, Bob 18, 34, 37, 50, 60, 85
ghettoisation 160, 169
Gibson, Robert 185, 196
Gogarty, Frank 170
Goldring, Maurice 35
Gordon, David 119
Gordon, Dawson 14
Gould, Matilda 132
Goulding, Cathal 168
Government of Ireland Act (1920) 8, 121–2, 126
Gowers Report 82
Graham, J.A.V. 37–8, 46–52, 57, 75–6, 87, 90, 93, 97, 99, 102, 121, 128, 132, 228
Grant, William 35
Graham, Jimmy 142

Hall, Sir Robert (and Hall Report) 84–7
Hanna, Frank 98
Harbinson, John 10–11, 46

Harland and Wolff shipyard 15, 88, 142, 162
Harris, Eoghan 169
Hassard, Jack 121, 181
Haughey, Charles 169
Hayes, Maurice 196
Hayter, Diane 221–2
Hayward, Ron 203, 209
Heath, Edward 159, 194, 203, 228
hegemony 2–3, 8, 14, 34, 105, 134, 229
Henderson, O.W.J. 102–3
Henderson, Tommy 32, 96
Hennessey, Thomas 169
Hepburn, Anthony C. 39, 208, 216
Hewitt, Jackie 219
Hill, John F. 45
Hobsbawm, Eric 161
Holmes, Erskine 127–8, 137–41, 148, 168, 196–7, 200–1, 230
Holmes, Henry 75
Home Rule movement 10–11
Horowitz, Donald 5, 229
housing 31–2, 53, 57, 144–5, 172–3, 179
Hull, Billy 208
human rights 135–6
Hume, John 148, 163–5, 177, 181–2
hunger strikes 222
Hunt Report 168

Independent Labour Party 11
Independent Unionists 14, 17
internment 78, 182–5, 194–5, 228
  see also detention without trial
Ireland Act (1949) 80–1
Irish Congress of Trade Unions (ICTU) 14, 16, 89, 96, 127, 134, 161, 180, 197, 218
Irish Labour Party (IrLP) 39, 45, 52, 133–4
The Irish News 73
Irish Republic 36, 61, 118, 168–9, 197
  Constitution of 19, 33, 200, 205
Irish Republican Army (IRA) 7, 9, 58, 70–1, 77, 85, 101, 117, 131–3, 145, 149–50, 169, 176–8, 184–5, 207–8

  see also Provisional IRA
The Irish Times 194, 200

Jenkins, Roy 125, 171
Johnson, A.A. 39–41

Kard, Frank 195
Kennedy, Norman 98, 100, 143, 149, 162
Kennedy, Paddy 169, 185
Kerr, John 79, 88
Kidd, Bob 200, 223–4
Kilfedder, Jim 93, 131
Kyle, Sam 11–18

Labour movement in Ulster 1–2, 13, 19, 34, 223
Labour Party *see* British Labour Party; Independent Labour Party; Northern Ireland Labour Party
Langhammer, Mark 221, 224
Lansbury, George 83
Lavery, Fred 22
Leeburn, William 34, 40, 50
Lemass, Sean 118–19, 97
Lister, Unity 78
Londonderry 17–18, 125–6, 139, 144–5, 148–9, 163, 167, 171–4, 182, 228
Londonderry Labour Party (LLP) 16–17, 92, 125, 138, 144, 171–5, 182, 227; also known as the Derry Labour Party
Longford, Lord 91–2
Loyalist Association of Workers 208
'loyalist' label 204

McArdle, Archie 183, 197
McAteer, Eddie 77, 91, 119, 148
McAughtry, Sam 119–20
McBirney, Martin 149
McCafferty, Nell 173
McCann, Eamonn 138, 141–2, 145–8, 173–8
McClenaghan, Dermie 173
McCluskey, Conn 120–2, 125

Index

McCluskey, Patricia 121–2, 125
McConnell, Brian 106
McCorkell, Dudley 18
McCormick, Inez 142
McDonald, Henry 206
McDonald, Jim 215, 219
MacDonald, Michael 172
McGarry, John 3, 92, 229
McGarvey, Paddy 200
McGonagle, Stephen 36–7, 174
McHugh, Pat 183–4, 197, 200
McIldoon, Douglas 99, 106, 139, 171,
    175, 181, 201–4, 209, 216–17, 228
McKee, Billy 195
Mackin, Brendan 137–8, 141–2, 167,
    175, 182
McMaster, S.R. 92
McMullen, William 11, 14
McQuade, Johnny 106, 201
Macrory Report 179
MacStiofain, Sean 199
Markey, Thomas 182
Martin, Neville 56, 73
Mater Hospital 77, 97, 166
Matthew Report 103
Maudling, Reginald 180, 183–4
May, William Morrison 87
May Day parade (1976) 218–19
means testing 18
Members of Parliament, social class and
    occupational background of 79
Mercer, Malcolm 17
Midgley, Harry 7, 11–18, 22–4, 37,
    138–9, 180
Miller, Maurice 124–5
Miller Andrews, John 16
Miliband, Ralph 100
Mills, Stratton 132
'minority participation' proposals 179
Mitchell, Billy 205, 207
Mitchell, Paul 229
Mitchell, Tom 131
modernisation theory 49
Morrison, David 220–1
Morrison, Herbert 42, 79, 142

Morrissey, Hazel 169
Moyle, Roland 197
Moyna, Bill 181
Mulholland, Marc 104, 118–20, 146
multinational companies 120, 160–1
Murray, Gerard 181

Napier, Sam 43–55, 76, 81, 97–101,
    107, 128, 137–42, 169, 171, 223,
    228
National Health Service 35, 77, 166,
    215
Nationalist Party 97–8, 117–19, 130,
    136, 144, 173
Neill, Ivan 53, 148
Nelson, Sarah 201, 204
Newell, Tommy 200
Newtownabbey Labour Party 142, 267,
    174, 214, 220, 224, 227
Nicholas, Sir Harry 126, 171, 178
Northern Ireland Civil Rights
    Association (NICRA) 123, 135–48,
    158, 163, 168–70, 177, 182
Northern Ireland Labour Party (NILP)
    collapse of 1–2, 87–8, 167, 217–24,
        228
    electoral fortunes of 16–17, 22, 24,
        33–4, 42–6, 50–2, 56–60, 72, 86–7,
        92, 98–9, 106–7, 131–2, 145,
        148–9, 163, 176, 183, 196,
        199–202, 221–2, 229
    financing of 46, 76, 84, 99, 171, 209,
        218
    internal divisions in 36–7, 40–2, 96,
        99, 148, 181–2, 185
    origins and formation of 10, 14
    policies of 56–60, 71, 77–8, 82–3, 90,
        104, 124–7, 182
    sources of support for 3–4, 45, 51–2,
        61, 85, 92, 97, 163, 183, 217–18,
        231
    symbols of 176
    see also Parliamentary Labour Party
Northern Ireland Office 198
Northern Irish state, founding of 7–9

The Northern Whig 70
Norton, Christopher 9–12

O'Hanlon, Paddy 163, 169, 177
O'Leary, Brendan 3, 92, 159, 185, 209, 217, 229
O'Leary, Cornelius 12, 96–7, 105
O'Neill, Terence 76, 87–91, 97–107, 118–33, 139–49, 158–60, 172
O'Neillism 120, 130, 149, 159
Orme, Stan 81, 124–5
Orr, Willy 44
Overend, David 132, 167, 219

Paisley, Ian (and Paisleyism) 93, 101, 104–5, 119, 126, 130, 132, 150, 167, 176, 206, 208, 220, 228
paramilitarism 176–8, 185, 195, 201–2, 206–7, 228
Parliamentary Labour Party (PLP) 15, 34–5, 61, 87, 99–100
as Official Opposition 73–9
partition issue 7–8, 33–47, 52–4, 59–61, 79, 81, 101, 126, 134, 180–1, 185, 194
Patterson, Henry 12, 32–4, 38, 51–2, 118–19, 125, 145, 158–9, 170
Patterson, Sadie 207
Payne, Stanley G. 7–8
People's Democracy (PD) 147, 169–70, 177–8
personation at elections 40, 92
Peters, Derek 220
Philbin William J. 129
Phillips, Morgan 37, 40, 43, 55, 73, 81–2, 230
political levy, contracting in to and out of 15
populism 8, 17, 21, 41, 78–9, 101, 130, 141, 206
Porter, Robert 166
power sharing 182, 198–205, 214, 217, 229–31
Progressive Unionist Party 19, 219
proportional representation (PR) 2,

12–15, 18, 180–3, 196, 200, 217, 222, 228
Provisional IRA 169, 176–7, 182–5, 195, 199, 222–3
Puirséil, Niamh 19–20, 45
Purdie, Bob 42–3, 121, 135, 140, 142, 160

Queen's University, Belfast 147
Labour Group (QUBLG) 123, 133

Rathcoole 103
Rees, Merlyn 203–4
rent control 57, 60
Richardson, David 21
rioting 19, 93, 100, 167–8, 178–9, 206
The Rising Tide (journal) 46
Robens, Alfred 55
Rose, Paul 124–5
Rose, Peter 80, 124, 126
Royal Ulster Constabulary (RUC) 8–9, 78, 93, 117, 120, 163, 167–8, 171–2
Rumpf, Erhard 39, 208, 216
Russia 8

Sands, Bobby 222
Sayers, Jack 86, 101
Schofield, Arnold 78, 84, 149
Scott, Clarke 13–16
Scott, Sandy 162, 200
Scullion, John 132
Second World War 20–4, 30, 32, 142
Secretary of State for Northern Ireland, first appointment of 55–6
sectarianism 4–5, 8–9, 12, 15, 19, 21, 30–2, 39–45, 48, 72, 77, 82, 85, 93, 100–2, 107, 119, 127, 129, 133–43, 148–50, 159–63, 167–9, 175, 178, 180, 195–208, 217–24
Shearer, Raymond 170
shipbuilding industry 84
Shorts Aircraft 86–8, 142
Simpson, George H. 22
Simpson, Vivian 73–4, 77, 84, 99, 106,

130–2, 143, 148–9, 166–7, 181–3, 195–6, 207–8
Sinclair, Betty 169–70, 207
Sinn Féin 7
Sloan, Gerard 182
Smyth, Hugh 219
Social Democratic and Labour Party (SDLP) 163, 177–86, 196–9, 202–3, 217, 219, 224, 228–31
Society of Labour Lawyers 136
Special Powers 81, 122, 145, 179
Spence, Gusty 101, 195
Stevenson, Delap 200
Stewart, Edwina 170
Stewart, Joe 77
Stewart, Reverend John 195, 200, 206–8, 215
Stewart, John D. 142, 168
Stewart, Sydney 106, 132
Stewart, William J. 19
Stockman, Hugh 74
strike action 60, 74–5, 85, 202–4, 208–9, 229–31
Stronge, Sir Norman 73, 77
Sunday observance 94–8, 107
Sunningdale Conference and Agreement (1973) 201, 205, 217

Tawney, R.H. 83
Taylor, John 79
Teevan, Thomas 45
Thatcher, Margaret 221
Toman, Cyril 147, 177
Tonge, Jonathan 181, 217
Topping, W.B. 43–4
trade unions 9–10, 14–20, 24, 31, 35–9, 46, 60, 71, 75–6, 79, 89, 96, 131, 134, 148, 161–3, 172, 174, 181, 204
Trades Union Congress 11
see also Irish Congress of Trade Unions

Ulster Defence Association (UDA) 205–8, 220
Ulster Defence Regiment (UDR) 173

Ulster Protestant Action (UPA) 101, 208
Ulster Protestant Volunteers (UPV) 149
Ulster Special Constabulary 9, 78
see also B Specials
Ulster Unionist Council 12, 119
Ulster Unionist Labour Association (UULA) 9–10, 102
Ulster Unionist Party (UUP) 1–3, 8–10, 14–24, 30–45, 52–61, 70–3, 77–9, 84–8, 92–3, 97, 100–6, 118, 121, 127–8, 132, 144, 149, 159, 166, 171, 176–9, 184, 197
Ulster Volunteer Force (UVF) 101, 132–3, 149–50, 201, 205–8
Ulster Workers' Council strike (1974) 202–4, 208–9, 214, 229–31
Underhill, Reg 220
unemployment 11–13, 16–21, 24, 30–1, 34–5, 51–60, 78–9, 83–4, 87–8, 100, 172–3, 194, 199
United Nations 147

Vanguard Unionism 176, 206, 209
Vatican Council 130

Wakehurst, Lord 87
Walker, Graham 13–14, 17, 19, 22, 32–3, 41, 56, 72, 80, 101, 104–5, 132, 138–9, 144, 230
Walker, William 11
Wallace, Armand 17
Walsh, David 95
Ward, Peter 132
Ware, Alan 5
Warner, Geoffrey 125–6
Warnock, Edmund 35, 73, 88
Watt, Sam 92
welfare legislation 9, 24, 31–4, 43, 60–1, 119, 126–7, 143, 215
Whitelaw, William 195–200, 203
Whitley, Bill 223
Williams, Len 81, 122
Wilson, Harold 81–2, 90–3, 100–1,

121–6, 142–5, 148, 158–9, 171, 183, 186, 194–5, 203–4, 208–9, 228–31
Wilson, Thomas 103
Wolff, Stefan 3
Woods, P.J. 14

Woodvale Labour Party 74–5, 94–7, 101, 106, 161, 180–2, 185, 206, 215

Young Hooligans 173–4
Young Socialists 180–1